THE MAGIC GOBLET

VALANCOURT CLASSICS

THE MAGIC GOBLET

A Swedish Tale

by

EMILIE FLYGARE-CARLÉN

Edited with an introduction and notes by
Amy H. Sturgis

Kansas City:
VALANCOURT BOOKS
2007

The Magic Goblet by Emilie Flygare-Carlén
First published in 1845
First Valancourt Books edition, August 2007

Introduction and notes © 2007 by Amy H. Sturgis
This edition © 2007 by Valancourt Books

Library of Congress Cataloguing-in-Publication Data

Flygare-Carlén, Emilie, 1807-1892.
  [Kyrkoinvigningen i Hammarby. English.]
  The magic goblet : a Swedish tale / by Emilie Flygare-Carlén ; edited with an introduction and notes by Amy H. Sturgis.
      p. cm. -- (Valancourt classics)
  Originally published: London : Clarke, 1845.
  Includes bibliographical references.
  ISBN 0-9792332-9-1
  I. Sturgis, Amy H., 1971- II. Title.
  PT9746.F6K93 2007
  839.73'6--dc22

                                        2007021520

Composition by James D. Jenkins
Published by Valancourt Books
Kansas City, Missouri
http://www.valancourtbooks.com

CONTENTS

INTRODUCTION

The Magic Goblet is not a cheerful book. It is a complex tale of how one generation inherits the consequences of mistakes made by actors long dead, a story of limited choices and unlimited selfishness. Most of the characters, while playing out their dramas before a backdrop of stirring and evocative settings, wrestle with intellectual and emotional demons before losing their chances at happiness and ultimately their lives. In its intricacy and artistry, as well as its sober tone, *The Magic Goblet* justifies the conclusion of *A Cyclopædia of Female Biography* in 1857: "Upon the whole, Mrs. Carlen appears to yield to few women of our day in original genius. Some of the passages have an approach to sublimity in the descriptions of nature, and of moral suffering."[1]

Emilie Carlen (also printed as Emilie Flygare-Carlén, among other variations) was during her lifetime one of the best selling authors of her native Sweden, as well as an international sensation; translations of her books appeared in at least ten languages before her death. At a period in which Scandinavian readers in particular and Western readers in general enjoyed a taste for so-called "light reading," sensational fiction of a Gothic flavor, paired with exotic coastal locales, met the demand well. Scholar Alrik Gustafson notes that Emilie "has been called 'the first professional Swedish author,' that is to say a literary practitioner who sensed what her public wanted and produced accordingly."[2] Her choice of subject matter and style reflected more than savvy business sense, however. Emilie Carlen's fiction sprang from a source very close to home.

The youngest daughter of a sea captain, Emilie Smith was born in Strömstad, Sweden on August 8, 1807.[3] In her introductory essay for the 1853 English translation of her novel *Gustavus Lindorm*, "To My

---

[1] Henry Gardiner Adams, ed. "Emily Carlen," *A Cyclopædia of Female Biography: Consisting of Sketches of All Women Who Have Been Distinguished by Great Talents, Strength of Character, Piety, Benevolence, or Moral Virtue of Any Kind*. (London: Groombridge and Sons, 1857): 150-151, 151.

[2] Alrik Gustafson, *A History of Swedish Literature*. (Minneapolis: University of Minnesota Press, 1961), 218-219.

[3] One of the best sources in English for a biographical sketch of Emilie Carlen is available in K. Margareta Horiba, "A Bibliography of Emilie Flygare-Carlén, 1807-1892." (M.A. thesis, University of Minnesota, 1971): 4-10.

American Readers," she describes her home in these words: "On the western coast of Sweden, among naked rocks and lofty mountains, and washed by the wild waves of the North Sea, is situated the small fishing village of Strömstad, renowned as the former home of the Vikings. Here I spent my youthful days, under the careful guidance of affectionate parents, upright and industrious persons..."[1] By all accounts, she absorbed the sea-faring stories of the harbor villages and often accompanied her father on trips along the Swedish coast. Her brother Edvard later encouraged her to revisit the scenes and settings of her childhood through her novels. In *The Magic Goblet*, Maria's experience in the fishing town of Fredsberg recalls the author's memories in a bittersweet fashion, from the perspective of an outsider: "All is activity and joy, thrift and contentment. I feel almost envious when I see these housewives, accompanied by their joyous children, go down in the evening to the strand to receive their husbands who beckon to them at a distance.... Are they not to be envied?"

This seemingly idyllic childhood ended for Emilie when, at twenty, she married physician Axel Flygare, a man fifteen years her senior whom she apparently did not love. She moved with him away from the coast to the rural inland province of Småland. Five years later, she returned to her parents' home as a widow with two children. Her daughter did not survive childhood. When Emilie did at last find romance, in the person of law student Reinhold Dalin, it ended in tragedy. The two lovers announced their plans to marry, but soon after Dalin died suddenly, leaving an unwed Emilie pregnant with their child. Due to the social stigma of her situation, she traveled away from home to give birth and left the baby girl in the care of strangers. Although Emilie pursued a relationship with her daughter years later, the two were never successfully reconciled.

The Magic Goblet repeatedly depicts similar plights of women with few or no options before them, who are forced to marry, to separate from their lovers, or to conceal the disgrace of unwed pregnancy. Much of the novel's dramatic tension derives from the inevitable approach of Thelma's arranged marriage to Count Albano: "And when her thoughts passed from the fearful intended bridegroom to

---

[1] Emilie F. Carlen, "To My American Readers," *Gustavus Lindorm: or, "Lead Us Not Into Temptation."* Trans. Elbert Perce. (New York: Charles Scribner, 1853): v-viii, v.

the approaching wedding-day, then she seemed to herself like a bride of death, and shuddered for fear and horror." When Alfhild's father, Provost Frenkman, announces his plans for his daughter to wed the heir to Great Hammarby, despite the fact she loves another man, she begs, "Say that you will not sacrifice your child," to which he replies, "What are you talking of *sacrificing!*... It would be more becoming in you to speak of *obeying*." At the center of *The Magic Goblet's* plot of revenge is the story of the fallen Sigrid, who, like her author, found herself unmarried and pregnant, seeking to protect others from her shame: "I have done penance, through sufferings, which words cannot describe."

Emilie Flygare found an outlet for her sufferings through the written word. Her first novel, *Waldemar Klein* (translated into English as *Julie; or Love and Duty*), appeared in 1838, and was sufficiently successful for her editor to assist in moving her to Stockholm, where she soon became part of the city's vibrant literary life. Throughout her career, she was compared to the older and more urbane Frederika Bremer, Swedish author, intellectual, and feminist, whom she met in Stockholm. The comparison was not entirely apt. Bremer was a highly educated and well traveled elite, while Emilie Flygare was the modest, untrained daughter of Sweden's fishing villages. Emilie apparently recognized her own deficiencies: very soon after arriving in Stockholm she married journalist Johan Gabriel Carlen (or Carlén), who for more than three decades became responsible for the final polishing and proofreading of her manuscripts.

Emilie's background did nothing to diminish her ambition, however. She regularly wrote two novels per year during her most productive writing period (1838-1852), and became one of the highest paid writers in Sweden, after only Carl Jonas Love Almqvist and Frederika Bremer. Women authors at the time were still something of a novelty, and her experience as a literary pioneer led her to sympathize with the suffrage movement and other calls for women's rights. She clearly criticizes "proud selfishness, the universal foundation of the male character" in *The Magic Goblet*, most effectively in the manipulative character of Rudolph Seiler, who abandons a strong, thinking woman to seek his ideal mate—in his words, "a being that lives in and through me, and that has no will, no thought, no feeling, but such as proceed from me." Yet the tale is not two-dimensional. The reader is aware of a certain irony when Alfhild is praised as a woman who "knows how to maintain and defend her dignity and her rights." Furthermore, the novel is more impressive for the fact that two of its most sympathetic, discerning, and noble characters are men: Bloom and Captain Sebastian Oernroos.

The Magic Goblet (published in Swedish as *Kyrkoinvigningen i Hammarby*) was Emilie Carlen's sixth book. Although it raised eyebrows for its portrayal of divorce and pregnancy—the *North American Review* later called it "a wild phantasmagoria of unmixed and unaccountable evil" (see the Appendix)—it was an immediate success when published in Sweden in three volumes in 1840-1841. In 1919, Rudolf Cronau noted in his book *Woman Triumphant* that "of Emilie Carlen's novels 'The Rose of Thistle Island' and 'The Magic Goblet' are most appreciated."[1] This seems to be confirmed by its enduring publication record: three separate editions of the book appeared in Sweden in the first half of the twentieth century alone.[2] Throughout her career, Emilie proved adept at moving between Romantic genres, from picturesque pastoral tales to tragic love stories, depending on her mood; *The Magic Goblet* in particular reflects her mastery of the Gothic tradition, incorporating such established ingredients as family curses, castle ruins, and deformed and deranged villains into what remains, at its core, a deeply personal narrative.

Emilie continued her remarkable output and duplicated her popular success throughout the following decade. Beyond writing her stories of romance, adventure, horror, and heartache, her passion was her son Edvard, who was named for her brother. Determined to give her child the opportunities she did not enjoy, she traveled with him across the country, sent him to the University of Uppsala, and after his graduation in 1851, funded his year-long European tour. Once again, however, tragedy struck: Edvard returned home badly ill, and he died on Christmas Eve in 1852. Emilie wrote nothing for six years after his death, and her biographers agree that she never recovered from her loss.

After burying a husband, a fiancé, and a daughter, Emilie already was intimate with mortality. In fact the text of *The Magic Goblet*, in

---

[1] Rudolph Cronau, *Woman Triumphant: The Story of Her Struggles for Freedom, Education, and Political Rights.* (New York: R. Cronau, 1919), 225.

[2] Horiba, 29-30.

which some characters compare themselves to ghosts and others imagine death as their bridegroom, is pervaded by this preoccupation. The book also is suffused with the language of loss: "Then the lonely heart made in itself a grave for its faded favourites, and on the little mound, for many a long sad day, pale Memory sat and mourned their early death." Emilie had not grown immune to grief through her repeated experiences; Edvard's death struck her so forcefully that she effectively abandoned her career after publishing twenty-four books.

The editor of the Stockholm newspaper *Aftonbladet* eventually lured Emilie from her retirement with an offer she could not refuse; he wished to serialize a new novel that focused on the coastal life of the everyday rural Swedish people. Carlen took this opportunity to relive the happiest memories from her childhood. The result was the 1859 serialization of *Ett Köpmanshus i Skärgården (A Merchant House in the Archipelago)*. The popular work renewed Carlen's visibility as an author, and in 1862, the Swedish Academy honored her with a gold medal for her role in elevating the Swedish language and culture. She wrote several more books, including the nostalgic nonfiction volume *Minnen af Svenskt Författarlif, 1840-1860 (Memories of the Lives of Swedish Authors, 1840-1860)* in 1878, which captured the reminiscences of her many years of participation in Stockholm's literary circles.

The death of her husband and collaborator Johan Gabriel Carlen in 1875, and her own increasing blindness, eventually brought a permanent end to Emilie's writing career. When she died in Stockholm on February 5, 1892, she left behind not only dozens of successful books, but also the legacy of three charitable funds: one for the assistance of teachers, in memory of her husband; one at the University of Uppsala, in memory of her son; and one for poor fishermen and their widows, in memory of her father.

It is difficult to understand how a woman deemed one of the "most popular Swedish writers" has been all but forgotten by English readers.[1] The fame of her novels cannot be questioned; not only were they frequently reprinted and translated, but they also inspired multiple dramatizations and sequels by other writers.[2] The consensus of critics is more challenging to discern. Some contemporary reviewers

---

[1] Cronau, 225.
[2] Horiba, 12-13.

considered her "among the second-rates" while others viewed her as "front rank among the novelists of the present age."[1] A portion of her detractors seem to have objected more to the genre in which she wrote, with its highly dramatic and sensational nature, than her novels themselves, while others objected to her risqué and controversial subject matter, perhaps more for political and personal reasons than literary ones. Comparisons to the accomplished Frederika Bremer, though arguably inappropriate, often did not help her literary reputation. Yet even in this, disagreement persisted: a reviewer in *Literary World* in 1853, for example, found that Emilie's fiction possessed "more life than Miss Bremer's works."[2]

In the end, Emilie Carlen was and is best understood on her own terms, as an author who offered a unique blend of nostalgia and disillusionment, a woman who criticized the prevailing social order while yearning for the traditional life of her childhood, an artist who used "popular, Gothic-style novels" and harnessed Romantic fascination with Scandinavia in order to tell intensely personal stories about her home.[3] Even as academics today turn fresh attention to the Gothic tradition, modern scholars such as Petra Broomans credit Carlen with laying the foundation for new movements in world and women's literature.[4]

The Magic Goblet is not a cheerful book, but Emilie Carlen's life was often far from cheerful. She lost all of those dear to her and chased the elusive memory of bygone happiness throughout the pages of her many novels. Her life and her fiction were intimately connected; in the words of Elbert Perce, in the introduction to his 1854 translation of Emilie's *The House in the Valley*, "When her mind is clouded by sorrow—and she has been oppressed with many bitter griefs—she seeks to remove the cause of her despondency by creating a hero or heroine, afflicted like herself, and following this individual through a train of circumstances which, she imagines, would

---

[1] *The Athenæum.* (London, May 4, 1844), quoted in Horiba, 17; *Bentley's Miscellany.* Vol. 30 (London, 1851): 212-214, 214.

[2] *Literary World.* Vol. 12 (New York, June 4, 1853), 461.

[3] Petra Broomans, *'I Have Heard About You': Foreign Women's Writing Crossing the Dutch Border: from Sappho to Selma Lagerlöf.* (Hilversum: Uitgeverij Verloren, 2004), 308.

[4] Ibid.

naturally occur during a life of continued gloom and sorrow."[1] Thus we have the central cast of protagonists in *The Magic Goblet*. Alrik Gustafson puts it in a different way: "Emilie Flygare-Carlén… as a born story teller was far more concerned in her novels with what happens than with what should happen."[2] Even in her most fanciful stories, her art imitated life.

Emilie's works, if they can be rediscovered by English readers in volumes such as this, may prove her enduring worth and appeal. Tales built on her models of doomed love and exotic adventure continue to thrill contemporary audiences. The subjects about which she wrote, such as mortality, morality, and inequality, remain at the heart of the human experience today. Her warning in *The Magic Goblet*, that "one half of our being belongs to earth, and it often draws the other half with it into the dust," is no less haunting in the twenty-first century than in was in the nineteenth. If nothing else, readers may learn why *The New York Herald* claimed "Emilie Carlen, like the author of 'Jane Eyre,' is perfectly original…"[3]

Amy H. Sturgis

May 2007

ABOUT THE EDITOR

Amy H. Sturgis earned her Ph.D. in Intellectual History at Vanderbilt University and teaches Interdisciplinary Studies at Belmont University. She is the author of four books and numerous book chapters and articles; she also is the editor of two books, including Valancourt Books' *The Magic Ring* (2006). Her official website is www.amyhsturgis.com.

---

[1] Elbert Perce, "Translator's Preface," *The Home in the Valley*. Reprint of the 1854 edition. (Fairfield, IA: 1st World Library, 2005): 5-6, 5.

[2] Gustafson, 218.

[3] Quoted in advertisement, in E.L.A. Berwick, *The Dwarf; or Mind and Matter*. Vol. 3. (London: Thomas Cautley Newby, 1855), 258.

NOTE ON THIS EDITION

This Valancourt Books edition follows the first English translation of *The Magic Goblet*, which was published in two forms in 1845, as *The Magic Goblet, A Swedish Tale* by H. G. Clarke & Co. in London (from which this edition is taken) and as *The Magic Goblet; or The Consecration of the Church of Hammarby* by W. H. Colyer in New York.

The translator remains unnamed in the 1845 volumes. Other sources attribute the English translation of the Swedish novel to Bernard Roelker (1816-1888). Although he studied philology while a university student, taught German at Harvard University, and produced multiple publications—he compiled *A German Reader for Beginners* and adapted Luther S. Cushing's *Manual of Parliamentary Practice* for German readers, for example—he remains better known as an attorney and legal scholar than as a linguist and translator. After graduating from the University of Bonn, the German-born Roelker emigrated to the United States and earned admittance to the bar. He built a successful legal practice first in Boston and then in New York. In 1863, he won the first legal-tender case before the U.S. Supreme Court (*Meyer vs. Roosevelt*). He wrote various legal treatises, such as *Constitutions of France, Monarchical and Republican, Together with Brief Historical Remarks Relating to their Origin and the Late Orleans Dynasty* (1848) and *Argument in Favor of the Constitutionality of the Legal-Tender Clause in the Act of Congress, February 25, 1862* (1863), among others, and remained a practicing attorney until the year before his death.[1]

Roelker's legal work did not remove him from the artistic life. He developed friendships with some of the best known literary minds of the day, including his Harvard colleague Henry Wadsworth Longfellow. In his autobiography *My Reminiscences*, geologist and explorer Raphael Pumpelly provides a clue about why translating *The Magic Goblet* in particular might have appealed to the ambitious young Roelker, who at the time of translation was not yet thirty years old: "Bernard Roelker was another friend in whose bachelor quarters I spent many evenings. He was a German of the old school

---

[1] James Grant Wilson and John Fiske, eds. *Appleton's Cyclopædia of American Biography*. Vol. 5. (New York: D. Appleton & Co., 1888): 304; and Henry Barnard, ed., "American School-Books," *The American Journal of Education*. 15: 40 (September 1865) 539-575: 548

of romance and philosophy.... It would be hard to overestimate the value of the Century to a young man interested in everything and still in the formative period."[1] Certainly Emilie Carlen was an author of international reputation by the time *The Magic Goblet* appeared; moreover, her novel delivers "old school" Gothic romance while expressing contemporary ethical concerns. Furthermore, the narrative of *The Magic Goblet*, which spans multiple generations and crosses national boundaries, both reflects its Scandinavian setting and draws on a larger European cultural heritage for its symbols and allusions, making it an ideal story for "a young man interested in everything."

The original spelling and capitalization in this text have been preserved, including internal inconsistencies, such as the dual use of "James"/"Jeames", "banns"/"bans", and "betrothed"/"bethrothed." The original punctuation likewise has been preserved. Obvious typographical errors (such as the absence of any punctuation mark at the end of a paragraph) and potentially problematic irregularities (such as the inconsistent use of single and double quotation marks) have been corrected to avoid confusion. In the 1845 edition, the text was divided both into two volumes and three parts. For clarity, the three parts have been retained, while a footnote marks the end of the original break between Volume I and Volume II. Furthermore, the 1845 English translation lists the author as Emilie Carlen; because she is more familiar to modern readers as Emilie Flygare-Carlén, however, this formulation of her name appears on the cover of the Valancourt Books edition.

ACKNOWLEDGEMENTS

The editor thanks Paige Carter at the Lila D. Bunch Library at Belmont University and James D. Jenkins of Valancourt Books for their invaluable assistance.

---

[1] Raphael Pumpelly, *My Reminiscences*. Vol. II. (New York: Henry Holt & Co., 1918): 582-583.

FOR FURTHER READING

Adams, Henry Gardiner, ed. "Emily Carlen," *A Cyclopædia of Female Biography: Consisting of Sketches of All Women Who Have Been Distinguished by Great Talents, Strength of Character, Piety, Benevolence, or Moral Virtue of Any Kind*. London: Groombridge and Sons, 1857: 150-151.

Carlen, Emilie F. *The Home in the Valley*. Trans. Elbert Perce. Rpt. of the 1854 edition. Fairfield, IA: 1st World Library, 2005.

Gustafson, Alrik. *The History of Swedish Literature*. Minneapolis: University of Minnesota Press, 1961.

Horiba, K. Margareta. "A Bibliography of Emilie Flygare-Carlén, 1807-1892." M.A. thesis, University of Minnesota, 1971.

Mitchell, Stephen Arthur. "Dialogue in the Early Swedish Novel: Studies in the Presentation of Speech from Cederborgh to Flygare-Carlen." Ph.D. dissertation, University of Minnesota, 1980.

Warner, Charles Dudley, Ed. "Emilia [*sic*] Flygare-Carlén," *A Library of the World's Best Literature, Ancient and Modern*. Vol. VIII. New York: The International Society, 1897: 3225-3230.

EMILIE CARLEN CHRONOLOGY

1807 – Emilie is born.

1827 – Emilie marries Axel Flygare.

1833 – Emilie returns home after Flygare's death.

1838 – Emilie's first book, *Waldemar Klein*, is published.

1839 – Emilie moves to Stockholm and marries Johan Gabriel Carlen.

1840-1841 – *Kyrkoinvigningen i Hammarby* is published.

1845 – *Kyrkoinvigningen i Hammarby* is translated into English as *The Magic Goblet*.

1852 – Emilie's son dies, halting her career for six years.

1859 – Emilie publishes her first work since her son's death.

1862 – Emilie is honored by the Swedish Academy with a gold medal.

1875 – Johan Gabriel Carlen dies.

1892 – Emilie Carlen dies.

SELECT BIBLIOGRAPHY OF EMILIE CARLEN

Waldemar Klein. Stockholm: Thomson, 1838.
First English translation: *Julie; or Love and Duty.* London: Bentley, 1854.

Representanten. Stockholm: Thomson, 1839.
First English translation: *A Lover's Strategem; or The Two Suitors.* London: Bentley, 1852.

Gustaf Lindorm. Stockholm: Bonnier, Thomson, 1839.
First English translation: *Gustavus Lindorm: or, "Lead Us Not Into Temptation."* With a preface to English readers by the author. New York: Scribner, 1853.

Professorn Och Hans Skyddslingar. Stockholm: Thomson, 1840.
First English translation: *The Professor.* London: Newby, 1854.

Fosterbröderne. Stockholm: Thomson, 1840.
First English translation: *The Foster Brothers.* New York: W. H. Colyer, 1845.

Kyrkoinvigningen i Hammarby. Stockholm: Thomson, 1840-1841.
First English translations:
* *The Magic Goblet; or The Consecration of the Church of Hammarby.* New York: W. H. Colyer, 1845.
* *The Magic Goblet, A Swedish Tale.* London: H. G. Clarke & Co., 1845.

Skjutsgossen. Stockholm: Thomson, 1841.
First English translation: *Ivar; or The Skjuts-Boy.* New York: Harper, 1852.

Rosen på Tistelön. Stockholm: Thomson, 1842.
First English translation: *The Rose of Tistleön. A Tale of the Swedish Coast.* London: Longman, 1844.

Fideikommisset. Stockholm: Thomson, 1844.
First English translation: *The Temptation of Wealth; or The Heir by Primogeniture.* New York: C. Müller, 1846.

Vindskuporna. Norrköping: Huldberg, 1845.
First English translation: *Marie Louise; or The Opposite Neighbours.* London: Ingram, Cooke & Co., 1853.

Bruden på Omberg. Stockholm: Huldberg, 1845.
First English translation: *The Bride of Omberg.* New York: Scribner, 1853.

Ett År. Stockholm: Thomson, 1846.
First English translation: *The Events of a Year.* London: Newby, 1853.

Enslingen på Johannisskäret. Norrköping: Huldberg, 1846.
First English translation: *The Hermit.* London: Newby, 1853.

Jungfrutornet. Stockholm: Thomson, 1848.
First English translation: *Maiden's Tower, A Tale of the Sea.* London: Bentley, 1853.

En Nyckfull Qvinna. Stockholm: Huldberg, 1849.
First English translation: *Woman's Life: or Trials of Caprice.* London: Bentley, 1852.

Familjen i Dalen. Stockholm: Huldberg, 1849.
First English translation: *The Home in the Valley.* New York: Scribner, 1854.

Romanhjeltinnan. Stockholm: Huldberg, 1849.
First English translation: *John; or Is a Cousin in the Hand Worth Two Counts in the Bush?* London: Bentley, 1853.

Förmyndaren. Stockholm: Huldberg, 1851.
First English translation: *The Guardian.* London: Bentley, 1865.

Ett Lyckligt Parti. Stockholm: Huldberg, 1851.
First English translation: *A Brilliant Marriage.* London: Bentley, 1852.

Inom Sex Veckor. Stockholm: Huldberg, 1853.
First English translation: *The Brothers' Bet; or Within Six Weeks.* London: Bentley, 1867.

Ett Köpmanshus I Skärgården. Stockholm & Leipzig: Maass, 1859.

Stockholmsscener Bakom Kulisserna. Stockholm: Fahlstedt, 1864.

En Hemlighet För Verlden. Stockholm: Flodin, 1876.

Berättelser Fån Landsorten. Stockholm: Flodin, 1877.

Minnen Af Svenskt Författarlif, 1840-1860. Stockholm: Bonnier, 1878.

Kerstin Marias Fästegåva. Stockholm: Bonnier, 1880.

Efterskörd Från En 80-årings Författarebana; Berättelser Och Noveller. Stockholm: Bonnier, 1888.

THE MAGIC GOBLET

THE MAGIC GOBLET.

PART FIRST.

CHAPTER I.

THE MAGIC GOBLET.

ON the first Sunday in advent of the year 1790, there stood in the newly-painted dining-hall of Provost Andreas Frenkman, a large table, of a horse-shoe form, spread with all the splendour and solid pomp which the festivity of the day rendered proper.

The building of a new parish church at Hammarby—the old one threatening to fall—had formed, for the last ten years, the constant subject of deliberation with the parish officers, at their regular meetings; and had been the topic of conversation between the provost and the Count H——, who had the *jus patronatus,* and on whom the final determination of the affair in question mainly depended. However much the latter allowed himself to be urged, he knew how to find excuses for refusing the renewed applications; yet Provost Frenkman steered with a practised hand, through straits and among rocks. And now the morning of the day had come at last, when the bishop of the diocese, together with the count, was to choose the site of the new church.

The service at church, with which this laudable work was commenced, was not yet ended. While all persons that were at all able to walk, and leave their domestic duties, were assembled in the old house of God, to witness the particulars of the celebration of the day, Alfhild, the charming daughter of the provost, walked round the solitary rooms of the parsonage, minutely examining the arrangements. She tarried particularly by the spread table, and looked with delight at the napkin on the plate for the bishop, which was skilfully folded in form of a pyramid.

"The place can be made still more handsome," said Alfhild, and a slight colour mantled her cheeks at the thought that a myrtle and a rose from her small greenhouse, might further ornament the place for the honourable guest; and she quickly brought the flower-pots and placed them before the plate. It is often that the most innocent thought bears the germ of a series of unlucky events, which not seldom end in the destruction of him who conceived it.

Alfhild, while hastily winding the sprigs of myrtle and rose round the top of the napkin, suddenly pushed her arm against a large cut glass goblet of high value. It fell to the floor, and the pieces flew with great clatter round the fire-place.

Pale as death stood the maiden, with the rose-twigs in her hand, which trembled so violently that the roses became loosened, and their leaves mingled on the floor with the fragments of crystal.

She looked with an expression of great anguish on the destruction. "The goblet!" was all she could stammer forth; but this word applied to an object, the value of which she had ever since her childhood suspected, though not clearly understood; and it was for this reason that she was now so much overcome by the misfortune. All she knew of this memorable goblet was, that about fifty years ago her grandmother had received it, with another similar cup, as a wedding present; and that a number of circumstances, which had always remained a secret to her, were connected with them; and that an old itinerant Finlander had prophesied, that the breaking of either betokened great misfortune to the family.

How the first goblet had been broken, Alfhild knew not. She had heard, however, that the death of her mother had been connected with it. Although this might have been accidental, yet the provost, who was a man entirely free from prejudices respecting other things, had become uncommonly careful of the remaining cup. The last words of her father that morning, as he left home to go to church, were still ringing in the ears of the trembling girl: "Alfhild," he said with a stern expression, "be careful of the goblet."

And it was now through her carelessness that she had spoiled, not only this beautiful glass, but also the good humour of her father for this day, and perhaps for several weeks. Alfhild drew a deep sigh, for she knew her father, and was conscious that many hours of trouble would follow her present sufferings.

Provost Frenkman was, in every respect, a severe man. He loved his daughter, but this love was only second in place with him; first came always his own iron will, to which all around him were forced to bow with submission. There was but one person in the house who dared to oppose him; and this one, hearing the ringing sound in the dining-hall as he passed by, now put his head through the door.

He was a man of about sixty-eight years, with a face uncommonly expressive for his age, and a frame which still showed that in former times he might have passed for a type of Hercules. Although Time's cold fingers had drawn many a wrinkle in his cheeks, and the winter of age had strewed snow upon his hair, there was yet alive in the old man such vigour and firmness, as indicated that he had fought many a battle with life and the world, and that the game had not yet lost its charms.

Captain Sebastian Oernroos, or Uncle Sebastian, as he was called every where, had been a younger brother to Alfhild's grandmother, and son of the former pastor at Hammarby. Of Captain Sebastian's former circumstances we only mention that, after having closed the eyes of his wife, and buried his last hope, a son ten years old, he felt lonely in his own house, and went to Hammarby, over which parish his elder brother then presided, and which came afterward under the pastoral charge of Provost Frenkman, no doubt in consequence of his marriage with the niece of the former minister, who brought him considerable property, and who was Alfhild's mother.

Captain Oernroos had lived many years at the parsonage, and been a witness of its ancient and modern history. Alfhild was his favourite and comfort. His even and kind disposition often healed the wounds which the iron will of her father inflicted on the delicate being. Alfhild, therefore, clung with gratitude and affection to the old man, who had always taken the office of mediator between herself and her father.

"What is the matter, my child? I hear a singular ringing." With these words, Uncle Sebastian crossed the threshold, and closed the doors slowly behind him. "What was it that rang so peculiarly?"

Alfhild did not answer; she only pointed with outstretched hand to the fragments of the broken goblet.

"God help us! God help us!" exclaimed Uncle Sebastian, as his eye caught the pieces. "The beautiful wedding present!" continued he, grumbling. "The fatal goblets bring fear and trouble, even to the third and fourth generation. Child! child! why must your hand touch this goblet? What brought the unlucky idea in your head of taking down the old monster, which has stood, dusty and forgotten, on the case yonder, for the last fifteen years?"

"Papa ordered me," answered Alfhild, with trembling voice, "to wash and place it by the plate of the bishop on this solemn occasion."

"If it had been by the plate of the count, one might see some reason for it," grumbled Sebastian, and with his eyes resting upon the fragments, his mind seemed to glide back to a time long past.

"Why by the plate of the count?" asked Alfhild, in whom even the sorrow of the moment could not suppress the besetting sin of woman.

"Vengeance certainly will come sooner or later," uttered Sebastian, almost inaudibly, and unconscious that his thoughts had taken the form of words till his eyes fell upon the face of Alfhild, which expressed the greatest astonishment.

"I am talking nonsense," he said quickly. "Gather up the pieces, child, and listen patiently to the lecture that awaits you. You have nothing to fear to-day, and to-morrow I hope to convince your father that the thing is not worth talking about."

"But this evening, after the visitors have left, Uncle Sebastian?" said Alfhild, with a timid look upon her old friend.

"It is then that I mean to set all right again. Now put the pieces out of sight, and wipe off your tears, that they do not betray you before them. Do not be troubled, my dove; Uncle Sebastian will not forsake you."

Alfhild obeyed mechanically, and when she had gathered all the leaves and pieces of glass in her apron she turned once more with a supplicating look toward the old man. There was something in his face and eyes, which seemed to be in contrast with the kind words he had just uttered, and this troubled Alfhild still more.

"Best uncle," said she, in a beseeching tone, "may I not come to your room this evening? I am no longer a child, so that you need not fear to tell me the secret history of these goblets."

"There is nothing to tell, my child. But you had better go now, and busy yourself with what is yet to be done in house and kitchen; and remember that in less than half an hour we shall have here the bishop, the count, your father, and all the potentates and dignitaries of the parish. You have to-day an opportunity of practising the difficult art of self-command, so indispensable for your sex, and I hope that my Alfhild will go through this first trial like a heroine."

Alfhild left the room in silence, being fully conscious of the necessity of following Uncle Sebastian's advice. The many arrangements entrusted to her care, consumed so much of the remaining time, that she had scarcely taken the last papillote out of her hair, when the maid Stina informed her that the people were coming from church.

Alfhild's simple toilet was soon finished; and a few minutes after she stood at the door to receive, as hostess, the high guests.

Not a parsonage in all Sweden could boast of a situation so beautiful as that of Hammarby. On one side a little lake faithfully mirrored the distant hills and forests; and on the other, a range of densely-timbered hills stretched away on either hand, shutting out as it were, the turmoil and confusion of the great world. Standing at the parsonage, the eye roved over a prospect which, even when winter reigned supreme, and the sun far off in the south forced his pale and fireless beams into the valley, might favourably contrast with many a scene of world-renowned beauty. At the extremity of the mountain range stood the crumbling walls of the old church, this day deserted and left to dilapidation and ruin. Over the weather-beaten steeple hovered a number of crows, frightened by the building committee out of the old walls, where they meant to pass the winter, and which they now appeared ready to leave. On the opposite side of the lake stood the white walls of the count's castle, the polished parapet of the balcony reflecting the sunbeams like a mirror. A little beyond, the ruins of the old castle met the eye; left entirely tenantless—for the count's antiquarian love was not sufficiently strong to induce him to preserve the home of his fathers.

But we are wandering too far from our story.

Fine and placid was the day, beautiful and calm the picture which, with many changes of light and shade, lay spread before the parsonage—beautiful and calm appeared the procession which was now approaching. The golden cross on the breast of the bishop shone brightly in the noon-day sun; Alfhild's eyes rested, as if spell-bound, upon the sacred symbol. The young girl thought of and saw nothing but this illustrious guest. She did not notice that the count walked at his right, her father at his left; nor did she hear a word of the kind speech with which the count introduced her to the bishop; and not till the latter had imprinted a light kiss upon her forehead, was she able to bid him welcome.

The glasses were already filled after soup, small pasties had been passed round, and the provost's elegant speech, and "the honour that had befallen his humble house," was half-finished, when his eye unfortunately fell upon the hand of the bishop, which was holding a common wine-glass. The provost stopped; a glance, which drove every drop of blood from poor Alfhild's face, told her that the dreaded discovery was made.

The provost, however, collected himself, and brought his speech to a close, with giving a toast in honour of the head of the church, which was succeeded by another, to the happy completion of the present undertaking. Now the bishop rose, and addressed the company. He spoke with dignity and warmth amid general attention; and his hearers were made to ask of themselves, what course things might take ere the time that the consecration of the new house of God should again bring them together?

After the excitement had subsided into the common channel of conversation, the question of where to find an architect arose. The provost produced a plan by a very skilful architect of Stockholm; but the count thought that this man would be too expensive; and a proper person might be found without going to the capital.

At these remarks, the provost's already gloomy brow began to darken still more; the following words of the bishop, however, had a soothing effect on him: "A young Norwegian, a skilful architect, with good testimonials, and of good education, was a few days ago recommended to me. He is travelling to study art, or as I have reason to believe, for pleasure, and intends to remain in Sweden a few years."

This proposal seemed to meet with general approbation, no doubt because it came from the bishop; for, in regard to its expensiveness, it, perhaps, gave no better prospect than the first. This, however, could not now be thought of; only Uncle Sebastian murmured to himself, "A Norwegian—and the goblet was broken this very day. This will not end well."

He could not express his displeasure, because the count gave his unreserved approbation to the proposition. Dissatisfaction and indignation, however, troubled him, which, no doubt, were caused by the memory of events of by-gone days.

The bishop and the count returned to the castle after dinner, and the other guests took leave one after the other, so that toward evening the moon, looking from behind the old church through the windows of the parsonage, found only a group of three persons round the fireside.

Alfhild had made a full confession to her father; but found to her great astonishment, and still greater grief, that a deeper feeling than mere anger affected him. He sat, with his head upon his breast, without uttering a single word. One hand rested upon the arm of the chair, and the other played with Alfhild's locks, while he was wholly absent in his mind, which was very rare with him. She had taken a seat at his feet, and felt pleasant and painful presentiments moving her breast, as she laid her head upon her father's knee for the first time since her childhood. It gave infinite joy to her heart to feel his caressing hand. Uncle Sebastian was walking, in short semicircles, round the fire-place, smoking his evening pipe. A harsh "hem! hem!" now and then breaking from his mouth, was the only sound which interrupted the silence.

"No! it will not do!" at length said the provost, in a tone which showed a determination to control the impressions made upon him; "it will not do. We must not give ourselves entirely up to our feelings. It must be the festivity of the day which excites me so unusually; and to this is added, that we have to-day the anniversary of a momentous and sad hour. Have you thought of it, my child, that this is the day your mother died? Have you prayed to-day, Alfhild?"

"No, dear father, not yet; but I will do it now," said Alfhild, in a pious tone. She could not help, however, feeling a slight shudder thrill through her, as her thoughts involuntarily passed from the death of her mother to the broken goblet. Yet these dark thoughts soon gave way to more pleasant images. Bright tears of joy coursed down her cheeks; it did her heart good to pray with her father. She had never known the affectionate caress of a mother, had never seen tears in her eyes, nor heard the warm prayer for the welfare of her child from her lips. Alfhild had nestled but few weeks upon the breast of her mother, when death called her away. Brought up by the hard hands of man, she had a dim feeling that something was wanting; and that, being a single weak tendril, she was growing up, though supported by two strong oaks, without a trellis round which she might twine herself.

Alfhild shed not bitter, but refreshing tears; and if ever a prayer from pure lips reached, on wings of devotion, the throne of the Father of all, that of Alfhild certainly penetrated there. Hope, comfort, and peace beamed from her eyes, as she rose. Leaning over to her father, she said in a low tone;

"Now I have prayed, and I shall never again forget it."

The provost touched, in blessing, the brow of his child, and said: "Go to your room, my child, we will take no supper."

Alfhild withdrew; the provost and Uncle Sebastian, however, sat in serious conversation till late at night.

"Why must this have happened just to-day?" exclaimed Provost Frenkman, while he rose and lighted a taper; "what has this history to do with the church affairs?"

"The ways of the Lord are inscrutable," answered Uncle Sebastian; "the future will lift the veil."

CHAPTER II.

THE NORWEGIAN ARCHITECT.

WINTER was gone, and already sprouted here and there a bud in the twigs of the high birch-trees that inclosed the court of the castle of Great-Hammarby. The coach, with the count's coat-of-arms on both doors, and drawn by four swift steeds that had not their equal in the whole country around, stood in waiting at the great staircase. Eager footmen were running to and fro in the long corridors, since the extraordinary event took place—that the countess and her sister, the "German baroness," (as she was every where called, having been married in Germany and returned a widow,) had the condescending intention of paying a visit to the "little people" in the neighbourhood.

After the carriage had been in waiting a long time, the ladies finished their game at chess, and seated themselves upon the sofa to take coffee at their leisure.

The two ladies were in a small saloon, which, by a glass door, was connected with the music-room. Now and then, while their fingers, adorned with diamond rings, leisurely moved the tea-spoons in the gilded cups, or moistened the lips with the aromatic potion, they listened or looked toward the glass door.

"Thelma's embroidery grows quite handsome," began the Baroness Ravenstein, leaving, with some difficulty, her comfortable position, and stepping to an embroidery frame, which stood near the glass door. Quite naturally, her look turned from the frame into the adjoining room, and with her finger on her lips, she motioned to her sister to come. The rising of the countess being always connected with some noise, and this being the case now, the countess lost the pleasure which the baroness had intended for her.

In the music-room likewise a movement was made—a few notes on the piano were heard, and immediately after, a young man of sallow, sickly appearance, entered the saloon. His figure, far below middle size, was so much bent forward, that one could hardly distinguish whether the sufferings of many years had given to his back the almost spherical form, or whether he was born with this defect. In his frightfully ugly face was most distinctly stamped, peevishness, ill-humour, and caprice; yet there could be seen here and there an expression that might be called proud and supercilious: his forehead was adorned with red, straight hair.

This person was the only descendant of the illustrious house, the hereditary count and heir to the estate.

"Do my mother and aunt intend to take a drive?" asked the count, throwing himself carelessly on a sofa.

"For a few hours, my dearest Albano," answered the countess, almost caressingly, and the tone of her voice distinctly showed that it was the indulgent mother who was speaking to her adored and deified son.

"My daughter shall entertain you," observed the baroness, with an exceedingly sweet smile; "and I believe she takes pleasure in doing it," added she, in a louder voice, since the silence of the count might be ascribed either to a momentary hardness of hearing, or to his usual absence of mind.

"On this point she should not be dictated to," answered Albano, dryly; "I do not like forced, involuntary company."

"Something has again passed between them," whispered the baroness to her sister.

The countess rang the bell; the waiting-maid came in with the cloaks, which the ladies put on, and then withdrew through the music-room.

Count Albano rose up to bow, as in duty bound, to his mother and aunt, and then seated himself again on the sofa, and sought to gain the most comfortable position possible. It was, however, a very rare case indeed, that he allowed himself to be guilty of the want of attention not to wait upon his mother to the carriage when she rode out. There must, therefore, be some particular reason why he left the duties of politeness thus neglected.

In the mean time the ladies exchanged, in the adjoining room, some half audible words together, and Albano's fixed and attentive look clearly showed that he endeavoured to catch them, though he remained motionless. When the outer doors were closed, and all was still, he murmured peevishly,—

"Probably new hints how a poor lady must conduct herself to catch a mis-shapen, but richly entailed heir. But they are of no effect, thanks to heaven! for, alas! ha, ha, ha, ha!—my appearance is not such as to make me succeed with my beautiful cousin on my own attractions; but, by my honour, they will not cheat me! I was near going into the snare, when I fortunately observed something of motherly anxiety in the baroness, and immediately fell from my new heaven. Besides I have nothing there to look for," added he, after a short pause, twisting himself on the sofa into different positions. "No; it is not possible to rest, sleep, or dream!"

Albano raised himself half up, and threw the sofa-cushion, which was entirely innocent of his want of rest, with such violence from him, that it flew clattering through the glass door into the music-room. Immediately after, the rustling of a silk dress was heard; a young lady opened the glass door, and stopped upon the threshold.

"Was this call intended for me?" asked Lady Ravenstein, in a tone half vexed and half surprised.

"Beg your pardon, it was done half against my will," answered Albano; while he rose, went to the window, opened it and called out to one of the many sluggards in livery, who were occupied in the court-yard with doing nothing.

The entrance of the servant appeared to be no unwelcome interruption of the *tête-à-tête*. The cushion was put in its place again; the fragments of glass were taken up, and the order given to have the door repaired by a glazier.

"Is my father at home?"

This question was made as if without purpose, as the servant was about to go out.

"No, your lordship."

"Then make haste to have it repaired."

The servant went out.

"Ah!" said Thelma, "how bright, clear, and fresh it looks out of doors!"

The tone, however, in which she spoke this, was far from that unmeaning indifference with which such remarks are generally made on the weather. Nor was it a want of other topics for conversation, which called forth this exclamation. It sprang from a desire to enjoy all those glorious things which nature unfolded without in all the splendour of spring. But she could not go there, since a command from her mother had enjoined her to stay at home and keep her cousin company, and Thelma had early learned to submit to the whims of others.

"My cousin, then, loves every thing that is fresh, clear and beautiful?" rejoined Albano, giving his words an emphasis that gave the young lady, who was well acquainted with his distrustful disposition, to understand, that he had found an object to vent his irritable ill-humour upon.

"Do you not love nature, Albano, and a pleasant, clear spring day?" she asked, gently.

"Nature? oh, yes; but in a different garment. A stormy October evening, with torrents of rain, that is something for me; that harmonises with my mind, which a spring day, with its calm beauty and its eternal green, can never do."

"Why not, Albano? tell me, why not?" Thelma let her hand and needle rest; her eyes followed her cousin with an unquiet beseeching expression.

"Why? You often trouble me with this word, Thelma, which has for me a peculiar, cold tone. I cannot tell you so as to make you understand me."

"Say it, Albano: it will comfort you to speak on what grieves you. I understand you perfectly,"

"No, dear Thelma, that you do not! I do not understand myself! how then could you understand me? One thing, however, I know; and this is, that you are too good and indulgent toward the outbreaks of my involuntary passion. Would that you were so, without others influencing your heart! But you are good, gentle, and patient to obey, from habit. My Aunt Ravenstein has studied the art of education excellently well."

"I do not understand you, Albano—at least I hope so; for why should it be your intention to hurt me?"

"No, that would indeed be a bad reward; that you, with the patience of an angel, the first degrees of a—"

Albano suddenly stopped; a lively colour covered his sallow countenance for a few moments. He felt a pain shoot through his breast, as he always did when the demon of distrust seized him; but a glance upon Thelma's gentle, innocent face, soon caused him to feel the wrong which he did her, and his suspicion gave way to a better feeling.

Silence followed, during which both felt themselves oppressed. Thelma shared, with many daughters of Eve, the weakness of breaking into tears easily. Albano, of course, should not see it; she, therefore, put her working-frame aside, and rose to leave the room.

"Thelma," said he, approaching her, "I did you wrong; I am a wild person, a monster who torments you; but, if you would understand me—but that is impossible! You cannot comprehend the pains I suffer, nor know the continual discord that lacerates my soul."

"My dearest Albano, we are now so much excited, let me go out for a moment. I am not dissatisfied with you nor offended; do I not know that you cannot be like other people? But let me go, Albano! It is so warm here."

"And it will grow so cold when you leave me. Do as you please, however, Thelma. Have you now no answer for me,—not even your usual *why?*" asked Albano, in a bitter tone. "But am I not a fool!" he continued, "I will take a ride; my horse has been saddled long ago; I shall——"

"No, Albano, you shall not do again as you did a few days ago," Thelma interrupted him. "You must not ride into the woods and stay away till late at night, so that we are almost frightened to death. That

you must not do, dear Albano, do you hear? Allow me rather to accompany you; I love riding so well."

"And if some one should meet us," exclaimed Albano, with a
disagreeable laugh; "he will think that a monster is eloping with a
fair princess."

"How can you jest so cruelly?" said Thelma. "No one will think
any thing of it, but that we ride to enjoy the fresh air. Come, dear
Albano, I look forward to our ride with the delight of a child."

"You, good angel, understand how to manage the poor sick patient. You wish to reconcile him to himself and to his fate, but this
task is not so easy. However, dress yourself, we will no longer dwell
on this."

Half an hour after they had gone a yellow *calêche* drove into the
court; an elderly gentleman alighted—it was the "old count," who
immediately proceeded to his separate apartments.

"Tell the old Borgstedt to bring me the letter-bag," was the short
order which the lord of the castle gave when he had reached his
room; whereupon he seated himself in a high-backed easy-chair, and
let his head sink back upon the soft velvet cushion.

He had rested but a few moments, however, when creaking footsteps, in even measured time, approached the door; and a head with
silvery hair was seen stuck through it, and then a small compact figure entered.

This was the old book-keeper, who, being born and brought up
at the castle, constituted, undoubtedly, one of the most valuable articles in its inventory.

"Give me the letters, and sit down meanwhile," said the count,
condescendingly.

The old man laid a number of papers upon the table before his
lord, and took a seat at the extreme end of a sofa near the door, where
he had sat countless times awaiting orders, or conversing with his
lord, when he allowed him the honour to commence a conversation
on what had taken place that was of interest.

"Well, obedient servant, have we at last the honour," said the
count, half in vexation, and half in pleasure, after having read the
signature of a letter by an unknown hand. Half audibly he read the
following short note:

"Highly honoured count: Various previous engagements which honour required me to fulfil, caused a longer delay in performing the promise I gave to the Right Reverend Bishop F., to come to Hammarby at the beginning of March. My business is now entirely finished, and toward the end of this month I shall have the honour to wait upon your excellency in person."

"With distinguished consideration,

"RUDOLPH SEILER, Architect,

"B———, 15th April 1791."

"You see, my old friend, this wish will now also be fulfilled," said the count. "Within a few days our Norwegian architect will arrive. Summon, therefore, labourers from all quarters, as many as you can get; for when the matter is taken hold of, I wish it should be done with vigour."

"Is it a Norwegian who is to build our new church?" Borgstedt asked, with a peculiar expression of voice; and this circumstance seemed to have withdrawn his attention from whatever else the count had said. Somewhat hesitatingly he added: "Your excellency had not mentioned a syllable of this before."

"Was it then worth while, you foolish man?" said the count, smiling. "Whether the architect is from Sweden or Norway can be indifferent, if he only understands his business, and that I have been assured is the case with this young man."

"Young man!" Borgstedt interrupted with a sigh; "then—young too."

"I believe, old man, you have to-day a crazy turn. What is the cause of your dislike of the Norwegians?"

"Dislike! Heaven forbid, your excellency! I have none. On the contrary, the Norwegians are, in my opinion, a bold and able people; but I wish that none of them would come here, for I think it is better that every one should stay at home."

It was probable that Borgstedt meant something that he did not wish to utter.

"Is Mr. Seiler to stay at the castle?" he asked, as the count was just about to dismiss him with a friendly motion.

"No; it is too far from the church. I have made an arrangement with Provost Frenkman, at whose house he will find accommodations. This will be best for all of us."

"Certainly; no doubt; but yet, your excellency, there is something in it that strikes one unpleasantly. It may be that I already begin to grow childish—but the whole matter will go wrong. It is only good," added he, "that the young count does not feel himself much attracted to the parsonage, and besides, he is very different from what young gentlemen of his age generally are."

"Hear, sir!" said the count, sternly, "I begin to fear that all is not right in your head—or has your age, as you observed, really made you childish? What has my son to do with all this matter? But, *àpropos*, is Albano at home?"

"No, your excellency; he just rode out with the young lady."

Borgstedt seemed to wish to change the subject of conversation, and he knew he should, if he only mentioned the young lady.

He had not miscalculated. With a more cheerful face the count said:

"Good; I am pleased with that. Thelma is exactly the girl for the sick youth. She is possessed of the first and most requisite qualities which the wife of a man in his condition should have; she is poor, gentle, and prudent. He would never have cast his eye upon a rich girl; but he must find something also in her that does not please him, as he does not begin to act in earnest."

"Oh, your excellency, what he is not pleased with is evident enough!"

"Well, what is it, then, old man? You have, perhaps, a fit of your former sagacity. Let me hear it. You may speak your opinion boldly."

"I think, your excellency, that all would go on in the natural way, if no one concerned themselves about it; but now comes her ladyship, the baroness, and puts her nose into every thing, excuse the expression, and tries to put in order what never was out of order. The opportunities brought about on purpose, the calculations and plans seen through, put the young count out of humour; and that is not to be wondered at, for in this way, he can never judge whether the friendliness of the young lady is voluntary or commanded by her mother."

"There you are not so very wrong, Borgstedt. I see you have not yet forgotten to make observations. But as regards my sister-in-law, the baroness, you must see that the bare hope for such a match is sufficient to turn the brain of a woman who has nothing except a daughter without dower, and a title without income. It is, indeed, no trifle for a poor young lady to be married to the heir of Hammarby."

"No, certainly not, your excellency, but when you look at it from another side, it is no trifle either, for a beautiful young lady to take the office of a nurse for her whole life."

"Borgstedt, you take too much liberty with the permission to utter your thoughts, which I gave you in consideration of your long and faithful services," said the count, with evident displeasure.

"Then I ask your pardon, your excellency; I shall never open my mouth again."

Borgstedt rose to go to his office.

"Wait, wait, I pray, you old bull-head, and sit down for a little while longer," exclaimed the count, in a jesting and pacifying tone. "You have, no doubt, something more in your heart. Speak, and let me hear whether it is any thing consonant with sound reason."

"No, your excellency, I have nothing more to say on this matter; I only wish, with all my heart, that it may be a good marriage; by which I mean that the heart may follow the hand, for then it is easy to bear the evil days. And, as far as I know the young lady, the best may be expected from her, if she be not continually tormented by the distrust of the young count. However, I said it, and say it again, he would have no suspicion if her ladyship, the baroness, would keep her hand out of the play; for I know he loves the young lady."

"Yes, that I also believe, and it would be well if we had the wedding soon. I shall take no joy in life and my excellent improvements, till I see yet another heir to my name and fortune growing up: for Albano's health promises no long life. And as I think more on what you say of my sister-in-law, I find that you are not so entirely wrong. At dinner, I shall give her a little lecture on this point."

With a smile of perfect satisfaction, the old man withdrew. The baroness was a thorn in his side, since her supercilious conduct often made him feel how little she regarded him for his fifty years' service. The baroness and the countess had their peculiar prejudices; a subordinate person was to them nothing more than a thing which is used when necessity demands it, but which is not the least noticed except then.

Not so the count. He also was proud, but in a manner which did not prevent him allowing, and acknowledging other merits besides the pedigree. He wished to be thought popular, a friend of the people, and gracious to everybody; in short, a patriot, and a man of fashion and education, and he was, therefore, courteous and civil to all that came near him. Yet, in reality, he contented himself with the outward appearance; he was satisfied if they believed him capable of those virtues; and how it was, in *fact*, in regard to all this, does not belong to our subject.

How few of our fellow-beings show to the world what they really are!

CHAPTER III.

THE ANTIQUE CHAMBER.

"WILL you come with me, Uncle Sebastian, and see how you like my little arrangements?" said Alfhild, putting her head, with a friendly nod, through the door of Uncle Sebastian's room.

"The new arrangements cannot be very great, as your rooms for visitors are always in the best order," answered Sebastian. "Besides, I have yet to look over several accounts," added he, with an uncommon coldness.

"I believe you are angry, dear uncle; but I hope it is not with me?" Alfhild's delicate white hands stroked the old gentleman's wrinkled face; "not with me?" continued she. "Do you hear? Do answer, and come with me. I shall not rest till somebody has admired my arrangements."

"What a singular girl you are! A bed with white covers, clean window curtains, and some glasses or vases with flowers, I have seen before. Let me alone; I wish that both the guest and the count, whom we have to thank for the first, were where the pepper grows."

"You certainly are in the most singular humour, dear uncle; so very much vexed! What am I to do to make you cheerful and good again? Do tell me! You, yourself, often told me, that to communicate makes the heart light. What in all the world has the count done to you, who are always so very civil; but what, above all others, has the architect done to you, whom you have never seen?"

"I have nothing against any body. You really seem to be anxious to see this architect; but he will come soon enough, and that is all I have to say."

"You feel thus when the weather is going to change," said Alfhild, jestingly. "I think, uncle, the horizon of your humour is this evening more clouded than usual; no doubt a storm is gathering—don't you think so?"

"Yes, that is what I mean; but leave me now, you little prattler! You will find something better to do than to stay here and argue with your bearish Uncle Sebastian."

"No, indeed, and we shall not remain good friends if you do not immediately come with me. I assure you that you will see something entirely different from a common guest-room."

"Well, to get rid of you, I will go."

The captain went, holding Alfhild's hand in his own, into the hall.

"Not here," said Alfhild, with delight. "Up stairs, up stairs, uncle, in the attic."

"In the attic! What does that mean? I hope you do not intend to lodge him there?"

"Only wait, you will see."

And Alfhild drew the old gentleman along up stairs into the spacious attic, the floor of which was strewn with green sprouts of fir. Here stood the red, blue, and yellow chests of the servants, and their bright-coloured Sunday dresses hung up in a long row along the wall. On one side of the gable she stopped, and put her hand into her small apron pocket to take the key.

"My child, I hope you have not intended this room for him?" asked Sebastian, while, at the same time, he pressed Alfhild's arm so tightly that she uttered a shriek.

"Why?—yes, I have, uncle."

She opened the door. Both now entered into a large square room, which was hung with old-fashioned, yet preserved tapestry, representing the scenes of Abelard and Heloise.[1] Its furniture was as antiquated and as costly as the former, and consisted of old, heavy armchairs, which were, however, easy and commodious, and a soft, well-stuffed

---

[1] Scholastic philosopher Peter Abelard (1079-1142) and his student Heloise (1101-1162) shared a tragic love affair that inspired a variety of artistic works.

sofa, covered with a black material of horse-hair. A beautiful table of oak, with inlaid work, stood before it; and over two smaller grey marble tables hung mirrors in frames of ebony. Between them, in a deep-carved niche, was the high window; two steps led to it; on the platform before it two arm-chairs were placed, whose richly-embroidered covers bespoke the taste and skill of the workman. On the right side of the window, opposite the sofa, stood a bed with snow-white curtains, which evidently belonged to a different age. Alfhild had taken care to change the heavy calico draperies, with large flowers on them, for light, airy muslin curtains. The rest of the inventory in the room was an old black writing bureau, and a fire-screen of the same material with the chair covers. But over the fire-place hung a picture, which was, perhaps, the crown of the whole. It was the bust of a young girl, of such beauty and expression as enchanted the eyes but chilled the heart. The black, flashing eyes had something undefinable in them, and the curled lip might be compared to the rolling ocean, of which we do not know what is hid in its bosom.

"Now, my dear uncle, is not this an excellent idea of mine?" asked Alfhild, clapping her hands for delight at her work. "Can you imagine any thing more handsome and comfortable than this room? There is something so grand, so—I do not know what to call it, that chains me here. But, I assure you, it cost me a great deal of labour to clear away the large quantities of dust and cobwebs. I had it at least six times scoured, and I rubbed off the tapestry with my own hands, and your finest brushes—which you do not at all know how I used, uncle—but they do shine for it as much as formerly. Indeed, you can't believe that such things want to be handled carefully. And the cushioned chairs—you should have seen how I beat them! I feared Mr. Amar and his company of love-rogues might run off with fright. But they held out faithfully, and now they stand there as if born anew, and look at me with their roguish eyes. But, dear uncle, you do not listen to me; you stand there as if dropped from the clouds. Have I done any thing wrong or wicked in arranging this room for our guest? But I have not yet told you why I did all this. Come with me to the window, and follow my hand with your eyes; there you see the old church which is almost tumbling down, and seems to give a parting sigh; and here the open ground, where the new one is to be built. Now imagine that our architect will sit here every morning and evening, and resting his arms upon the window-sill will view his work. The contrast between the old and new will inspire him, I hope; or what do you think, uncle, does an architect not need inspiration?"

"May God be with us!" sighed Sebastian, extremely oppressed at this moment; "God be with us. Inspiration!—I tell you, girl, that inspirations are good for nothing; they are the work of the devil, and do more mischief than all other things together. I ask you what else is it but a cursed inspiration that induced you to this foolish undertaking of putting this room in order, which had stood untouched for more than fifty years?"

"But what is there wrong in it, my dear uncle? On the contrary, it is useful and good, for the room had to be put in order, at all events, sooner or later, and—"

"And——You are a blind child, going madly on as if there was nothing in the world but jest and play," interrupted Sebastian. "Now, Alfhild, this room gives you delight; you have looked forward to this joy, as you did formerly to a new doll, and as you will in future to any other fancy-work. I will tell you a fable, which teaches how it often happens that, having obtained our wished-for ends, incidents occur which make us wish that we might recover our former position. A peasant found that a calf, which he had sent to the pasture, had been soon after stolen. The peasant fell on his knees and prayed: 'Great Pan,[1] I will sacrifice to thee a buck if you will show me the thief.' Pan granted his prayer; a terrible panther came rushing toward him. 'Great Pan,' now prayed the peasant, 'deliver me from this monster and I will sacrifice to thee two bucks.' Believe me, my child, our wishes are of the same kind, and generally similar in their consequences."

"You are very unkind to-day, my dear uncle," said Alfhild, plucking him by the beard, with a roguish smile. "Why are you so grave and singular, as if it regarded some unheard-of mishap, while it concerns only the most insignificant matter in the world. You have no eye for any thing to-day; you praise neither my industry nor my arrangements; however, this shall not disturb me. I know you have your whims sometimes; yet I like you nevertheless. However, you must promise me one thing, and that is, that you will be kind and friendly

---

[1] According to Greek mythology, Pan, the god of nature, watches especially over shepherds and their flocks.

to the expected stranger; for I can imagine how painful it must be to be treated unkindly in a house which one enters as guest. But, dear uncle, do drive the clouds away from your brow."

Alfhild's tone had changed from the lightest jesting to the tenderest request. She pressed her head close to the shoulder of her uncle, and her hand strayed between the coat-collar and the red silken neckcloth which Uncle Sebastian wore. The consequence of it was, that the temperature of his heart began to rise, which could be perceived most clearly by the tone of his voice, as he spoke in his usual good-natured manner,—

"Well, well, my child, let it be so. Perhaps it will not turn out so bad as I fear. Does your father know of this?"

"Yes, indeed; papa entirely agreed with my proposal; for, being obliged to receive guests so very often, we can, indeed, hardly refuse one of our common rooms for strangers for a long time. But, uncle, we agreed not to tell you any thing of it till all was ready; for we feared your spirit of contradiction, which always shows itself in finding fault, if the question is on an innovation."

"Indeed; but you did not hesitate to turn every thing topsy-turvy when my back was turned."

"Now you are good again, uncle."

Alfhild, at the same time, kissed the old man's forehead, and then turned, with a roguish expression of countenance, the conversation upon the accounts that were to be examined.

"That's true, my child, your thoughts hit upon the right subject. Good-bye then; I suppose you have still many things to do. But just come here and place yourself against the light; I want to see whether there is any resemblance between you and the picture up there."

"Yes, so do. I have often looked at that portrait myself, and it seemed to me that it resembled me a little. Who is it?"

"Your grandmother, my late sister; but, heaven be thanked! your eyes have not the same fire, though they are as clear, and the smile round your mouth is not the same. Your eyes and lips are a faithful image of your soul, and innocent sentiments. But not a word more on that. All this is long buried, and peace be with the dead."

"But, uncle, why does not this portrait of grandmother's hang with the rest in the dining-room?"

"For the reason, because this room was occupied by some one

who loved this picture very much, and chose this place for it: but afterward things took place, connected with your mother, which caused... But why do I pass the time here in prattling on things... Forget what I told you, my child, and instead of it, remember to send me my hyssop tea very soon; you know my cough does not abate."

With these words, Sebastian left the room, his eyes still lingering on his darling. Alfhild fell into a sombre mood, and with an almost fearful feeling she turned her eyes from the portrait and stepped to the window, which she opened to breathe the fragrant spring air.

The sun was just disappearing behind the hills, his last rays glimmering on the faded gilding of the old church steeple. Evening was drawing near, and sad and gloomy feelings awoke in Alfhild's soul. The future was the theme of her musing; and she longed to know whether friendly stars would light her earthly path.

She rested her face upon her hand and pensively listened, while from the old church tower pealed out the solemn tones of the evening bell, with which suddenly mingled the rattling noise of an approaching carriage.

"There he is! there is the architect, most certainly!" exclaimed Alfhild; and her heart beat more restlessly. She had always looked with delight for the arrival of the guest, yet now she trembled through fear of Uncle Sebastian's ill-humour. There was now, however, no time for trembling. She ran quickly down stairs into her father's room, who had heard the clattering of the carriage, and was exchanging, in all haste, his gown for a black official garment, in order to receive properly the guest that had been recommended so particularly by the count.

When father and daughter—for Alfhild represented the hostess—came into the front hall, all was still. They went out, but they saw no carriage. They looked to the right and left, and then with surprise at each other. No carriage was to be seen either near or far; all remained quiet.

"We must have heard wrong," said the provost, looking up the road.

"No, certainly not, papa," answered Alfhild; "it certainly was a carriage, and I even heard the snorting of the horse."

"You foolish girl! you see that it was a mistake, since no one has come, and nothing is to be seen around," said the provost. "But let us go in; and do not mention it to your Uncle Sebastian—he would only laugh at us."

They went back into the room. The provost filled his pipe and took a newspaper, and Alfhild some work; their thoughts, however, were occupied with things wholly different.

About half an hour had passed, when again they distinctly heard the clattering of a carriage and the snorting of a horse, close by the house.

"If this is an illusion," exclaimed the provost, rising, "then the devil is at play!"

"No, papa, the carriage stops at our door," said Alfhild with animation. "Now certainly we are not deceived."

Alfhild was right. When they went out a cabriolet stopped, and out of it sprang the expected architect.

Rudolph Seiler, our architect, measured nearly six feet, and had a highly-arched chest, and athletic shoulders, on which he seemed to be able to carry no insignificant burden. His face was oval, and showed a profile whose whole proportions proved, as far as one could judge by them, a noble, aspiring mind. His arched forehead, which was crossed by two large veins, projected somewhat, and formed a deep wrinkle between his dark eyebrows. His complexion was of a kind that becomes a man; not like cream and strawberries, but brown and vigorous.

Thus stood the architect before his host. Was he handsome or ill-favoured? That Alfhild would not say, however closely she regarded him; but when he stood in the room, and bowed with the ease and winning manner of a polished man of the world, and asked to be allowed to share their home, then light sprung up in Alfhild's soul, and she was astonished not to have seen at the first glance that the architect was the most beautiful man she had ever beheld.

Though the provost did not think with his daughter, yet he thought the guest at least a very polished, handsome young man, with whom, to judge by the beginning, he hoped to harmonize. In consequence of it, he immediately offered him a pipe, and told Alfhild, in a whisper, to send for some of the beer two years old, which was distinguished both for its good taste and its beautiful colour.

The two men took a seat on a sofa. Seiler had, in a short time, with an easy, skilful tact, brought the conversation upon the building of the church, the count's family and castle, and the ruins, and had then passed over to a comparison of the past with the present, in a political point of view. Besides, the architect had exercised so much skill in the difficult art of entertaining a stranger, that the provost felt very happy to have under his roof a guest who promised to give him, in his monotonous life, such various entertainment.

Alfhild now came with the beer, and placed a table before the gentlemen. The large tobacco-box of the provost, the meerschaum-bowls, and the glasses, looked well by the side of the polished silver cans, containing the beer.

"We generally drink it with sugar," said the provost, "for it is very strong, you must know."

"I, too, will thank you for some," answered Seiler, and with a pleasant expression, reached his glass toward Alfhild.

"Upon my honour," exclaimed he, drinking off the foam, and casting an animated look upon Alfhild, "I believe even Valhalla[1] could not afford a better drink!" and he emptied the glass to the bottom.

At this moment Uncle Sebastian entered, and the provost introduced him to the guest. The countenance of the architect assumed a higher colour; but this probably arose from his surprise at Captain Oernroos's strange salute, which consisted only of the words, spoken with great absence of mind:

"Yes, indeed! ha! I imagined so!"

CHAPTER IV.

THE PORTRAIT AND THE OMENS.

THE first rays of the morning sun had not yet drunk the dew-drops, when Seiler was up, and sat in his morning-gown in a corner of the sofa. He had not slept well, and therefore he had risen earlier than usual. He was now occupied with looking over some papers that lay before him on the table.

If one had judged from his examining eye, which settled now on this and now on that piece of furniture in the room, and then again

---

[1] According to Norse mythology, Valhalla is the hall of the slain, where heroes who died gloriously in battle feast and drink with the god Odin.

with rapidity ran over some lines in the manuscript, one would have been induced to take him for a traveller who, guide-book in hand, sails along a river looking for every place that is mentioned. At length he laid the pamphlet aside, and sank, with his arms folded, in deep thoughts; but they could not be of a friendly and cheerful nature, for his face grew darker, and the wrinkle between the eyebrows deeper.

"The bed-curtains with large flowers are not here," said he, in a voice hardly audible; "the innocent angel has put white ones instead. Ah! one does not sleep very well behind these pure white hangings, unless the soul is also white and pure. But is there not something moving outside the door, in the empty garret? I hope no listener has come."

Seiler rose and went to the door, which he slowly opened. Nobody was to be seen. All was silent as the grave, only now and then a draught of air waved one or other of the Sunday dresses of the servants hung up there. A slight shudder crept through Seiler's soul. It seemed to him that these black frocks with white aprons were unfriendly ghosts, nodding to him their morning salutes.

"It is a stupid and bad custom to deck out the walls in this manner," thought he, being out of humour. "If we consider that all these outward covers, which hang here like culprits on the gallows, but a short time before inclosed beings with a restless soul within them, then the exhibition of these masks makes a ghost-like impression. However, they are not worth dwelling on longer."

Seiler again shut the door, and began pacing up and down the beautiful spacious room. Soon other chords began to vibrate in his soul, of which his beaming eye and smoothed brow again bore witness.

"Oh! ye wonderfully beautiful notes, swelling up from the heart-strings like sounds of sweet music!" said he, half whispering; "from what source do ye come, and whither do ye go? I have lived—I have enjoyed the fairest scene of life, and have drained to the dregs the cup of misery, held to the lips of the children of the earth ever since the first transgressor lost Paradise and happiness; and yet—yet—why do I hasten restlessly onward? Why do I not stop at the goal already found in my bleak native mountains, which promises quiet and repose? Away with the thought! It is weakness—unworthy weakness—that should never dwell in the breast of a man. The victory, the independence of man's will, is his heaven—or his hell!"

At the conclusion of this soliloquy, Seiler's countenance resumed its expression of gloomy sternness, and his piercing eyes, fixed upon the portrait over the fire-place, blazed like a meteor's in a moonless night.

"By heaven! it is she! it can be no one else!" he exclaimed. "Ha! what a look! what a mouth and smile! what an expression in the whole face! Oh, woman! thou wast called once an angel; but—yes, yes! Ye are beautiful images of innocence and fidelity. But she has long since appeared before a higher Judge, as have also the others. One spark, however, yet glimmers beneath the ashes, which vengeance will fan into a flame, to light, by its clear blaze, the villany hid in darkness, and condemn the secret transgressors."

A motion at the door interrupted his musings; it was Stina, who entered with coffee and a plate of bread. Seiler's countenance instantly assumed an expression of lawless indifference.

"Good morning, fair Stina!" said he. "Do you always take coffee at so late an hour here at the parsonage?"

"Why this is not late: that, I think, no one can say," answered the girl; "but if the gentleman wishes to have his coffee earlier, that can be done to-morrow, for Miss is always up in time."

"Well, if it will be no extra trouble, I should like to have it between five and six o'clock. Is the provost already up?"

"No, neither he nor the captain."

"Bring me quickly some water for shaving, Stina; and let it be quite warm. And, if we are to remain good friends, you must always be as quick as lightning. Take this, and run."

The commanding tone and air of Seiler, but particularly a shining dollar, (which she had, however, well earned by the repeated scouring of the room,) made Stina, who was generally very slow in her movements, the most light-footed of beings, and hardly had five minutes elapsed, when she reappeared with the water.

"You want your boots brushed?"

"My travelling boots you may brush at some convenient time; I shall now take another pair."

"But your clothes?"

"Also at some other time; those I wore yesterday I shall not wear to-day."

"But those were, I think, very handsome. In the afternoon we have more time, and then all shall be done at once."

"Very well. Now, Stina, as poor as I am dressed, I shall go out; then you may fix up the room. But Heaven be merciful to you, if you put the least article of my things in another place from where you found it! We shall not remain friends if you do."

"Stina, Stina!" cried a voice from below; and with the exclamation: "Why, the captain is already up and stirring, and I have not brought him yet his hyssop tea!" Stina flew down stairs so fast that her hair and hoop-petticoat fairly streamed in the air.

The sitting-room below had been swept, aired, and strewn with sprouts of fir, and waited for its usual inmates. Alfhild, neatly and simply dressed, was gliding about with the brush, to free mirrors and tables of dust.

She was a charming and fascinating girl. Over her whole manner lay spread a maidenliness so pure and lovely, that it would have been sacrilege to have doubted the harmony of her soul with her appearance. Besides, there was a certain childish roguishness in her motions that became her extremely well, and often manifested itself in conversation by particular turns in words and thoughts. This it was that made one think they saw a changing child that had just left its playthings, and not a full-grown young girl.

"Ah! you are already up, Mr. Seiler?" exclaimed Alfhild, as she saw in the glass, which she was just dusting, the image of the architect, who stood in the open door.

"Is it permitted to enter so early in the day?" asked Seiler, with a light bow and a speaking look upon the young hostess.

"Certainly; as soon as the room is in order, every member of the house has admittance. Every one goes and comes as he pleases. Did you sleep well under our roof, Mr. Seiler?"

"I did not sleep at all. The appearance of my room, which, by its old-fashioned, but at the same time beautiful and interesting tapestry, and through the solid splendour of its furniture, is so enticing for a lively fancy, and the singular contrast it bears to the large, waste garret-space, and its curious wardrobe—all this called up strange thoughts in me, which drove away all sleep. Waking, I dreamed myself into past times, times when all those objects which occupied my mind were new, and intended for another guest, who, no doubt, dreamed, waked, and felt as I."

"I am indeed sorry," answered Alfhild, with a slight touch of vexation, "that these thoughts and imaginations deprived you of sleep, after a fatiguing journey. When I asked of my father permission to arrange this room for you, I hoped its prospect would be pleasant and of use to you. But if you cannot sleep in it, that is, if you converse with the ghosts that, for nearly half a century, may have haunted there, you can this very day exchange it for one of our common rooms for visitors, in the side wing. But then I shall believe that Uncle Sebastian was right when he said, that my preference for this chamber would bring its own punishment."

"No, by no means; I wish to keep it!" cried Seiler. "Having now seen it by day, and become familiar with its furniture and the charming prospect, I would not exchange it for another for any price; for I am convinced I should be the loser. But what did you say about ghosts? My curiosity is indeed excited; may I ask for a further explanation?"

"Ah, Mr. Seiler," said Alfhild, so low that one could only call it a whisper, and at the same time she cast an attentive look upon the door, which led to the room of the provost; "it is perhaps not right of me to speak of things of which I am to know but little; but an old tradition which has been preserved for a long time in our family says, that some fifty years ago this room was the stage of some gloomy, mysterious family scenes, the recollection of which affected so disagreeably the succeeding minister at Hammarby, Uncle Sebastian's brother, that the room was closed and has not been used since. But I think this may have been done because it is not very convenient; and besides, it has the disagreeable entrance through the attic. Other rooms for visitors were built, and this has in course of time been forgotten. As regards the costly furniture, it is said to have been brought here from the count's castle, shortly before those mysterious events; and although it is the best in the whole house, yet no one has ever attempted, as far as I know, to take it down."

"I thank you for these communications, which are quite interesting," said Seiler, while he passed his handkerchief over his brow, as if he would conceal the deep colour glowing upon it. "Yes, indeed, they are very interesting. They only increase for me the value of the room—for I have a weakness for all that is wonderful. But what is that about the ghosts?"

"Oh, that was only a jest," answered Alfhild, smiling. "But still, our people maintain to have sometimes heard noises in the old room; but these poor people are full of superstition. I myself sat many a summer's night, till twelve or one o'clock, up stairs at the window, without hearing a single sound which might not be explained in a natural way. I have an irresistible desire to stay in that room; and you cannot conceive the joy I had when I saw it put in order again. If there is any thing inexplicable in the whole affair, it can only be the firm belief that haunted me, that of all our rooms this one would be the most agreeable to you."

"Then you conceived and understood me before I crossed the threshold of your peaceful home," answered Seiler, while, with a look that cast a kindling spark in Alfhild's innocent heart, he took her hand and pressed it. "There are certain presentiments," added he, "which the understanding of man cannot explain; do you believe in such?"

The tone, the question itself, the inimitable softness of voice, and the mystic character of the subject, entirely embarrassed the young, inexperienced girl. Softly trembling, like a child that feels fear at a story, and yet listens again with an irresistible desire, Alfhild answered in a scarcely audible voice: "I believe in them. Yesterday evening I felt something similar, when the clatter of your carriage so wonderfully mingled with the ringing of the bells; you, however, arrived here half an hour after the ringing."

"What!" exclaimed Seiler, with a singular awe, "a foretoken—a presentiment?"

"Yes, even so! My father and myself both heard it. We went out, but, as I just said, we found nothing till your real arrival called us a second time to the front door."

"But it may have been some one else who rode by. I do not see why we should trouble ourselves to hold the simplest, most natural occurrence, for a mysterious foretoken," said Seiler, and strove to dispel the thoughts which rose within him.

"But," rejoined Alfhild, "the path from the main road leads only to the parsonage, and to no other house."

"If you really did not hear wrong, I must own that this is very singular," Seiler added with a smile. "It would then be a confirmation of what I said before."

The continuation of the conversation on this subject was interrupted by the entrance of the provost.

After the gentlemen had breakfasted, the holsteiner, that had once been green, drove up. They first stood on some ceremony in regard to the seats, but soon agreed, and set out on the road to Great Hammarby. Seiler was to pay his respects to the count and family.

CHAPTER V.

THE DINNER.

IN her solitary room in the east wing of the castle sat the Baroness Ravenstein, writing letters. Thelma, for once exempt from tiresome lectures and jealous inspection, stood in a window recess, whence she observed, through the half-open blinds, her cousin walking in the court-yard; apparently more bent down and weaker than usual, and supporting himself with a cane, as though oppressed by the weight of a hundred years.

But it was not Albano alone on whom her looks rested: they were attracted, with irresistible power, by a tall, strong figure, that with a kind of unwilling yet refined politeness, checked his bold step to accommodate it to the creeping walk of the sickly young count.

This was the architect, who had not found the old count at home; but as he was expected back every moment, Seiler preferred, instead of paying his respects to the countess, as the provost did, to stay in the court with Albano, who, however, did not seem by any means delighted at the politeness of the stranger.

"Who can that be?" Thelma asked herself. "No doubt some nobleman from a remote part of the country. Never have I seen a man of more beautiful appearance and bolder bearing. Ah! how small and insignificant Albano appears by his side. What charming motions, and——"

Thelma sighed—at what? That she did not ask of herself; but a bitter feeling of unhappiness mingled with her emotions, when she forcibly brought herself to think on the good qualities of her cousin, of which she knew many—which were, however, incapable of re-conciling her to the want of a beautiful exterior.

"If he would only be less distrustful!" this wish was accompanied by a bitter sigh. "I *do* understand him," she thought; "and also mother, uncle, and aunt think——But my heart! ah, the poor heart! How it is roused when they say, that poor young ladies must have no heart, and have nothing to do but their duty. And is it my duty to sacrifice my heart, my life, and my whole self, for the benefits that were for many years bestowed upon my mother and myself, to a man like Albano? His sick, bent-down, mis-formed body, his distrustfulness, his violent passion, often glaring with rage, excite my compassion; but when his eye is burning with a consuming fire, for which I have no name, then I feel a shudder, a trembling, and abhorrence at the thought that I am to be his own. Oh! I would rather die than ever rest in Albano's arms! Yet, no more of these lamentations, my poor heart! Thou must suffer thyself to be buried alive in the dreary tomb of gratitude!"

Thelma was drawn from these painful thoughts, by her mother reminding her that it was time to dress for dinner. With a long look upon the stranger, and a shudder at the involuntary comparison of Albano with him, she went out of the room. Had she waited a few seconds longer she might have seen the old count return, and invite the stranger to dinner; for the horses were quickly taken from the holsteiner, and the gentlemen entered the castle.

In the small saloon in which the noble family generally stayed, sat, a quarter of an hour before dinner, the countess and the provost at the chess-board. The first-mentioned preferred a game at chess to all other amusements, and as the provost fortunately was a very skil-ful player, he was in great favour with her, and never came to the cas-tle without being welcomed with a gracious look, and drawn to the chess-board. This time the game had lasted several hours, and both had forgotten the architect, who had not yet been presented, as well as the count, the dinner, and all around them.

The entrance of the baroness with Thelma recalled the players from their reverie. The countess suspected it must be pretty late; the provost recollected that he had not yet paid his respects to the count. They rose, with the understanding of finishing the game after din-ner; when the count entered, accompanied by the architect, and pre-sented him to his wife.

It is impossible to describe the expression in the face of the illustrious lady, when they presented to her the elegant and neatly-dressed gentleman, who moved with an ease and a bearing that might have done honour to a nobleman, simply as "Mr. Seiler, the Norwegian architect, who was to build the new church."

The countess found herself greatly discomposed. To the fascinating, polished stranger—and that he had those qualities, was shown by his whole manner—she wished to show all possible attention; to the architect, on the contrary, nothing but the polite, scantily-measured condescension of a patroness. But what was she to do, to take a proper medium? The case was delicate, and the natural consequence of this unnatural attempt was a considerable increase of that stillness which was innate with the countess. One might have taken her for a statue, seeing the manner in which she listened to Seiler, as he, in chosen expressions, spoke of his good fortune to be allowed to pay his respects to her ladyship the countess.

The count, who did not lack a certain sharpness of look, saw at once how affairs stood. He therefore hastened to shorten, without ceremony, the formality of presentation.

"My sister-in-law, Mr. Seiler, the Baroness of Ravenstein, and Lady Ravenstein," said he; and casting a glance through the room, he asked: "Where is Albano?"

He had not yet made his appearance. While his father was looking round for him, the architect directed his gaze from the smooth, graciously and proudly smiling face of the Baroness, upon Thelma; and it lasted long enough to prove to her distinctly, that she had made no unfavourable impression upon him.

The perception covered her cheeks with a deep blush, which was observed by none but him who caused it. He was, however, perhaps the most dangerous confidante she could have—at least, it would not have been unjust to think so; for a smile of triumph round Seiler's mouth, and a motion with the eyelids, had in them something of the joy one imputes to a demon when he thinks he has allured an innocent soul into the snare.

Albano now entered, and returned, with a negligent indifference, the polite, almost deep bow of the architect. How disgusting did Thelma find the one in this moment, and how fascinating the other!

A man of refinement and education seldom allows himself a pre-

meditated incivility, if he is only called upon to observe the customary little rules of intercourse; but Count Albano despised all forms,
acted only as he pleased. Seiler, however, had too much natural and
acquired tact not to act as if he observed nothing of the want of education in the young count. He immediately directed his attention to
the baroness, with some trifling question.

A few moments after was heard through the door of the dining-
room, the welcome "All is ready;" and after they had seated themselves at the table, the restraint relaxed a little. The company took
part in the conversation, which the talent of the architect succeeded
in introducing, sustaining, and guiding. He had been much in foreign
countries, and not without profit to himself. He also knew how to
draw advantage from it, and now depicted, in an animated and picturesque style, the master-works in Rome, and its architecture. The
capitol, the church of St. Peter, the triumphal arches of Trajan, and
the bloody catacombs, all were discussed; yet, in a manner that had
nothing forced or talkative in it, but quite natural, and at most only
showed the laudable design to entertain the company during dinner.

"Why, surely!" whispered the baroness to the count, while, hovering between the desire to eat and to listen, she directed her look now
upon the dishes and now upon Seiler, "the man is not so stupid—he
has manners. Upon my honour, the man has seen the world—has *ton*,
wit, taste; and an architect, my brother!"

"This is nothing very uncommon, my gracious sister," answered
the count in a low tone. "He is an artist, has an artistical mind and
head; and, what is more, an artist's exterior. To a great talent, my
dear sister, and to an artist who appears like this one, and conducts
himself like a nobleman, we may give the honour of our intercourse,
without compromising ourselves in the least. Besides, the bishop has
taken him into his special favour, and recommended him to me very
particularly."

The baroness nodded assent, and remarked:

"Certainly! certainly! my dear brother; especially in the country,
where we need not be so very particular."

The attention was again turned upon Seiler, who saw very well
the advantage which he gained every minute, and endeavoured to increase it by new turns of conversation. Only upon one of the company his arts had no effect. Every ingenious idea, every pointed phrase,

shivered and recoiled at Albano's coldness, like an arrow shot against a granite rock. He grew even more silent and gloomy, the oftener he looked upon Thelma's animated features. Forgetting all prudence, during the few moments of so rare an enjoyment, she gave herself up to the enchanting pleasure of taking in all the images and ideas, which the much-travelled stranger brought before her mind, letting them have full sway over her. She did not think of incurring the re-proof of any one, until her eyes accidentally fell upon Albano, and she saw in his face displeasure, pain, and chagrin struggle together; nay, read even the condemnation of her innocent enjoyment. Now, suddenly all the blood rushed from her heart to her face, and she lost the thread of Seiler's interesting conversation.

None of the company had perceived these incidents except old Borgstedt, who had his seat at the lower end of the table. He alone saw, and understood how new threads were tied together, and how the old ones became entangled. He also noticed what Albano could not see—sitting on the same side with Seiler—the fiery glances with which the architect now and then consulted, as it were, Thelma's taste. But Borgstedt had made such observations for many years, and under several counts, without communicating to others a single word. He only now and then made an exception in favour of Captain Oernroos, with whom he had from boyhood stood in near and friendly relation. However this may be, suffice it to say, to make observations was his province, and every eclipse of the sun or moon, every planet that rose on the count's horizon, every erratic star that threatened to come in collision with other heavenly bodies, his eye caught immediately; and he computed, in all silence, from his humble observatory, what constellations might come of them.

The table was removed. After coffee had been handed round, and the provost, by a gracious sign from the countess, had been called to the chess-board; the baroness, impelled by a mother's pride, pro-posed to her daughter to sing at the piano. They accordingly went into the music-room.

Thelma felt weak and fearful; her performances did not go be-yond mediocrity, and yet the baroness had praised the talent of her daughter in a manner that might have placed the most skilful artist in a false position. Thelma, therefore, was in a very painful embarrass-ment; as caprice and bashfulness were to the baroness synonymous in such cases, she was obliged to take her seat at the instrument. Seiler placed himself behind her chair. From the interest he took in the music, and the accuracy with which he followed, and turned the leaves at the proper time, the baroness seemed to draw the conclusion that he understood something of the art himself, and therefore asked him whether he was musical?

"Yes, a little," Seiler answered, with a smile.

"I mean whether you play on any instrument,—the piano for instance?"

"Very little indeed, and for the most part nothing but my own phantasias, for which I first composed words; but they are mere fragments without connection or value; only re-echoes of cheerful or sad hours, by which I sought to heighten the enjoyment of the former, and lessen the bitterness of the latter."

"Really! You are then a poet and composer in one person? Indeed a very talented young man! I pray, let us hear one of those compositions; we shall be very much obliged to you."

"My feeble musical attempts are entirely unworthy to be produced before an audience so refined; yet I will not refrain from obeying your command."

"Your chivalric courtesy would not allow this," said the baroness, obligingly.

Seiler seated himself gracefully at the piano, which Thelma had just left, and struck a few chords, which he, by degrees, united to a free phantasy, and by which he produced a powerful effect upon the hearers. It was not music, according to the rules of art; but the soft and charming notes that alternated in wailing and fiery strains, and the peculiar transitions from one key into another—all this proved him possessed of a love for harmony, and of deep feeling. After a short pause, Seiler sang, with a beautiful full tenor voice, one of his songs.

"Hope waves her torch, as when the world began,
    To light the path of life so deeply shaded,
  Yet little trust she kindled in the man
  Who farther to enjoy nor wills nor can
    Since all his stars have long since wholly faded.

"Still of the worlds beyond the earth he thinks,
    And dreams, with fondness, till life's last light closes;
Blow on, ye storms! the grave, from which he shrinks,
Is quiet; there the weary wanderer sinks—
    There, after years of strife and anguish, he reposes."

The power and beauty of his voice and performance made a strong impression upon the persons present. For some time after the singer had finished, the hearers sat still, mute, and almost unconscious; admiration glowing on each countenance.

After he had left the castle, there was but one opinion, with the exception of Albano's, concerning the architect; that he was a highly ingenious, refined, and talented young man. The countess had gone so far in her condescension, that she had left the chess-board, and invited Mr. Seiler and the provost to dinner for Sunday next. This was a distinction only few could boast of; and on their way home the provost endeavoured to make the architect comprehend this great honour, who listened politely, yet with a doubtful smile.

CHAPTER VI.

THE EVENING STORM.

FOUR months fled away. The building of the church had greatly advanced, when one beautiful but cloudy evening in August, the architect, tired with the exertions of the day, returned to the parsonage. With a feeling of delight he seated himself upon the already damp turf-bank, in front of the house; which, encircled by a hedge of roses, invited him to rest.

This, his favourite seat, was before one of the windows of the common sitting-room; and, almost every evening Alfhild, while occupied with some domestic work, waited here to receive him with some elder-juice and water, or with a glass of the excellent beer, two years old, according as the weather made it agreeable. This evening, however, he did not find Alfhild here, although he returned from the building somewhat later than usual.

Seiler threw expectant, restless looks upon the open house door; the grass-bank grew damper, since a fine rain had begun to sprinkle the earth; yet the warmth of his feelings prevented him from perceiving it, and only the brow, round which the dark locks played, grew cold. But as Alfhild remained absent, his brow, by degrees, became wrinkled, and grew darker as the evening advanced.

"What can detain her? Why does she not come? Shall I go in? No! If she does not come out, I shall take no evening meal."

Seiler remained yet a moment longer sitting upon the bank, in a listening posture. All was still in the house; only the even-measured steps of the provost and Uncle Sebastian, who were walking up and down in the parlour, were heard. Impatiently the architect shook his head, sighed once, and thought:

"This evening, then, her friendly look is not to chase away, with its beneficent warmth, the dark clouds that lower o'er my brow, and darken my heart. Alfhild, thou being from a better world, only when I am in thy presence do I feel well! Then I forget all, past, present, and future. An inspiration of bliss moves every fibre, and when I am near thee, I at once become a trusting, hopeful child. Then sleeps the serpent in my bosom, and the tiger dares not approach where the angel of innocence keeps watch. Oh, thou pure one! why lie yet some bitter years between our hearts? And why have I not courage—the bond——? Yet no, it would be cruel! Many things must first change; but first"—Seiler's eyes shot fiery sparks—"my work must be finished, and the account closed."

With these words he rose quickly, and his lofty figure shortly after disappeared among the bushes, which encircled the borders of the lake.

A boat lay on the shore. Seiler unfastened it; after having cast a searching look around, he stepped in and let the light bark glide upon the blue surface. He kept close to the land, and approached, after having scarce an hour plied the oar, a rocky hill that stretched into the lake, and with its white shells, and snail-houses, lay there like a great swan. Seiler, with a skilful hand, forced the boat through the dense, high masses of rushes, and landed on the north side of the hill. Several clefts formed here a kind of staircase. He reached this, but stopped, however, several times, and seemed to check his breath, to listen: not a sound was, however, to be heard.

"Do all deceive me this evening?" said Seiler, as he stood on the peak of the cliff, and from thence looked down to a spot on the oppo-

site side, where, of some loose block of rock and trees, a commodious and spacious grotto was erected, to which a well-beaten path led
from the east side of the park attached to the count's castle.

Seiler seemed undetermined whether to descend or remain. As
he stood listening, his ear caught the echo of sweet music from the
grotto; the tones seemed those of a soft voice, accompanied by a
lute. The music suddenly ceased, as his own deep voice burdened the
echo. Soon after, all was quiet—so still, that the very motion of the
leaves could be heard. The castle clock struck nine, as a light figure,
illumined by the moonlight, glided along the dark path between the
grotto and the park.

Seiler remained on the peak of the cliff. Not a word escaped his
half-closed lips, round which played a subtle smile; but his eyes followed the white dress that inclosed the charming, hastening figure;
and when this, at the end of the path, timidly turned and made a
motion with the lute, as if taking leave, then Seiler bowed to her in
a manner which expressed as much the finest gallantry, as the most
bashful, warmest admiration.

Lady Ravenstein immediately after vanished in the dark alleys of
the park.

The architect now descended, not without difficulty, upon the
uneven path to the grotto, and reached it in safety. In the grotto itself he tarried but a moment; he stood, however, much longer at the
broad barrier which separated the small space before it from the deep
abyss. On this side of the rocky hill there was no landing-place, as
it was much easier to get to the pavilion from the park and garden
than from the lake. The architect occupied himself, for a short time,
with examining the pavilion and the hill from all sides: he then appeared gradually to change his thoughts, and to meditate on other
things than those relating to locality. His eyes turned upon the moon,
which, beaming between some dark clouds, was reflected in the lake,
and upon the stars that sparkled in the heavens.

"How magnificent and great," said he aloud, "are the works of
God, compared to our miserable creations! What is the greatest and
highest master-work that human mind can produce, compared to a
single dew-drop in the chalice of a flower? Nothing! a shadowy image—a dream! What else but shadow and dream can be the inheritance of man? The heart, full of unspeakable desire, drags itself along

in darkness, and is not able to obtain for itself light enough to take one look into the future. We regard with envy the winged beings that hasten through spaces which our eye is not able to measure. They fly? The thoughts of men also fly, and are able to soar higher than the birds; and yet we envy them for their wings. Oh, how miserable! Farewell, ye shining stars, wandering through the silent night! Bear a friendly greeting to the beloved valleys of my youth—to my native home, with its giant mountains. How gladly would I go with you, if all were yet as formerly. But my path leads not upward; no! downward, downward, into the dark deep!"

Pale, and wet with the dews of night, Seiler stood resting his arm upon the barrier of the grotto. The beams of the moon fell bright upon his figure; and whoever had seen him at this moment, would have owned never to have met more manly beauty.

The sky was suddenly clouded over; the moon disappeared behind masses of vapour, the stars veiled their silver light, and impenetrable darkness fell upon the earth. Anon, rivers of red fire hissed through the air and tore the cloudy pall, and the awful thunder rolled with a dull, heavy sound along the horizon. Seiler stood in deep thought, regardless of darkness and danger, until streams of rain warned him to shelter himself in the grotto. He entered, and seated himself upon the bank of turf that ran along the walls. His thoughts were now turned back to the parsonage and Alfhild. What might they think of his staying out so late? Alfhild's image, with all its signs of anxiety, came before his soul. He saw her increasing pain, with the increase of the tempest and the advancing night. He determined finally to undertake, however difficult it might be, the slippery way up the hill, and thence down the other side to his boat and, in spite of wind and rain, to get back to the parsonage. He was about to rise to execute his purpose, when hasty steps from the park approached the grotto.

Seiler was not a man who was easily embarrassed by unforeseen incidents; but still, he now felt his face glow at the thought of being discovered here. What excuse, what reasonable pretext could he give, to justify his late and singular visit within the limits of the castle? To come to the grotto by the usual way, he would have had to go across the court of the castle and through the garden, where he would have surely lighted upon people who, as the evening was fair, must have been there. To pretend that he came this way could not therefore be thought of; but, on the other hand, to confess that he had stolen thither by unusual paths, might have given rise to suspicions which would be unpleasant to him.

"Why did I not go home immediately?" muttered Seiler, between his teeth. "I never found delight in these night-adventures."

In the mean time, the steps had approached quite near, and Seiler saw, through the half-opened door of the grotto, the small figure of a man, in a short frock-coat, take the place at the barrier which he had just quitted. Seiler remained quiet, and the other, who seemed to devour with his eyes the grand picture of the contending elements, did not perceive that he had a witness. Single words, without connection, struck Seiler's ear; but the sounds died away amid the powerful rolling of the thunder and the streaming down of the rain. The few syllables which he caught were, however, sufficient to convince him that his neighbor was Count Albano, whose presence, of all others, he desired least at this moment. About half an hour thus passed. Thor's car[1] rolled heavily, but more distant; the masses of clouds, driven by a strong wind, moved along the sky, now partially clear, in fantastic forms, and the rain gradually moderated.

"Now, I hope, he will return to the castle," thought Seiler, drawing himself deeper into the grotto. But he had miscalculated. Fatigued by the exertions of body and soul, and shaken by a severe chill, Count Albano suddenly entered to seek rest for a few minutes. He intended to let the wild thoughts pass by which chased each other within him, and had also driven him out into the stormy night.

"Who is there?" called out the count, as in opening the door he perceived that some one was in the grotto. "Who's there?" he called out once more, in a deep and angry voice, which one would have hardly expected of his feeble body.

"A friend of more peaceful scenes of nature, your lordship, than those just ended," answered the architect, while he rose and made a courteous bow. "The beauty of the evening allured me out upon the lake, where the tempest surprised me, and compelled me to land here and seek shelter."

"To land?" asked Albano, with a sharp expression of voice. "You seem to forget that there is no landing-place here."

"Oh, yes; on the other side of the hill."

---

[1] Thunder. According to Norse mythology, Thor is the thunder god.

"Indeed? That would not have entered my mind! Then Mr. Architect has made a pretty long and laborious promenade to find shelter, which he might, in my opinion, have obtained as quickly, and with less trouble, by returning to the parsonage; for I think it must take no little time to climb up the bare rock, and go down the other side, to come here—especially in such weather!"

"Not so very much, if one is nimble and accustomed to such labours," the architect remarked carelessly.

"To such adventures, you had better say," rejoined the count, irritated by Seiler's answer. "As it has now cleared off," he added, collecting the last remnant of his self-control to remain calm, "you need shelter no further; and I request you now to leave this place to me. I had this grotto constructed that I might be undisturbed."

"As your lordship commands," answered Seiler, with much composure. "Allow me to assure you that, if I had known the entrance to this grotto was forbidden to strangers, I should not have sought it. My ignorance of this circumstance excuses, perhaps, the liberty I have taken, and shall not take again."

At the conclusion of this formula of politeness, Seiler made a slight bow; and a few minutes after he climbed, like a practised huntsman, up the cliff, and soon disappeared behind it.

CHAPTER VII.

THE FIRES OF JEALOUSY.

"Satan!" exclaimed Albano, gnashing his teeth, when Seiler had left the grotto, "you will not make me believe that you came here without a particular purpose!" He struck his forehead, and, in the same moment, he knocked his foot against a light object that lay on the ground. "Ha! what was that?" he exclaimed, seeking with his hands for the token of Seiler's hated presence. "A pocket-book containing— what? Can it be that he left it behind on purpose?—can it——Oh! ye powers of darkness! ye change my blood to fire! my brain is burning, my senses feel seized upon by the demon of madness! Could he, perhaps——No, no! Away, abominable thought!—And yet, how did not she gaze on him the first day at dinner! With what eagerness, with what delight, did she take in each word that came over his cursed lips! And since that time how shy and reserved she appeared to conceal the sympathy she felt, when he approached her with his refined impudence. Did she not blush, and grow pale, and tremble, when I surprised her exchanging looks with him? Unfortunate girl! if it were possible—if my senses do not deceive me, then tremble! Love, which now makes me a miserable fool, would then change into revenge, and make of me a man—nay, a devil! When I met her in the court an hour since, did not she then come from here? She was so warm, and told me that she had been running, not to miss the evening meal. Her warmth might come from something else. No, no, not so; that cannot be! I am a timid child that sees spectres in the clear light of day. She is pure; yes, Thelma is pure as an angel of heaven. But I must see what this pocket-book contains."

Count Albano now closed carefully the door of the grotto, then put his hand into his pocket, and found a key to a small closet. He opened it, and took out implements to strike a fire, and a lamp, which was soon lighted and placed upon a stone table; at length he seated himself near it upon the moss-bank, with the pocket-book in his hand.

The ungainly figure, in the dimly lighted cavern, made a very disagreeable picture; and the cold, closed grotto, with its dark, damp walls, built of large rocks and trunks of trees; the moss-banks, the stone-table, the ugly form of the exiled count, his rolling eyes, the entangled red hair, the lateness of the hour—all gave to this night scene a ghostly aspect; and when Albano, with satanic caution, but with devouring eyes, took from the pocket-book accounts of buildings, drawings, letters, and other papers, and also two small cases of red maraquin, he resembled, at this occupation, an inhabitant of the lower world, who has come up to hold a charnel-house examination. Upon each new object he fixed his staring eyes, and when the pocket-book was at last emptied, and all the things lay on the table, a demoniacal smile curled round his mouth.

For some moments he seemed undecided where to begin; finally, he took one of the two letters. He opened it, and found it signed by a name entirely unknown to him. Nevertheless he read it, half-aloud, as follows:—

"BROTHER RUDOLPH—The proof of friendship you desire of me,

is as unnatural as it is incomprehensible; and I will hope that it was only an unhappy, quickly passing excitement, that induced you to decide upon a step that wars against the laws of morality, and would be a sure means of exposing you to the odium of the world. Far from complying with your wishes, I shall not, therefore, mention a word to the unhappy woman to whom relates this affair; convinced that, when the excitement in which you now live is past, you will see your folly, and ask me to keep it secret.

"Excuse me, therefore, if, under the present circumstances, I hold you unworthy of receiving information on what, otherwise, would have made the main subject of my letter. I have now only to bid you farewell, with the wish that you may soon become again rational, that you may be further loved by your friend,

"BLOOM."

A host of confused thoughts and dim ideas were reeling in Albano's head. He read the letter three or four times over; but with the exception of the circumstance—which presented itself clear as the sun—that Seiler was in love, and found himself, at present, in an intoxication of bliss, all remained dark. But what more wanted Albano to know? Was not this enough?

"He loves!" Albano exclaimed; "loves Thelma, my future bride!" His lips quivered, while he tried to press them convulsively. "But what stupidity, to believe that he will soon recover himself, and forget his paroxysm. Ha! to burn and hope for Thelma, that some favour may comfort and cool the burning heat! Such thoughts only he can harbour who has never seen her, and never came near her irresistible circle of enchantments! But, by heaven! let this Norwegian adventurer try to snatch but one drop of the cordial for which my soul is thirsting, if he dare! She shall be *mine*, and that soon; and may he then thirst and burn till his heart falls to ashes!"

Thus Albano raved till his strength was nearly exhausted, and the soul could bear the straining no longer. Now he seized another stimulus, another letter. The same hand, the same signature, as in the first. From the date it appeared that Seiler had received it quite recently. Albano mechanically trimmed the lamp and began to read:

"Rudolph! By the friendship that bound us together from youth, by the vow which you, three years ago, confirmed with an oath, I call upon you to come to yourself and to us. Leave Hammarby—give up the building of the church—flee the alluring syren-voice—in short, leave all which destroys the peace of your soul and the happiness of the future. Oh, Rudolph! is it you whose power I so often admired? Is it you who is not able to tear himself away from the magic spell in which your reason and your noblest feelings are stifled, by sipping the intoxicating foam?

"It is vain that you state your reasons; with me they avail nothing; and never—I tell it you for the last time—shall I lend my hand or my name to a plan that would brand you and your accredited agent with disgrace.

"BLOOM."

"I cannot comprehend this—my head grows dizzy and burns," said Albano. "What does he want? the wretch! It cannot be to elope with her! Oh no, impossible! Such bold adventures are buried with the age in which the violent exploits of knights did cease. But there is something in these mysteries that is incomprehensible to me. Some plan is preparing, the object of which is to cross my designs. Worm!—do not stir; creep in the dust where thou belongest, and stretch not thy hand toward a fruit which hangs too high for thee!"

He was silent for a few moments, looking steadily upon the last lines of the letter; then he hastily ran over the other things. The drafts of buildings he replaced. Now he came to a pamphlet with gilded edges, of which he read only the title "SKETCHES FROM JEAMES LEGANGER'S LIFE, DURING HIS TRAVELS IN SWEDEN IN 1741 AND 1742."

"Old stuff!" said Albano, taking up one of the maraquin cases. The little spring opened at the first pressure, and the young count's eyes fell upon the glorious features of a woman's face, whose fiery speaking looks defy all attempts at description.

"Here I am entangled in a new labyrinth, from which I see no outlet," muttered Albano, while his eyes rested upon the portrait. "Is it *she* whom he loves? Truly a beauty! but the original cannot be found with us here. No, that cannot be; perhaps a sister."

With a lingering hand he put the portrait into its case again, and took up the other.

This was the picture of a young man with regular and extremely animated features. Albano looked at it very carelessly, and as he put it down he read on the back side of it "Jeames Leganger," the same name which he had seen on the pamphlet. Too much occupied with his own thoughts, he hardly noticed this circumstance, and put all things again in their places.

But now the question arose with Albano: has the architect left the pocket-book behind on purpose, or has he lost it? In the first case his design might be that Thelma should read the letters, and conclude from them his passion for her. He rejected this thought, however.

"Such a daring fellow would be capable of writing to her his passion with fire and blood; or would even have the boldness to express it to her in words," said the count. "Hence, that he has lost it is the most probable conclusion; for if Thelma were in the play, it would have answered his purpose to leave only the two letters. He will no doubt come and look for it to-morrow. It may remain lying here, for she will not be up before he will make his morning visit here."

Albano, entirely exhausted, let his head sink upon his hand, and gave himself up without resistance to the fantastic dreams which his excited imagination called forth in consequence of what he had just passed through. It seemed to him as if he saw Thelma with the bridal wreath round her pale brow, silent, patient and meek, resigning herself to her fate, and reaching to him her hand for life. Anon, he saw her upon her knees with dishevelled hair, crouching at his feet, and asking him to spare her. In vain his arms clasped her with wild violence; they were wrestling with each other. She freed herself from him, but he seized her again; at last she sank down exhausted, and in her look which she fixed upon him once more, there was inexpressible meekness and resignation.

Albano's gloomy mind was deeply stirred by the ghostly picture which moved before his soul. His feelings, strained in the most painful manner, found relief in a flood of tears. He wept convulsively. With lamentation he called upon Thelma's image, to stay and not leave him to a future of unbounded misery. Caressing, entreating words flowed from his lips. The expression of his face grew milder, more resigned.

Had Thelma seen and heard him now, who can tell what effect this hour might have had upon her. But when he was with her he was constantly ruled by pride, artificial coldness, distrust, and petty revenge. It did not occur to him to reveal to her this boundless love, which in its paroxysm bordered on madness. Albano apprehended, perhaps not without reason, that this glow of passion in a body like his, might excite disgust, nay, perhaps sneers. The breast of the pitiable youth heaved violently in the struggle that passed within him, and his tears burned like fire upon his cheeks.

Steps were heard at this moment, the door opened, and a dark shadow appeared on the threshold. Albano gazed on it till he at last recognised the bent figure of old Borgstedt.

"Almighty Heaven!" exclaimed the faithful servant, "who would have expected your lordship here? I had no rest in bed; I saw you go out, and feared some mishap might have met you, as I did not hear you come back. How wet you are! and you have not taken your cloak with you. For heaven's sake let us go home; I see you are shaken by a fearful fever. You must not stay here on any account."

"Let me alone, Borgstedt," Count Albano answered, slowly returning to reality. "Go home, and never again disturb me in my wanderings, which I undertake for the purpose of being alone. I excuse you this time, on account of your good intentions; but don't do it again; for, you comprehend, old man, that I cannot wish to have witnesses in such moments."

There was, as usual, something commanding in his tone; but it was now so mingled with pain, sadness—nay, perhaps even shame, to be found in such a state, that Borgstedt could not refrain a tear, which fell upon the hand of the count, as the old man was leaning over the table.

"What now!" exclaimed Albano with vehemence, while he withdrew his hand as if stung by a wasp. "Is it come to this, that my servants weep over me for pity? Go, old man, go! You are too faithful and devoted; I need not, therefore, command you to be silent on what you have heard and seen here."

"No, your lordship, I cannot go till you go with me; my anxiety is not caused by what I heard and saw. I have lived to see yet more curious things, and it does not surprise me that a man should have feelings which he pours out to himself, since no one else understands them. Believe me, in the time of your grandfather I saw very peculiar things; and one may have confidence in an old servant like myself, to whom, for upward of half a century, all family secrets are known.

Many secrets lie buried in my breast, and they will all die with me. But you must go back with me, absolutely; it is high time that you go to bed. We shall see tomorrow if all this exposure passes by without bad consequences."

In the voice of the old servant there was something which Albano, usually stubborn, could not resist; and this time the highly uncommon event happened, that a subordinate exercised power over him. He rose in silence, put out the lamp, locked it up, threw the pocketbook upon the ground where he found it, and left with Borgstedt the mysterious grotto.

As soon as Albano came out in the coolness of night, he felt his wet clothes cling to his burning limbs. A severe chill came on, and shaken by cold so that he could hardly keep himself upright, he at length reached his room. The old servant lit the wax candles, and put his young master to bed. He gave him some cooling medicine, and covered him closely with all he could find. After all this was done, and a sign from the fatigued count had informed him that his kind services were no longer needed, Borgstedt withdrew, yet no farther than the next room, where he lay down on a sofa.

"The cursed love-fever!" muttered Borgstedt; "if that attacks a brain which was not quite right before, madness is complete. And the worst of all is when a soul all fire and flame gets into such a body. Poor Albano! His grandfather, of blessed memory, had a different appearance. But was that better for him? No! He turned the heads of half a dozen misses and ladies in one year. God be merciful to him, and let him find forgiveness for the sins of his youth."

CHAPTER VIII.

ALFHILD'S VIGIL.

SEILER having fastened his boat, and cast a sneering look toward the rocky hill behind which the grotto lay, hastened toward the parsonage. Although it was past midnight, Seiler observed with agreeable surprise, a light which shone toward him, and the window from which this pleasant message came was that of Alfhild. Seiler saw a shadow move to and fro behind the window curtains. Caro, the faithful watch-dog, had already announced by a friendly whining, that an acquaintance approached the house; and as the architect opened the door, Alfhild came to meet him with the light in her hand.

"Oh, Mr. Seiler, where have you been? You frightened me almost to death!" Alfhild looked so pale, that it was difficult to decide whether watching or tears had made her eye-lids red.

"I wandered about on the lake," answered Seiler softly. "As I, an hour before sunset, came home, tired by the labour and heat of the day, and longed for the drink which I always relish so much when I receive it from your hand, I seated myself outside the door upon the grass-bank, and waited patiently a long, long time, but she whom I expected came not. A restlessness came upon me; I walked away, unfastened the boat, and rowed up the lake. The evening was still, and the lake smooth. Alfhild's image danced before me on each little wave, and I bent down to kiss it—"

A flash-like beam of northern light trembled on the cheek of the maiden; she veiled the eyes with the delicate lashes to restrain a falling tear. Seiler would fain have kissed it away, but he dared not.

"Since through my negligence you might have taken injury on your night-excursion," said Alfhild, with a motion of invitation toward the door of the sitting-room, "it is no more than proper that I try to make amends. I have saved you a portion of our evening meal."

The architect followed her into the room. Alfhild lighted a lamp, and now Seiler noticed, to his great delight, a small spread table. All on it was arranged with great neatness and taste. Seiler's favourite dishes stood together; his favourite flowers shone out in the blue porcelain vases, and also his favourite drink, the old beer, which Alfhild mixed with sugar, as on the first evening, stood there in the polished silver cans.

Seiler, cheered up by the sudden change of scene, relished his meal, and the young hostess, with delight, saw him take one favourite dish after another. It was long since he had taken his dinner, he had never had a better appetite, he had never enjoyed a more friendly care, and had never been waited upon by more willing hands.

How his large black eyes sparkled! Alfhild knew that they, in certain moments, had an expression which she could not bear, and she felt, without looking up, that such a moment had come now. Her hand rested in his, yet she drew it back as with an electric shock, as she felt his lips burning upon it.

"Did you fear during the thunder-storm?" Seiler asked, as if nothing had happened.

"Ah yes—no—not much——only very little!"

"But where were you, Alfhild, when I returned from the building ground! I have not heard that yet."

"When you came home I was in the lower part of the village with a sick person. I expected to be back before you, but stayed longer, as I found Lady Ravenstein at the same place and with the same intention. As I accompanied her, in going home, I came, without being aware of it, near the castle, and from there to our house is, as you know, a good distance."

"Lady Ravenstein! Then *she* too visits the huts of the poor? That is indeed very praiseworthy. In the company in which she lives, I should not have thought such feelings possible."

"And yet it is so," Alfhild answered with animation. "No person can have a better heart than Lady Ravenstein. But unfortunately she is obliged to hide her noble feelings; for if she should speak of them to her mother or aunt, she would, at best, only be laughed at, and be called a silly enthusiast. Also Count Albano, though he is said to be good and just toward his inferiors, never allows Thelma to visit the houses of poverty and sickness in person, because all this may be done, as he maintains, by messengers. Thus poor Thelma is almost like an imprisoned bird. The garden, with the adjoining park, constitutes the narrow world in which she is allowed to breathe the fresh air."

"But how could she venture this evening to go so far!" asked Seiler.

"The countess and baroness were gone to the city, and were not expected back before ten o'clock; both the counts were at a dinner-party of gentlemen, in the neighbourhood. Thelma therefore flew, like a bird that finds the door left open, beyond her limits for once. We met, and spent a very pleasant hour together."

Seiler had finished his meal, and turned to the hostess, thanked her for her care, and then in a somewhat softer tone, asked her pardon for the alarm that his long stay from home had caused her.

"Oh, mention that no more! It is now over, and all well again!" said Alfhild, with a smile, while she rose and trimmed the lamp.

"Would that you were right! Would that heaven would make all right again!" exclaimed Seiler, looking in her eyes with an expression suddenly changed and painful.

"What do you mean, Seiler?" she asked, with a slight trembling.

"For you, pious Alfhild," Seiler resumed, "whom none of the dark shadows that are contending in my breast dare to approach—for you all is well as soon as the thunder-clouds are scattered and the sun shines again."

"And is it not the same with you?" asked Alfhild, blushing.

"No, alas, not so! many clear moments send their friendly rays to scatter the clouds in my heavens; but when they and the angel that gave them to me, have disappeared, the clouds gather again more threatening and in blacker masses. The breast of a man may be likened to a battle-field, where the combat never ceases—where every conquered combatant lies bleeding, and only waiting for the moment to renew the fight."

A light shudder thrilled through Alfhild's frame. "What do you call all these secret powers, that combat each other?" asked she gently.

"What are they called?" A singular smile curled round Seiler's lips. "Yes, Alfhild, I will tell you, although you will not understand me. These powers, however invulnerable they are, may yet be divided, in the main, into two classes. To the first we count *honour*, to the other belong false pride, revenge, love, reproach, the first to reach the goal after which we strive, and a thousand others. In short, on this side we find all the wild passions which we received as travelling companions on our journey through life. They follow us faithfully, but they are of a nature too heterogeneous not to be continually in open or secret warfare with each other. But not even the most distant sound of their tumult must approach your ear. Pardon me that I have, this evening, being particularly excited, touched upon a subject which I shall endeavour to banish entirely from our company."

"Oh, Seiler, would that you might and could banish every thing that causes in your soul such direful and ominous struggles! Try it at least, dearest Seiler, try to have gentler and milder thoughts, and it will grow ever clearer and more peaceful around you!" Thus Alfhild entreated and assured in a caressing and friendly tone.

"Thou pious innocence!" said the architect, with suppressed emotion, while he passed Alfhild's hand over his burning brow, "to combat, banish! Indeed I might try as well to live without air as out-ride this circle in which I drive myself—though without peace—con-tinually about. Good night, Alfhild! When your pious prayers, like smiling angels, approach the throne of the Highest, send up a sigh also for me. Will you promise me that?"

"Oh yes," she answered, "to-day and every evening, always will I pray for you, Seiler. But how your forehead glows! you have almost burned my fingers."

"How much more would you burn them if you placed your hand upon my heart? But that you will not do; you will not know its vio-lent beating, or hear how it struggles for relief."

"Seiler!" Alfhild said nothing further, but in this word there was an emotion and devotedness which electrified the architect. At one moment he came near yielding to the rushing waves that threatened to carry him along; but a deep look into her trustful eyes, that beamed so friendly upon him, restored to his excited soul the power of con-trolling the weakness of the present hour. "Good-night, Alfhild! May the genii of innocence keep faithful watch by your side! Revenge is dying, the storm is abating, and the heart finds rest; thy angels spread their olive branches over the battle-field!"

Seiler took the light, hastened up stairs, and disappeared in the attic.

Thrilled with happy, singular forebodings, Alfhild entered her quiet chamber. It seemed to her as if she had this evening lived more than in her whole former life. While it was, however, impossible for her to become distinctly conscious of all these painful and pleasing impressions, she put the development of them, full of trust, in the hands of Him to whom she now prayed for herself and for him who, she felt, would always be the chosen idol of her heart. All the gloomy words which Seiler had spoken vanished like forms of mist, and the better words only kept company with Alfhild's smiling dreams.

In the mean time Seiler had entered his room, but Alfhild's angels had not followed him there. From his restless walking up and down, and the deep wrinkle between his brows, which he contracted more than usual, might be inferred that dark thoughts were working in him powerfully.

At length he sat down at the writing-desk.

"As I shall not get to sleep very soon, I will once more read

Bloom's letter, and then answer it," muttered Seiler, and felt for his pocket book, which he, to his inexpressible surprise, did not find in its usual place. "Lost!" said he, "perhaps on the water—perhaps in the grotto with Count Albano!"

A cold shudder ran through him, and his whole manner showed a most violent concussion. "If," said he, half aloud, "if the suspicious man should have found it, and taken it home; if the sketches of Jeames Leganger should, at this moment, make a subject of entertainment for Count Albano—cursed!"

Seiler, in the most painful earnest, threw himself from the one sofa corner into the other. Chill and heat alternated in his body and soul. In this suspense night crawled on like eternity. At length day dawned; and as soon as it had grown sufficiently light, Seiler put on his cloak, went down stairs, opened softly the house door, and hastened with quick steps to the spot near the lake where the boat lay. On the same way, and with the same difficulties as on the preceding evening, he reached the grotto, and found his pocket-book. His eyes flashed fire when he saw the treasure lying on the ground where he lost it. He was now convinced that the eye of no stranger had unhallowed its contents; for Seiler, of course, could not suspect that there were here materials for striking a light; the little closet being fitted in so accurately that it was impossible to observe it on the wall, which was covered with moss and wood.

The architect felt, therefore, perfectly calm, and after he had hastily opened the pocket-book, and convinced himself that the ribands with which the pamphlet was tied were untouched, he had no longer a doubt left. In the great haste with which he ran over the things in the pocket-book, it was, of course, impossible for him to notice what could not have escaped him in a calmer state of mind, that all the articles lay huddled up in disorder; Count Albano not having taken the trouble to return each item to its proper place.

Without farther loss of time, Seiler returned with all speed to the parsonage. He required some hours of rest before going to his usual daily occupation, and he found in the arms of sleep a short relief for his many and intricate troubles.

CHAPTER IX.

SEILER TO BLOOM.

A few days later, Seiler sent the following letter to his friend Bloom, before mentioned:—

"You say you will lend neither hand nor name to this game. What do you really think? Is it not a far greater crime to deceive each other daily by silence, than to speak, since, this must be done sooner or later? And, by heaven! Bloom—it must be done. You know me; you know that I cannot isolate myself as you do, who creates for himself of his ideas and the execution of his plans a world of his own, with which fancy has nothing to do. And even if I could do so, such a state would be unnatural with a character like mine; and every digression from the eternal laws of nature carries with it punishment to the transgressor, either early or late.

"Bloom—my friend, brother and companion in joy and sorrow! with emotions of joy I call back by memory the hours when the man that was broken down by the labours of the day, was again restored by your company, and when the soul recovered new elastic power for the coming time. I call to mind the time when, buried among large volumes, I had come near dreaming away my whole life. But I then met with you, and you taught me to understand myself; and I began to see that the narrow path of a man in office was, for my thirsting fiery soul, the way to the grave. I threw off the heavy burden, and free, with buoyant spirits, and longing for an occupation more suitable for me, I hastened to Italy to study the art to which I was to devote body and soul.

" 'Why do you mention things?' you will ask, 'that are perfectly well known to me? What have they to do with this subject?'

"Yes, Bloom, they have something to do with it. Remember that I overcame every difficulty, and removed every obstacle when the object was to attain a certain end after which my unfettered spirit strove: and I ask you if you believe, or rather if you can believe, that I will desist in the matter in question?

"I know you will say, that obstacles like the present ones have never before crossed my way. True; but the greater the difficulties are, the more ardently my burning soul desires to conquer them.

"Bloom, my friend, I know full well that you hold the powerful feeling which we call love, to be something entirely subordinate, to be a thing that should be considered by a man only after his civil relations or political duties, and many *other* things; and with such notions of love it is not to be wondered at that you cannot comprehend how it is possible to undertake to break the fetters by which it is trammelled. But you ought to know that certain duties, when based only upon the cold forms of honour and custom, weigh heavier than the chains of a galley-slave.

"But, Bloom, throw off the cold thick veil of prejudice. Imagine to yourself an improved relation; and this *must* be brought about ere my heart can find repose. Do you believe that I can find repose among my native mountains? I have been a stranger to peace ever since that soft, but nevertheless unendurable chain, has weighed on me. What was it think you that drove me from my home? You do not know it; it was dark mysteries which my burning imagination could not interpret; for they were shrouded in mist when I left Norway. It was not till I came here that I understood them, and this in awful clearness. It is not this, however, which I wish to speak of. No, I wished to convince you that, if I had found comfort and peace of heart at home, the dark forms which beckoned me to come to Sweden would have done so in vain. I should have never desired to change my circumstances, and never have thirsted to empty the cup of revenge.

"But now it is otherwise—the die is cast. I have sipped the foam from the cup, and it has no disagreeable taste. I sometimes feel a satanic desire to empty it to the very last drop.

"But no! I believe it will not come to this. An angel stands by my side and holds me back; but, Bloom, I stand on a brink between two precipices; nothing but a narrow ridge of rocks lies between them and thence I might soar to heaven; and if once there then earth with its base passion for revenge, its paltry prejudices and unnatural social relations, would vanish. This ridge of rock I know, and I must pass over it.

"I can never speak on this subject without falling into excitement so unnatural, that I always swerve in some manner from the proper object of my letter. This object was to tell you that I shall apply directly, and in my own person, to the proper place. You might have assisted me in this delicate and painful affair with counsel, comfort, and aid; but I find you, for the first time, reserved, cold, and even repulsive. Is what I desire a crime? Speak no more of the laws of morality, they have been settled long ago; the *municipal* laws are the only point of question left.

"You, Bloom, have your own thoughts and notions on human affairs and their mutual relations. They are your own, and I esteem them; but take care lest the same feeling which you now condemn so severely in me, play you the trick of overthrowing all your wisdom. I could almost wish it on amount of your present conduct. You only give trivial admonitions, one after the other, that I ought to return, almost like the prodigal son. You are brief, bitter, and disagreeable, in the highest degree. You no longer show even your art of arguing and convincing. Something must be the matter with you. Let me know it; although I have head and heart so full, that both are near bursting, and will yet do so if a small spark should fall into the combustibles that lie heaped up in them; yet like an honest faithful comrade in life and death, I am ready to throw off my burden and hasten to your assistance.

"Farewell, Bloom! That I may not be over hasty, I will take the subject into consideration a few weeks longer; after which it shall be pressed with greater earnest. Fear nothing. Neither delicacy nor candour shall be wanting in the execution of it. This promises, sacredly,

"Your faithful

"SEILER."

"P. S. Know, when I sometimes view from the highest scaffolding of the new church, or here from my window, the new temple that is rising, I sometimes feel a purpose of heart and a trembling, such as I imagine that to have been which tradition tells us seized the architect whose genius created St. Catherine's church in Stockholm. I fear, like him, that my work may fall in and crush me. Such fancies are generally foreign to me, and I do not know, indeed, how it happens that they have sway over me now. It will grow better with me as soon as all the threads which now cross each other and become entangled in my head, shall be properly arranged. I often make in my mind a large interrogation mark after the little word when?   THE SAME."

CHAPTER X.

THE LUNATIC COUNT.

"Well, dear father, how are things at the castle?" asked Alfhild, when Provost Frenkman had one evening returned from a visit to the count.

"Bad, my child, very bad. Count Albano's sickness increases in violence. He has attacks of such raving madness, that persons stand constantly by his bed-side ready to hold him. The physician shakes his head, and looks very doubtful."

"Then her grace, the countess, I suppose, felt for once like *other* people?" Uncle Sebastian drily remarked, and blew clouds of tobacco-smoke into the air with his usual exactness of manner.

"Yes, like other parents who fear they will lose their only child. This is quite natural."

"Certainly—and to lose the heir to the entailed estate that was to transmit the illustrious name of a race, whose heroic exploits are yet living in the memory of the present generation—that would be too much! Heaven itself could not look upon so much grief without being moved; the tears of nobility must not flow like those of common people. No, that will not do. The exalted family of the count must have something apart in this as in other matters."

"Why! brother Sebastian, what is the matter with you? Is it possible that your unnatural hatred against the present count's family, from whom we never received any thing but good, can go so far, that you, in your blind thirst for revenge, mock at its misfortune— that you scoff at the best and holiest feelings of humanity, the grief of parents at the sick-bed of their child? That is indeed malicious, Sebastian," added the Provost, in a grave tone. "It is wrong to cherish such thoughts, and it is yet more wrong to utter them in the presence of a child, who cannot understand your foolish prejudices, which, however, by no means justify the bitterness of your attack."

"No, of course not; but it is not wrong, nor sinful, if a 'high lord' commits the greatest outrages under the shield of his rank, his name, and authority: if he contrives the most abominable plans, and robs an honest man of his reputation, honour, and the whole prosperity of his future life, to throw, by these means, a veil over what was done. Ha, I grow mad! My old blood begins to boil even now, when I think of all the heroic deeds, written in blood, in the annals of the exalted, noble family!"

"Indeed, I see that you actually grow mad," said the Provost, coldly. "But recollect also, that the time which you so often speak of, is long past, and its events have gone to rest. May you at last give rest to the shades of memory. It is not good to rouse the lord when he would sleep."

Uncle Sebastian did not answer. Having knocked the ashes out of his pipe, and placed it aside, he now began, with his hands on his back, his usual promenade, between the sofa and the fire-place. A jarring "Hem!—hem!" was the only sound, that in shorter or longer intervals, passed over his lips; and the old gentleman seemed to reflect how he, who scarce ever indulged in loquacity, had come to be carried away in this manner. He no doubt felt somewhat ashamed of it; and as the Provost defended and honoured, in every respect, the privilege of nobility, while Sebastian would gladly have annihilated them with one blow, he felt himself at this moment more than usually alone with the "shades of memory," as the Provost called them. He, therefore, thought it best to retire to his solitary chamber.

"You may send my supper up, my dove," said Sebastian gently to Alfhild, "I shall stay in my room."

"But, dear uncle Sebastian," Alfhild rejoined, with a tender look—she was not allowed to express her sympathy in any other way, except by the tone of her voice—"Pray, do stay here! The servant is just calling the architect down; he is always so very polite and friendly, and will, no doubt, cheer you up."

"No, my child, this evening nothing but solitude will do me good. Good night! I am going to rest; may God grant that I go very soon to eternal rest!"

Uncle Sebastian shut himself up, but Alfhild whispered through the door, "as soon as we have finished supper I shall come to see you, uncle—you may depend upon it."

"What was the matter with the old gentleman this evening?" asked the provost somewhat gruffly. "Has any thing happened during my absence, which awakened recollections of the old traditions which he can never dismiss from his head?"

"No, papa, I know of nothing. I only observed that he lost his patience as you began to speak of the sickness of the count; he has been all day in his usual good-natured mood. But, dear papa, uncle Sebastian is old, and has gone through so many hard times, that we must indulge him with his recollections."

"Indulgence! If I have not practised it for more than ten years, then I do not know what indulgence is. But this you do not understand, my daughter. Do not, therefore, interfere in things on which your father has already spoken. You women are not—pay good attention to what I now say."—But what women are not, Alfhild did not hear to-day, for Seiler entered at this moment, and her father dropped the subject.

The host and guest appeared to be on the very best terms. Provost Frenkman, who loved pleasant, refined company, and found in Seiler an attentive listener, as well to his philosophical deductions, as when he unfolded his creed of politics, was well pleased with the company of the architect, who made it his particular task to study the peculiarities of his host, and to accommodate himself to them. He took pains to be as fascinating and interesting as possible, when the provost in the course of the day, came to see him on the building ground, or engaged him in conversation after dinner.

"Well, my dear Mr. Seiler," said the provost, "you have been obliged to wait a little for supper. I stayed away too long; but the count's family was so kind not to consent in their grief to let me go."

"That I can easily imagine," answered Seiler, politely. "Your happy talent, to unite the qualities of a good companion with those of a good pastor, must naturally, under the present circumstances, find so much the more acknowledgment in the count's family."

"Well, well, one does what one can, my dear Mr. Seiler; but by the by, I fear the prospects of the noble family to retain the majority are very slight. This sickness may easily annihilate all hope; for the young count will either die or become crazy."

"Does he, indeed, rave so very badly?"

"For the last three days like one possessed: and beside other foolish things, he has taken a fixed idea into his head, which is so mad, that he will never get rid of it unless there is means to persuade him that what he wishes is done."

"Cannot this wish then be fulfilled?" asked Seiler, astonished, as it seemed, but in reality only with a view to conceal his feelings, which lay too deep for the provost to suspect them, for he answered immediately:

"No, that God knows, and I likewise who was very near being strangled for my official zeal in visiting him. Only think—indeed, he must be mad—he desires to be married to the young Lady Ravenstein without any further delay. Of course, he does not consider at all the publication of banns, the consent of the future bride, and other requisite formalities; and the least contradiction, though made in the gentlest manner, renders his sickness worse."

"Then the young lady must be in the most painful state of anxiety," remarked Seiler.

"Certainly she is; and she has the greater reason for it, since her mother asked me some questions which indicated that she is not adverse to gratifying the wishes of the young count—for instance, whether the publishing of banns were admissible in such cases, and several more of the kind. I, however, gave the selfish lady a look and a few words, which forestalled all further effusions of her confidence; and, like a shy, timid dove, the poor young lady looked upon the only man who perhaps alone of all around her, thought it a sin to chain the young child to the bed of a madman."

"But how do they answer his wild, mad fancies? To do this properly certainly requires much sagacity." The architect seemed to wish to know more about the affair, and the provost was by no means averse to speak farther on the subject.

"Requires much sagacity, you say?" he therefore continued. "It does not require much sagacity to invent new excuses. Old Borgstedt can best get along with him. I will tell you an instance of it. As I, well instructed by the count and countess, came to him, he was sitting upright in his bed, fixing a stare upon the door with his wild, bloodshot eyes. 'Well, it is kind in you, Mr. Provost, to come at last,' he called out to me. 'You let yourself be waited for a long time?' 'Did your lordship send for me?' I asked very humbly, as I had been told that he desired, in his present condition, a slavish obedience from every one, a peculiarity (between us) which he also has when he is well. 'What?' exclaimed he, highly irritated, 'do you dare to deny that you have been ordered by several messengers to perform the rites of marriage? Borgstedt, you can bear witness that I sent several messengers. Is it true or not?' 'Perfectly according to truth,' Borgstedt assured him with all gravity; 'but unfortunately the messengers, as I said before, did not find Mr. Provost at home.' 'Yes, that is true,' observed he more calmly. 'I now recollect it. Well, I am glad to see you. Take a seat till my bride comes. My father will, perhaps, be so kind as to tell my cousin to make haste with making the bridal wreath. She must be here within half an hour.' 'I will tell her to make haste,' answered the old count, who had accompanied me to his own room, and, glad to have a pretext, he left the apartment. 'Give me my watch, Borgstedt,' said the sick man as soon as his father had closed the door: 'I will see if she is punctual. But, Mr. Provost, where is your official gown and your book? You knew that you were to perform a marriage ceremony, and you cannot do it without your robe.' 'My dearest count,' said I, somewhat embarrassed, 'I had the honour to come here entirely by accident, and was very far from suspecting that it was your wish that your servant should perform so important an act to-day. Besides, I thought that you would have due publication made, as is usual in such cases.' He then contracted his eye-brows, and fixed his looks upon me with an expression that surpassed in awfulness all that I had ever seen. 'Ah!' said he in a sharp tone, 'You wish to find subterfuges; but they will be of no use to you now. It is your duty to marry me with or without gown or book, published or not published, when I command it. Have not you heard, moreover, that I shall stay here but a few hours longer? I must join my regiment; before I march, however, against the enemy, I wish to have my personal affairs arranged. I intend, also, to make my testament, but of course I must first be married, to be able to do something for my wife.' 'Certainly, certainly,' answered I, somewhat disturbed; 'but without a book your lordship must see nothing can be done.' 'Well, then, send a messenger immediately to the parsonage,' commanded he in a harsh tone. Much perplexed, I observed that the book and gown were in a closet that I alone understood to open. 'You mean to deceive me, priest!' exclaimed he, with the wildest expression of madness; and before I had time to draw back, he seized me by the throat with his long lean fingers. There I was sitting as in a vice, and should have been undoubtedly throttled like a dog, if old Borgstedt had not helped me out of my double dilemma. 'Your lordship,' whispered he, while he listened toward the door, 'I hear the footsteps of your bride. She would die with fright if she saw what is here going on. For heaven's sake keep yourself quiet.' 'Ah, is she coming?' said he in a low voice, and at the same moment the fiendish expression disappeared from his countenance, my throat was released, and I quickly withdrew into the remotest corner of the room, from where I observed how, lying almost without motion, and with his eyes fixed upon the door, he strove to watch the remotest sound that might confirm him in his happy illusion. 'Where may she have gone to, Borgstedt?' he asked, after having patiently waited for a few minutes. 'Go and see; she has perhaps heard something, and been alarmed.' The old servant immediately obeyed the command, and returned with a face that indicated the poor patient had been right in his supposition. 'My dearest count,' said he in a sympathising and beseeching tone, 'the young lady, actually intending to come here, heard something of the violent scuffle, and became so much alarmed, that she fainted, and had to be carried back to her room. Ah! women are so weak; they cannot bear to hear the least sound of an angry man's voice without falling down like flies. I hope, however, your lordship will excuse her; she cannot help her feeble constitution, the poor lady.' 'Hush, Borgstedt,' the count answered, with an expression of his usual pride. 'Thelma does not require your apology. You must see that it is I, on the contrary, who must be inconsolable for having alarmed her. Mr. Provost, convey to her my profound respects, together with my sincerest regret, that I have placed her in that condition. The marriage ceremony, you see yourself, must now be deferred at all events; but to-morrow morning at ten o'clock you must be here to perform it.' He made a dismissing motion with his hand, and thus, to my delight, the scene ended."

"That was an unpleasant audience," answered Seiler with a slight shudder; "to-morrow, I suppose, it will not be much better."

"No, that is certain; but I shall take care not to go and see him again. The doctor told me, as I related to him this scene, the only thing that could operate upon his state, was Thelma's presence; but the poor girl is so full of fear, that she almost faints when they speak of a visit to her cousin. We shall see if she will not at last be persuaded to it."

During this conversation supper had been finished and Alfhild, almost dissolved in tears at the fate of poor Thelma, soon after left the room to fulfil her promise to uncle Sebastian.

The provost, tired by the fatigues of the day, went to his chamber; but Seiler hastened to the shore of the lake where the boat lay. This time he carried something under his arm, which he had first taken from his room. It was a mandolin, a reminiscence of his stay in Italy. When he had arrived at the rocky hill, he did not stop at the usual landing place; he thought himself obliged to fulfil the promise he had given to the young count; and he, therefore, sailed a little further along the rocky shore. At a short distance from the grotto he laid the oars down, took the mandolin and sang to it the following song:

Thou evening beam, but lately lighting
The stranger's solitary way,
Thou sawest a heart that time could never
Gild with hope's shortest, slightest ray.

But lo! a star is now appearing,
That shines so rich with hope, so mild;
There dwells henceforward in his bosom
An angel form, a heavenly child.

Now go thou down, thou sun of evening,
For then my lonely heart shall rise;
For the first time in this pure starlight,
My life's true sun illumes the skies.

Wrapped in a large shawl that covered her face, Thelma Ravenstein was leaning over the barrier near the grotto; she listened to the melodious notes without suspecting the danger for her young heart. She felt, indeed, a kind of gentle reproach, when, instead of going to sleep, she stole every evening through the damp coolness to the grotto to breathe the air, in a double sense, after the laborious oppressive day; but, after so many sad words it cannot possibly be a sin, thought she, when she was listening in the darkness to the timid notes that flowed from the lips of the architect.

"Indeed he has never spoken to me. To be on the water and sing a song to the mandolin can be no sin."

However this might be, Thelma's cheeks burned with increasing glow; all grief, all sorrow and trouble which she suffered at the castle, were forgotten. She lived only in the enjoyment of the present moment. Nothing is of greater effect upon ardent sensibility and a heart half awaked, than mystery and fear in love.

After Seiler had finished his song, he put his hand upon his heart, took off his hat, bowed, and turned the boat toward the other side to return to the parsonage.

Thelma did not see the look he sent after her, for she had already vanished.

CHAPTER XI.

LOVE AND CURIOSITY.

AUTUMN was approaching, and the frequent rainy weather, as well as the increasing darkness of the evenings, made the secret visits of the architect more seldom, till they at last ceased entirely.

The condition of Count Albano had remained about the same, only one other symptom was added—namely, that his violent attacks of raving were often succeeded by a long and lasting feebleness. He then suffered himself to be treated like a child; yet the greatest care had to be taken in the choice of expressions, for he was easily roused to new paroxysms by a single word or an unforeseen turn of his thoughts.

Until now all attempts to induce Lady Thelma to visit Albano had remained fruitless. However, she had promised, (that is, her mother had extorted the promise from her), that as soon as his mental disease had abated, she would no longer refuse to hand the medicine to the patient, who was now only with great difficulty to be persuaded to take any thing. The eyes of the unhappy man were constantly fixed upon the door. It was evident that he expected somebody; he had, however, ceased to speak of marriage, though there continually occurred in his wanderings allusions to the bride, and her not appearing. He spoke most of the grotto, and this in the most painful manner, which no one knew how to explain.

While the affairs at the castle became more gloomy and monotonous, those at the parsonage assumed a clearer and more friendly aspect. Seiler's affection for Alfhild became more evident, and the bashful, lovely looks of the maiden, her quiet, tender attentions for him, were favourable answers to his feelings.

With a true father's joy the provost looked forward to the moment when the architect, who had become endeared to him, would open his heart and ask for the hand of his daughter. That Seiler had not done this of Alfhild was certain; and the provost highly esteemed his delicacy of feeling, which prompted him to ask first the paternal consent.

But day after day passed by without producing any result, though the provost by his increasing friendly and affable conduct, showed clearly enough that he was not averse to Seiler's plans; he felt a certain uneasiness, yet he could do nothing else but let things go on in their natural course, and calmly to abide the issue of time.

One evening, (it was the last day in the month of September,) the family at the parsonage sat as usual round the cheerful fire-side, and conversed with all heartfelt familiarity, which justified the inference of a more intimate relation. Even uncle Sebastian was milder than usual. The great horror which he had entertained against the architect on their first acquaintance had now entirely disappeared, in consequence of his pleasing and affable manners. Far from deeming him a being that might justify the gloomy, unhappy forebodings that had preceded him, the stranger stood on the contrary in the clearest and warmest sunshine of favour with Uncle Sebastian, and he looked with a kind, hopeful expectation upon the two young people, who sat close together by the fire-side. While Alfhild's fingers busily knitted at some work for Uncle Sebastian, who, to escape from the blinding glare of the fire, had moved farther back toward the provost, Seiler bent over to the beautiful young maiden and whispered: "Oh, happy he who will be so fortunate as to sit, as we do now, by his *own* fire-side, and delight his eyes on the happy housewife!"

This wish might be of an entirely general bearing, and no answer encouraged Seiler to continue; yet he added:

"If this time should ever come, Alfhild, then—then the housewife must be like the beautiful smiling image I have now before me."

Yet Alfhild answered not a word; but the glow on her brow and cheeks burned deeper, and more busily flew her fingers at the knitting work, though many meshes were dropped, and had to be taken up anew.

"I see, Mr. Seiler," said the provost, more cheerful than usual, "that you are not entirely displeased with Sweden. A peaceful evening, like the present, is one of the greatest enjoyments for a man who has taste for the joys of home."

"Yes, indeed," answered the architect, "I love Sweden, though her sons did not always show to Norwegians the same hospitality which I have received from you; and what I love above all things, is the quiet life at home. This tames and quiets my disposition, which is mild by nature."

The provost and Uncle Sebastian interchanged looks; and while the brow of the latter became wrinkled, that of the provost brightened more and more, as he said very frankly:

"Well, if you are pleased with Sweden, Mr. Seiler, then make it your future home. A skilful man of your profession can want neither work to support him, nor hearts that love him."

"It is some time, Mr. Provost, since I have taken into consideration what you just alluded to," answered Seiler. His voice betrayed something evasive and uncertain, which showed that he was embarrassed. The only answer of the provost, when no continuation followed, was a long—protracted "ah, ah!"

"Yes, as I said," observed the architect with delay, "I have often thought on it: but many circumstances in which I am involved require yet some time to be arranged. I hope, however, that the future will give fulfilment to my wishes in this respect."

"Circumstances—intricate," remarked the provost sharply, "are not what I like, and I pity every one who cannot openly follow his conviction, where the destiny of his future life is in question, but must consider secret relations. I did not know that this was the case with Mr. Seiler."

The architect blushed. He felt the poignant remark of the provost, and the more he felt himself touched by it, the more it grieved him, to see through his silence, a shadow fall on him, which he would so gladly have avoided. To extinguish, as much as possible, the bad effect of the turn the conversation had taken, he rose, and replied with all the self-control and captivating openness in his power:

"I think there may be circumstances in the life of every one that influence his will and actions. But even the most intricate knot may be solved, and when this has been the case with mine, then I desire nothing more than to call Sweden my home, and——"

He interrupted himself. In the condition in which he was he had said enough. Another word would have been not only superfluous, but would have had a colour of over haste. He bowed in silence and resumed his seat.

The provost was by nature not prone to great distrust. Besides, the declaration just made, had something so simple and natural in it, which struck him favourably. He was by no means inclined to give up all hope of having so energetic and handsome a man for his son-in-law. He was, therefore, induced to accept Seiler's answer as satisfactory, and reached his hand to his guest with an expressive smile, by which he wished to make amends for all. After this storm all felt the air to be purer and lighter. The atmosphere had been once put in commotion, and the evening seemed to be destined to bring to the parsonage clouds of all kinds.

"The mail is very late this evening," said Uncle Sebastian. "Let us play a game at draughts till the papers come."

"I should like to play," said the provost; and Alfhild rose to prepare a table.

The game had lasted about half an hour when the door opened, and Stina entered with the mail-bag.

"Hum!" said the provost, as he began to empty it. "I am anxious to hear what news there is at the capital. Here is a letter for Mr. Seiler. Ah! what a neat lady's hand; perhaps from mother or sister?"

"No, I have neither mother nor sister, but I have yet a few lady acquaintances."

Seiler took the letter. The provost paid no attention to him, for an official writing absorbed his whole attention. But Alfhild observed the embarrassment in the architect's manner, and the painful constraint he imposed upon himself to answer the question of the provost.

"Will you not read your letter?" said she. "I will place the small work-table near you with a light."

"No, no, dear Alfhild, it requires no haste. I will wait till I go to my chamber. It contains nothing of importance."

"But, to judge by your appearance, dear Seiler, it seems, indeed, to be something of importance. May I look at the fair lady's hand, which papa just praised?"

With a forced "certainly you may," he handed her the letter. She took and held it against the fire.

"That is, indeed, a very fine hand. I would like to know what it contains; and if it contains nothing of importance, as you say, I, perhaps, may gratify my curiosity without incurring your displeasure."

By way of jest, she placed her fingers on the seal as if she would open it.

"May I?" said she with a smile.

"Why not, if it gives you pleasure?" replied Seiler, with the same exertion to appear indifferent.

"Well, if you have no objection," said Alfhild, with animation; and instantly the seal was broken and the letter unfolded.

Now Seiler grew pale, and his short broken breath indicated a vehement emotion of mind.

"Take care, Alfhild, you will burn yourself!" said he, in a changed, suppressed voice; while he, with a quick movement, took the letter from her, and put it in his pocket.

"It is then something important and secret, as your confused features show," remarked Alfhild, in a tone which had in it something of that sensitiveness which does not become woman very well, but still is often found in the best of them. "I see you only wished to jest with me. But I really do not believe that a letter from a lady to you could contain any thing else but those little trifles which every body might read; and you yourself tried to give it this appearance."

"Alfhild," answered Seiler, in so low a tone that only she alone could hear it, but with a deep, serious voice—a voice which found its way to her soul, and moved every fibre in her whole being—"Alfhild, if you will be like other girls—if I find that you are little, envious, distrustful or whimsical, then my respect ceases; and a girl that I cannot respect I thrust from my heart, though I loved her even to idolatry. *Confidence*, Alfhild, is the basis on which our most beautiful feelings rest, or on which at least they *ought* to rest. Tell me, do you feel at this moment, though you see a letter from a lady in my hands, the contents of which you do not know—do you feel your confidence in me stand immoveably fast?"

Alfhild's little peevishness was over. Tear after tear coursed down her cheeks. She was unable to answer: she was moved too violently and intensely. She felt burning pain and remorse at having offended the man whom she idolized from the centre of her soul. But who can find words in a moment when he has an excess of feelings?

It was easy for Seiler to comprehend all the wonderful fibres that trembled in Alfhild's soul; but men are seldom contented at what they see. They always wish to feel every thing with their coarse hands, to convince themselves of the existence of things. Seiler read Alfhild's answer in each tear that fell upon uncle Sebastian's work, at which the poor child, in her anxiety of heart, knitted with all her power; notwithstanding this, he repeated his question: "Will your confidence stand immoveably firm, Alfhild? Will you rather die than give up your faith in the honesty of my heart?"

"Yes, Seiler, that I will!" answered Alfhild so lowly, that only the delicate organs of a lover could understand it. "I know it would be easier for me to die than give up my belief in...."

She had no courage to finish. She cast her looks down upon her hands, which she, with an expression of pious resignation, folded and pressed against her breast.

"My *love*," said Seiler. "Thanks, Alfhild! Now it is spoken—now we understand each other and trust firmly!"

With a hasty, almost convulsive motion, he pressed her hand, and left the room.

Unobserved by the gentlemen who were engaged in reading, Alfhild went softly into her chamber.—

"*My love—now it is spoken*," repeated she several times. But she did not conceive why this word, which she had always fervently wished to hear from his lips, now that it was spoken, did not fill her with all the bliss she had expected from it.

She felt nothing of bliss; she felt strangely, incomprehensibly; she appeared strange to herself, and such a state could not be pleasant to her simple, innocent heart. She wept till she was tired; and this was the first fruit of the important confession of being loved.

In the meantime the hour for the evening meal had arrived, and Stina announced by a loud knocking at Alfhild's chamber door, that it was time to dispel the love-thoughts from her mind, and to begin to prepare for supper. When Alfhild, with tears in her long eye-lashes, and a little shawl round her head, to excuse the burning of her cheeks by a pretended tooth-ache, entered the kitchen, she was initiated into the first elements of the infinitely long catechism of love.

"Dear Miss," said Stina, "we have been long waiting for eggs for an omelet; the cook will get entirely out of patience if she does not get some immediately."

"Ah, Stina, my teeth ache dreadfully. Hold the light while I open the closet and hand you the eggs."

"But in heaven's name, what are you thinking about, Miss?" exclaimed Stina, astonished. "The eggs are not there. How would the architect laugh, if he saw Miss Alfhild so absent!"

"Oh, hush your talk; here are the eggs!" And without thinking of their fragility, Alfhild dropped them on the ground, instead of putting them in the dish which Stina held for her.

"Will supper soon be ready, my dove?" inquired uncle Sebastian's voice through the door; "I begin to feel hungry."

"Soon, dear uncle!" And with a silencing motion to Stina, Alfhild gave out other eggs, and then began the work with double energy. Through the united efforts of the cook and Stina, the supper soon stood on the table, yet half an hour later than usual.

"I thought you had forgotten us entirely," said the provost, who, in regard to the meal hours, loved punctuality, while he rose to take the cordial, which it is customary in the north to take before meals. "But what in all the world, Alfhild—how you look! red as a turkey-cock! What is the matter—I believe you have cried?"

"Cried, papa! No; why should I?" Alfhild trembled: she did not dare to look up.

"That you must know best. I indeed do not know; perhaps it is the heat from the kitchen fire."

"Yes, that is generally the case when one stands long at the fire; it makes one very red."

"But of what use is the cook if you place yourself before the fire? You must not do so; I do not wish you to look like a cook when you come to the table. I hope you will observe what I now tell you. But where is the architect? Have you a seat for him?"

"Yes, dear father, he will be here directly." But instead of the architect, Stina came and announced that Mr. Architect was not well, and should not come to table.

"Indeed, that is sufficient reason. But half an hour ago, when we spoke with him here, he seemed to be in very good spirits. Come, brother Sebastian!"

The provost filled his glass and put it to his lips; but with a thundering: "What cursed business is this!—Who put in the liquor?" he placed the glass upon the table with a force that made its contents fly.

"The liquor, papa? It was I who filled the bottle; what is the matter with it?" asked Alfhild, trembling at the severe expression of her father's face.

"What is the matter with it?" exclaimed the provost, angrily; "it is vinegar, you goose! I believe you are not in your right mind this evening!"

"Well, well; let that suffice," interrupted uncle Sebastian. "You see, my dear brother, that both casks being exactly alike, a mistake is very easily made. Do not cry, my child, but go and get us other liquor."

The provost shook his head: "You are always ready," said he, grumbling, "when there is an opportunity to spoil her."

Alfhild, in the meanwhile, ran to the cellar to correct her mistake.

"And you are always ready to make much ado about a trifle," replied Sebastian, drily.

The evening meal was finished at last, the table removed, and Alfhild at liberty to go to her chamber. There she wept afresh, and thought that love was indeed a very singular thing. She had all the evening experienced nothing but disagreeable sensations. Alfhild wept, for in her dreamings she had imagined love something entirely different from what she found it at present.

Morning came, but with it came no joy. Seiler did not make his appearance at breakfast. He had gone to the building, and did not return till the moment they were sitting down to dinner. And how did he look! Pale, reserved, almost repulsively serious. Once only his eye rested on Alfhild; yet this was done with an expression of deep grief; and as soon as the company rose from the table, he took his hat and went again to the church. During the whole evening he stayed in his room, and kept the door closed.

Poor Alfhild had, therefore, time enough to give herself up to the most painful thoughts, which weighed upon her the more heavily, as they were the first which she had not courage to communicate to uncle Sebastian. The only enjoyment in her new world was that of suffering alone and for him.

CHAPTER XII.

GLOOMY PICTURES.

NOVEMBER's chilly storms raged in the deserted halls of Hammarby castle. The count's mansion was no longer the place of meeting for the fashionable world; it was no longer, as in former days, crowded with guests who sought a comfortable home; no more its little coteries planned the evening's dramatic entertainment, and calculated the expense of the next masquerade. Musical and dramatic *soirées*, masquerades and card parties, and the delightful *tête-à-têtes*, in the deep dark window recesses, had passed away, and all was silent, dead, and lonely. Thus had it been ever since all things were done according to the will of the Count Albano, who had declared his explicit aversion to every kind of sociability and enjoyment. Both in doors and out the young man was so repulsive, so cold and reserved, that the few guests who still visited Castle Hammarby, began to withdraw; and the splendid new castle became more lonely and unendurable than the ruins of the old one.

The wind whistled through the high windows of the saloon, the curtains slowly moved to and fro, and the lights of the chandelier gave a faint waving light, so that the bent form that sat on a high-backed chair near the stove, resembled more a shadow than a real man.

After a little while, a servant came in and spread the tea-table, and lighted a pair of wax tapers. The countess and baroness entered, preceded by a servant who carried a light, and opened the folding doors. After a friendly but yet peevish salute of the count, who only mechanically nodded from his corner, the ladies took a seat upon a divan. In silence and with a stiff monotony, as if they were at a funeral where one is obliged to stay till the end, for appearance sake, the noble family sat round the tea-table. No sound was heard save the noise of the boiling water in the silver tea-kettle. When the countess, by a motion of her hand, had signified that the table should be removed, and the servants had withdrawn, the Baroness Ravenstein broke the silence.

"My brother-in-law, I promise myself from this evening the happiest success. We have attained much—nay, the most difficult part, by prevailing on her to go and see him. The rest follows as a matter of course; I guarantee—for I know my child—she will not be able to see his suffering and striking face without doing every thing that duty and feeling command her, to console and comfort him."

"I fear," said the count, "that his face, which my sister calls striking, will strike her most dangerously, for he looks, indeed, awful! and will, perhaps, frighten her so, that she at the very first visit will lose courage for all the rest."

"I think you may fortunately be wrong in this, my friend," began the countess; "for if this was the case, she would not stay with him half an hour, and it is already longer that she is in his room. I think with my sister, that we may hope for the best; and if Albano can only be calmed, says the doctor, he will be entirely well again, and also recover from the fits which occur even now but very seldom."

"Heaven grant that it will turn out well!" said the count; but a doubtful shake of his head proved that his faith was not very strong. "The life," he began again, after a short pause, "which we have led already for several months, is a slowly killing poison, which is consuming all my strength, and takes from me all desire to mingle in politics or society. Do not we three sit here like pale monuments on our own graves?—and all that is wanting, is to be carried down into our gloomy family tomb."

"What awful images!" whispered the Countess Ravenstein, in a trembling voice, and shrinking farther into the corner of the sofa.

Loud and moaningly howled the storm without; a violent gust of wind burst open the door of the anteroom, yet no one seemed inclined to close it, and its creaking and slamming echoed dismally through the lofty rooms.

"What terrible weather! It might make one feel weary, even though there were no other causes," said the countess, only in order to say something. "I am curious to know how it will be with us a year hence."

No answer from any human lip was heard; but from the music-room came a sound, which, though quite natural, was yet awful in the extreme to the excited nerves of the noble family;—a string of the piano broke.

"Let us do something," said the count, whose manly self-control awoke at the low "ah!" which escaped the lips of the ladies. He rose, closed the door, and rang the bell for a servant to arrange a card-table.

Silent, pale and quiet, like shadows, the members of the count's family sat down to the amusement which was to restore the equipoise of their minds.

Let us in the meanwhile pay a visit to Count Albano.

In a large, square room, lighted by a glass lamp suspended from the ceiling, stood a wide pompous bed, with red silk curtains and rich gilded ornaments. It was one of the antiquities that had been retained from times long past, and was remarkable for the circumstance that Louise Ulrike[1] had slept in it when she had once thought it worth the trouble to honour Castle Hammarby with a visit for several days. On this bed lay now, completely dressed, a pale yellow, almost an ashy-grey form, whose red hair and beard formed a frame in which the frightful face with dark burning eyes was set. The fits of madness under which Count Albano had suffered during the first six weeks of his sickness had gradually given way, and the disease had taken a different character. When his mind sometimes began to wander, no violent attack like those he had before endured need be feared. On the contrary, it seemed that he had grown melancholy, and that his spleen had increased. Curious, however, was the extreme care that he appeared to bestow upon his exterior. No one was allowed to hint, but in the remotest way, at his looks; this he would not suffer, though he often had the looking-glass brought to him, holding it for a whole quarter of an hour before him, and revelling, as it were, in the contemplation of his awful ugliness. Frequently upon these occasions his mouth contracted into a peculiar smile; whether from grief, joy, or madness, no one could say. He was unable to sit up at the most more than two hours in succession every day; he then went to bed, and lay in a motionless state. He spoke little, and answered still less; his only occupation consisted in staring incessantly at the bronze ornaments of the canopied bed.

In this state he lay when Thelma came to see him. It was evening. She took a seat on a chair by his side, and the lamp-light fell upon

---

[1] Louise Ulrike of Prussia (1720-1782) became Queen of Sweden after marrying Adolf Frederick of Sweden.

her, so that her pale, suffering face could be distinctly seen. The great struggle of self-denial was painted in every feature; and an indescribable mildness was expressed in her countenance, which made her appear like an angel visiting a life-weary son of earth. Farther back in the room, behind a large screen, old Borgstedt was busily stirring to and fro; but he belonged to the back-ground of the scene, and we will busy ourselves only with the fore-ground.

"Have you no friendly word to speak to me, dear Albano?" Thelma asked, suppressing a slight shudder, and bending over Albano, who kept his staring eyes fixed upon her.

"You had no friendly word for me, Thelma, not a single one for three months that I have been pining here," answered he in a low but not reproachful tone. And as Thelma sighed, he added: "What has induced you to visit me?"

"My wish to see you, Albano! Would I were able to do you some service."

He smiled and shook his head without answering, but in his smile there lay a deep and bitter grief.

"You do not answer me, Albano; are you not pleased with my coming here?"

"Yes, indeed, pleased as a poor dog who gets a few crumbs thrown to him out of pity, that he may not starve."

"Do not speak so, Albano, you pain me; your words pierce like daggers through my heart."

"Then I shall be silent, Thelma; that I have learned already."

"No, do not be silent; do not look at me so gloomily, dear Albano, you frighten me," said she, leaning her head against the bed.

He passed his emaciated, long, and cold fingers over Thelma's warm forehead; and as she calmly suffered this, he raised himself half upright, and after having some time played with his left hand in the folds of her white dress, he gently laid his arm around her waist. Then the poor girl began to tremble in all her limbs; she hardly dared to move, or even to breathe.

"Are you alarmed? You tremble like the aspen leaves near the grotto, on the evening that I met you on my way thither. Do you remember, Thelma? It was an awful evening. Ha! how it thundered, lightened, and rained! Seiler, the coward, took shelter in the innermost recess of the grotto. I found him there, and ordered him to leave the environs of the castle. But it seemed that you thought him an interesting, fascinating, beautiful young man, as beautiful as one of the statues by Sergell[1]—is it not so?"

Thelma almost died with fear and torturing anguish. She writhed like a wounded worm; but his arm enclosed her firmly.

"Do you fear?" he asked again, and he bent toward her till she felt his red shaggy hair touch hers.

"Yes, Albano, I do fear! I shall die with anguish if you do not let me go," she replied, making an effort to free herself.

"Fear nothing, Thelma! I shall do you no harm. I will only hold my arm thus. I love no one more than you; all others vex me; but you, you hate me, because I am ugly and misshapen, and yet dare to have a heart—a heart, Thelma, which, if you desire, would gladly sacrifice its last drop of blood for you. Oh! you do not know what it is to suffer such torments as I have suffered; you do not know what is to be obliged to despise one's self, and to be despised by the woman whom one is compelled, to his own torture, to adore; and yet not be able to resign all claims to life's happiness? You do not know what it is to feel one's heart torn by the furies of jealousy—to be tormented by distrust—to rave and destroy one's own self in the hell of madness— to sink down upon the couch of sickness, to feel a thousand pains gnawing at the miserable body in which all passions are contending with each other. Ah, Thelma! all this you do not know, do not comprehend; for all this you do not care. You even despise and abominate this wretch! But, Thelma, my love! do not do so. Know that, however miserable I may at present be, I will not be despised!"

"I despise you, Albano? No, certainly not. I suffer with you—I weep for you; but let me go, for mercy's sake! I shall suffocate if you do not let me stand up."

"Ah! you only say so, Thelma, to get away from me; if I let you go you will leave me and never come back again."

"Yes, dear Albano, if you release me now, if I may sit quietly on a chair beside you, without alarming me by your violent outbreaks, I will stay with you so long as you desire it, and come again to-morrow, and every evening till you are well. Yes, that I will, and I will bring with me my lute to sing you to sleep. Would you like that?"

"Ah, thou alluring syren-voice! How beautiful thou art, and yet

---

[1] Johan Tobias Sergel (1740-1814) was a celebrated Swedish sculptor.

how false! See, now you are free, Thelma; be now grateful and do not leave me."

He sank back into the pillows which she kindly put in order; and he then lay quiet, alternately staring upon her and the ornaments of the bedstead.

In this way a long hour passed; at length the unhappy sick man fell asleep, and Thelma stole away to the room of her mother, where she, in complete exhaustion of mind, sank upon a sofa. The roaring of the storm sounded to her like a mysterious, nightly Æolian harp; and by the notes of its gloomy cradle-song she sank into dismal dreamings.

When the Baroness Ravenstein shortly after entered, to divert herself after a tedious evening, by the examination of her daughter in relation to her visit to Count Albano, she found Thelma asleep. A light touch awoke her, but she besought her mother in the most loving terms to be allowed to retire without speaking to-day of what she had passed through. She was very tired, and wished to go to bed.

The baroness would not oppose her. Thelma's eyes, sore with weeping, were either powerful advocates in her behalf, or the mind of the mother had been softened by the dismal evening; she contented herself with marking this day, the 15th of November, with a cross in the almanack.

The morning sun shone brightly when Thelma entered her mother's room, at the summons of a servant. "Well, my child!" With these words the baroness commenced her invitation to relate the great events of the preceding evening. "You have risen very early to-day, I see. I thank you for it, and must give you a kiss. Bashfulness and affection, you see, and all other foolishness of this kind, I never could bear, and we have already had enough of this. To speak candidly to you, my dear Thelma, I must tell you that I have been indeed ashamed of your conduct of late. You have shown not the least proof of the good education which I have given you from a child."

"How so, mother?" asked Thelma, while a burning colour spread over her face. She believed—but we can hardly say that she *believed*, she was too excited for it; it was only a suspicion that flashed over her mind—that her mother had become acquainted with her secret visits to the grotto.

"I perceive, with a deep and proud mother's joy your repentance," began again the baroness. "The blush on your face proves that you see yourself how foolish it has been in you. I have, however, wished to leave it to your own feeling, in the conviction that you would see at last, that in this way you will ruin all of us. Indeed, my child, you have almost crushed the heart of your mother; a mother who through many lonesome nights, especially of late, has watched and prayed for you."

"Oh, my beloved, dear mother, was it then a sin?" asked Thelma, in the most painful embarrassment, convinced that her secret was discovered. She put her burning cheeks in the hands of her mother, and then with a beseeching look, pressed them to her heart.

"Not so, not so, my love!" said the baroness, somewhat embarrassed, and caressingly stroked the locks from her daughter's brow. She did not comprehend Thelma's excited state, and took it to be the effect of the speech she had just addressed to her. Believing that she might, for the present, rest satisfied with this victory, she did not wish to torment farther the frightened sensibility of the poor child, but said kindly:

"Be calm, my dear child; I speak not of a sin, but only of your obstinacy. But since you repent of this, and will no doubt make amends for your fault by complying with the long expressed wish of your mother, all is forgiven and forgotten. And, dear Thelma, how sweet is the consciousness of fulfilled duty! You know when your father died, all our property was attached. Every thing was sold to pay his debts, and we suddenly found ourselves in utter misery. Being alone in a foreign country, without connections that might have assisted us, we should have been reduced to beggary, if my brother-in-law had not extended to us a caring hand. He himself came to Germany for us. He gave us a new, peaceful home under his own roof. He took care of your education, and loved you like a father. My sister, your aunt, has shared with me a mother's care, and always considered you as her daughter that would, one day, brighten our old days. Judge now, yourself, Thelma, if it would not be the blackest ingratitude, after all the generosity on their part, if you should refuse to show your gratitude in the only way that is at your command—if you should refuse, I mean, to resign yourself to a fate that hundreds of others would seize upon with delight."

The flood of words gradually abated; but even had it continued as copious as on its first outbreak, Thelma would not have attempted to check it. She sat silent and thoughtful, having found that her dear secret was not discovered, and only a misunderstanding had made her tremble and blush; and now she feared that the tears and words thus called forth, would prove weapons in her mother's hands, for she would interpret them to be signs of contrition and repentance of her refusal to accept the addresses of Count Albano. Poor Thelma suffered dreadfully, and she had not a single being in the whole wide world to whom she might have confided the pangs of her young heart.

"Now, my dear Thelma, you really are yet like a child, that may be excited by the least word. However, we will pass that over now, and come to the main thing. How did you find your cousin?"

"Dreadful," answered Thelma, and a slight chill shook her at the recollection of his embrace. "But let us not speak of this, dear mother. I can assure you he frightened me so that I have entirely lost the remembrance of what he uttered. Yet I have promised him—and I shall keep my word—to come every evening with my lute, and play and sing him to sleep."

A ray of joy beamed from the eyes of the baroness. "My beloved child," said she, smiling, "more I need not know; for I know that your singing will lull to rest all the gloomy thoughts that have so long held possession of poor Albano. He will grow well, rational, and almost like other men. It will be your work, and believe me, my child, you also will yet be happy. The dismal solitude, the desolate dreariness will cease, and you are the saving angel to whom he and we all look up with gratitude."

At the conclusion of this speech, the baroness embraced her daughter with much affection. It was not possible, thought the world-experienced lady, to see a more interesting scene, as well in relation to the outward effect as to the impression which it had made upon the tender sensibility and youthful heart of her daughter. Alas! Thelma knew but too well, that it was only the concluding scene to a great gala, and this conviction affected her unfavourably.

Days came and went. Thelma sang and wept; and wept and sang. Count Albano became more calm and quiet. He got up, shaved himself, had his hair put in order, and began, as the baroness expressed herself, "to become pretty much like other men." Nevertheless storms raged without; and within the house things would not grow entirely well. This autumn was, at Hammarby, more solitary and drear than ever. The count read the newspapers and played *solitaire*; the countess and the baroness played chess, and Thelma profited every free moment to steal into the library, the windows of which looked upon the lake. But there also all was quiet—all was joyless, desolate and drear as in her own heart.

A wandering sunbeam once fell upon her poor heart, and called forth by its genial warmth a few beautiful half-blown buds; but autumn came, the sun disappeared behind the mountains, the dew congealed, and the buds fell off. Then the lonely heart made in itself a grave for its faded favourites, and on the little mound, for many a long sad day, pale Memory sat and mourned their early death.

CHAPTER XIII.

THE SEPARATION.

ONE morning on one of the first days of December, Seiler came into the sitting-room, where breakfast was ready, in his travelling dress. He was to leave Hammarby for a few months. Since the building could not be proceeded with during the winter, he had determined during this time, to take a journey to Norway. Certain affairs in his native country required his personal attention. With the bitter feeling of separation in his heart, he now came to bring to iron necessity this severe sacrifice, to exchange with his beloved the last friendly look for a long time.

Since the evening when Seiler received the letter, the contents of which Alfhild was so curious to know, he was no longer the same. The strength of his affection for Alfhild seemed to have increased; yet he gave less often utterance to it in words than before. His looks and every action, however, spoke an intelligible language, and the heart of the young maiden gradually began to find an unutterable delight in this silent, sad love, which had a powerful ally in the gloomy and brooding melancholy expressed in Seiler's countenance, and which only her presence had power to drive away. The architect did not love at all these melancholy musings. He intended to shake off for ever the fetters that oppressed his mind, and to restore to it freedom and peace. To effect this he resolved to separate from Alfhild for a few months—for he was of opinion that he was better able in Norway to work for the happiness of their future, than by staying during the winter at the parsonage. As soon as his determination had been matured, he communicated it to Alfhild. She became pale, and fixed her eyes upon him, which spoke more than words of grief and despair could have done.

"There is no help for it; be strong, Alfhild, for it must be done!" said Seiler.

"Must be done!" said she slowly, folding her hands. "Why then must it be done, Seiler?"

"For our happiness, Alfhild, for the sake of your future I must leave. But console yourself, I shall not spend the time that I am separated from you in vain and I will always be with you in the spirit."

Seiler bent down and kissed a tear from her cheek.

"This is well," answered Alfhild, a little consoled; "but you will not be with me; I shall not see you. Wherein shall I be happy?"

"In the future, my beloved! We cannot reap before we sow; we cannot obtain happiness without sacrifices; we can never pay too dear for it. A short time of sorrow and trouble soon passes away. You must not grieve. When all shall one day be clear around us, you will thank me for not having laid the heavy burden of harsh reality on your weak shoulders."

"No, Seiler! I shall never thank you for it; if I knew what you are musing on and what troubles you, I should feel much better. It could not be worse than now, for my imagination doubles every thing. Oh, I beseech you speak! I am not so weak as you think; try my fortitude!"

For a moment Seiler seemed to consult with himself. To waver was not his nature; he therefore turned away from those beseeching, dangerous eyes. He was convinced that she would suffer more by the truth than by the uncertainty in which she was suspended; and since that was his conviction, it must be so, whether right or wrong.

"But Alfhild!" said he, "you must not, in this manner, abuse the power which love gives you over my reason. Do I not try your strength to the utmost, when I desire from you the courage for a separation, the cause of which I neither will nor must acquaint you with; when I demand that you shall have trust and faith, that only the desire to secure our future happiness can induce me to leave you?

See, my love, if it was not stern duty that calls me away from you, why should not I be perfectly happy when near you; why should you see me melancholy and dejected, when I enjoy the happiness of your society? No, I must go away, away in order to work! No happiness can dwell in my breast till then."

"I do not understand you, Seiler, and that pains me most. But I know that I love you, that I can suffer, and if necessary, even die for you. Do as you please; but one thing you must promise me—speak to my father before you leave. It grieves me unspeakably—nay, surely more than you can believe, to have a secret from him and uncle Sebastian. Ah! Seiler, I see by your looks that you intend to say 'no' also to this. Do it not!—in this case do not let me ask in vain."

"Oh, it grieves my heart to be constrained to afflict you thus, dear angel!" said the architect, with an expression of the deepest grief. "But believe me—I conjure you not to doubt the truth of my words. The reasons that prevent me at present from asking for your hand, are of such a nature that my honour would be branded if I did not regard them. Time is required to remove all obstacles. On my return I shall be at liberty to speak to your father. And you, my dear Alfhild, cannot for a moment give room to a thought that I would cause your heart sorrow, if it was in my power to save you from it. I know what grief my refusal gives you; but whatever you may suffer, it cannot be compared to the grief I feel, to have implicated you in these gloomy, turbulent relations of things. Alfhild, can you pardon me—can you love me still, since I must, Heaven knows, against my will afflict you so deeply!"

"Every thing, Seiler, every thing I can pardon you; I can suffer for your sake every pain, since I am yours. The heart of no other woman has the least share in your heart, or the least claims upon your fidelity. These treasures are, indeed, mine, and with them I will gladly and patiently wait till the hour of remuneration arrives."

A dark cloud hung over Seiler's brow, a deeper colour shone in his face; but leaning upon Alfhild's shoulder, he whispered: "Noble being! to you, to you alone and exclusively I devote my whole life. Your every feeling is love—thus woman should love—at least the [woman] whose heart beats for me!"

Alfhild was happy. Words like these, from his lips, filled her whole being with an inexpressible delight. Now she felt herself to be able to bear all.

During the days that passed before Seiler's departure Alfhild displayed much fortitude. Seiler should see that she was strong. She attended to every thing with the greatest punctuality, and never came to the table with eyes red with weeping. On the last morning, however, she could not succeed in repressing the outbreak of her burning grief, and conceal its visible traces. Her eyes were dim, and her cheeks glowed, when, after having been called three times, she entered the room to take leave of Seiler.

Breakfast was finished, and the architect had already shaken hands with the provost and uncle Sebastian. Now entered Alfhild. They had not a word to say to each other; but as he printed his parting kiss upon her hand, he let slip into it a billet. She looked up. Seiler's eyes were not capable of tears; but their fiery lustre was darkened by a moist veil of mist, which vanished not till the parsonage was far behind him.

And now he was gone. The provost found it proper not to notice Alfhild's emotion; uncle Sebastian, however, was not a man of cold calculation. He took his doveling by the hand, led her to his room, and sat down by her.

"You need not be ashamed, my child," said he, with heartfelt sympathy. "Though it is now many years since I cherished such feelings as now move you, I have not forgotten them on that account. Weep to your heart's content, my dove; uncle Sebastian's heart has not yet grown cold."

Alfhild leaned upon the breast of the old man. It was soothing to her to be able to breathe out her pain without being obliged to lend it words; it was relief to her to give vent to it by a stream of hot tears.

But it was not Alfhild alone who wept during these days; far more bitter tears flowed in the library at the count's castle. There sat Thelma in a solitary corner; she had no human being on whom she might lean. She hardly dared to own to herself the feelings that dwelt, with destructive power, in her breast; for the day before the architect had paid his farewell visit to the castle, and his look had been colder than ice. To-day he was gone—he, the only being that had taught her that there are in life also points of light. He was gone, and *cold*; she in a prison at home, and *warm*: dangerous opposites.

The short winter's day was soon gone. The wax candles were lighted at the castle, grief was buried near the fallen buds, the tears were dried, and Thelma took her lute to go to Count Albano. The poor maiden indeed, was not in a mood to sing; but yet she sang that she might not be obliged to speak.

When uncle Sebastian, after an hour, left Alfhild, she opened the billet. It contained a small medallion with Seiler's portrait. On the paper she saw only the words; *"Be patient and have faith. Only in death shall I resign the hope to call thee mine!"*

Alfhild's delight in having a portrait of Seiler it is not possible to describe; it formed a glowing contrast to Thelma's silent grief. We will leave both, and follow the architect on his journey to Norway.

CHAPTER XIV.

SEILER IN NORWAY.

NEAR the bay of Trysseldals-Elf lay the small estate which Seiler had inherited from his father. To this place he now directed his way.

It was a dark evening on the Sunday before Christmas. The snow fell in thick flakes, and had nearly covered the whole road, so that it was only with difficulty the architect could keep the path. It ran in many windings up a steep hill, on which stood a small, white painted house, with green window shutters, and protected against the snow-storm by high pine-trees. The nearer Seiler came to it, the more distinctly he saw through the windows of the sitting-room the glimmer of the fire. His heart was oppressed by feelings that were too powerful to be expressed by words; but from time to time he laid his head upon his breast, as if he wished to check its violent beating. In that house he was born; in it he had played as a boy; dreamed as a youth, and struggled as a man. His father and mother lay under the cold earth; but, to the mind of the son, their venerable forms yet distinctly appeared before him. He saw the gentle, pious mother, with the peaceful smile upon her lips, walk to and fro in the little house, and spread order wherever she appeared. He thought he yet heard the tone of her voice, as she reproved the often wild and wilful youth; and as then, so now, his mind relented at her beseeching. The beseechings of a mother—oh, what irresistible power they have!

Then came the image of his father before his soul. Did he not sit yonder in the corner of the sofa, holding his pipe?—the shade of a hero, even when in a sitting posture. Seiler's imagination was excited so strongly, that he seemed to hear every word with which his father, now and then interrupting himself with whiffs from his pipe, related his adventures in former times encountered at sea, and which he had more than a hundred times repeated on the long winter evenings at the fire-side to his attentively listening son. But now appeared in the shadow, in the corner near the black earthen stove, a third figure. This was his venerable grandfather, a man, who, even after his death, exercised a powerful influence upon Seiler's fate.

Seiler had at last reached the door, which was already locked. He knocked in his familiar way, and immediately was heard the well-known whining bark of Castor from the yard. But when the door opened, and instead of the old faithful servant, a small red-haired girl came out, then Seiler awoke from his short dream; reality, the naked truth, the object of his journey, all stood before his soul in awful clearness.

"Good evening," said he, with a suppressed voice; "is my wife at home?"

"Yes; then you are the gentleman?"

"Certainly! help to carry in the things."

Seiler walked before into the little ante-room, which was dark; a pane of glass in the door which led to the sitting-room, however, showed him the way, for a ray of light fell into the dark chamber. He put his hand upon the latch, but could not immediately summon courage to open it. He looked through the glass, and beheld a beautiful young woman on a chair near the stove. On her lap lay a child more than two years old, as pale as the white night-dress it wore. Low, broken, plaintive sounds passed over the pale, ashy-grey lips, yet they subsided, when a soft "hush, hush!" reached his ears. The young woman sat with her face bent over the child, so that only a part of her brow could be seen. On it was seen a fine wreath of her glossy, black hair; the rest was covered by a small white lace cap.

A deep sigh straggled forth from Seiler's breast; his eyes turned involuntarily from this group to the window. There sat a man of middle height, of a pale countenance, which the light from the fire made still paler. On his brow lay furrowed deep wrinkles, and one of his hands was mechanically moving in his thick hair. Now and then he cast a look upon the young mother, and then his eye seemed to flash forth fire, till he let his eyelids sink, and turned his face again away.

This man could not properly be called ill-looking, though he was far from being handsome; there was, however, in his face a certain firmness and earnestness, softened by a gentleness of expression which invited sympathy. One seemed to see a man who had practice in the difficult art of self-control.

"He forsakes her not," thought Seiler. "He stays faithfully by her; but how he is altered. Honest Bloom, you do not know, have never known, nor will ever know the power of love. And yet thy cheek is pale, and thy brow is furrowed. There are yet sufferings entirely different."

The architect softly opened the door, and stepped over the threshold.

The young woman rose suddenly: she uttered a faint exclamation of surprise, while the child began its low wailing.

"Fear nothing, Maria, it is I! Pardon, if I alarmed you. How is it with little Waldemar?"

"Ah! he is very sick. Excuse my sitting down again, the child cannot bear to be so—" not my violent emotion, she might have added without infringing upon truth; for her emotion was, indeed, so strong that she was near fainting. She bent low her pale face over her sick child to conceal her feelings from him who had just entered.

"Good evening, friend Bloom," said Seiler. His voice, however, was not so firm as usual, and his hand which he extended to his friend, trembled.

"Welcome to your native home, Seiler," answered Bloom, "and pardon that I have, during your absence, taken interest in your household. As a neighbour and friend, I could not see your wife in solitude."

"I thank you for your kind care, by which you oblige me much," answered Seiler coldly and civilly. He felt offended, and turned now from Bloom to his son.

"Has he been sick long, dear Maria?"

"It is now several weeks. It will be soon over with him; soon shall I be alone."

She looked up;—her tearful look met that of her husband. Seiler took her hand and kissed it with the indifference of a man who shows to a lady some slight attention; afterwards he looked not upon Maria, but only upon the child.

He took a chair and sat down by his wife. Bloom paced the room in long strides. Anger, grief, and still *another* passion contended within him. He several times drew near his friend, but always withdrew again.

The servant now opened the door, and asked where the gentleman's things should be carried.

"Into the blue corner room; and have a fire made there," answered Seiler hastily.

"You must take something warm," said the young woman, whilst she rose with difficulty and put her child, now sleeping, on a little bed that stood in the room.

"Do not trouble yourself, good Maria; I want nothing."

Seiler rose and offered her the chair with the native politeness which he never forgot.

"Permit me to leave you for a moment," she asked, whilst she strove to overcome her violent emotion. "The little one sleeps best in the cradle; I will put him there."

Seiler perceived how it was with her, and did not attempt to make her stay. She took the child upon her arm, Bloom opened the door to the sleeping-room, and both men remained alone.

Having been silent for a few moments, whilst he evidently struggled with his pride, the architect said: "Bloom, have I no longer the least share in your heart?" and he extended his hand to his gloomy friend, who was still walking up and down.

"If you can behold this sight, and remain unmoved," answered Bloom, "then you have no longer a share either in my heart or in my respect. If you can behold this lovely being, in her double grief as a forsaken wife, and soon also as a bereaved mother; if you can behold this tender being, your son, with his pale face disfigured by suffering, on which death has already printed his seal—if you can behold all this, and then not feel what duty demands of you at this moment—if you can still refuse a *reconciliation*; then, Seiler, I have nothing more to say. You are then sunk so low that nothing can restore you to reflection, and the discharge of your most sacred duties."

"I am not sunk so low as you assert," answered the architect with

pride. "I feel at this moment that the most powerful impulse ani-
mates me, not to destroy, through untimely weakness, the execution
of which I have just begun—a work, the completion of which will be
attended with peace and blessing; for respect without love is a barren desert that never brings forth flowers. And you know, Bloom, the
grief that awaits me and affects my inmost soul—the coming death
of my child—just this it is that gives me the double conviction that
the step which I have proposed is the true one. God himself therefore loosens the only real tie that in some measure binds us together.
However, till the little heart has ceased to beat, and the heart of the
mother has recovered from the deep grief which bows it down, this
subject shall not be mentioned. With the same respect which I always
entertained for Maria, I shall continue to treat her. We will live like
friends who understand each other, and who by degrees accustom
themselves to a thought, the execution of which both consider as
right, but out of regard to the world, do not like to touch them. Yet
some time the deed must be done; but it will always be and remain
my most zealous and warmest endeavour to show to the world that
it was necessity, and not aversion, that separated us. No breath must
fall on Maria's reputation; she will stand pure; and if a shadow must
fall upon either, may I be the one."

"No breath must fall upon her reputation? Indeed, that I willingly believe!" answered Bloom, contemptuously. "Nor do I know
from whence it should come; if there were any body who was bold
enough to breathe it, I should stand up as the protector of the forsaken woman. But you, Seiler, you cast a shadow upon your character, your morality and your social influence, which, in my opinion,
could be removed by nothing in the world; and what is worse still,
this shadow will step in between yourself and your conscience."

"No, by my life and my honour, never will it do that!" exclaimed
the architect, while his face burned deeper, and his eyes sparkled.
"Have you forgotten how my marriage with Maria was brought
about, or have you never heard of it?"

"I have never learned it exactly," answered Bloom. "We are now
alone—relate it to me. Maria will not return very soon."

"The moment is not well selected," began Seiler, "but you have
set my blood in commotion; I must give myself relief. You shall hear,
and will then, I hope, judge less harshly:—

"My father had, as you must have heard, in Maria's father a truly devoted friend. They both had in their younger years, made many voyages together in a large merchant ship, and had, in many a trying hour, opportunity to search each other's hearts, in which they found, on both sides, nothing but generosity, self-denial, and honesty. Time passed on, they grew up to be men, and began business for themselves; they owned vessels of their own, and married to enjoy their good fortune the more completely. It has been often asserted, that the ardent and imaginative affection which young men conceive for each other, continues very seldom to manhood, and that all illusions of youth disappear before the manifold events of life. That the *illusions* vanish, may be true, but yet sometimes remains the better part. This was the case, at least, in the present instance.

"Maria's father made several unfortunate voyages in succession, and at last lost not only his ship, but also her whole freight. My father, who had become a wealthy man, procured for his ruined friend a new ship, in whose gain and loss they would share equally. This vessel, which my father built himself, was called 'the Union.' She made remarkably fortunate voyages, and within a few years made up the losses which Vern, Maria's father, had sustained.

"During this time I had grown up; and when my father found I had no inclination to maritime affairs—the branch of ship-building, however, excepted—I was sent to a university to study. Once, in the Christmas vacation, I came home—I was then twenty-one years old—I saw Maria for the first time. She had, after the death of her mother, been educated by an old aunt in Copenhagen; but since she also had died, her father took her home again, having made an agreement with my parents that she should, in future, live at our house. Maria was beautiful, nay, I thought I had never seen a girl more so; yet she made, nevertheless, no impression upon my heart. But out of common politeness I gave her a certain preference above other girls, which our parents misunderstood, taking it for a serious affection. One evening—I shall never forget it—we sat at table round a bowl; the glasses were filled to be drunk to the successful voyage of 'The Union.' When this was done my father filled the glasses again, and said without farther ceremony, in a true seaman's manner: 'We will drink one more glass to the Union! Rudolph, my son, what say you? Maria is more beautiful than Rachel, and you will get off with half the time of serving; for I see that you have no longer much patience. However, that is no sin. I was many years older when I wooed your mother; yet I had no rest till I was married to her. I therefore think that the sooner a young man marries, the better it is.'

"At that time, dear Bloom, I had not yet that spirit of self-reliance which afterwards developed itself in me; and besides, my father was a man who understood the art to exact respect and obedience. I therefore did not dare to utter the displeasure I felt when another took the liberty to determine, without farther question, on the most important point of my life. Perhaps I should have done it, if we had been *alone*; however, to take such a step in Maria's presence, which would certainly have created a stormy scene, my sensibility and pride would not permit. I hoped through the indifference with which I now resolved to meet henceforth my betrothed, to make my father observe that this union was not likely to fulfil the joyous hopes which it was not possible to destroy in the first moment.

"What Maria at this moment felt, I do not know; however, when our eyes met, she appeared to be as little satisfied as myself. Yet also she uttered not a word, and our blushes and silence were taken for consent. The health of the betrothed was drunk, and it was agreed that the wedding should follow after the lapse of a few months. I should first finish my studies, and Maria, under the instruction of my mother, make herself a skilful housewife.

"During the remainder of the vacation, which I had this time to pass in my father's house, the heretofore friendly, unembarrassed relation between myself and Maria, became now timid and reserved, and it often happened that we treated each other coldly or avoided a meeting. My mother, perhaps, observed it first, and called my father's attention to it; for it lasted not long before he took me aside and questioned me in regard to it. Now I had courage to be candid. I declared plainly that I could not love Maria either now or ever. My father became at first almost raving at this statement. He was not accustomed to allow that any body else should claim to have a will after he had expressed his own. His violence, however, abated sooner than I had expected, and he requested me not to speak on the subject again till some years had passed, and I had examined my heart more thoroughly.

"I objected that this would be practising a deception on Maria;

but he would not yield on this point, being perhaps deluded by a secret hope. He begged me to grant him this request, and since it was the first time that my father *asked* me for any thing, I could not possibly refuse him. My peace, however, was broken from this time, for I knew what this request included.

"At my departure Maria showed herself very cold, and my pride was wounded not to find in her the least sign that might have indicated any feeling at our being separated for several years. The vexation at this removed me yet farther from a heart that had never been very dear to me, and I left without alluding with a single syllable, to the relation we had been brought into by the will of our parents.

"You know yourself how soon I became weary of the profession my father had intended for me. It was you, Bloom, who first opened my eyes on this point. I wrote to my father and humbly asked for his permission to be allowed to leave the sciences to men worthier than myself, and to go into the world and devote myself to my present vocation.

"The old gentleman was very much displeased not to see his son become a learned man, when he at once set his mind upon it; but through the persuasion of my mother and grandfather, and perhaps also for the purpose of laying me under a new obligation by this indulgence, he granted my request. I received money, and began to travel.

"As I have once before mentioned my grandfather," said Seiler, interrupting his narrative, "I cannot omit telling you, that it was he, in fact, to whom I owe my first education, the bent of my character, and in a word, that power and freedom of soul which makes me despise all those petty things to which people in general give so much importance, that they can sacrifice all their lives to their attainment. My grandfather, I assure you, was a true man. He had suffered much, and struggled with fate, which had crossed his way in the person of a villanous count. Death took away from him the victim, whom he deemed too despicable to inflict any other revenge upon than that of deepest contempt. My blood boils when I think of the hours in which the noble man unfolded to me the dark leaves in the book of his life, in this very room, and on this very sofa. He could speak of sufferings, Bloom; but I forget myself, which I always do when I come to speak of him.

"You know that I stayed several years abroad. During this time, 'The Union' made several voyages, of which the one was still more fortunate than the other. At last she was wrecked, and Captain Vern and the greater part of his crew perished. Grief at this misfortune, I believe, was the cause of my father's sickness, of which he soon after died. At my return I noticed a great change in my father's house. My old, much-beloved grandfather had gone too, to the land whither he had long wished to go, and my mother went about in her solitude, patient as ever, yet longed to be re-united with that husband, without whom she seemed not to be able to live.

"I must own that the conduct of Maria during that time was most exemplary. Never tended a daughter her mother with greater love; but never flowed either warmer praises from the lips of any mother than those which mine bestowed upon the patience and perseverance of Maria, who, in her early youth, knew how to bear the hardest trials with so much fortitude.

" 'But when I shall be no more,' often sighed my mother, and pressing my hand very significantly, 'will Maria be without protection, and without a home? Will she be thrust out into the world, which is a stranger to her, to gain her livelihood with the work of her own hands? Poor Maria! will that be your reward for all the nights through which you have watched at our sick-beds, with indescribable love and patience? And in this house you can remain after my death, only under one name.'

"These were the words of my beloved mother, which I can never forget. She was too much a true woman to expose herself to my contradictions, by arguments on right and wrong, and by admonitions of duty. She only put into my hands the fate of her unprotected darling. She knew the weakness of her son, and her hope did not deceive her. I should not have been a man if I could have let her die in this uncertainty.

"Maria did not hear our conversation on this point, but she no doubt suspected it; for when I asked her one evening at the sick-bed of my mother, if she would become my wife, she answered proudly—nay, almost repulsively:

" 'I have never considered the agreement of our parents as binding on you, Rudolph, and wish that you also would not consider it so.'

" 'Maria, *but I do it*,' interrupted my mother, and looked upon us both with her mild and friendly eyes. 'I should be so much rejoiced if I could bring to both the departed, the glad tidings that their children regarded their wishes even after death.'

"I will not expatiate, Bloom; in short, a few days after, Maria became my wife. You came, at that time, into these parts, and first saw Maria as a bride. She was beautiful, but cold. Our hearts did not learn to understand each other. Meanwhile my mother died, in the conviction that what was now wanting to our happiness would come in time of itself, when we should be left entirely alone and to ourselves. But, alas! she deceived herself. As long as she was alive there was one bright point in which our feelings united; but when this point vanished in the night of eternity, a coldness remained between us, which our most strenuous efforts could change into nothing else but constant study of our mutual wishes and caprices—a polite exchange of *thoughts* and *words*, but not of *feelings*. Bloom, I do not know whether you understand me, when I say that this relation stunned me. The very air became to me an oppression; my soul pined after freedom and a new life. Three years I dragged myself along in this manner, and almost froze to death by the side of my wife, who showed herself indefatigable to make my domestic life pleasant; but then I could bear it no longer. I went to Sweden, whither an inward longing impelled me to go. Here accident or a peculiar fate came to be joined to newly-awakened recollections, which, though they did not properly concern myself, exercised a powerful influence on my restless mind. But it was not this alone, alas! other circumstances made me look upon my present condition in a different light. I became acquainted with a girl whom I must ever love with all my heart and soul—a girl for whom I could lay down my life, and for the possession of whom I am now struggling. Oh, Bloom, you should see her! She is innocent as a child, and pure as the dew-drop in the chalice of a lily. She is all heart rather than head. Woman requires, generally speaking, not much of the latter; unfortunately there are many who follow their heads more than their hearts, which ought to be the mainspring which puts and keeps all their feelings and actions in motion. Alfhild is a stranger to disguise; she cannot restrain the tears when sorrow calls them forth. She is all love, a being that lives in and through me, and that has no will, no thought, no feeling, but such as proceed from me."

Seiler remained silent. Bloom stood before him with folded arms, and regarded him with that compassion which we bestow upon a blind man, who at clear daylight seems to grope in the dark.

At last he asked him with a cold and bitter sneer:

"Does your wife want these qualities, because she is possessed of sufficient strength of soul to conceal the misunderstood feelings of her injured heart under the veil of external calmness? This power we must respect as well in man as woman. It is the sign of a soul which is too elevated to succumb even under the bitterest trials. But you—you want to have a puppet into which you can, like another Prometheus, breathe a soul after your own liking; a spirit of mere air and moonshine—a spirit which every second asks whether you grant it permission to exist. It is abominable, Seiler, to see a man whose selfishness oversteps all limits of reason."

"You may call it what you please, but these are now my views of love. Maria is a proud, haughty being, that has too little feeling. She does not love me, and has never loved me; but from reasons which are entirely founded on her pride, she rejects, with contempt, a separation which would give her more advantage, and happiness than a marriage like ours."

"Ah! how unworthily and ignobly do you speak of a woman whose least action is too lofty to be comprehended by your levity—a levity which is so much beyond all measure, that you overlook the simplest facts that form a glaring contrast to your assertion, that she has no feeling and has never loved you. Your ingratitude, your hardness of heart and selfishness are unparalleled! But a time will come, I am persuaded, when——"

Bloom suddenly stopped and drew back; Maria entered.

The least traces of tears had disappeared. Calm and serious were her manner and tone, as pointing with an inviting motion to the door of the adjoining room, she said:

"Supper is waiting; the gentlemen will excuse me if I cannot bear them company; my place is at the cradle of my sick child."

"How is it with your nights, good Maria?" asked Seiler, with a certain sympathy.

"I watch through them," answered Maria, with a painful smile.

CHAPTER XV.

THE MARRIAGE.

WHILST the gentlemen were at table absorbed in conversations which it would be too tedious to relate, as they treated only on the material question, the separation itself, let us meanwhile look closer at the lights and shadows of the picture, which we have so far held before our readers only in general outlines.

Maria Vern was only sixteen years old when she came to live in the house of their future parents-in-law. Her distinguished beauty had already received testimonials of homage, which, though they had not made Maria vain, had yet made her aware that she was capable of attracting those around her; and she was, therefore, surprised that Seiler treated her with so little attention, for she had been given to understand by the glances of many men, that her presence was not without effect. Although Maria felt hurt by it, she was too wise not to conceal her slight vexation, which, however, was soon sunk in a bitter sorrow, for a deep feeling drew her towards him. Womanly bashfulness and a kind of instinct, however, commanded her to banish every trace of it in his presence. In this manner, the almost unnatural coldness in her manner, was produced, which Seiler, with a little more experience and sagacity, would have recognised as a wall with which the heart, already captivated, was surrounded to protect it from glances which might spy out its true condition.

During the whole of the time which Seiler spent in Italy, Maria's feelings were put to a hard trial. Though he showed toward her by far more friendship and respect than before, yet the flame that was glowing in her heart burned without being returned. She now withdrew more and more within herself; yet many painful hours she spent in acquiring this external coldness, and she was induced to surround herself with this icy veil, only from the consideration how contemptible she must appear to him if he should perceive her weakness. She would have at least his respect, if she could not win his love.

Ah, how warm were those tears which Maria shed unseen by all; how fervent was her prayer in the sleepless nights, that she might win but the smallest share of his heart! Soon came the dreaded hour when he offered her his hand and name, that he might give her further protection. But his tone, his look, and whole manner, told her that it was nothing but a feeling of honour which drove him to this action. She had the courage to refuse the offer; but the vehemence of her emotion in doing it, caused this refusal to appear prouder and more offensive than she had intended. This was, however, to no purpose; her motherly friend knew her feelings; she had long observed them with inward joy, and therefore did not give up her dearest wish till she saw it accomplished.

Maria became Seiler's wife. During the holy act which united her for ever with the man whom she adored, her heart was swelled at once with joy and pain. But even on the first evening a little scene occurred which drove back her warmest feelings to the deepest recess of her heart, and caused her to resolve to seek to find out the wishes of her husband, and to promote his comforts, without ever influencing his conduct and himself by an intimation of any feeling of love.

Seiler said to his young wife, as he took his seat by her on the sofa in the solitary bridal chamber: "Dear Maria, to restore at once a friendly relation between us, it is necessary that we should closer examine our hearts, to learn what we may expect from each other. We must, for once, be entirely candid. You know that our fathers wished for our union, and that we had not the courage to oppose an authority which we were accustomed to obey. It is true we might, afterwards, have broken the engagement which had not our consent, but—" Seiler made here a pause; he was not so cruel as to tell her what she could guess. After a few moments of the greatest torture for poor Maria, he continued:—"A harsh fate would not grant that, we learned to love each other; and I believe the mean cause of it was, that the determination of our fathers was an encroachment upon our future rights. Do not you also think so?"

The young wife felt her blood rush to her face and tears to her eyes; but she forcibly repressed them, and the colour gave room to a death-like paleness, when Seiler added,—

"Do not blush at your want of love, my excellent Maria. I have no right to demand it, since I myself have none to offer."

She now rose. In her face was depicted cold pride, and far more of this than his words really deserved; for they showed at least an openness which deserved acknowledgment. But her look and tone

almost approached the freezing point, as she said:—"Why is it necessary to speak what we both know so well?"

"Maria, we owe it to each other, to express in words what heretofore was only a conjecture. We therefore know now that we do not
love each other at present; but we know not if it will always remain
so. Our feelings may, perhaps, change. And since we are once married together, it is our duty to endeavour to smooth our paths, and to
think as little as possible of the moment, the mention of which must
always be painful to us."

"Good Seiler," replied Maria gently and calmly, and no longer
coldly, "we certainly have so much respect for ourselves and each
other, that we shall surely succeed in making our life together as little
bitter as possible."

And herein both kept their word. Neither spoke any more of
want of love in the other. On the contrary, they strove to give to their
home an appearance of comfort which in fact was wanting: for when
both were alone and unobserved, she sighed over the coldness of her
husband, and he over the constraint he was obliged to put himself
under to appear contented.

A few years passed by; Maria had given her husband a son. The
common duties appeared now to bring them nearer to each other;
but a trifle, a word, a turn of thought separated them again. Maria,
with her warm feelings, was much too sensitive; and he, with his
coldness, showed himself much too indifferent. Thus it grew worse
with every year. She forced herself to lay upon her burning heart an
icy crust, and he assumed an unnatural warmth.

The only mediating genius that stood by the side of the young
married couple, was Bloom, their neighbour, who from a taste for
agriculture, had established himself in the country. He was possessed
of property, and had invested it in real estate, to have ample scope
for the manifold experiments in this occupation, to which he was devoted with peculiar zeal. Bloom was a man of indefatigable activity
and patriotic sentiment. He never grew wildly enthusiastic; but he
became warm and animated when the point was to carry out a conceived idea; and his ideas generally were of such a kind that a sound
reason could not but approve of them. Bloom's lands bordered upon
Seiler's estate; and the friendship which they had formed for each other, already before Seiler's journey to Italy, grew still closer, after they

had become neighbours. But Bloom soon discovered with pain, that Seiler, who was able to grow warm for a masterpiece of art, stood cold before a masterpiece of nature; and such he considered Maria. He often was witness of those small domestic scenes from which an acute observer can conclude upon the inner state of hearts; and he became convinced that Seiler tormented beyond measure, his young wife, by his cold politeness.

"He is the cause of it," said he; "he does not love her." And Bloom did all that a friend can do in such delicate circumstances, but the bond of marriage is too sensitive to allow of the interference of a third party. He, therefore, was forced to content himself with bringing them in an indirect manner nearer to each other and to happiness. But in this he did not succeed. One frost after another destroyed Bloom's young, feeble seedlings, and he saw, with grief, his hopes unfulfilled.

As Seiler's profession required him to be often absent from home for months, Bloom went constantly over to the young wife, and endeavoured by his conversation and attention, to induce her to forget the absence of him who was unutterably dear to her, although he did not return her love—to fill his place in her heart, Bloom knew to be impossible.

No one was more grateful to Bloom for his friendly exertions than Seiler; for no one could wish more sincerely than he, that Maria might have some resource and joy. And he often told her:—

"Dear Maria, do bestow upon Bloom a grateful look. He lives for you like a true knight, without ever casting a look upon any other woman."

Seiler meant nothing particular by it. He knew Bloom, and could safely intrust to him his wife, his honour and his house; but Maria felt offended by such expressions, and once answered with ill-concealed bitterness.

"You would, perhaps, have no objection if I favoured this chivalric attention. A man who does not love his wife does not care for her feelings."

"But so much the more for his own honour, madam!" replied Seiler, and for the first time in a tone that thrilled through Maria's heart with an icy coldness. She turned pale and put her hand upon her brow, without saying a word.

"Well, why do you try me by such foolish suppositions?" added he, somewhat calmer. "You cannot but know, Maria, that thoughts of this kind must offend me. But let us no longer speak of it. I know Bloom; I know you also, and thank God sincerely that, through our mutual friend, you have entertainment in many a lonesome hour during my absence. I believe, besides, that he understands you better than I do; and I am not jealous, Maria. I have too much regard for you to be so."

"No, you are not jealous, that is true," said Maria in a tone which proved that her woman's sensibility was offended. But she could experience nothing more bitter, thought Maria, than to hear her husband thank God that a stranger was the support and friend of his forsaken wife. She left the room, deeply offended; but when they met again at noon at table, she was again herself. Every thing went calmly on in its usual course, and Maria neglected none of her duties. By degrees, however, the few flowers that adorned the chains withered; and at last only thistles were found enveloping the links.

The heart grew void and desolate; cold summers, rapid winters, cheerless days and tearful nights, could not satisfy it. Maria suffered, but never complained; but she suffered not alone. Bloom understood the bitterness of her grief, and shared it. It became *his own*; for the young, proud, suffering woman, was to him dearer than he perhaps knew himself.

During Seiler's stay in Sweden, Bloom's tender attentions to his fair neighbour and her child went on increasing. They were to him like an intrusted treasure; and when he sometimes searched in his heart for the cause of the zeal with which he endeavoured to give some pleasure to the young woman, nay, was almost hourly occupied in cheering her, the answer always was, that it was his duty.

"But is it also my duty," thought he then, "to find no longer any pleasure at home, and in my usual occupations! No, it is sympathy with her misfortune which follows me, and continually compels me to visit her." And thus things remained till Seiler's letter arrived; in that letter he spoke, for the first time, of his plan to be divorced from Maria.

But this was a thing Bloom had never before thought of; and it was for the lively feeling of joy which he had at this news, which first made him clearly perceive his actual relation to Seiler's wife. But a man like Bloom, of moral principles, abominated as well the law which allowed a divorce, as also those who made use of it to free themselves from fetters, which had in time grown too offensive for them.

"As to the law, however," said Bloom, walking up and down, and debating with himself, "it must be granted, that the country where it does not exist is not to be envied, since there can really be circumstances in marriage under which it is not only allowed, but even— even—no, right it can never be!" He broke out with animation,— "What God has joined together man *shall not* put asunder. All very well; but may they not be considered as separated when they cannot be happy together? There is the knot which it is not easy to loosen.

"By marriage it is understood, or at least ought to be understood, the union of souls, and what is material has nothing to do with it. If now, two souls cannot be united into one, but on the contrary, tend in two different directions, would it not be better then not to lay any constraint upon them? Indeed, it certainly seems so. But the *external* tie is also a sacred one, and public opinion never fails to brand the separated husband or wife."

Bloom had great respect for public opinion, or rather, a certain fear of every action which might appear to have a double meaning, and he therefore carefully avoided it. He did this, however, never at the expense of his conviction. Before he formed a resolution, he anxiously weighed the *pro* and *con*, and did not cease to look at an affair in question from all sides, until it stood before him in the clearest light.

It is, therefore, not to be wondered at, that also in the present case, he abstracted it entirely from his own heart, and endeavoured to consider the question of divorce as a disinterested inquirer.

"Seiler does not know his wife," thought Bloom; "that is the only cause; for if he knew her he could not but love her. Maria's beautiful soul is for him yet an undeveloped bud, and it requires longer than a day to cause her to unfold herself into the most resplendent blossom; for her reserved, and so often repelled feelings, withdraw and conceal the splendour of their glorious colours. But would not he be a fool who said: of this bud no rose will come; I waited all day and it did not blow. He would be a still greater fool if, in order to make a rose of it at once, he forcibly opened the bud and unfolded the leaves. Every thing, both in the physical and moral world, requires a certain time for its development; and with man, too, should not all likewise be harmoniously done?

"But Seiler's restless violent soul will hear nothing of waiting; he goes along like a whirlwind, and will tear out with root and branch the beautiful tree that is rooted in his own heart. The rash man! Who can comprehend and fathom all the springs that operate upon each other, in one so violent and headstrong? He has, however, wished for what is right and good; he has struggled and striven, and I have observed that sometimes an appearance of calmness shows itself upon the surface. But the powers of nature cannot be checked; soonest after they have been erected and brought into conflict by some imprudent art, lightnings appear, whose main object is, by restoring the lost equilibrium, to bring back the calm which generally succeeds every storm." Here Bloom suddenly stopped; he had come to the chapter on the laws of nature, and a powerful voice which represented, God knows, what secret potentate, strove with all might to overpower that one which had chosen for its special task the defence of public opinion.

Bloom was in a very difficult position. To argue with one's self on right and wrong, is by far more dangerous than to do it with others, if we are not sure that no selfish feeling corrupts our judgment. It was this last fear that clouded Bloom's clear sight. He resolved, lest he might come into a labyrinth of thoughts and opinions, from which it would be difficult for him to extricate himself, to answer his friend Seiler, now only in general, shortly and in the negative, upon his intimation of making the overtures to the divorce between him and Maria.

Having sent a letter to this effect, the honest Bloom felt himself more calm, and on this evening he was more free and unembarrassed with Maria than he had been for a long time. It seemed to him that she also treated him with a degree of friendship, which increased in warmth with every day. All, therefore, went on well, that is, as well as could be, when Seiler's second letter came.

Now arose new struggles; yet it may be taken for granted, that Bloom's last refusal was owing more to an uneasiness to be a third party in an affair like this, than to a fear to offend public opinion, for through daily reflection he had come to allow, that, as no relation in the world remains standing still, but rather rises or falls, so likewise a marriage relation must either improve or grow worse; and as things stood between Seiler and Maria, an improvement could hardly be any longer thought of. Since, considered from a moral or religious point of view, nothing can bind a man to live in a hell which he himself created, he must be also permitted to leave it. However, this view, entirely new to Bloom, he kept for himself. He would have considered it highly unworthy and rash to give to Seiler the slightest hint of it before the other party, the most important one, was asked. What would Maria say and do? It was she, and she alone, who must give the final decision. And Bloom could not bring himself to laying this question before her to decide.

Some weeks passed without the occurrence of any thing unpleasant. Though Seiler had written that he himself would apply to his wife, Bloom believed that he would take the matter into consideration once more, and then leave it to take its own course. But he found himself to have been in error, when, one evening on his entering into Maria's room, he found her for the first time, as far as he recollected—in tears. She had her sick child on her knee, and the letter of her husband in her hand.

"What is the matter, Madame Seiler? have you received unpleasant news?" His voice trembled and he could hardly bring out the words.

"Yes, indeed, Mr. Bloom, very sad news," answered she, while she hid her face to conceal her emotion.

Bloom was not able to inquire; he was too much excited to utter a syllable. In silence, but unquiet, he seated himself by the dejected young woman.

"Will you read the letter of my husband?" asked she, giving it to him.

"I see that you are already acquainted with the matter in question; yet your sensibility was too delicate to allow yourself to be the messenger of such news. Read, and afterwards we will talk over the matter."

Though Bloom ran through all the pages, yet at the conclusion of the letter, he did not know what it in fact contained. He only saw Maria's tears, felt the burning pain which in this moment tore her breast, and heard constantly the words, "Read, and afterwards we will talk over the matter." And was it he who was able to speak on this affair? Was he able to give advice? His soul was in a storm of feelings of the most different kind; and in his heart he wished himself far from the torture which an upright man feels who has to struggle with his passion, his duty and connection, especially when it concerns a being for whom he is willing to lay down his life.

"Well, what do you say, Mr. Bloom? What do you say to the proposal? Certainly one cannot ask a man to do more for a wife that he wishes to get rid of."

There was a cold scorn in Maria's tone and look. The feelings in her heart changed so quickly that they assumed a new form in every second.

"What do you mean by 'doing more,' Madame Seiler?" asked Bloom, stammering. He hardly knew what was meant; but he suspected that it referred to her future support.

"Ah, it is too hard, Bloom! You know not how it pains me to be obliged to bear a disgrace which is a thousand times more bitter than death; and, moreover, to see it expressed as ingeniously as if one was inhaling the fragrance of flowers. But—what do you think of it?"

"I have scarcely any thoughts at all," answered Bloom, in a monotonous tone, taking the letter in hand once more to compel himself to read it with more attention.

We lay the letter before our readers in the following chapter.

CHAPTER XVI.

SEILER TO MARIA.

"DEAR MARIA:—Pardon that I left your last letter unanswered longer than I had in fact intended, but there are certain feelings, thoughts, and ideas that require a long and earnest consideration—and this was the case at present. I wished to speak to you much, and with a deep and heartfelt feeling, yet what I wished to say required the most delicate treatment, and I delayed to accustom myself first entirely to the thought.

"Good, dear Maria, thou sisterly friend! I must give you this name, since you always were rather a loving and anxious friend than a loving wife. Can you suspect the object of my present letter? Do you still recollect what occurred on the evening of our wedding? We promised each other to bear our common fate with faithful fortitude—although without love, and we have honestly striven to keep our word. Yet it is not our fault, that *duty remained* a duty, which in time grew more oppressive. No, Maria, man cannot command his heart—this we have experienced in ourselves, but we are masters over our will, our resolutions, and views of things. And these views are perhaps not so unlike as you may think at the first sight of the proposal which I am now about to make to you.

"Let me yet tell you first, dear Maria, that you do not yet know yourself. And this is very natural, as you have but of late begun to lead a reflective life; but continue to do so, and the chaos will yield ever more to the light breaking in, that lay heretofore sleeping in your inner self. And when it will one day have become entirely clear—when your eye is able to reach beyond the limited circle of common life,—when you will have before you a different future, a different belief, and a different hope from that of a martyr-crown; then, Maria, you will understand what I am going to say to you, and you will perhaps bless the hour when the thought came into my mind which helps us both to light, peace, and freedom.

"And now, Maria, be not frightened at the word itself! You are no common weak woman that trembles at a breath; you have strength—you have suffered and borne much. Be also now the calm, resolute being to comprehend what the present moment demands. I lay before you the question,—will you consent to a separation, since we cannot become happy together?

"I can easily imagine what horror must arise within you at the word—divorce. But you women often start back when it is required to take a step which may be judged of by the world in a double way, and you are capable of leading a miserable life rather than expose yourself to that opinion and be free and happy. But, Maria, this ought not to be so. Woman is as much a self dependent being as man, although civil order and an ancient abuse, which still resist enlightened reform, seem to intimate that you are destined for a kind of domestic beasts of burden. But whoever of you feels strength, will, and capability in herself, to walk her own way—whoever feels that she is able to step beyond the narrow circle which men prescribe for you, she only does her duty, unless love holds her back in breaking these fetters.

"It would be easy for me to allege a number of other reasons to confirm the doctrine which I set forth; but I will content myself with only one, which will convince you that a marriage without love, a marriage which, in general, rests on no firmer basis than ours, is of highly baneful consequences for the growing generation! I refer to the example which discontented parents give to their children. For is it conceivable that parents that live only in an artificial harmony, and therefore may often forget themselves, are qualified to give a proper education to the children that grow up around them? See, Maria, it is at this time that the picture of an unhappy marriage shows the deepest shadows, and that the scenes are witnessed by those who ought never to see such things.

"The sense of right and wrong is perhaps keener in no one than in children, and the fault of the parent might easily make their children contemptible, unprincipled, nay, perhaps abominable men; for where the examples of love and religion do not stand as guardians to growing youth, there is nothing to be hoped for, but every thing to be feared. At first an unhappy marriage operates only upon the parents, but afterwards it affects the future, and God alone knows to what generation.

"Dear Maria! these are no vain shadows which I invent to influence your imagination. No, unfortunately, experience furnishes us with more examples of this kind than are necessary to show us what we knew before; namely, the moral influence of marriage upon our posterity. I have only wished to show you what we, like others, may have to expect under the same circumstances, and now leave it to your decision whether it would not be better—nay, whether religion and duty do not urge us to be separated, instead of exposing ourselves to those incalculable consequences. The simple way in which we have to proceed in this, is that the one party leaves the other. We will remain for three years separated from each other, after which time a divorce is established in fact in our country.

"To set you at rest in regard to all that concerns your future, I will here allege for once and all, that Bloom who has ever been my agent, shall arrange this entirely according to your wish. Our little estate, with all its appurtenances, falls to our son. You will have the entire disposal of it till he comes of age without my interfering with it in the least, whatever arrangements you may make. As regards the most difficult point—that of our common tie, the boy shall stay with you up to the completion of his seventh year, after which he will probably want a manly treatment, and he shall then not stand in need of a father, who will educate him with all that love which the remembrance of his esteemed mother demands, if the most sacred voice of nature did not speak in his favour.

"And now, Maria, I have unfolded to you my whole plan, on which I have long reflected. I have, perhaps, been too diffuse, but this subject requires much space, and when thoughts are set down in black and white, they do not come to their result so quick as when they move in their free, unchecked course.

"I have already before this written on this subject to our common friend, Bloom, and therefore hope that this letter may not find you entirely unprepared.

"However this may be, I know that you are strong; and since the object is good, the means must not deter us, for of two evil things it is best to do that which is the least evil. The opinion of the world must be consulted last; we have a judge within us which never leads us astray. Farewell, Maria! When you will have arrived at a determination, which I wish you would consider well, hasten to communicate it to

"Your obedient,

"SEILER."

While Bloom was reading the letter, and endeavouring properly to comprehend the import of it, Maria had brought the child to sleep, and came now to consult with the tried friend on the answer. She seated herself on the sofa by his side, but started back with fright as her eyes fell upon his staring look. He still had the letter in his hand; his mind was too much occupied with the present and the future to notice that Maria had taken her seat by his side, till she had taken, and gently shaking his hand, with the words: "For heaven's sake, my good Bloom! what is the matter with you? Are you unwell? I almost believe so, for you are pale as death!"

"No, I am not unwell; it will soon be over. Allow me to ask you, Madame Seiler, what answer you intend to give. I need not first mention, that whatever your resolution may be, you will find in me a friend and brother, whose life and property you may command at pleasure."

"Ah! do not I know how good you are, Bloom! Has the forsaken wife not often had occasion to bless her protector? I am convinced that I may consider you my sincerest friend in all conditions of my life. Do not you think with myself, Bloom, that there is but one answer that can possibly be given to this letter?"

"No, that I do not see," he answered, with an unsteady voice. "It seems to me—I believe—I mean to say—I imagine—if a husband makes such a proposition to his wife, and developes it in a manner that leaves no doubt—then it is clear that also the other party must take this point into deliberation, and—but you know what I mean."

"I believe, at least I guess what you mean," she said, in a low tone, and some wrinkles formed themselves on the brow generally so very smooth. "You mean to say, Bloom, that I——"

"I mean to say nothing, my best Madame Seiler. I would not for any thing in the world influence your resolution by a single word. No, heaven forbid that I should thus abuse a confidence in me; and if you consider my wishes but in the least, then have the kindness to tell me of your resolution not till it stands irrevocably firm, and is communicated to your husband."

"But, Mr. Bloom, you indeed wished, just now, to know what I intended to answer."

"It is true, but it was wrong in me. I therefore beseech you now the more to grant my wish, and this especially, if, as you intimated before, that you think but one answer upon this letter possible."

"Yes, so it was, Bloom; and to comply with your wish we will speak upon this matter no farther. If you come to see me to-morrow evening, I will hand you a copy of the answer which I intend to draw up this night, and send to my husband to-morrow at noon."

"Good!" said Bloom. And in this single word "good" there was an expression that seemed to show that a great burden had been taken from the heart of the poor man. He now spoke with calmness on various other subjects; yet he went home earlier than usual, to give his friend time to answer, and in order to collect and compose his own excited thoughts.

Yet it may be said with all truth, that during the time from this evening to the next he rather dreamed than lived. The wavering between fear and hope, and the whole question which he had already for some time considered as fully settled, but which now came before his soul with renewed vigour, had so much affected him, that upon looking at himself he feared to alarm the young woman, and all his strength was scarcely sufficient to command his features as he entered her room the following evening. He found her more calm, and though pale as a corpse, yet occupied with some work.

"You are welcome, Mr. Bloom. The worst is now over—it is now finished!" and she gave him at the same time a written paper.

"Your confidence will not be abused, Madame Seiler," said Bloom, and an ice-cold shudder ran over him, as he bent forward to take the paper from Maria's hand. "Allow me to read it in the adjoining room." He did not wait for an answer, but withdrew into the next room. He sat there for some minutes in the greatest agony without moving. At length he took courage and read it. It was the same letter which threw the architect in the gloomy mood that brought him home. We will communicate it in the next chapter.

CHAPTER XVII.

UNREQUITED LOVE.

"Rudolph,—

"In my half-broken heart tremble yet some notes that never yet found a response, but still could never die away, for they were the gift of the great composer who bestows on us the feelings of life—notes from those strings that vibrate only in eternal love. But, Rudolph, though these notes sound yet softly, they form no longer an harmonious whole. The strings have slowly rusted—one after the other is loosened, and there is but yet an echo, which now must also die away.

"Perhaps you do not understand me; it may be that you *will* not understand me. This I almost fear, for you have always maintained that there is no love in our marriage. But it is you, Rudolph, who determined that there should be none. And when I saw the earnest with which you indulged in this once conceived idea, I had not the courage, the strength to throw myself upon your heart, to clear at least myself from this harsh opinion. Perhaps you may grow displeased, if you see that in a moment when I should show most pride I give signs of a weakness which I heretofore strove to conquer. But, Rudolph, in this weakness there lies perhaps my greatest *strength*. For you may believe it is, for the pride of a woman who knows herself to be rejected, no trifle to open her heart to that man who never wished to read in it. I am, however, convinced that my duty as wife and mother commands me to suppress every feeling of pride. I will show myself as I am, that you may not misjudge me in future. And if you should despise me on that account, then—it would be but one pang more, surely one more bitter, perhaps more painful than the rest, yet rather this than not to have been candid at this fearful crisis.

"Yes, Rudolph, so it is. In my heart there has burned a feeling as deep and true as can glow in the breast of woman, and it burned alone. The sparks of this flame have often hovered around you, but they were quenched by the icy breath which you breathed upon them; and the heart—the poor heart trembled with coldness at the same time that it was consumed by its glow. But you know that I have suffered and been silent. Even now I should have spared you the pain which my confession may cause you, had not your proposition of a divorce caused an uproar and storm in my soul, which I must try, at every hazard, to still; and it has seemed to me that I should grow more calm, if I have no longer a secret from you that dimmed the sun-rays of our domestic relation. I am not so infatuated as to hope that feelings which you never cherished should rise in your soul just now, while you are throwing off those which you heretofore have had for me—a feeling of honour and duty; only I do not wish you to be able to say that want of mutual love is the reason that induces you to the cruel plan of separation. No, you must allege *another* reason; whence you will draw it I do not know, nor do I wish to know, for my resolution stands firm; I shall never accede to your proposal of divorce.

"Do not think, Rudolph, that it is through weakness or any thought of my sad condition, that I seek to maintain for myself the rights which belong to me as your wife. No, indeed, no; for I well know that my life will be in future much more desolate and joyless than heretofore; but I do it for our child, and the respect I have for the sacredness of our tie. And then, Rudolph, what have I done to you that you wish to brand my name before the world, and draw me before a judge who will condemn me to death while he passes sentence on my honour? For dark shadows always follow a divorce, let the cause be what it will: and this is natural. If husband and wife dissolve the holiest of connections, some great fault on the one side or the other must necessarily be the cause of it, at least the world thinks so. The pictures you hold up to my eyes of the independence of women, who are at present trodden under foot by men, are, I fear, more imaginary than true. Has not God himself ordained that they should be subordinate? And they will do well not to violate the laws of nature, and force themselves upon the field where man is accustomed to rule. Woman need, on that account, be no 'despotic animal.' She has her peculiar power in her heart, which must suffice when outward storms are raging around her.

"The picture which you draw in relation to the children in an un-lawful marriage is gloomy, but I ask you if there can be more unfortu-nate beings than those who grow up without having properly, either father or mother, since they stand equally removed from both, and have no home-like fire-side round which they may gather in child-like delight? You will, no doubt, answer 'No' to this, unless you have determined both to speak and act against nature; and with this 'No,' you may also admit that the example of separated parents must be of a still more baneful effect upon the moral education of children, than that which you portrayed in colours too glowing.

"Oh, Rudolph! if you will not spare *me*, think at least of your son; he is innocent, and yet you mean to cast a shadow upon his tender head, you mean to sow in his heart a seed of discord which will shoot up between him and us—for who is right and who is wrong? Is it our child who is to decide? No; he will not be able so to do, and therefore his young heart will close itself against us both. If we had not this child—and if I were perfectly convinced that you could not become happy, and ever find joy in life unless separated from me, then I think I could say 'Yes' to your unnatural request, though my heart should break by it. But now hope is whispering to me that time will bring up some friendly star that may give light to the present night. But, however this may be, so long as our son lives, I deem that my own honour, as well as the care for his future, demand from me to say, 'No,' to your proposition.

"Rudolph! I cannot bring you back to us, and yet my very soul shudders at the mere thought to put my name to a paper which would deprive me of all hope of happiness.

"MARIA."

Now the blow was over—the matter was decided. Hope and fear exercised their dangerous influence upon Bloom no longer. He rose with manly composure and folded the letter. He paced the room up and down a few times to recover his usual calm deportment, and he succeeded better than one would have believed after his violent emotion. But it is not seldom found that men are more tranquil after an important affair which has a powerful influence upon their lives than they were before.

Bloom walked, as mentioned before, up and down, and was mainly thinking on the impression this refusal would make upon Seiler. He was not able to judge properly of the strength of passion which Seiler had conceived for the young Swede, but he concluded it as settled, that this relation must necessarily cease of itself after Maria's letter; for Seiler could not apply for a divorce against her will. In regard to the open confession of her love to Seiler, Bloom was of opinion she might have omitted that; but it occurred to him soon after, that Maria had not the least suspicion of his affection for another woman; of his unfaithfulness she had not yet the slightest intimation, and he therefore allowed that she was right to try every means which duty, love, and motherly affection afforded her, to lead back the infatuated man.

"Would that she had made the confession which no doubt was highly painful to her pride, at least not in vain," thought Bloom. "May she not experience the humiliation that he treats her feelings with coldness and distrust, for he will not believe in the sincerity of her feelings, since his own heart has already given way to another passion."

And Bloom was right. Seiler was, indeed, deeply moved by the letter of his wife; but it was not so much through the confession itself, as through the impediment that was thrown in the way of his plans. As his eyes flew over the lines of the letter, he must allow, against his will, that, as she really loved him, and had never in the least offended her conjugal duties, a separation was out of all question, despite his passionate feeing for Alfhild. Without her consent he had no hopes of being freed from the yoke which he could bear no longer.

It was this uncertainty—for he could not resign himself to the thought that all was lost, notwithstanding the distinct refusal of his wife—which depressed Seiler's spirits and made him gloomy, melancholy and taciturn. Perhaps he also felt remorse, that in the same moment when he received the letter of his wife, without informing himself first of its import, he had broken silence regarding his affection for Alfhild, and had let her look into his heart, where she could imbibe only poison from the flowers. This act, through which he lost something of his independence, offended the proud man, for he felt that nothing was now left him but to bend to his fate.

The thought of what his wife during this time suffered occurred to him but seldom. The selfishness of man has no time to occupy itself with the sufferings of others, if he himself is a prey to pains whose weight oppresses his breast, and checks the full flow of his blood. Besides, Seiler thought, when he sometimes felt himself drawn to his wife by a secret power and against his will, "Who knows if a word is true of all she writes to me of her feelings. She only intended to put a new and stronger chain on me by this invention. I will inform myself of it more minutely. I will see with my own eyes."

And he might have added, I will be blind, lest I might be disturbed in the execution of the plan that I have formed.

The consequence of it was, that Seiler resolved to return home, and attempt to induce her to consent by appealing to her generosity; and he was so certain that Maria would become happier by the separation, that he conquered his pride, which would otherwise have forbidden him to call upon the generosity of a woman.

The answer which he sent his wife, after a long delay, was cold, short, expressive of regret, and evasive. The allusion to her love to him was so subtle and calculated, that it could hardly be found; and the letter stated, in fact, nothing farther than that he would come home by Christmas to consult with her on the affair in question personally.

Seiler had put the love of his wife, with the greatest skill, in such a light, that poor Maria could throw her eyes neither upon the letter nor upon herself without blushing at her weakness. It answered, therefore, perfectly its purpose. The rejected heart, offended, withdrew within itself. All hope was now gone; but she would have despised herself if a sound of complaint had escaped her lips.

In the meantime her child grew worse, and the hours in which she watched in prayer and tears were full of all that earth can approve most—most anguished and oppressive.

When Seiler unexpectedly arrived—he had not appointed the day of his arrival before—there was little hope left for the life of the boy. With what grief did the mother see the hour approach when her last hopes should be carried to the grave!

CHAPTER XVIII.

THE YOUNG MOTHER.

CHRISTMAS-EVE was come, and with it a violent storm, which made the dreariness of the room in Seiler's house, which was lighted up on account of the holyday, only more dismal. It seemed as if not a living being was in the parlour, where a fire burned in the fireplace, and the Christmas table stood prepared with lights and cake on it; but if a stranger had entered, he would have said at once, even if he had found the room full of people, that the best was wanting here—peace and comfort. There was by no means a want of order; on the contrary, all was neat and clean—but without life. The spirit of love did not hold here the sceptre; one would, therefore, have seemed to be rather in an empty tomb than in a room where a family festival was to be celebrated.

In the adjoining room there was nearly the same scene as on the evening when Seiler looked through the pane of glass. Maria was also now sitting on the small settee near the stove, with the sick child on her lap—Bloom on the same chair, and at the same window. He even passed, as on that evening, now and then, his hand through his hair, but his look was more gloomy, for it rested uninterruptedly upon Seiler. He stood with his back against the stove, and regarded with deep emotion the slow death-struggle of his child. In this moment he was only father. The presence of the angel of death checked all feelings that lay beyond the circle which he described with his white wings. The language of grief is silence; no one had a word to say to the other.

Slowly passed the hours. Maria's breast struggled for free air, and the light of life of her child flickered ever fainter, for it was expiring.

"Oh," thought Maria, "would that also my time had come—that I could follow my child, and soar with him to that land where there are no sorrows! Here all is so narrow and dark. After my child is gone,

I shall remain behind—no ray of sun will any longer warm this poor heart!" But her wish remained unfulfilled. The rattling of the little breast had ceased, the small lips no longer quivered in convulsive motions under the kiss of the angel of death—the eyes were no longer contorted by pain and struggle; they had closed for eternal sleep; yet Maria lived on to struggle yet longer in the death-struggle of the soul.

There now sat the young mother with her dead child on her knee, and longed for a heart whereon to lean her weary head; but lonesome, awfully lonesome and forsaken was she, although he whose eye she sought lies on his knees by her side. His soul, his thoughts followed the child; but her, the crushed wife, he saw not; he offered not to her his open arms, though she herself was near dying. Maria could bear it no longer; the child fell from her knee, and was taken by Seiler. Bloom caught the fainting mother in his arms, while his eyes darted a dark look upon Seiler. He, however, noticed nothing; he sat in silence, and pressed to his breast the broken link of the chain he hated.

When Maria returned to consciousness, to a clear consciousness of her grief and misery, it was Bloom, who stood by her side; it was his warm, inexpressibly sympathising look which sought hers; it was his hand which, by a gentle pressure, drew her back to live and to struggle.

She moved; he lifted her up and laid her head on his breast; she suffered it, for she felt a human heart beating there. And its beating and its warmth relieved her own heart, and she felt less alone.

"Dear, dear Maria, are you now better?" whispered Bloom, in a tone that penetrated to her very soul. It seemed to her as if she had heard the sounds before; they appeared to her so familiar, and yet at the same time so strange. The reason of it was, that she had so often in her waking dreams spoken in a similar manner to her husband, but never received a response.

"I grow better," answered she with a broken voice, while two hot tears fell on Bloom's hand. Seiler now drew near. He had, though late, yet at last, felt that also he had to fulfil a duty towards his wife, and after having laid the dead child upon his little bed, he went, if not to bring comfort—which it would have been difficult to find—yet to show to Maria that attention which she had a right to demand from him.

Seiler took her hand, which she let him take without visible signs of yielding or resisting. He kissed it, and said mildly and kindly, but without warmth of feeling,—

"The trial of this hour is hard, Maria, very hard, but I thank God that you are pious and resigned with all your heart."

"Yes, indeed, and this is very necessary," muttered Bloom. Maria's lips, however, contracted into a painful smile. She had no more words for her husband, but her look met his, whereupon both cast down their eyes. They had exchanged their thoughts,—no words were required for a mutual understanding.

The day of burial was passed. Friends and acquaintances—they had no relations—had left the house of mourning; and, exhausted by her violent exertions, Maria walked with tottering step about the desolate house. When she felt herself overcome, she seated herself upon the footstool near the stove, where she had commonly sat with her child; but now no sound was heard but that of the funeral bell which continually re-echoed in her ear. She always sought this place in the quiet twilight-hour; her hands lay folded in her lap, now empty, on which her tearful eyes would gaze incessantly, but no eye met hers—the beating of no heart was perceived. All was still, and Maria shuddered for very loneliness.

The men, in the meantime, walked with measured steps up and down the adjoining room. It was as if they yet felt the presence of death, and this forbade them to touch upon the common subjects of every day life. However, all conditions pass by at last.

The snow-storm had soon covered the path bestrewn with small green pine tree twigs, on which the sable train had passed with the little coffin; the windows were opened, the odour of the perfume had vanished, and though the tears in the eyes of the mother, and the grief in her anguished heart, did not cease so soon, yet also *her* deportment became gradually more tranquil.

Days and weeks passed slowly away under such circumstances; but yet they do pass by. We say in the evening, Heaven be thanked that also this day is at an end;—and in the morning, Heaven be praised that another night is passed! But it is a sad life, if the mere vegetating of the body can be so called. The soul must be roused from its slumber, and awakened to a new life. So thought the architect, at least, and determined one morning—it was in the beginning of February—to begin the execution of his plan, which could be delayed no longer, because he was obliged to return to Hammarby by the middle of March.

Poor Maria had expected this moment long before. Although she believed that it would be better if all was over, yet she knew how to estimate in her husband the delicacy of feeling which caused him to defer this matter as long as possible. Now, however, the hour had come; her blood rushed to her heart with unusual violence as Seiler entered her room and said, "Good morning, Maria! If you feel strong enough to hear me, I should like to speak with you;" after which words he seated himself by her on the sofa.

She was not immediately able to answer; as soon as she had recovered her breath, she said with as firm a voice as possible, "Yes, I feel strong enough, Rudolph, let me hear!"

Her state of mind, the trembling of her voice, and the open, loving, and resigned expression in her look, affected Seiler. He could not at this moment conceal from himself, that he was indeed deeply and fervently loved; but he believed and hoped—because he wished it—that this feeling for him was now for the greater part conquered. This was, however, not the case. He read in Maria's looks besides love, something else which he blushed to make clear to himself. He hovered, for a few seconds, in a feeling between shame and remorse.

"Maria!"

"Rudolph!"

Again a pause followed which was highly painful to both. At last Seiler began to be ashamed of his weakness, as he called it—and overcame, with some exertion, the dissatisfaction with himself which everyone feels when he is called upon to communicate something which he knows will deeply wound the heart to which it is addressed.

"What I have to tell you, Maria," said he with considerable composure, "you are already acquainted with through my letter; but since a new reason has been added to those others already stated, I believe you will much the more readily accede to my proposition. However, I will speak of this subject only if you yourself give me permission so to do."

Maria now turned suddenly pale again; her breast heaved, sensations never known before rushed through her heart; she only said in a very low voice, "I will listen," while she folded her hands, which was her general custom. Her head was bent, her eyes were fixed in a gaze on one corner of the room, and her lips quivered.

Seiler moved nearer to her. She felt his breath on her cheek, and a convulsive sensation compressed her breathing; every fibre was strained; the torture was slow.

"You will listen to me, dear Maria? Thanks for this word! My heart will beat lighter if no secret oppresses it longer. But how shall I find words that are significant enough to describe to you the state of my mind—the state of my heart? However, you will release me from seeking for them; you are too high-minded to regard much form. Know, then, Maria—I—I—I love—love from my deepest soul the only woman that is suitable for me—the only one that can make me happy—a being that satisfies and ever will satisfy my heart."

"A very *naïve* confession!" said Maria, with a terrible artificial coldness, while her blood seethed in her veins. The wildest storm is harmony compared to the stunning discords that in this moment tore her heart.

"Not so *naïve* as true and human," answered Seiler, somewhat offended. "Perhaps I acted wrong in making this confession to you; but the mistake carried its punishment with it. I have rendered myself, I see, in your eyes yet more detestable than I was before."

"And is not this just what you wish?" asked Maria, trembling.

"Far from it! I am not so contemptible as to base the hope for our separation on so low a motive. No! on the contrary, I wish that you would be impelled by the same motive which induced me to take this step, and which is the conviction that we cannot possibly henceforward be happy together, nay, hardly longer even live together. And, as we find this, and are convinced that this will never be otherwise, we may also have courage and resolution enough to break this outward, formal tie. The other, if ever there was one—excuse this word—is torn already with the last sigh of our child."

"You are cruel!" replied Maria, while she pressed her hands with force against her breast. "But let it be enough; I am perfectly convinced, and willing to fulfil your wish. But no disgraceful law-suit. My love, my peace, my life, the most sacred ties of nature, you have trodden under foot—leave me my honour, at least, that something may be left me, now that I am thrust into the world alone, forsaken and without protection, in which no one belongs to me and I to no one.

"I have no one!" she exclaimed once more, with a deep, trembling voice, and her eyes looked up to heaven, which, calm and clear, looked down upon the sufferings of the earth. No ray would come from thence and give light to the poor tortured heart. The ruler of the heavens, of light, and of the hearts of man, was putting Maria's faith to a terrible trial—the battle was not yet quite finished.

"Pardon! oh, pardon, Maria, that I cause you such grief!" said Seiler, moved by her unbounded sorrow. "But believe me, I too suffer at this moment beyond expression. I am indeed no fiend; I can no longer see your true heart writhe under the tortures of our conversation. Maria, I confess to you, nay, I take God for my witness for the truth of my words, had I known in the first year of our marriage that you did cherish a powerful and warm feeling for me in your heart, then would certainly my own feelings have awaked, and this hour of pain and trouble would never have come. But, Maria, you mistook the choice of your means to obtain my love; and your constant coldness, although it never made you neglect a single duty, produced a want of happiness and comfort which made our domestic life hateful to me, and called forth in me a desire for new relations. This much I tell you, Maria, that you may see at least that I am a man. And now, after we have exchanged the unhappy secrets of our hearts, nothing more remains to be said. I have nothing further on my heart—no request, no wish, but I place the decision of our mutual fate into your hands. I have never read in your soul so much as now. Oh, pardon, that you must suffer so much through me! Farewell, Maria! I go to Bloom for to-day. We shall not meet again till to-morrow!"

Seiler bent down, pressed a light kiss upon the hand of his wife, and left her in the greatest excitement.

END OF THE FIRST PART.

PART II.

———

CHAPTER I.

ALFHILD'S DEPRESSION.

THE winter months passed, both at the parsonage and at the castle, very slowly. From the former all spring of life had fled in a double sense with the departure of the architect; and in the latter every trace of comfort lay buried through Albano's continuous sickness, which consisted less in physical suffering, than in a highly excitable and gloomy state of mind.

Of Alfhild's life we may say that it was composed of an uninterrupted chain of hope and disquietude, of longing and painful want. Seiler was the centre of all her thoughts. What was he doing now? Were his thoughts with her? Could he now, at last, give an explanation of the incomprehensible mysteries that enveloped him? And in what do then those hinderances consist of which he spoke at his departure? These questions tormented her incessantly. As soon as it grew dark in the room, and she could no longer distinctly see the thread at her spinning-wheel, she went quietly into Seiler's room; and in the corner of the sofa where he used to sit, she laid her head upon the cushion, and brooded and dreamed till it had grown quite dark, and uncle Sebastian's well-known steps called her back into the real world.

"Girl, you will die by your broodings," said the old gentleman, one day, as he felt with his long, dry hand tears in Alfhild's face. "I tell you, child, this will not do! Indeed, you will grow as thin and slender as a stick, and as red-eyed as our cock, if you continue in this way much longer."

"In what way, my good uncle?"

"If it were not so dark here, Alfhild," answered he, in a reproving tone, "I should, no doubt, see how you blush at this question. Fye! my child, will you cast dust in the eyes of your old friend? In former times it was wholly different; when someone troubled you, you went to uncle Sebastian for consolation and advice. Do I now love you less, or have you less confidence in me than formerly?"

"Ah! no, dear uncle, not at all; but it is indeed very hard, you may believe me, to tell all—and I—certainly I cannot tell it to you."

"Well, you need not trouble yourself farther, my child; I understand you sufficiently, and know that you girls always find it difficult to speak on certain things. That is as it should be; for modesty becomes a woman, and it is her most beautiful ornament. But moderation, my child, moderation must be in all things. That has always been my principle, and therefore, though you will not speak on this subject, yet at least you may hear it spoken of. I will only tell you that I knew long ago how it is with your heart, even before he left and your lamentations began; and what is still more, I also saw that he loved you sincerely, and believed every day that he would, like an honest fellow, ask for your hand. But that he did not. Well, he perhaps had his reasons for waiting; may be that he is an honest fellow, notwithstanding. I say no more on this point; but this I say earnestly, that if you do not leave off pining, grieving, and weeping, I shall really be angry with you; for I do not wish that a girl who has been brought up by men, in a nature full of vigour and beauty, should conduct herself as if she had been fed from her childhood on moonshine. That is not good at all. You must resolve to be rational, my child, and you have the more reason so to do, since no misfortune is at the door. All can yet turn out well. When the March sun shall melt the snow on our fields, then your grief will also melt away, I hope."

"May heaven grant it, dear uncle; but I do not know why I am so fearful and anxious. I cannot help it. I am glad, however, that you know my secret, and that I can speak with you about it without having told it to you. Ah! life indeed is sometimes quite beautiful and delightful; but sometimes, nay often, it also is so gloomy that one hardly knows where one is. You are right, uncle, formerly it was much better. Then I always was unembarrassed, free, and cheerful, and enjoyed every pleasure, even the smallest, with all my heart; but now I no longer take pleasure in any thing, at least not in the same manner as formerly; for a certain earnest, a singular, powerful feeling, that I was then an entire stranger to, follows me every where."

"Well, my child, that is the usual effect of love. Before we have any thing to do with these cursed things, we hardly know that we live. It was just so with me in my younger days; but that does not belong here. I mean only to say that every one must come to this, for love is a sickness which nobody can escape from if he has a heart within him. But we, of course, aggravate it, like any other sickness, by our ill-treatment; and I fear that this is the case with you, my child."

"How, dear uncle? I do to it nothing at all; it does, on the contrary, something to me."

"So I believe, and that is just the misfortune. You ought to keep a certain diet, and not live entirely on feelings and tears, like a gourmand on his favourite dishes. You know we have in all sicknesses to take care of ourselves, and not eat of all things we like. If we do this in spite of all prescriptions and experiences, we have to lay the bad consequences to ourselves."

"But, dear uncle, that is indeed singular. If I was not so very sad I might laugh at you; say, then, what diet should I keep? I do not suffer of a physical ill, and cannot, therefore, be treated like an invalid."

"No, no; nor do I speak of a treatment of starvation, and suchlike; but a sickness of the mind is exactly like one of the body, and must, therefore, be treated, in my opinion, in a similar way lest it grow worse, for then it is incurable. See, my child, I think that if you for instance, instead of remaining in bed in the morning and thinking of him—which hurts you for the whole day—should get up as soon as you are awake, drink three glasses of water, and, as at the springs, walk the room up and down, your blood would no doubt, become lighter; and if, nevertheless, irresistible power should impel you to hover with your thoughts round him; they would at least be more cheerful and bright, and not cause you continually to weep, which I cannot bear at all. And if you then, moreover, let Peter give you a ride in the sleigh on the lake every day before dinner—of course only when the weather is fair—and would snowball with your old friend for half an hour after dinner, I think that this exercise—for you have no conception what influence the exercise of the body has upon the mind—would do you good, and free you from these obnoxious broodings. By the time that evening comes, you will then be so tired that you will not only want to go to bed, but will also go to sleep directly, without being troubled by sad thoughts."

Alfhild shook her head doubtingly. She could not possibly take confidence in this treatment which uncle Sebastian prescribed for her. She, however, loved her old friend too much to find it either ridiculous or contemptible. She only answered, "if it would help—but—"

"You can at least try it, my child! Besides, we can in the mean time do nothing till the physician arrives, who will be more successful in the cure. You know we are now in the beginning of February."

Alfhild sighed.

"But now leave off sighing," began Sebastian again. "To-morrow we begin with our regimen; will you, my child?"

"Yes, because you wish it, uncle Sebastian, not that I expect the least improvement from it."

The following morning about six o'clock uncle Sebastian came to Alfhild's door, knocked, and called out: "Are you awake, my child?"

"Yes, dear uncle."

Alfhild opened the door; but she did not dare to afflict her uncle by telling him that she had been awake ever since four o'clock, and spent the time as usual.

"Well, my child, only keep up courage," said uncle Sebastian; "a bright fire is blazing in the parlour, and the water is waiting for you. Come down, and as we are promenading up and down, I will tell you a story of the count's mansion, which I heard last evening. Old Borgstedt was with me, and told me something that will, no doubt, excite your attention."

"What is it, dear uncle?"

Alfhild put on her shawl, took the light in one hand, and with the other the arm of her old friend.

"Only wait a little! you women always are so very curious; this sin you inherited from your first mother, therefore we cannot blame you so much for it. But do not believe that I shall begin the story at once. After you have drunk the first glass of water, I will tell you the first chapter of my news."

They went into the room, and after Alfhild had accepted the first glass, though she could not but laugh at her water cure, she began with uncle Sebastian her regular promenade through the room.

"You see we have now commenced the cure," said uncle Sebastian, "and now listen. You know that Count Albano's health has remarkably improved since Christmas—I mean as regards his madness. Though it has grown clearer in his mind, and he conducts himself again in most respects like other people, yet he has not yet, by any means, overcome the cause of his evil—namely, his unfortunate affection for the young lady. With this you are no doubt acquainted, though you have for some time past hardly cared about any thing else but what related to yourself. But let us proceed.—The baroness and the countess have recently schooled the poor girl. You know what I mean to say.

"These two illustrious ladies have taken a notion—may God forgive them their sin—that it would make for the happiness of the family, if Albano would marry the lady, in a word, if it were possible to bring about a better edition of a new heir to the entailed estate than *he* is; and so, since the young count has improved in health, they have continually harassed poor Thelma.

"The old count, for his part, remains entirely passive, but the women do not want to hear of neutrality, and storm her with exhortations and commands to pay the debt of gratitude which she ought to bear the count's family. Well, I can pardon the *countess* for it, for mothers are always partial if the welfare of their children is concerned; but it is entirely different with the baroness. She is influenced by nothing else—(God forgive me!) but the grossest selfishness, and sacrifices her poor child to wealth. But what was I going to say? We should never put in our observations when we relate any thing, for we then fall out of the common track, and mix up the thread of our thoughts with that of our story. Well, the sum total of it was, they walked like the cats round hot porridge. Count Albano went silently, like a dark spirit, through the empty rooms of the castle, and ogled with his red burning eyes, the lady Thelma, who had in her distress no one to whom she could apply, but old Borgstedt. He consoled her as well as he could, and spoke to her of the power of religion over afflicted hearts in severe trials, of the joys after death, when the earthly sufferings are overcome, and what else he could think of to comfort the poor girl; for he did not dare, though the fate of the young lady struck deeply to his soul, to advise her that she should oppose the injunctions given her. Indeed, this would not have been good at all: the matter must take its course, according to the will of heaven. Yesterday morning, now occurred the remarkable event which you shall hear after you have drunk the second glass of water."

Alfhild emptied it without the least resistance, that she might the sooner hear the continuation of the story. She had not been at the castle for several weeks, partly because her own sorrows made home dear to her, and partly because the baroness showed, at Alfhild's visits, a certain anxiety. She always remained in the room as long as Alfhild spoke with Thelma, and wished, no doubt, thereby to prevent an intimacy and familiarity between them. Alfhild had sagacity enough to see that the baroness did this not from haughtiness, for formerly the young girls had been often together, and always unobserved—but rather from fear that Thelma might confide to her friend her affliction in regard to Albano, and thereby receive the comfort of a sympathising being. Alfhild, therefore, staid at home, and had for a long time heard nothing of the state of things at the castle.

"Well, uncle, what did come then?" Alfhild placed her empty glass upon the table, and began again her promenade.

"Yesterday, now, the young lady came into the parlour, with eyes red with weeping, to pay her respects to her gracious aunt. The baroness, the baboon, had no doubt the evening before belaboured her sufficiently, so that Thelma, exhausted by the long struggles, had consented to be made a sacrifice of. Borgstedt read all this partly in her face, and partly had he learned it from the chamber-maid's chronicle, in which he sometimes turns over leaves. Yesterday, however, at the catastrophe itself, Borgstedt was standing in the saloon, eating his breakfast, when the young lady passed through it.

" 'Count Albano is in that room, dear lady,' said he, in a low tone; for she always went out of his way, and the old servant thought to do her a service by telling her so. But she shook her head, sorrowfully, and answered in a tone so piteous that old Borgstedt was almost choked with emotion: 'It is all the same.—I suppose I must become accustomed to seeing my bridegroom.' With these words she entered the room, but did not shut the door behind her. Borgstedt, therefore, heard every word, and even saw some things, while he walked up and down eating his breakfast, and approached the door as often as he could.

"The first thing he heard was the voice of the countess, who said in a honey-sweet voice to her who entered, 'Good morning, my Thelma! What a beautiful colour you have to-day! But I assure you, my child, the embroidering by candle-light spoils your eyes. You must promise me, sweet Thelma, not to be so industrious in future.'

"Do you perceive how cunning she was, the old cat?" said uncle Sebastian, interrupting himself in his usual manner. "No doubt her eyes were red by embroidering! But the poor child answered meekly and resignedly, 'As you command, dear aunt!' and then she courtseyed to Count Albano, who rose, and taking her hand, gazed upon her as usual, attentively with his rolling eyes.

"She seated herself by him on the sofa, and conversed with him on something, heaven knows what; Borgstedt believed it was on the book which lay before them. Now came the Baroness Ravenstein from the other side of the room, and seemed to have something of importance to speak to her ladyship, her sister. 'Ah, my best Clementine,' said she, while she feigned not to notice her daughter and the young count, 'will you come with me for a moment into the cabinet?' And with that both withdrew—a real satanic trick, you understand, to leave them both alone.

"When the ladies had disappeared, Borgstedt stepped nearer to the door, for he knew well that the bethrothed did not think of watching the door. He saw distinctly the count move closer to the young lady, who grew paler and paler, while her bridegroom said, 'How kind and charming you are, Thelma!' and he began, at the same time, to stroke her hand. She sat quiet and patient like a lamb, and did not utter a word. Seeing that his first manœuvre met with no resistance, he took courage and greater liberties. Borgstedt had forgotten what he said to her, but it was most confoundedly high-sounding language, and amounted in the whole to this—that he felt himself unworthy of the good fortune to call her, one day, his wife—the most rational thing he could say—but that, if she would sacrifice her life to a poor sick man—which is asking not a little—his gratitude, and God knows what else! would have no bounds. What else he said I have forgotten, and am angry with myself for having so bad a memory. She said, at last, 'Yes,' as what else she may have said; in short, he took her into his arms, which he otherwise would not have done. But when she felt his bony hands on her body, she closed her eyes and fell fainting to the floor. No; now I tell an untruth; she sank back into the sofa, as you can easily imagine. Then Count Albano called out for help with all his might. Borgstedt came running from the saloon, and both the ladies out of the cabinet, and there was an ado, a running about and fussing, such as never was seen before. When the young lady came to herself, she looked, as Borgstedt vows, like a corpse risen out of a coffin; but Count Albano looked round with a proud and defying air, and said, 'I wish that my bethrothed, which she now is, be not troubled with any questions.' Thereupon he bent down to her and sang in the finest and most disgusting voice, 'My sweet, dear girl, I shall not now disturb you;' and then left the room with Borgstedt.

"I believe the poor girl must have wanted rest after so much torture. At dinner champagne flowed, and the old count proposed the health of the bethrothed, which was drunk with much solemnity, and thus the great festival was concluded.

"To-day, no doubt, a messenger will be sent with this news to your father. Borgstedt, however, came last evening, and opened to me his heart, and I had no rest till I had communicated the news to you. But the water, my dear child, the water must not be forgotten; you must drink yet a third glass."

"But, my dear uncle, I am so excited! Oh, the unhappy Thelma! Ah, do not trouble me with the water!"

"By no means. If you are excited, which I find very natural, you have the more reason to cool your blood. And afterward it will be time to prepare the coffee for your father."

"Ah, how disagreeable you are, dear uncle! I assure you I shall get the dropsy in this manner."

"It is better to get the dropsy than the love-sickness."

Uncle Sebastian himself filled the glass, and Alfhild, after some resistance, drank it to please her old friend.

But the cure had not yet been finished for this day.

At noon, when the provost had been called to the castle, our heroine had to undergo a sleigh-ride on the lake, and in the afternoon followed the more fatiguing pleasure of snow-balling. Either in consequence of Uncle Sebastian's cure, or because her sorrow over Thelma's unhappiness had exhausted her strength, suffice it to say, Alfhild slept this night much better than usual, and did not awake the next morning until the old gentleman called her.

CHAPTER II.

"Ah, if woman's tears easily flow, does not a woman's smile pass by
faster still? And the former is mere appearance far oftener than the
latter."—JEAN PAUL.

WHEN the provost came home from the castle, he presented the
compliments of the ladies to Alfhild, together with the request that
she would come to cheer up by her company the young betrothed.
There was an entirely different life at the castle since Thelma's engagement with the young count had been effected; in the opinion
of the provost, however, it was there still as gloomy and desolate as
ever. He observed no other change in the atmosphere than that the
old ladies now spoke out loud what they had before only *whispered* to
each other, to wit, some commonplace remarks on the happiness, the
delight, the quiet and peace that would succeed the wedding which,
at Thelma's most urgent request, should not take place till the autumn. This delay, however, caused some differences in the family; but
as Albano took the side of his future bride, the others had to yield.
Thelma felt a gratitude which almost bordered on happiness, when
she saw yet a few months between her and the time when she was to
take upon herself the hateful yoke.

The next morning old Borgstedt came for Alfhild.

"All is true," said uncle Sebastian, as he saw from the window a
fine black steed harnessed to the count's sleigh, stopping before the
door. "You are to be taken to the castle like a princess."

Alfhild was soon seated in the sleigh, and the ride was most
charming, but the half-loud conversation which Borgstedt held with
her gave her so much sorrow, that she entirely forgot how well her
little person was situated.

At her arrival, she was received at the steps by the old count in
person.

"You are welcome, dear Miss Frenkman! You make yourself indeed so scarce, that we are obliged to send for you, if we want to have the pleasure of seeing your handsome, gentle face."

Though the count was always a polite man, he had never been so friendly as now. But things stood very differently now from what they did before the engagement. The daughter at the parsonage had ever been very beautiful, and the counts at the castle had never been without taste for art, as the count chose to express himself; and he had, therefore, carefully avoided the acquaintance of Albano with the handsome daughter of the parson. The anxiety of the count proved in the present instance unnecessary. Albano's heart was not constituted that it could burn for several objects at the same time. His father, however, could not conceive this, as he in his youth had never been enflamed for less than half a dozen ladies at the same time.

Through Albano's engagement, all apprehension had been removed, and as the old count, moreover, saw the necessity of allowing to the young intended bride pleasant company, Alfhild was received with a hearty welcome as a desirable friend. With a smile of delight that a little sunshine would be spread in the gloomy castle, he conducted his fair guest up to the family, who were, as usual, assembled in the parlour.

Thelma hastened to meet her dear friend, whom she had long desired to see, with heartfelt joy; and when Alfhild had made her best and deepest courtsies to the ladies, who honoured her with a kiss, she received with emotion and but hardly restrained tears Thelma's sister-like embrace.

"I pray you look pleased!" whispered Thelma to her, and looked at the same time like the angel of resignation. Alfhild strove to smile, but when she turned from the future bride to the intended bridegroom, whose pallid countenance, deep-lying eyes, and projecting cheek-bones, almost forced from her a shriek of terror. She had not seen him since his sickness; she trembled, and Thelma's fate appeared to her so dreadful that, thinking on her own fate, she believed herself to be in heaven.

"I am glad that we have little Miss Frenkman here," said the baroness, who found the long silence of the young girls dangerous. "I know Alfhild has much taste; she must therefore assist Thelma in selecting from the many designs for embroidery which I have sent for two, for the bridal footstools."

Poor Thelma, who believed that all these things were yet far distant, blushed deeply, and cast a beseeching look upon her mother. But the baroness and countess laughed at her as at a child that has a work yet before him, which he thinks impossible to perform, but still must attempt to do.

"Perhaps I may be permitted to express likewise my opinion in the choice," said Count Albano, while he approached his betrothed.

"Yes, of course!" exclaimed the baroness; "that is no more than proper. The future husband chooses the design for his intended wife, and the intended wife that for her future husband." And with this the baroness rang a silver bell that stood upon the table, whereupon a woman entered, who was ordered to fetch from the room of the baroness the basket with the designs.

The company took seats round the large table before the divan, where the designs were put.

"Well, my little Thelma," said the count, while he stroked the cheeks of his future daughter-in-law, "on which one shall Albano kneel at the altar? Is it to be that basket of flowers, or this wreath of roses?—but I hope the thorns will not prick him."

Thelma was near breaking into tears at all these remembrances of her inevitable, cruel fate. "I have no taste," said she, half aloud and evasively; "I can, therefore, not choose."

Albano's eyes, that had until now an uncommonly mild expression, now darted a gloomy, threatening glance upon the trembling Thelma. In his violent excitement, he seized all the designs, and a second later they would have all been destroyed, if Thelma had not, with most remarkable strength of mind, prevented the outbreak of his wild passion by stretching her hand over the table, and laying it, with a friendly expression, upon his, while she said, "The poor designs shall not suffer for my fault, Albano! I will now choose; I will try to have more confidence in myself."

"And in your taste," answered Albano, appeased. He took Thelma's hand, and pressed it to his loathsome lips. The baroness and the countess nodded to each other, the count coughed, and Alfhild sighed. The samples were again spread out and examined anew.

After many deliberations, Thelma's choice fell at last upon a landscape which had great resemblance to the environs of the grotto in the rock—Albano's favourite place; while he himself decided on a design which pleased him no doubt on account of its peculiarity. It represented a lake in twilight, over whose water-plain an eagle hovered, holding in its strong claws a swan.

"What do you say to this, Thelma?" asked Albano, as he gave her the design. "It may be that I have not chosen as happily as you; but I find this design so peculiar and so simple that I choose it. The idea of it has struck me forcibly."

Thelma could not repress a shudder. She thought it, however, a little silly in herself to be frightened by such a trifle, and, that no one might notice her emotion, she endeavoured to show her particular satisfaction with Albano's choice.

But a universal dissatisfaction was now expressed, as well with regard to the design as to Albano's peculiar taste and Thelma's yielding.

"Is it not uncommonly ugly, dear Alfhild?" asked the baroness, as she reached her the design.

"Certainly it is; and I find it, besides, gloomy, dreary, and cheerless," answered Alfhild. "If I should ever be a bride, I would certainly not choose such a design."

"And would you not do it if your lover had selected it, and asked you to find it handsome?" asked Albano, and scanned Alfhild with his sharp reddish eyes.

"Not even then, Sir Count. I hope, however, that my lover, if I should ever have one, will care more in such trifles about what pleases me than what has his approbation."

"Indeed, Miss Frenkman knows how she wants to have things," said the old count, and smiled in his fine manner. "I like to see ladies take the part of opposition; then they prove true to their nature."

"And I am pleased if they do not do so," answered Albano, with a strong emphasis. "I believe my father mistakes when he supposes that women are destined by nature to opposition."

"I cannot decide, indeed," replied the old count, pleasantly, "whether nature appointed this place for them, or whether they chose it themselves. It is, however, certain that they have, ever since the creation of the world, maintained this place with honour, and will maintain it also in the future. This is beyond all question!"

"My good friend, we go too far from the main subject," objected the countess, impatiently. "But this is always the case with men; they can never adhere to the point in question, but go over to other things which have not the least connection with them. We forget the design while you are demonstrating."

"No, dear aunt, here it is," answered Thelma, thereby putting an end to the discussion. "I will prove to uncle that the old saying is yet true—'no rule without an exception,'—and will not oppose Albano's wish, but begin to-morrow to embroider it. The design is, indeed, quite beautiful."

The baroness shook her finger at her daughter in a threatening yet pleasant manner, and thought she did not yet know how to bear herself in her new situation. Albano triumphed. The tenderness in her friendly looks, however, frightened poor Thelma, who feared his love as much as his anger. The announcement of dinner being ready, put at last an end to the quarrel, and after dinner the basket with the designs, which the baroness wished had never been brought down, was removed.

Alfhild stayed at the castle a whole week, and had during this time often opportunity of admiring Thelma's self-sacrifice and patience. When she came home again, she was calmer than before. Uncle Sebastian, not knowing what favourable influence Thelma's society had exercised upon Alfhild, ascribed this change to his cure. Alfhild smiled, and did not contradict him. Besides, their conversations in the morning were so pleasant, that she never regretted the hour she passed in uncle Sebastian's company.

One day the provost, wishing to give his daughter a little diversion, said, "Alfhild, I think it would give you pleasure if you would ride with me to the fair at B——. If you feel inclination you may accompany me. I purpose to sell my yoke of oxen, and see if I can find a pair that are younger; and besides, I intend to sell my black horse. The rogue, however active and handsome he is, has his faults. In short, my child, various business will oblige me to stay there till the next day at noon. It will be so much more convenient for you to go now, as I shall take the large waggon, for the roads are too bad to go on the sleigh; and I mean to leave the coach with the wheelwright, and buy me a new one, for if I should some time go with you to Stockholm, the other would be, I suppose, too old-fashioned."

"You are very kind, papa, and I feel very grateful to you," answered Alfhild, and kissed her father's hand. "If you think I shall not be in your way, I should be delighted to accompany you. When do you go?"

"On Friday morning; but do not keep me waiting, as women generally do. At six o'clock precisely I am to be seated in the coach, so that we are at the place by noon."

"I shall not, dear papa, and shall certainly be ready."

Alfhild was any thing but delighted at the prospect of a pleasure like that which her father proposed; but she knew that a friendly question of her father, "Will you ride with me to this or that place?" meant only, "you *shall* ride with me there;" and therefore Alfhild made no further objection, but complied with the proposal with a good grace.

On Thursday afternoon Alfhild rode over to the castle to inquire whether the ladies had any commands for the town. This attention was received with great acknowledgment, and while the old ladies went out to prepare a schedule of the things which Alfhild had to purchase, she remained alone with Thelma. The old count was not at home, and Albano had the politeness to molest the two young girls no further. He was, as mentioned before, no great friend of company, and avoided, in general, every third person that came in between him and his betrothed; but he did so at present the rather since he had conceived a certain aversion toward Alfhild ever since she had expressed her opinion so boldly at the choice of the design. When, therefore, Albano observed that Thelma found pleasure in Alfhild's company, he retired to his room, where he continued his incessant wanderings to and fro which he had begun in the saloon. His spleen had not entirely disappeared before the long-desired happiness, and though he delighted in this good fortune, yet there were many things that caused him vexation. Dark thoughts, gloomy images, and black imaginations kept yet always company with him when he was alone, though he tried to banish those spirits whenever he was with his beloved.

"Thank Heaven that he has gone!" said Alfhild, with much candour, after he had withdrawn, while she embraced her friend.

Thelma heaved a deep sigh from her compressed breast. "Ah! Alfhild," said she, "how delightful is it to have for once a free moment, a moment when we can be natural, and look into a heart that understands us. This good fortune has not often been my lot, and I

cannot expect to have it often in future. An hour like this we have
not had for some time. Tell me how you find him—no doubt quite
detestable."

Alfhild had not the courage to answer; she took Thelma's hands
and put them to her moistened eyes; this was sufficient answer, she
thought.

"But he is often so good, Alfhild," said Thelma, with that delicacy
of feeling so natural to woman, of putting constraint upon herself
before others, at the expense of her own heart. "You must not hate
him, Alfhild; he loves me with so much fervour. Would to God he
did not half so much, for even this half I should find too much," she
added, with a light sigh, while she hid her face on Alfhild's shoulder.

"Poor Thelma!" The pure dew-drops mingled on the cheeks of
the young maidens.

"And if he could guess my wishes before I knew them myself, he
would endeavour to fulfil them; but—of what use is it, Alfhild? Oh!
Alfhild, answer something. I see by your looks that you think me very
unhappy, and you do not know yet all; no—you do not know it!—See
here!"—she laid the hand upon her breast—"here is a pain which no
one suspects, and which is more bitter than all others, and against
which I daily struggle in vain."

Alfhild looked searchingly in Thelma's eyes; she knew not what
she meant. But Thelma was strong; she would not lay the burden
which oppressed her upon the shoulders of another. Moreover, she
feared to touch upon a subject on which she had never as yet dared to
utter a syllable to any one.

"Whatever it may be," said Alfhild, with great sympathy, "it is
impossible to find anyone who would bear the cross more patiently
than you do. Would I possessed but half your strength!—for know,
Thelma, I too have sorrow, have a deep grief...."

The countess entered and put an end to all further interchange
of feelings. Alfhild received a number of commissions and minute instructions how every thing should be, and many admonitions not to
mistake any of the orders. Soon after the baroness also came with a
long catalogue of commissions, and Alfhild was indeed startled at the
great activity she was to display at the fair. After the many marks of
favour that had been bestowed upon her to-day, any objection would

have been high treason; she therefore lodged the documents in her bag, took leave, and drove home.

CHAPTER III.

UNWELCOME NEWS.

THE following morning, as the clock struck six, Provost Frenkman put his foot upon the coach-step. He had the morning pipe in his mouth, and the brown tobacco-bag hung suspended from a button-hole. As soon as the provost had duly adjusted his furs and his foot-bag, Alfhild took her seat.

"Wrap your cloak closely round you, my dear," reminded her uncle Sebastian, and covered the feet of his darling in the furs and shawls that had been put in the coach on account of the severe cold.

"I hope you have not forgotten any thing," said the provost, casting an examining look upon the things around.

"Not the least thing, papa; all is in the best order," answered Alfhild.

"Well, then, drive on, Peter! But, stop a moment; if you should see Lars with the oxen, before we get to B., then tell me; I have yet to speak to him before he drives them to the cattle-market."

This order being given, he said: "Good bye, brother Sebastian! Look to the house! Good bye, children; Stina, do not turn any thing upside down in the room when you sweep it; and you, Sisa, take care of the fire. Now drive on, Peter."

The Holsteiner now passed through the gate of the court, where Stina and Sisa stood to whisper to the coachman yet some more commissions.

Without describing their overtaking the oxen, we go directly to the stage of the various market scenes at B. As it was already noon when the provost arrived, the crowd was at its height, and not without much delay Peter succeeded in walking his nag through the farmers and country-women. At last, however, he reached in safety Paerman's Hotel. The provost and the host frequently transacted business together, and for several years past, a room was always on market-days kept in readiness for him. The way to it led through the large room for strangers, and while Alfhild waited in it for her father, who had stopped on the staircase to speak with somebody, she examined the motley groups around her.

The provost gave her ample time to look around; for he had met with an old acquaintance, a Norwegian, with whom he had often traded, and who was willing to purchase his black horse. The provost, however, would give for the new horse which the Norwegian offered to him, only his old one and a young one which he had at Hammarby. It was, therefore, agreed that the stranger should on the next day go with him to the parsonage to look at the young one. This being settled, the provost entered the guests' room to take his daughter, whom he had at the bargaining entirely forgotten.

"I am glad you have come at last, papa!" said Alfhild, delighted. "I felt entirely lost among these many strangers."

"Bless me!" exclaimed the provost, "I entirely forgot to give you the key to the room."

He opened the door of his room, and soon after Peter came in with all the things. Now they made their toilet; the provost put on his best wig and a new neckcloth. Alfhild took the papillotes out of her hair, curled her locks, fastened a new veil to her bonnet, and put on a clean collar. They then took coffee, and determined to take dinner in company of a few friends after they had finished their business. The provost took the arm of his daughter, and Peter followed them with two large baskets. Thus they set out on their wandering through the undulating crowd of people.

The motley crowds, and the crying of the most various voices mingled up together, gave Alfhild not half so much pleasure now as formerly, and she scarcely noticed the curious, friendly looks that were cast upon her from all sides. She had eyes only for the commissions of the countess and the baroness, otherwise she would have, no doubt, found pleasure in the comic scenes around her. There a woman with her cloak gathered up in one hand, and with nose lifted up, was hunting from booth to booth after a bank-note that had been stolen from her. She had put it down from her hand to put some sugar-bread in her basket, which a gentlemen had made her a present of. "And it was at this booth!" she cried out with great indignation—this assertion she renewed at each booth, and from each she was dismissed with taunts. "It is shameful!" she called out to an acquaintance that was passing by, "I but just put the bank-note out of my hand, and the same instant it was gone."

At another place two small boys were seen, setting up a terrible crying after their "mamma," whom they lost sight of while looking on the tricks of a dancing bear.

Now a young gentleman with an elegant mustache appeared, clearing his way with feet and elbow, to look a handsome country-girl in the face—not to mention a great many other figures.

Alfhild did not care about any thing, but thanked heaven when she had got through with her commissions, and could, on the following morning, seat herself in the new carriage to return to Hammarby. But she was not a little astonished, when having some time waited for her father, she saw him coming with a stranger, and she was still more surprised to hear that this tall Norwegian stranger would accompany them home.

The day after the arrival at Hammarby was a Sunday. The guest and uncle Sebastian were at church to listen to the sermon of the provost; and Alfhild had, in the meantime, some domestic business to attend to. After she had finished this and read a few pages in a book of sermons, she arranged the things she had bought at the fair for the count's family, intending to ride over to the castle after dinner to deliver them.

However much engaged she was with these things, yet she felt a certain disquietude of mind which she had never before felt in the same degree, and she was troubled by misgivings without being able to assign a reason for this singular state of mind. Several times hope whispered to her, "March will soon come now;" yet despite of this, the gloomy mood would not leave her.

The creaking footsteps of the gentlemen in the entry awoke her from her dream-like condition. She hastened down to offer to the gentlemen some refreshment, and after this they sat down to dinner.

The provost sharpened his carving-knife, and while one piece after another fell from the roasted joint, he remarked to the guest, in order to make an agreeable host:

"It is quite pleasant to me to hear once more at my table the Norwegian accent, and to have a true Norwegian by my side. For you must know that we have become so much accustomed to it, that we really miss something since your countryman, the architect, Seiler, is no longer with us. You know Mr. Seiler, as you told me before, when we were speaking of the new church."

"Yes, indeed; he is a very fine man," answered the Norwegian, flattered by the remarks of the provost on his countryman, to whose pleasant person he was partly indebted for the friendly reception he had found at the parsonage. "A very fine man; I had, about two years ago, the pleasure of passing a day at his house, and on that occasion I became acquainted with his lovely wife. Indeed, she is a very fine woman, and even celebrated as a beauty in the whole country round, and justly so."

"Is he married?" asked the provost, and the carving-knife dropped out of his hand. He sat thus motionless—a picture of the greatest astonishment.

Uncle Sebastian's eyes darted fire, and the violent trembling of all his limbs and the swelling of the veins in his face, proved that twenty years ago he would certainly have fallen into raving madness at this news. He was now old; yet his spirit had not lost all its fire. This was shown by his sudden rising and pushing the plate back with vehemence, and springing towards Alfhild, who was now sinking lifeless from her chair. The arm of the aged uncle seemed to have recovered its former strength. He drew his darling to his breast, and carried her lifeless into her room. The provost hastened after him, and both men united their efforts to recall Alfhild back to life. Her dress and boddice were untied; one glass of water after another was passed over her face, and all kinds of perfume administered to her to smell of. At length the surgeon who had been sent for arrived. He opened a vein, and as soon as the blood flowed, she opened her eyes. Though she had returned to consciousness, yet she lay still silent and faint, without moving a limb.

When the provost believed that all danger was over—which he considered as perfectly certain—he returned to his astonished guest, and the dinner that had grown cold in the meantime: for Frenkman, though a man of refinement, belonged to that class of people who can return to the table with the same appetite, though they meet with the most unheard-of accidents.

Uncle Sebastian, meanwhile, sat by the side of Alfhild's bed, and held her hands in his. Neither of them spoke; but when she sometimes looked up and fastened her almost dying look upon her old friend, then his heart ached so much, that he had to collect all his military feeling of honour to prevent his shedding bitter tears. So much the more, however, he pressed and rubbed her little hand, and breathed upon it, and endeavoured in all ways to warm it a little.

"That is the finger of God!" murmured uncle Sebastian in his teeth. "The wretch is only the instrument of a higher power! Punishment, alas! alas! I felt that from the beginning."

"Uncle Sebastian, I pray you with all my heart, do not speak such awful words," said Alfhild, with a tremulous voice. "Let us not break the staff over him. I knew, indeed, that a dark cloud was drawing near to hide from me the light of the sun. Ah! it was the sin of my love! Great God, let me die rather than live with the annihilating feeling of loving the husband of another woman! Do you not believe, uncle Sebastian, that God will pardon my sin? Indeed I was ignorant of it!"

"Yes, indeed, my dove; you are white and pure like snow, and innocent like an angel of God. You have no guilt upon you; but he, the villain...."

"Oh, do not speak it out!" asked Alfhild with indescribable anguish; "do not utter so wicked a thought; be patient for my sake, for the sake of poor Alfhild. I too will be patient, and suffer and be silent; for God demands a victim for the sin. The husband of another—hu! My heart quivers, and it is as if all its fibres were breaking! But tell me, where shall I hide myself when he comes back? I cannot see him, and even his image I must tear from this poor heart; for since now all is clear to me, I must no longer enjoy the past joys even in recollection."

"You do not hate him, then?" interrupted uncle Sebastian. "You appear prepared, I believe, to pardon the wretch!"

"Hate him?" said Alfhild, while she fixed her large beautiful eyes upon the old man, which induced him to cast his down. "How could I hate him—and what is there I could reproach him with? Does he not share my fate? Our feelings were involuntary. They were sinful, but we *both* are guilty."

"Are you so blind, my child, that you do not even see how abominably he acted, to awaken a passion, and to nourish it in his own breast, while the most sacred tie was binding him?"

Alfhild was silent. It seemed to her that she had loved the architect from the beginning, without any encouragement on his part; but it hovered before her mind only dimly, and she did not know whether it had been actually the case, that he had awakened and sought her affection. That he had *nourished* it could not be denied; yet she shrunk back, with trembling, from examining into any thing by which he, whom she adored, must sink in her esteem. It was a secret which she determined to bury in her heart. Alfhild did not answer, and uncle Sebastian had too much delicacy of feeling to force from her a confession which her feelings forbade her to make.

Long and sad days and nights followed this unhappy discovery. Alfhild soon left the bed again, but the young, cheerful girl waned evidently, and she soon walked about like a shadow.

Uncle Sebastian spoke no more of his water-cure. He endeavoured in vain to think of something that might be applied as an antidote to rear Alfhild out of her sad condition, but he found nothing; and all he could do was only to share in the silent grief of his darling. The provost continued with the method which he held for the best; he saw nothing but the pale cheeks of his daughter, which induced him to take a physician, who declared to the father's great satisfaction, that Miss Frenkman had taken a violent cold.

It was true, Alfhild did cough, and the doctor was not entirely wrong, in a certain way. But this was an outward symptom; the real cause of the sickness remained unknown. Sadly passed now one day after another. It was so cold and desolate at the parsonage, that it seemed winter would never end. With each grain of sand that ran through the hour-glass, however, the fearful moment of Seiler's return drew nearer. Provost Frenkman, without stating to the count any particular reason, had contrived to rid himself of his former guest for the ensuing summer, and there being no other fit place very near where Seiler could stay, the count determined to take him while the church was building, under his own roof.

But we must now return to Norway to see what progress things are making there.

CHAPTER IV.

THE DIVORCE.

NIGHT had spread her dark mantle over the earth, and the day, so bitter for Seiler and his wife, which we described at the end of the first Part, had sunk in the wide ocean of eternity.

Maria lay on her knees in her solitary chamber, and prayed to God to give her strength and courage to drain the bitter cup. But peace would not come to her breast. At each look into the future she startled, for she saw herself alone, without the slightest hope of mending her condition, and doomed to bleed to death from the wounds of her breast. Yet Maria did not cease to pray, and not only for herself alone, but also for him who had caused her those bitter pangs.

The love of woman, though she cannot but condemn it as a weakness, remains, if it was true love, so entirely without selfishness, that she forgets herself on account of the beloved object. Maria had loved her husband thus, and loved him still, after the last star in the heaven of hope was quenched, and the last rose lay scattered at her feet.

This night became for her memorable for ever. It had seen her struggle, her prayers, her tears and her anguish; it became also witness of the victory in the painful struggle with her heart! It was long past midnight, when trembling with cold and excitement, she sought her lonely couch. Mechanically she stretched out her hand, as she was wont to do, toward the place where the bed of her child used to stand. It was empty, and as her hand sank powerless by her side, she felt a violent pain shoot through her heart. Sighs heaved her oppressed breast. Ah, how long and dark was the night for the poor wife, on whose brow cold drops of perspiration stood! But God is kind; morning will dawn,

> "And on the thorn of pains springs up,
> The rose of pure delight."

Also this night was succeeded by a morning whose first pale beams woke Maria, and dried the last tears that hung on her eye-lashes. She dressed herself, and breathing with her warm lips she made an open spot on the frozen window panes, and looked through it up to the Creator of the world. Now that day had come, she felt a hope and trust which night had not given her; a certain peace came over her soul, and gradually her self-control obtained full power again. She knew now what he was going to do—she knew what sacrifice iron necessity demanded of her, and she was ready to make it.

Patient and beautiful in her infinite grief, Maria entered the sitting-room, and arranged the breakfast-table herself for the first time since the return of her husband.

When Seiler entered, she rose and went, more bashful perhaps than a young bride, and blushing, to meet him. He gave her his hand in silence, but when he felt its light trembling, and her indescribably charming confusion, he could not but own himself that he had never before looked upon her with impartial eyes.

"How do you do to-day, good, dear Maria? Your cheeks appear to me to be fresher than they have been of late."

"I am glad if you find that! Indeed I feel somewhat better. But the coffee grows cold; allow me to wait upon you to-day."

At the word "to-day," her voice became evidently tremulous; there lay an almost superhuman exertion in her usual tranquillity.

Husband and wife took seats opposite to each other, and Maria was even able to smile as she reached to him the cup. But there are hours in life when a smile pains us more than the bitterest and sharpest word. This was now the case with Seiler. Maria's smile pierced through his soul, and caused him more pain than a thousand tears and reproaches would have done. He knew her, and was aware that her deeply wounded feelings forbade her to show the real state of her soul; and that with death in her heart she was strong enough to smile, in order not to excite his compassion, since she could no more excite another feeling.

"By heaven!" thought Seiler, and brought Maria's hands to his lips with a degree of respect and emotion which he had never shown before—"Bloom is right! I never knew her before. She is a noble, high-minded woman; and had she not been so proud, so politely cold while my heart longed, often in past years, for a warmer ray of sun; or if she had only tried to conquer it in the usual ways of little stratagems, she would certainly have succeeded. But now, now it is past. My heart has found a being that does not know what is disguise, or what is the meaning of such strength of mind, which commands her to conceal the warmest feelings, and to show an icy coldness, while the blood is seething in the veins, and each beat of the pulse announces to the restless heart that another second is passed without hope. No, Alfhild, my pure white dove, she clings with warmth and yearning desire to my breast, seeking there protection, and her cheek reddens or grows pale, according to the expression she finds in my looks. Thus, thus must be a woman's love; wholly given up to and dependant on the man to whom she devotes herself. All her thoughts, feelings, and conceptions must unite in the one consciousness that she loves. She must have desire for nothing else. The word of her beloved, or husband, must suffice her; her confidence in it must be her world, and his will the only thing that she consults. The only arithmetic which she needs to understand is, 'to be able to calculate the change of his humour.'"

In thus comparing the love of his wife with that of his beloved, which he carried through with the greatest selfishness, he forgot entirely, which is frequently done, to consider justice; for he took into no account all *his own* behaviour toward the two beings, which if he had done so, would have convinced him that he had to seek for the cause of the different conduct of the two women in *himself*, and not in *them*.

During his long, silent soliloquy, Maria sat regarding him, to understand how, after having kissed her hand so friendly, almost lovingly, he became all at once so thoughtful, and seemed to forget all around him. "It is impossible for him now to think that there is in the world yet a being who is his wife," thought Maria, and rose from her chair to leave him alone. She would so gladly have spoken to him, but his thoughts were far from her.

The motion she made when she left her place, brought him back to himself.

"Why, good Maria, will you leave me so soon?"

His voice had no longer the least warmth; it was mild, but without feeling.

"I thought you wished it, Rudolph."

"By no means; something only occurred to me just now. Pardon me, and do not go yet, Maria."

His look was so speaking; she resumed her seat; fearing, however, that one of those unpleasant pauses might follow, which is more painful to the mind than an unpleasant conversation, she suppressed her emotions, and said;

"I also have reflected, Rudolph, have considered, and have come to a resolution."

She began to stammer; it became difficult for her to bring the words over her trembling lips; breath failed her. And yet she must at last speak, for it could not remain as it was now. The strength to speak out her resolution lived in her strong soul, yet her voice trembled and denied service.

"Dear Maria, I believe I understand you." Seiler's eyes became again animated and shone brightly, while the veins of his forehead swelled; but he too could speak no farther. A feeling of shame which is painful to a man who deems it impossible to do an act which offends, but in the least, against the laws of honour, who, however, sees himself compelled to compromise, in some measure with this almighty sovereign, in order to convince him and himself that he is acting according to his commands—such a feeling Seiler had at this moment, and this hindered him from continuing his speech. In restless suspense he looked forward to what his wife would utter next.

"Yes, I have determined, Rudolph...."

Maria spoke with so much effort that she was obliged to fetch breath anew between almost every syllable.

"I have determined to accede to—to—to—your proposition!—I have no objection, you understand—I give my consent to the divorce."

At Seiler's ill-concealed emotion of joy, which he had not delicacy of feeling enough to conceal, Maria's heart shrank convulsively; but all was not yet over; one word of awful meaning remained yet to be spoken. Who of the two was to be the deserted party? If she stayed, which would have, no doubt, been most convenient, she must have been the one who, according to the Norwegian laws, had to make the application for a divorce. Maria could not become reconciled to this thought, this idea had for her something highly unpleasant, that she should be the one who—no! this was impossible. She would rather go away and leave to Seiler liberty to act as he pleased.

"The way and manner,"—she began again, after a painful pause, without being able, however, to continue the commenced sentence, and said then, "I wish—I should like—"

"What, good Maria?—Whatever you wish, shall be a holy duty for me to fulfil. Speak entirely, openly!"

"Well then, Seiler, I wish to be allowed to go away, and that you—you...."

Seiler easily imagined the reason that induced Maria to leave her quiet, neat household, that had become dear to her, and he anticipated her wish with that delicate attention which now again awoke in him, and was always reflected in all his actions.

"Best Maria," said he, with feeling, "leave all this to me and Bloom; we will arrange every thing entirely according to your wish."

"Then, Seiler, nothing is left to be settled," answered she with a tremulous voice, sank her head, and intended to leave the room, when Bloom entered. The great importance of the present hour gave her yet for a few moments sufficient strength not to succumb to her emotions. She took Bloom's hand, and said in a firm tone:

"May I consider you in future, as heretofore, my real friend? I stand now in double need of your protection, since I have no longer a proper protector. I have entered into a voluntary agreement with Rudolph to dissolve our marriage relation."

Bloom's eyes wandered with a peculiar expression from the one to the other.

"To dissolve your marriage relation!" exclaimed he, in a tone as firm as it was possible for him. "And is this done voluntarily on your part, Madame Seiler? Do I hear right? is it really so? but have you well considered this step?"

"Voluntarily, Bloom," answered Maria. "And I have not wanted time to bethink myself. I am perfectly convinced that after what has happened of late, no re-union can be effected, and therefore may then also the mere appearance of it vanish!"

"In God's name, be it then!" said Bloom, "although we ought not to call upon the name of God in such an undertaking, whose love tied the bond which is now dissolved again. But yet I say, in God's name! And may it have been done at the right hour, since it can no more be altered. And now, Madame Seiler, I beseech you fervently to choose me as your friend, brother, and protector. So far as it is in my power you shall repent as little as possible this so-called voluntary separation, which is, and remains nevertheless, a forced one."

Now was Maria's strength exhausted. When she put her hand into that of Bloom, which he proffered, she was only able to answer in a faint voice and with tears: "Now it is over; I will repair to my room."

Bloom conducted her as far as the door; but on the threshold she turned round once more, and her eyes sought those of Seiler. Pale, mute, tortured by feelings which were not to be envied, stood the architect motionless in the room.

"Farewell! Rudolph," she said; "we see each other this moment for the last time. You must depart first, and then—I. God be with you!"

She stretched her arms out towards him. The feelings which now stormed her heart drowned all others.

"Maria, heroic woman! From this hour forward, though we separate for ever, you shall be dearest to my heart after her. Forgive, Maria, that I learned to know your worth too late."

Seiler clasped his trembling wife in his arms. Maria's brow rested for some minutes on his breast, and in the hour of departure the first warm kiss was imprinted on her lips. Bloom conducted the exhausted and severely tried young woman to her room, and then returned to discuss with Seiler the necessary preparations for the important step which was to be taken.

A few days after, the architect left his home. He purposed to take a journey through Denmark, and to return to Sweden not before the end of March. Seiler was conscious that he must seek to recover not only the necessary composure, but also the lost elasticity of his mind before he could make his appearance in Hammarby.

CHAPTER V.

THE JOURNEY.

DURING the first days of these scenes Maria's state of mind was most painful; but an attempt at describing it would be too bold, and might fail. She sat motionless and cold like a marble statue; she did not weep, she did not speak, nor take any nourishment; she seemed to have no feeling either for pain or joy, and Bloom's endless efforts were not able to bring even a single syllable from her. Knowing, however, her wishes, he walked in silence to fulfil them.

He knew that she preferred the most profound and complete solitude to every thing else. Through a friend, he had discovered a place which he deemed proper and suitable for her; besides, it was so far removed from her present home, that no one from there could easily discover it.

With the tenderest regard for her comfort, he arranged every thing; and as soon as he received information that her new home was ready to receive her, Bloom's handsome sleigh, with its fastest horses, appeared one beautiful forenoon before Maria's door.

When Bloom entered her room in his travelling attire a light tremor seized her. She would rise, but could not. He approached her in a manner which showed the most heartfelt sympathy,

"Best Maria," said he, in a gentle tone, "make your departure brief; all is ready. The little strength you have left, you must save for the journey. Promise me to keep your composure as much as possible."

"I have already taken leave," answered she, in a low voice, and cast a long look upon the spot where once stood the cradle of her child. He wrapt a cloak and shawl round her, and rather *bore* than conducted her to the sleigh. When all was properly arranged, he seated himself beside her, and ordered the coachman to drive off.

After having proceeded some stages from her home, Bloom sent back his own horses, and now they went at the most rapid rate, with post-horses, through the Norwegian mountains. The roads were good, and the riding seemed to have a more wholesome effect upon Maria than all the former attempts to cheer her up. She slept at night, and was also able to take some food to please her friend. On the third day they reached the borders of Sweden, and stopped to rest a little at one of the pleasant inns near Idefjord.

While the hostess arranged the neat set of china before them, Maria, for the first time, looked round her, observing the outward objects, and addressed to her protector the question, whither he intended to bring her?

"Into the neighbouring country, best Maria, but not far from the borders. I think it best that you do not remain in Norway for the present."

"But in Sweden, Bloom? What do you think of? This is the same country where—"

She was silent.

"It is true it is the same country, Maria; but the places are at a great distance apart. Surrounded by rocks and cliffs, and remote from all intercourse with the world, lies the house of a poor country clergyman,—there, to the solitary Fredsberg, I will bring you for the present. The people that are living there are simple and unpretending, yet peace and comfort are dwelling with them."

"And there I am to go? Shall I find there a female being with whom I can associate?"

"I hope so, Maria. I do not know personally the young hostess; but I have reason to believe that my friend who served me in this matter would not have chosen Fredsberg, if the place did not afford what I pointed out to him as the first requisite. Of course, we must not expect a woman of distinguished education and social talent; and such an one is, perhaps, less desirable to you than a quiet, good-natured, amiable person, of sufficient sensibility and intellect to understand you, and shorten the weary hours of the day by a heartfelt kindness, which heightens the value of the slightest attention. Moreover, my good Maria, you yourself expressed a desire to live at a place far remote from your home, in a place which would afford peace and quiet."

"It is true, Bloom, and I am content; for how can I wish for company in my present condition—and if I had any, how could I bear it? Indeed you have acted right; when can we get there?"

"If we pass over the river Idefjord this evening, we shall sleep to-night on Swedish soil, and shall be at our place of destination to-morrow evening."

It had begun to grow dark, and Maria was not without some fear, when she thought of the distance of several miles she had to pass over the ice of Idefjord. They would, however, have moonshine, and the preceding cold weather warranted the firmness of the ice. They determined, therefore, to continue their journey, and as soon as they had taken their coffee, they resumed their seats in the sleigh.

Swift as an arrow flew the little horses with their light burden over the Idefjord. Bloom's arm rested on the back of Maria's seat; and, in order to protect her from the cold, he held her cloak-cape close around her. A sharp north wind was blowing, yet he had more warmth within him than was necessary to render him insensible to it.

"I am yet a little afraid," whispered Maria, while she moved closely to her friend and protector.

He had hardly sufficient breath to assure her that the ice was firm, and nothing need be feared.

The dangerous way was successfully passed over. Having arrived at the first stage on the Swedish territory, they found the roads so difficult that Bloom was obliged to alight and walk by the side of the sleigh, to secure it against upsetting. Having at last reached the open highway, he found it quite pleasant to be able again to take a seat by Maria.

"That was a very bad road," said he, glad to have it passed; "there was no danger, however. I hope you felt no anxiety, Madame Seiler?"

"Oh, no; not since we have again firm ground under us. But you had a great deal of trouble."

"I no longer think of that. Have we not fine moonshine? We must ride yet a little distance farther."

"As you think best, Bloom. The farther we go, the more agreeable it will be to me."

The journey of our travellers was now continued almost without interruption till they descried, on the following evening, the small solitary house where the poor country clergyman was living with his wife, almost totally ignorant of what took place without his narrow circle. The environs were desolate and bare, as every where in this region, and only now and then the eye fell upon a single rock or cottage. The naked strand was covered with spray by the restless waves of the sea, over which now and then a shrieking seagull was hovering.

Winter had just now covered the whole landscape with its white snowy cloak, which was for the benefit of the interior of the houses. The whitewashed walls of two small but very neat rooms, shone before the fire in the chimney-place, and a candle which stood on a small table gave light to the persons grouped around it.

On the one side of it sat a young woman, in a brown woollen

dress, with a yellow-speckled neck-cloth modestly pinned up. She was spinning, and singing gaily an old fashioned waltz. While she drew the thread from the yellow flax with the one hand, she held together with the other the little cloak of a sprawling child that lay in her lap, and was quite impatient in its inconvenient position. Opposite to this woman of blooming freshness and good-natured appearance, sat her husband, the minister. He was a man of middle age, and had the calm expression in his manner which is the sign of content. He was busily engaged in making a fisher's net.

At the entrance of the strangers both rose, and it was a pleasure to see their emulous efforts to show the guests all due attention. "What the house could afford" was immediately served up; and when the natural, well-meaning hostess conducted the fatigued Maria after the meal was finished into the small inner room, which henceforth was to be her own, they both understood each other perfectly, and Maria had the good fortune, long missed by her, of being able to weep out her grief on the feeling breast of a woman.

Bloom remained a few days in this little secluded world. He employed his time in taking walks with Maria. When they sometimes stopped before one of those huts, which during sunshine were wholly covered with sea fishes to be dried, they looked at each other, and thought that men can be happy with very little, if habit has not changed the simple wants of nature into craving after luxury and pomp.

"What do they do with the fishes?" asked Maria.

"They sell them; for without this only article of their traffic, they would not be able to procure even the most indispensable necessaries of life."

Maria sighed.

"Let us go in," said she.

They did so, and took the greatest interest in examining how these people of nature establish themselves for the long winter. The men boiled oil and mended their implements for fishing when the weather was too bad to promise a good draught on the sea between the cakes of ice. The women spun and twisted yarn for new nets; the children were sitting round the chimney fire, roasting potatoes in the ashes.

When they had left the hut to return home, Maria said, in a low tone:

"Even so, I should have been happy, Bloom, if he had loved me."

At this remark, a piercing pain shot through Bloom's heart. He had not for several days spoken of Seiler. With a great effort to appear calm, he answered:

"No, good Maria, I do not believe that. To feel happy in a situation like this, more is wanted than love. Habit and custom from childhood is necessary for it, and, besides, one must never have seen any thing better, if one wishes to be happy in it."

Maria smiled; but there was something in the smile which it was not difficult for Bloom to interpret. It told him that she considered him incapable of understanding any thing beyond the sphere of common feelings. This offended him.

"You, probably, think me as cold as those cliffs on the strand," said he, with a slight touch of vexation.

"Not that, best Bloom! You are certainly as warm and good as a man can be; yet for those who love there is a different kind of warmth, which is understood only by lovers."

"And you think that I shall never be wanted among them?"

"I know not, Bloom, what may come to pass; I only believe that neither habit nor an entire ignorance of something better are required to feel perfectly happy in a desert like this, if one lives there with the person whom one loves and by whom one is loved in return; for then there is no room in us for other feelings. Love gives life to the most dismal place, and when the soul is warm it finds nothing cold around it. But pardon me, Bloom! I seldom indulge in fancies, yet now I cannot refrain from them entirely. The most glaring contrasts sometimes awaken our sympathy."

"Yes, at a certain time," observed Bloom; "but the soul seeks that which agrees with it, and before this is found no harmony is possible."

"Ah, Bloom, how can you say so! What is to become of those that never find a soul attuned to theirs?"

"That was a dismal thought, Madame Seiler! No one is so unhappy as not to find during his life one soul harmonizing with his own."

"Yes, one," answered she, gloomily; but hastily breaking off, she took up another subject for conversation. "But, Bloom, it is very painful to me if you make use of the two words which can no longer be united,—which are 'Madame Seiler.' Show to me that friendship, and call me in future simply 'Maria,' as you did in former times."

"As you wish it, Madame Sei—, best Maria. It will make me doubly happy to be allowed to call you so in future."

They went home—and if Maria had heretofore deemed her friend cold, she changed her opinion when at his departure she read in his face the most intense pain. They agreed that Bloom was to visit her about midsummer time.

At first, the days at Fredsberg crept for Maria very slowly along, and only now she began to see what Bloom had been to her; afterwards, however, she found in her new abode that peace which blessed all its inhabitants. She learned to love her hostess, the friendly Eliza; ever more, and also the minister won her favour by his great love to his wife. Maria shared in her occupations and diversions. She longed not to leave a solitude which many other women in her condition would have deemed a kind of imprisonment or a grave.

Maria thought thus: A woman who is to be separated from her husband does well to give the world as little occasion as possible to speak of her; and her deeply wounded heart also felt best in this still, uniform life.

CHAPTER VI.

AN UNEXPECTED DISCOVERY.

The March sun had already kissed away the winter snow, and April made its appearance, but not the least information was received from Seiler.

"This good Mr. Seiler is, I must say, a fine fellow," said the count one day to old Borgstedt. "But if he does not condescend to come now, I shall send for another architect."

"Heaven grant it," answered Borgstedt. He had his own views on this subject, for he had heard the notes of the sweet serenade, which in the autumn had resounded before the grotto, and at the same time observed a figure quickly walking under the old Linden trees of the park; and the delicate proportions of it left no doubt to his old eyes who it was. However, Borgstedt would no farther meddle with such dangerous things, he was therefore silent, and only said:

"God grant it! Your lordship could do nothing better."

"Why so, Borgstedt? What do you mean? You must remember that Seiler is a very skilful young man, and, moreover, he has been recommended to me by the bishop. You will, therefore, find it necessary to treat the matter with a little consideration. I shall think on it still farther."

"Certainly, sir count; but...." Borgstedt stopped at this "but." He had no sufficient reason that he dared to allege; and the count who considered this lame objection, unsupported by a tenable reason, mere idle talk, resolved to do nothing before the end of April. If the architect should not come then, he would get another.

On the same day, Count Albano walked with his intended bride in the afternoon in the picture gallery up and down.

"How stately your grandfather looks in the beautiful uniform. This picture was made, no doubt, when he was in the full bloom of life," said Thelma, while she looked with particular sympathy on the fresh and lively features of the man with whose degenerated grandson she was destined to pine away her life.

"His appearance is undoubtedly imposing; but he is said to have been a wild fellow, a man of unbridled passions, and the terror of all mothers who had cause to fear the levity of their daughters. Perhaps you want to see him closer by," added Albano, with a contemptuous smile round his mouth, and took down the picture. At this movement he held it so that the back of it became visible; and on it stood a name which had for some time lain dimly in his mind, without being able to recollect where he had first heard it; it was the name of "James Leganger."

"James Leganger!" The count read it several times in succession with his lips convulsively contracted, till the recollection of the night in the grotto, and the pocket-book with its mysterious letters, which painted a secret passion of the architect for Thelma, stood, at once, clear before his mind.

His sickness, and the subsequent aberration of mind, had put the cause of it entirely in the back-ground; and when Albano's thoughts sometimes strove to clear up those dim recollections, he was only able, at most, to throw a very dim, uncertain light upon them, which confused him still more. But now this single name threw a clear light into Albano's soul, and through it all demons and wild spirits of jealousy suddenly awoke again. They hungered and thirsted after this long fasting.

"Good heavens, Albano! what is the matter all at once? what are you reading? you look so pale that you frighten me!" Thelma took him by the arm, and moved him gently. He had the appearance of a sleepwalker.

"What I am now seeing and reading I know not exactly," answered he, slowly, "but this name reminds me of a man who awakens strange thoughts in my mind, thoughts which made my head grow dizzy, and my brain burn, till the fire laid it in ashes. You recollect, Thelma, you once said that I was crazy; or was it not so?"

"Dear Albano, do not speak of it!" Thelma was seized with an awful shudder. She recollected, but too well, the visit she paid him after his madness had somewhat abated.

"Well, Thelma, I will not speak of it; instead of it I will put a question to you, which I have forgotten heretofore to make. On the evening before my sickness—you know that I met you in the walk when you returned from the grotto—had you seen Seiler that evening, I ask?"

Albano's eyes fixed a penetrating look upon his betrothed; he seemed to wish to read the deepest bottom of her soul.

Thelma first blushed, and then grew white as the lace collar that covered her neck. She stammered hardly audibly, "Seiler—I really do not recollect that now."

"Indeed! you do not recollect that now? Why do you change colour? Perhaps you do not know why! Take care, Thelma!" Albano's voice trembled with rage; his eyes sparkled fire. "Take care! I can be kind as a lamb toward you; but do not provoke me, for then the lamb might change into a tiger, that suddenly devours his mistress, who reaches to him with her white hands a few crumbs from a table where others have already revelled their full."

Thelma sank into a chair, and covered her face with her hands. Her bosom rose and sank under the vain efforts to fetch breath. This was only a prologue to the tragedy of their marriage. She wished inwardly to die before the curtain should rise for this dreadful drama, a curtain which, as her mother maintained, was to show her the entrance to the temple of happiness.

"Do not be afraid and grow peevish, Thelma," said Albano, in a milder tone, while he raised her head with his hand to lay it against his breast. She trembled violently. She always did so whenever he touched her; but now this motion was conclusive. It seemed to her as if the tiger approached her throat to clasp it with his claws.

"Let me go! let me go!" she prayed anxiously, and tried to free her hand from Albano's grasp.

"Ha! you shudder at me! Ha! ha! ha!—a loving bride!"

He let her go, and walked up and down in the most violent agitation.

He did not dare to decide whether that which he now saw, spoke against her or not; for he had sufficient common understanding to see that fear and fright might have induced her to answer his question indistinctly. Perhaps she had actually not seen the architect.

"No, I will not condemn her upon this uncertainty," thought he to himself. "I must first have clear proof. My suspicion is perhaps nothing but an abominable birth of my jealousy. I must watch her wanderings by day and by night, and, like a skilful huntsman, go on the look out to catch my game by stealth. It was a good idea in my father to take him into our house during this summer. I shall watch him closely, yet not show the least distrust, for I might scare the dove without learning first whether she has eaten of the corn that I strewed for her."

During these thoughts Albano's face assumed a less disagreeable expression. He strove to give himself the appearance of composure, as much as it was possible for him after so stormy a scene.

Thelma observed his face through her fingers; she noticed with a calmer beating of her heart that the anger was gradually disappearing from it, and that it assumed the expression of its usual dark melancholy. At last she dared to take her hand from her face and look up. He now stood before her, and gazed on her with a heartfelt, almost supplicating look. The heart of woman is easily moved and reconciled.

"Best Albano!" said she, "I am sometimes unreasonable; don't be angry with me." She reached to him the extreme points of her fingers, that he might see she was sincere.

Albano touched them lightly, and answered in a friendly tone,—

"Indeed it is not to be wondered at, good Thelma, if you sometimes act like a child that has seen the chimney-sweeper. I have often looked at myself in the glass when my face, ill favoured by nature, became yet more hideous by some strong emotion. I promise you, however, to make an effort in earnest, henceforth to control my wild disposition. And believe, what I asked before relating to Seiler, had no meaning. I cannot entertain for a moment the supposition that Lady Ravenstein could open the doors of her heart to receive as a guest an itinerant adventurer. My sweet Thelma, be entirely calm. An evil moment became master over me. This name here stands in connection with some stories I heard when a boy. This brought me upon my grandfather, of whom I recollect yet clearly many a secret adventure was whispered about, when he was yet dwelling in the old castle, which is now a ruin, as well as the renown of our ancestors; for the present offspring—no doubt the last—will gather no new laurels."

Albano spoke the last words with an expression, for him, unusually soft, almost painful. He had touched a string in his soul, which produced a cutting discord; for even in a being so neglected as Count Albano, are found dreams of honour and glory, though they are and remain only abortions in the soul of him who cherishes them. But perhaps for the reason that they can never become any thing else, because alike the moral and physical power oppose their realization, they burn, perhaps livelier and more passionately than with healthy natures.

Astonished, and unable to comprehend the sudden change of conduct in her cousin, Thelma congratulated herself on the change which his thoughts had taken. She blushed, however, at his confidence in regard to the architect, and felt a little offended at the remark he had allowed himself as to her heart; but as things stood at present, she considered it a real wonder, a dispensation of providence, that at this dangerous moment he had recovered his composure so suddenly.

Having conversed awhile longer, in a very general way, on Albano's ancestors, they returned to the parlour; but soon after, Thelma, desirous of being alone, and pretending a violent headach, retired to her own room. She seated herself in the corner of her little sofa, put her feet upon a cushion, and leaned back to enjoy the luxury, for once, of indulging in her thoughts, undisturbed and unobserved.

In the evening about eight o'clock, a young, handsome girl came in—she was Thelma's waiting-maid. She brought tea, and served this favourite beverage to her young mistress with much delight.

"How is your headach now, your ladyship?"

"Not much better, Anna. You may arrange my bed, however. But how are things at the parsonage? You visited to-day your sister Stina."

"Ah! I believe Miss Alfhild is not well at all. I heard some strange things whispered."

"Strange?—how so, Anna? The provost told me that Alfhild's cold and pain in her chest had increased with spring, so that she is obliged to keep her room; but that is nothing so very strange. She took a cold at the fair and she has not been well since."

"Yes, no doubt, the fair was somewhat the cause of her sickness; but whether it was the *taking of a cold*, I will not say. Do not you think, my lady, that there may be some other things at the bottom?"

"No—I do not see why! I was, myself, several times at the parsonage, and heard that she coughs very badly, and cannot see out of her eyes for the cold in her head."

"For a cold in her head!" exclaimed Anna, with a roguish smile; "it sometimes happens that also the eyes of my lady are likewise red and swollen, but not from a cold."

Thelma slightly blushed. Her desire to speak now and then with some being, and though only in the subordinate position of a chambermaid, had given to Anna a certain liberty and appearance of refinement which was not at all found in her sister Stina; but she was no chambermaid, nor had she the natural propensity to refinement and ladylike behaviour, with which Anna appeared when she met at church or at the parsonage, with her friends or acquaintances.

A short pause now followed. Thelma was nibbling at a rusk; and though she was very curious to know what Anna knew, yet, after the last remark of her chambermaid, she did not dare to put another question.

"Does my lady command some more tea?"

"No, Anna, I thank you. But I had almost forgotten—did you ask Miss Alfhild for the pattern which I lent her, and now want myself?"

"Bless me! I forgot that entirely; but I know, my lady, if you had seen my utter astonishment when Miss Alfhild stood before me, you would certainly pardon me. Oh, how thin she has grown! Would to God the man had never entered her house! But the provost has always been something of a dealer in cattle; and so it happened that the Norwegian from the cattle market was invited to the parsonage to dinner."

"What are you talking about, Anna? What Norwegian, and what dinner? What has that to do with Alfhild's sickness?"

"Good God! my lady: this is just the very thing. Miss Alfhild was yet, in the forenoon, as well as could be, and arranged the purchased things to bring them here after dinner, and deliver them to their ladyships the countess and the baroness; but then happened the ugly incident at dinner, and spoiled all."

"And what incident was that?"

"Well, my lady, you can imagine that they meant to keep it a secret; but Stina is not so stupid. She knew at once why Miss Alfhild fainted when the Norwegian, who was to buy some cattle at the parsonage, related that the architect was married in Norway, and had so beautiful a wife that it would be difficult to find the like of her in all Norway."

"The architect married! You speak in a dream, Anna!"

Thelma at this news was suddenly taken by a cough like that of Alfhild, though that of the latter was natural, but this of Thelma nothing but an innocent means of concealing from the sharp-sighted servant the impression which her story made upon her.

But this was not necessary, for Anna's sagacity did not go so far as to suspect the possibility that the swollen eyes of Alfhild and her lady could have the same cause. She only supposed that Thelma would not believe her words, and therefore answered somewhat sensitively:

"If I speak in a dream the Norwegian has probably done the same, when he said that he had been in Seiler's house, and had seen his wife, who could compare with the fairest in the land. And you can imagine, my lady, that Alfhild did not faint for nothing. No, it is certain that she was so much overcome by this news, that she could not recover herself at all. Besides, every body at the parsonage knows that she liked the architect; and when the poor girl heard that he was married, one can easily imagine how it must have affected her. You, my lady, can easily imagine yourself in her place."

"Be silent, Anna!" commanded Thelma, in an uncommonly severe tone. "Your prattling increases my headach. Go and get me a glass of water from below, and then go your ways. I shall ring when I want you."

The little Anna, who was not accustomed to be put off in this manner, thought to herself, my lady shall wait long before I shall tell her again any news; for since her news found no better reception, she believed them wasted.

In the meantime Thelma lay there, covering her burning face with both her hands. What news!—Seiler married! and loved by Alfhild, and she thought of herself. The room grew too close for her, and her breast too narrow, so that she feared she would be suffocated. Good God! was then Seiler a villain, an abominable despicable man, who made use of his beautiful figure, and his captivating, dangerous manner, to entice young, inexperienced girls into his snare, and who was capable after seeing them caught, of laughing with fiendish joy at their torments, like a simple boy who delights in the writhings of a tormented worm? No, no, that was not possible! Those large, black, sparkling eyes did not lie with every glance they sent—and those lips, that could smile like no other, certainly did not open to mock what is best and noblest in this world. But on the other hand, what had these dangerous lips spoken to confirm her in the illusion in which she herself indulged with too much weakness? Thelma put this question to herself, and she could not but own, that no word had ever come from his lips. Deep, bitter sighs tortured her breast, that was already cramped to the utmost, when she thought on the evening walks to the grotto, and the serenades, and the star that he sung had risen in his heart. Was it then so very clear that all this referred to her, and not, perhaps, to Alfhild? But no, if so, then the song would not have always resounded from the grotto, and only before it. Fear and hope were thus contending for the possession of her heart. Now was a deep shadow thrown between them. It was the recollection of Seiler's icy coldness when he took leave at the castle of Hammarby. Thelma trembled. The die of hope showed its blank side, and it retreated in a deep abyss, which her eyes could not fathom. Another ghostly shadow now joined the former, and assumed gradually Albano's figure, commanding her to suppress every feeling, and to die; for he alone was master over this heart.

Thelma lay motionless with her eyes closed; her cheeks had ceased to burn, as well as her heart; and all was cold and drear.

"Ah! if he only be no despicable man," sighed she. "Why has he concealed from us that he is married?.... But the rumour is, perhaps, unfounded; the provost has said nothing of it."

Thelma wished to put only one question more to her waiting-maid. She entered now with the ordered glass of water, which she had been very long in bringing; for Count Albano had met her, and desired to know how his bride was, and she had not been able to get away from him very soon.

"Hear, Anna," began Thelma, without any further introduction; "if the story you told me is true, can you then explain to me why it is that Provost Frenkman, who generally likes to tell news, has not told a syllable of it here?"

"Oh, I can easily imagine," answered Anna, "the reason of that. You know, my lady, that the architect when he comes back, is to stay here at the castle; it is, therefore, evident that the provost has declined taking him into his house on account of Miss Alfhild; and it is not to be expected that he should speak of his own affairs here at the castle. No, that is certain, and this the more so, since the very same evening when Stina was in the room to wait—the Norwegian had left—the provost said to Captain Oernroos, as if accidentally; 'Hear, Sebastian; the matter is by no means so certain. This Norwegian cattle-dealer is a great storyteller; and I never liked scandal. If the architect had said himself that he was married, there would be an end to it: but if he is not, we should do him no agreeable service by telling that he is. And therefore,' said he, 'I would advise that no one in my house should spread this rumour among the people.' Stina now knew how matters stood, for the provost gave her, at the same moment, a wink with the eye, that she was near fainting herself; she collected herself, however, but she trembled so much when she offered a dish to the provost, that he looked at her kindly, and said: 'You must not take things at once so much to heart, Stina! I only mean to say that the rumour of the marriage of the architect should not be spread from here; for this talk might injure Mr. Seiler!' Stina bowed behind the chair as low as she could, and thanked heaven when the gentleman left the table, and she could go into the kitchen to breathe freely. If we now put all things together, then we see, my lady, that all is very plain and natural."

"Yes, indeed, Anna, you are not without sagacity; but, as the provost does not wish at any event—and I think he is entirely in the right—that such rumours should come from his house, you will see yourself that it is your duty to be silent likewise on what you have heard from your sister. And I, too, shall speak to no one of this matter, which in fact does not concern us at all."

"No, my lady, it does not concern us at all; but poor Miss Alfhild has so much more concern in it," replied Anna. "You can think that her grief about this abominable man will break her heart. And is it not shameful that he deceives her in this horrible manner? It is indeed a shame for a married man. But you know, my lady, that I can keep a secret."

After Anna had given her the glass of water and finished her speech, she withdrew, and Thelma was left alone with the stream of her thoughts. She had never believed that the proposition of the count to let the architect stay at the castle, would be accepted, as her aunt was always opposed to it; but after what she had heard from Anna, she doubted of it no longer, for it was very natural that the provost, under the present circumstances, could not take the architect into his house. It was, therefore, certain that he would come and live under the same roof with her, and that she should see and hear him every day. Thelma made an effort to turn her thoughts from this subject upon Alfhild. The kind, good, dear Alfhild—what might be her sufferings? Thelma felt it deeply, and the only thing that was incomprehensible to her was, that she had not long before observed that Alfhild loved her guest. She certainly believed him unfettered by any tie, and he had perhaps practised his dangerous art upon her also.

"No, he is not a good man; he is a...."

Thelma's thoughts here stopped; a bitter pain gnawed at her heart, for it was here where all her efforts to excuse him concentrated as in a focus; and it is a painful feeling to be obliged to despise him whom one loves.

CHAPTER VII.

SEILER'S RETURN.

UNCLE SEBASTIAN marked the past day with a large cross in the almanac. It was the twelfth of April, a real day of sorrow. His old, faithful horse, which, like a dear comrade, had shared joy and sorrow with him, had grown so decrepid by age that he had been obliged—though with a heavy heart—to condemn him to death; and it had this morning been, with all solemnity, shot through the head, which put an end to all the sufferings of a useless life.

Uncle Sebastian, who no longer possessed many beings to whom he was devoted with true affection, had loved the old horse particularly; and it might be almost said, that Alfhild and this old horse were the only objects of his care. To this was added, that uncle Sebastian, being himself old, could not help thinking that, after Polle was gone, his turn would come. All this had put the old man so much out of humour, that, in order to indulge undisturbed in his thoughts, he locked himself up, and did not want to see any body.

The provost was absent on a journey of business; Alfhild sat alone in the sitting-room, and was spinning, but the fine thread she drew from the flax would not become even, and broke every moment. She tied it together again and again, but to no purpose. Fatigued, she left, at last, the spindle alone, let her hand drop on her lap, where she mechanically played with the scales that had fallen down.

After a few moments she took out a chain which she wore round her neck under the kerchief. To it was appended the golden medallion, holding the portrait of the architect. Alfhild held it up to her eyes; but the falling tears soon covered all its features. "Oh, Seiler, Seiler!" she uttered this name in a low tone, and the last time it was interrupted by a sharp, continued cough, which she could not get rid of, and which, in spite of all applied medicines, grew worse and more dangerous. The deep grief which gnawed at her young heart contributed to increase its pain. She wished, however, to show herself strong, and would not allow herself to be sick; but continued to attend, as usual, to her domestic duties.

When the painful fit of coughing had ceased, she held the picture up again, and after a few moments struggle, she touched it with her lips; but during this her limbs were shaken by a light chill, and she pronounced Seiler's name in a painful wailing tone. At this moment the door opened. Alfhild's mind was far away, and she did not see or hear till she felt herself clasped by two arms, and pressed to a heart which constituted her world, her happiness and life. She rested on the breast of the architect. He covered her burning brow with kisses, and only one wish was in her soul—this, that she should never awake from this blissful dream. But, alas! she soon awoke; the image of Seiler's wife stepped in between the two. With the whole force of her delicate, emaciated hands, she thrust him off.

"What do you wish, love?" was all she could utter, and covering her face with her hands, she turned from him lest he should see her horror at the sight of him.

"Alfhild, is this you? what is the matter?" asked Seiler, and stepped back with great surprise.

She was not able to answer. The cough which she had restrained broke out anew with greater vehemence. The architect held her in his arms, though she strove to free herself, and showed the greatest feeling of horror at every motion. It was of no use, his other hand supported her head.

"My only, my dearest Alfhild! I know not if it is perhaps an evil dream; but certainly you have not been careful of your health," said Seiler, complaining in a heart-rending tone.

Her look, which met his, reflected the affliction of her mind; her lips, however, quivered too much to be able to speak. He conducted her to the sofa, and adjusted its cushions into a comfortable seat. The pain at her heart increased while her physical pain abated. She lay still and gave rest to her body and soul; Seiler stood for a few minutes silent before her.

"That was a gloomy and singular reception, my dear beloved Alfhild," whispered Seiler in her ear, in a caressing tone.

She answered with great effort:—"How can you speak to me so, Seiler,—so—so?—Know that I—that I have found out, at last, your dissimulation;—you are married, and speak to me of love?"

She buried her face in the sofa-cushion, not to see the man blush for shame whom she adored.

Yet Alfhild might have looked up, for Seiler appeared neither ashamed nor embarrassed; the only sign of strong emotion of mind was the deep wrinkle between his eye-brows. He lifted up with his hand Alfhild's face, and turned it towards him.

"My only beloved," said he calmly and composedly, while his look expressed the warmest and holiest confidence. "It grieves me, it cuts to my very soul, that you should have heard this from any body else but myself. I was induced, however, to be silent, through a hope that I might save you the first pain, till the affair on which depends the happiness of our future, should be settled. I now see that I was wrong in my calculation; but since you know it, be patient, pious, and reasonable, my beloved, and do not believe that I stole your young heart to deceive it in its hopes, and rob it of the happiness of life. No, Alfhild, my will to make you happy and conquer all obstacles that oppose your happiness, is as firm as my love to you is warm, pure, and constant. The time I spent absent from you has not been spent in vain. A divorce from her who was my wife is in process of being effected. She has left Norway, and if she stays away three years, the bond is severed according to our laws."

"O God, what do I hear!" exclaimed Alfhild, horrified and almost motionless with fright. She had, for a few moments, listened to Seiler's voice, unable to interrupt the defence of his conduct, which was so calm, decided, and dangerous to her heart. "A divorce on my account!" she continued, "Ah, that is dangerous—that is sinful, Seiler! Is she then so disagreeable a woman, that you have not strength enough to bear the cross which you yourself have laid upon your shoulder? I have heard her spoken of in the most flattering manner."

"Alfhild, God forbid that I should confirm you in your suspicions! Maria, far from being disagreeable, ranks, on the contrary, among the best of her sex; she is beautiful, more beautiful than even you, my beloved—you hear I am not partial—but our hearts do not understand each other. We remained cold toward each other, and not a single spark would kindle the flame in our breasts. There was but one tie between us. We had a son, but God hath taken him away, and I have seen in this an approbation of my intention, which I had previously conceived and communicated to Maria. I will not conceal from you, my Alfhild, that my wife always loved me, as I have heard but now. But from this a still more unnatural relation arose between us, and we both became convinced that the only expedient for us left, was to sever a tie, entered into from duty and obedience, the minute circumstances of which I will relate to you anon. And now my dearest, my only girl, now you know enough not to disturb you any longer. Depend upon my love and my honour. After three years I shall be free, and as soon as law has spoken we shall celebrate our marriage, and I shall settle for ever in your country."

Alfhild was silent. Singular thoughts, both pleasant and gloomy, ran through her burning brain. They could not become arranged, for they had no resting point through love, which was somewhat shaken.

Engaged to the husband of another woman, married to the divorced husband, whose wife must mingle her tears in the cup of joy—could that be right—could it be acceptable to God—could that satisfy her innocent heart, which, in order to be entirely happy, must feel free from every wrong and disquietude?

Alfhild had no answer upon Seiler's consolation; the main thing was wanting, peace, which his words could not give to her. She shook her head with a painful, sad expression, and put it upon the cushion with an expression as if she did not think it worth while ever to lift it up again.

"You are now too deeply moved, my beloved Alfhild, to be able to judge rightly of me and my feelings," said Seiler, and strove to banish from the tone of his voice the displeasure which he felt, when he saw himself not justified before her who was to cherish no other thoughts but his own. "I hope, however, it will grow better when I can daily and hourly speak courage unto you. You have suffered too long alone."

"Yes, Seiler, I have suffered long enough, but not alone. Uncle Sebastian understood me from the beginning, and sought, as much as possible, to console and support me in my reverse trial. But, Seiler, what you said of speaking hourly comfort to me, will be entirely out of the question; for my father has stated to the count that he had no longer room for you. You are to reside at the castle. If my father was at home, or if uncle Sebastian had not accidentally, on account of some grief, locked himself up, we should have certainly not been allowed to speak together. My father is very angry with you, I know, though he never speaks a word about you."

Alfhild did not observe that the old familiarity which had formerly prevailed between her and Seiler had imperceptibly stole in again; but to speak with him and be cold and reserved was more than she was able to do.

"By heavens, that is very disagreeable news, my dear Alfhild," answered the architect, in a gloomy tone. "The castle would be the last residence which I would have chosen myself, since I return here a different man in body and soul. What unhappy accident is it that leads me to the scenes of my gloomy broodings just now? Singular—inexplicable!—"

He seemed to speak only to himself; his look flew through the time in which he had been absent, and through the changes that had taken place with him. His firm, true, and great love to Alfhild, it was, that had driven away from his soul all feelings of revenge and bitterness. He had therefore delayed, he would be entirely sure of himself, and as he now returned with the firm resolution to fulfil the obligations he had entered upon, now that only the hope for a happy future with Alfhild, was the star that shone for his heart; the first he meets with are the doubts of the beloved, and the second a summons from the dark powers which had once carried him along, not to let the opportunity pass unimproved. Seiler rejected, however, with disdain, every thought of giving up his love, which he had sealed with a vow, for it was too sacred for him to forget it, because of other passions.

"What is then the danger that awaits you at the castle?" asked Alfhild.

"Danger?" exclaimed he; "there is no danger! But—but—oh, you do not comprehend the feelings that are raving here!" Here he laid his hand upon his breast. "Here, my Alfhild, it has before raged as the waves of the sea in a tempest. I still feel the beating of the waves, but it is no longer dangerous. No, by heavens, it is not!"

He bent down, and his lips touched Alfhild's brow.—She was silent.

"And you say your father is angry with me? He has no reason for it. I was not obliged to inform him of my circumstances; and yet I gave him clearly to understand that there was hindrances against the fulfillment of our mutual wishes, which might, however, be overcome. He had no reason to doubt the truth of my statement."

"But this is asking much," said Alfhild, conciliating.... "Appearance was against you when the Norwegian, who dined here one day, spoke of your marriage. You must recollect that my father could not have the slightest suspicion of what you just now related. And as for the rest, Seiler, since matters stand thus—"

"Yes, since matters stand thus," interrupted Seiler, "he will approve of my reasons, and not be unreasonable. Three years are no eternity. We both are still young, and besides, during these three years, I will stay in Sweden so much, that my Alfhild shall not find time to cherish gloomy thoughts till the sacred bond shall unite us for ever."

"Ah, Seiler, many things will have changed before that time comes. I cannot, pardon me, I cannot possibly become reconciled to the cruel thought of having obtained my happiness at the expense of a noble competition. I pray you, speak no more of this. I start back from all these relations; they cloud my understanding, and love is a feeling too partial to allow me to give decision in this manner alone."

"What decision?" asked Seiler, while his lips violently quivered. "What do you mean, Alfhild?"

"I mean, Seiler, that we must no longer think on a union, of which we have at present hardly the right to speak. The future may decide this; it will develope what it bears in its bosom; yet we must not lift the veil with bold hands, and load our hearts with a burden still greater than the one they bear already. Act as if nothing had happened until you are free, and have again the right to speak of love."

"My Alfhild, you are now a real child," said the architect, while he tenderly played with her locks. "To act as if nothing had happened! That is impossible. I have your word and you have mine; the three years will soon pass over, and with exultation I shall then call you mine before God and men!"

"Yes, but till then, Seiler!"—Alfhild looked beseechingly into his eyes.

"Until then we must be patient," continued Seiler; "we can see each other sometimes, but not so often that it would give to people topic for conversation. I hope you will then be contented, and have no longer any doubts. We have also done what our circumstances demand to remain undisturbed."

"Yes; but it is not the public opinion which we have to fear most. The voice in our own breast is a judge far more dangerous than the world.—To be engaged to the husband of another woman!—My soul shudders. For the sake of my rest, my peace of heart, for the sake of my eternal salvation, Seiler, let us consider our connection broken off till—your divorce is obtained."

"Alfhild, you desire a thing which can have more dangerous consequences for both of us than the scruples that now make your heart tremble. Consider the matter well before you form a resolution which is to be decisive, and might have great influence on me. Alfhild, my only beloved Alfhild, if you could look into my heart, if you could see its trembling at the mere thought that I shall no more hold your hand in mine, then you would suppress your childish whims for fear of conjuring up again the wild storm in my breast, which your pure love, and the conviction of belonging entirely to you, has conquered and overcome."

The architect was silent; but his eyes, in which a strange dark fire glowed, spoke a powerful language, and the heavy clouds which chased each other on his brow, gave a reflection of the violent storm that raged within him.

Alfhild felt an uncertain, sad foreboding. The word of concession was already hovering on her tongue when steps were heard in the lower entry, and immediately after Provost Frenkman appeared in the door.

CHAPTER VIII.

THE SURPRISE.

"AH! your obedient servant, Mr. Architect, welcome to Sweden!"

We know that the provost flattered himself to possess a certain tact; and he would have thought it a mark of little politeness to show, but in the least, the vexation he felt at Seiler's being here. He was to suspect only gradually the contempt which the provost entertained for the *"hypocritic adventurer."*

Seiler advanced a few steps to meet him. Both gentlemen touched their hands slightly, not without visible signs of embarrassment. Hereupon the provost, casting a disapproving look upon his daughter, who rested on the sofa in a half-reclining position, said:

"Your position seems to show that you are not well; in which case no hostess is obliged to do the duties of hospitality. Go to your room; I excuse you for to-day of all domestic duties."

Alfhild rose. She was so weak and agitated that she could hardly walk through the room. But when Seiler approached to give her his arm, the provost advanced quietly, took the hand of his daughter, and opened himself the parlour door, as well as that of her room.

The trembling Alfhild was left alone; the host returned to his restless guest to continue the conversation.

"Well, Mr. Architect, you will find some changes at your return. Certain reasons, which delicacy forbids me to explain, have compelled me to forego the pleasure of your company at the parsonage; and the will of the count is, that Mr. Seiler reside at the castle."

"Indeed! That is any thing but pleasant. The castle is far from the place of building, and that is very inconvenient."

"As regards this inconvenience," replied the provost, "the count has fast horses, and Mr. Seiler has, no doubt, had opportunity to practice riding, unless he prefer to use his own vehicle."

"The castle will not and cannot, notwithstanding, afford the pleasant things which I enjoyed at the parsonage," rejoined Seiler, somewhat encouraged by the calm, though cold and polite manner of the provost.

"No, that is true. You killed here two birds with one stone," answered Frenkman, in the bitterest tone. He thought Seiler calculated too much upon his politeness, since he, Seiler, allowed himself to provoke him by so clear an allusion to what had happened.

It pained Seiler to have offended the provost, and he wanted to try whether he should succeed if he frankly stated to him his present position. In a well calculated and shrewd manner he began:

"The justice of this reproach is for me a sure sign that my most secret thoughts have been frustrated by your sagacity; this conviction gives me courage without any preliminary remarks, to express my regret that Norwegian laws dissolve the bond of an unhappy marriage not so soon as the Swedish, which allow that all may be settled within one year. In my country one of the two parties must have been absent three years before the other can sue for a divorce."

Provost Frenkman looked highly surprised upon his guest; it was difficult to determine what thoughts and resolutions were forming in his head. He answered briefly:

"Then you intend to be divorced from your wife? That is not at all handsome."

"Handsome or not handsome," answered the architect, with a slight shade of vexation, "this step is no doubt the most correct, if persons cannot live happy together. However, here the question is not about the right or wrong of the matter; this I have settled with my conscience, and our laws will do the rest. What I wished to say—and all I have just mentioned, is only an introduction to it,—is nothing more than the open, candid question whether, when my marriage is dissolved, and I ask for Alfhild's hand, you, Mr. Provost, will intrust to my care the happiness of your child, who is dear to me above all things here on earth?"

"That is a very difficult question," interrupted the provost, with great sharpness, "indeed, a very difficult question; I, therefore, hope you will allow me to defer the answer till a more proper moment presents itself to discuss this affair."

Seiler's blood began to rise. He was one of those natures that best like to tear all fetters to attain the end of their wishes. A violent storm of passion raged in his breast. Was he to have suffered all these pains, to have passed through all these struggles, that he should pine, for three years, in uncertainty at the result of his endeavours? What was to support him when the image of Maria, in her patient sorrow, with her dying child upon her arm, came before him, entreating him to return where duty and love called him? No comfort, no certainty as to the future should stand shining by his side, and drive away the dark demons. He was to remain solitary, as he was now, without other company except doubt, revenge and recollection of the victim living far from him. Was it possible to bear all this? Can any pain be compared with the torments of uncertainty? He was not to know whether a regard was waiting for him when the goal was finally attained.

In the convulsive play of the muscles in his face were shown all the changing emotions of his mind, though he strove to overcome them. The provost had never seen either him or any body else in such a state, and he was surprised at the tumult of passions. "The calm and smooth appearance of this man," thought he, to himself, "conceals passions which the love of no woman is able to soften, or to govern. He now wants to be separated from his wife, upon whom the greatest praise is bestowed; a time might come when Alfhild should meet with the same fate. No, indeed! This is out of all question."

The silence lasted very long. Seiler awoke at last from his dreams—he awoke to reality. The uncertain, or rather not very uncertain answer of the provost, stood before him in all its clearness, and slowly, with suppressed impetuosity, he remarked:

"Am I to consider your resolution as unalterable, Mr. Provost? Is there no other tribunal to which my love, my offended pride, can appeal? And Alfhild's happiness, her peace, her life, in short her whole soul that is attached to me for ever, faithfully and warmly, have they no claims to be considered by her father?"

"I hope," answered the provost with a coldness which deprived Seiler of all further hope, "I hope Alfhild, with the education she received, and with the principles of religion and virtue which I sought to inculcate into her from her tenderest infancy, will not doubt for a moment, what the duty toward herself, toward her father and the world, demands of her. It is possible that she loved you while she believed you free. I know this, however, not for certain, for I have not wished to touch upon that subject; and still less do I know whether her feeling speaks yet at present for you. The surprise by your sudden arrival may have given her, probably, the appearance of cherishing feelings which are, in fact, out of all question. Indeed, I flatter myself with the thought that she has too high an opinion of herself to be the betrothed of a married man, and that she has been able, long ago, to banish from her heart also the remotest idea of such a mis-alliance."

"Is it this you hope, Mr. Provost? You may possibly be right," interrupted the architect, who exchanged suddenly his warmth for an icy coldness. "Alfhild will be strong enough to despise the man who ventures his honour, his peace, and the warmest drops of his heart's blood to possess her. She will not degenerate from her first mother. Sigrid's blood flows in her veins. But remember that James Leganger's spirit is hovering over this house, where he drank the cup which blackest treachery offered to him, that he might drink health to his own disgrace, and consider that vengeance does not die, though it lie buried for more than half a century. Do not awaken the dead from their graves! Until now peaceful grass has grown on the mound; let no storm-wind pass over it and tear it up. May there be peace on earth, in heaven, and in the souls that long for it."

Provost Frenkman had strong nerves; but in the moment, when the last words of Seiler's deep full voice died away like the roaring of a violent hurricane, the rolling of which is yet heard though it has already passed by, he felt in all his limbs a motion like a trembling. The muscles of his face were distorted; cold perspiration stood on his brow as he recollected the first Sunday in advent, the broken cup, and many other things, which, since the present hour itself had something appalling in it, had now a violent effect upon him, and shook his frame. He strove in vain to drive away these dark thoughts; he could not succeed, however much he strove to consider them mere superstitions.

"Mr. Seiler—Mr. Architect," began he at last, in a somewhat wavering voice, "I know not how, or in what manner, you have come to know family circumstances which have long slumbered, and which have nothing to do with the present affair, nor will I ask for it; but I think that no prudent man will call up such things, which must be entirely indifferent to him, and cannot be connected, in the least manner, with the present events. We are no children that can be frightened by ghosts. Allow me, therefore, to ask you what you intend by these strange allusions?"

"What I intend, I think, you must know! If my words, however, were not rightly applied, I have nothing farther to add; for if this hour does not bring us nearer together, another will hardly do it!" answered the architect proudly, and seized his hat with a degree of self-control, which no doubt cost him much at this moment.

The provost appeared undetermined. He was like a man, who, on the border of a ditch, bethinks himself whether to jump over or to stay on the same side, because he does not know whether the leap will be successful.

"Mr. Architect," said he, hesitatingly.

"Mr. Provost!" interrupted Seiler; "permit me to bid you farewell, and to thank you for the kindness which you showed to me at your house before. What I mentioned of your family matters will be between us. Words like those we interchanged one does not like to repeat, and you may rest assured that the circumstances which made me acquainted with James Leganger's fate in Sweden will be buried with me; for though I warned you before, it cannot enter into my mind to wish to disturb the peace of your house as a return of thanks for your former kindness. Yet a higher power rules over us, and holds in its hands the invisible threads that guide our fate. By it all things will be judged that appear before its seat of justice."

Seiler advanced to the door with hasty steps. When he was already on the threshold, he was held back by the provost, who said to him with the utmost emotion:

"Mr. Seiler, we do not part as enemies. I have no right to inquire after your family connections; but I begin to suspect that there is a bond of relationship between yourself and the man whose name you before mentioned. Mr. Architect, I am a man who loves peace, and am an enemy to all violent scenes. I beg you, therefore, with all my heart, that you will let all we have here spoken together remain between us; for my relation and friend, Captain Oernroos, lived in those unhappy times, and his memory is yet filled with many pictures and suspicions respecting that period; so that I, who have nothing to do with this affair, but only wish rest to the departed shades, should be worried to death with the stories from the old man, if he once knew that a second James Leganger had been at the parsonage; and besides, under circumstances that are highly gloomy and dubious. I, who have lived more in the world than my good Sebastian, know well that the dice of life may turn up very singularly, without the world of spirits having any thing to do with them; and, in order to convince you of my perfect confidence in you, I wish to make the agreement with you, in all secrecy, that when you are in possession of the decree of divorce, you may renew your suit for Alfhild. If the girl remains faithful, and you persevere in your intention, it may be done in God's name. I give you my word of honour, the most sacred thing I can pledge, that whatever course things may take you shall have Alfhild for your wife, if she will have you, and your present tie is completely severed."

"This promise comes late enough," replied Seiler, with a peculiar twitching of the under lip. "I accept it, however, and I assure you that I shall demand the fulfilment of your promise when the hour for it is come."

There was something cold, almost sneering, in the tone of the architect. With a half bow he stepped over the threshold, and hastened through the entry to throw himself into his cabriolet that had remained unharnessed.

When he passed Alfhild's window, he saw her sitting thereat, with her head resting on one of her hands, wrapt in melancholy thoughts.

When she heard him she started and looked up. The blood rushed to her cheeks; she looked with a painful expression upon the beautiful figure of Seiler, who, with pale countenance, hastened past, and saluted her only with a light motion of his hand toward his head-cover.

"What was that?" exclaimed she, rubbing her eyes as if she wished to chase away some illusion. "Was that Seiler? Is it possible that hearts can be estranged in less than an hour? Ah, it is my father," sighed she, "who has brought this about!"

When the provost had re-entered the room, he exclaimed: "He is a devil of a fellow! He would be capable to undertake the utmost! God preserve my peaceful house from the fate of becoming the scene of events such as passed here fifty years ago!—But what fate can have brought him here?—fate?—Nonsense—fate?—Do I also come now upon the hateful subject which Sebastian is continually harping upon?—(Perhaps I may yet be converted to the same belief.) However, fate or no fate, destiny, God's providence, or, what else it may be called,—singular is the matter, notwithstanding! And it is just as singular that I suddenly feel myself attracted toward the man with irresistible power, but at the same time also repulsed by certain glances of his eyes and certain features of his face. To provoke such a nature would be impolitic, which a man of some experience must allow himself to be. I was, therefore, obliged to give him my promise. In four years—and his affairs regarding the divorce cannot possibly be arranged before—many things may be altered.—The main thing, for the present, is to be silent. My family, my honour, and clerical dignity, require that no stories should be spread abroad. People have always enough to tell without giving them topics for it."

While the provost thus soliloquized, Seiler's cabriolet flew towards the castle; but he sat in it more resembling a statue than a man. That defying expression was still about his mouth; his cheeks did not resume their color, nor his eyes their fire, till his cabriolet flew rattling over the stone pavement of the court-yard of the castle, and at one of the windows a certain face, well known to himself and us, showed itself. Yet then no fire glowed in Seiler's eyes, but—bright flames flashed up in those whose gaze was fixed on him.[1]

CHAPTER IX.

SEILER AT THE CASTLE.

"WELL, my brother, is not the person who alights there from the cabriolet, our genteel architect?" asked the Baroness Ravenstein, while she put on her spectacles and directed her eyes from the traveller upon the count, who sitting at some distance at a table, was engaged in making a plan for a new stable.

The count went to the window, and saw as he smiled graciously, and nodded to the architect, that it was so.

"Yes indeed, there he is!" said the count. "If he had not come now, he would have lost the building of the church at Hammarby; for I was on the point—but—He is a very handsome, skilful young man, and he comes just in good time to assist me in making the plan for the new out-building."

The countess sat at the other end of the room, and followed with motherly attention the expression of Albano's face. He stood in the middle of the room, busily engaged in his favourite occupation, which consisted in teazing the favourite lap-dog of his mother; but at the first mention of the arrival of the architect, he gave, suddenly, the poor dog a violent kick, and looked at the same time like an irritated tiger.

The countess said nothing; she felt, however, that the sudden change in her son from thoughtless quietude into the greatest excitement, was partly caused by the arrival of the architect, and it was not the first time that the countess observed the aversion which her son had to him. She did not know the cause of it, but hoped, however, to find it out at last.

A few moments after, steps were heard in the adjoining room, and the count himself opened the door of the parlour to give a welcome to Mr. Seiler.

The architect did not fail to make the deepest bows in all direc-

---

[1] This marks the end of Volume I in the first edition.

tions, but he did it with an ease and a manner far from all restraint, which made his whole appearance attractive. There was not the slightest trace in his face of the violent emotions which he had just now undergone at the parsonage. His travelling coat, garnished with rich cords, gave him the appearance of a cavalry-officer, which pleased particularly the baroness, who took much delight in this class of the sons of Mars.

Hereupon our hero made some handsome excuses for his unpardonable boldness in appearing before the ladies in his travelling costume; but—he smiled and shrugged his shoulders.

"But Mr. Architect did not know where to make his toilet," interrupted the count, to help him out of his dilemma. "That is the fault of old Borgstedt, who has not paid attention, though he had directions, to show Mr. Seiler to his room in the north wing. However, I believe you are handsome enough as you are. Please, sit down by me; I wish to speak with you. You have been at the parsonage?"

"Yes—I had the honour, in passing by, to thank Provost Frenkman for the hospitality shown to me; but as I heard that your lordship had been pleased to surprise me with a change of my residence, I did not wish to have my horse unharnessed, but immediately continued on my way hither."

"Well, that is good. But you have let us wait for you very long."

"Yes, it is true, somewhat; on the other hand, the weather has as yet not been favourable for building. But now I will proceed with it with double force."

"I have no doubt that you will make all effort after you have once begun;—but now come here and cast a glance at my plan; you will not, perhaps, dispute my talent for architecture. I intend to build a new stable: what do you think of this plan?"

Seiler made, with great politeness, his objections and changes, and the count was highly delighted at the insight he gained by it.

During this time Count Albano had so much overcome his first impressions of Seiler's arrival, that according to his pre-conceived plan, he stepped to the table and appeared as unembarrassed as possible, to view the bold objections and the new lines which the architect had made through the plan of the old count.

"It gives me great joy, Sir Count, to see you restored," remarked Seiler, while with a hasty glance he viewed Albano's angular features.

They were apparently calm like those of the architect; at times, however, evil looks, unobserved by the rest, fell upon each other from the eyes of each.

"You find, no doubt, Mr. Seiler, that Albano looks now in better health than at the time you left Hammarby," said the old count. "This is, however, not to be wondered at; you can also congratulate him, for he is betrothed to his charming cousin, Lady Ravenstein."

"Indeed!" The eyes of Seiler sparkled as brightly as if he were himself the bridegroom, and his congratulations breathed nothing but the choicest rose-fragrance.

The countess, who thought the familiar tone of the count toward the architect very improper, seemed to be least satisfied; and it struck her as still more improper, that the count invited the gentleman to remain in the parlour in his travelling attire,—a thing which offended all rules of propriety. Seiler pacified her, however, on this point, for he himself found it improper to try her patience any longer; and after having perfectly satisfied the count in regard to the plan, he withdrew to take possession of his room.

The countess, in whose estimation he had, for the moment, risen by this proof of his sense of propriety, turned her head a little, and seemed even to wish to smile with her pale lips, while she said to the architect that they would be happy to see him at tea, which would be served at eight.

As Seiler passed over the court-yard to the north wing, which he was to occupy, he again cast a glance towards a certain window in the east wing. The same form appeared there, but vanished again suddenly; and behind the quickly-closed casement Thelma stood now with a heart beating, far more than on the day when she, a year before, viewed the dangerous architect for the first time.

In the meantime Seiler was received by old Borgstedt, who excused his delay by some necessary business he had been obliged to attend to, but now, with great zeal, opened the door to the small handsome rooms, which were intended for the architect.

Seiler expressed his perfect satisfaction with them, and took immediate possession of them by ordering his things to be carried here, and taking all the trifles from his pockets. Among them Borgstedt's sharp eye noticed, to his great astonishment, the same pocket-book which Count Albano had had lying before him on the table in that stormy night when Borgstedt entered the grotto.

"Ah! do things stand thus?" thought the old man, while a ray of light fell into the labyrinth of conjectures in which he had long been roaming about without finding any outlet. "It belongs, then, to the architect—was forgotten by him, and found by the count, who opened it, and found there things that were sufficient to shatter his understanding. I wonder what the young count will come to now that the enemy is in the house, since such a mere trifle could turn his head. And this was—hem! hem! I don't understand. They cannot have interchanged love-letters. I will stake my life on it; they have not yet gone so far."

Seiler was too busy with himself to pay attention to old Borgstedt; and as the latter soon found it proper to continue his musings in his own room, instead of indulging in them in the room of the architect, he asked whether the guest had any farther commands, and after a few trifling questions and answers he withdrew.

As soon as Seiler was alone he barred the door, and threw himself upon the sofa. In this moment he threw off also his mask. It was painful to see the tumult that arose in his features, heretofore so calm. They were first shrouded in dark night; gradually, however, a sneering smile developed itself. Hereupon day conquered night, the shadows vanished, and it grew light enough to see the struggle between the outward and inward powers that fiercely attacked each other. The eyes shot fire, the brow glowed, the lips were contorted convulsively, and the teeth behind them gnashed.

In the breast of the architect, which but a short time before had been an abode of love and peace, the visit at the parsonage had awakened a number of hostile powers, which, bridled by him during his visit to the noble family, had now free scope, and began to rage so violently, that all the fibres, pulses, and drops of blood seemed to try their strength against each other.

The architect himself was not conscious of it, for he was an involuntary victim of his own passions. A proud selfishness, the universal foundation of the male character, formed the beginning and end of all his feelings and actions. It is, therefore, easy to imagine that he was offended by what had taken place at the parsonage, in a manner which can be comprehended only by him who, like Seiler, wants to be a god for her who loves him.

Eve was driven out of Paradise for her sin; Alfhild, however, could not be punished so severely, for the angel who guarded the paradise of love in the breast of the architect, took side for her, and would have certainly conquered, if the allusions of the provost to the state of his daughter's heart, as well as his first refusal of Seiler's sincere and open request, had not provoked and offended his proud self.

This state of irritation induced the architect to allude to certain events which he certainly would not have done in a calmer state of mind. He regretted this step; but the coldness and indifference of the provost drove Seiler to madness, though he was yet able to conceal it under an external cover of snow and ice. As is generally the case, his irritation was yet heightened by the feeling of having exposed a weakness; and, therefore, the friendly proposal which the provost made afterwards, found no longer the way to his heart. Stormy passions and gloomy thoughts barred it; and it had come with him so far that he felt a sharp pain shoot through his heart at the sight of Alfhild, which caused him to pass by her only with a light motion of his hand.

Gradually, however, the storm in his soul subsided, and on the excited sea only calm, regular waves beat at last. The architect passed his kerchief over his brow, wiped the drops of perspiration from his face, and sought to collect himself. The watch, which he took up mechanically, showed a quarter to eight; the hour for tea was near.

"Oh, Alfhild!—Alfhild! thou angel in my distant paradise, do not deceive me, or I must banish thee from it, and then all is over—it is over with both of us! Let thy faith be firm and unshaken; but a four years' trial does no longer satisfy me, and I will not grope in the dark for the goal after which I am striving."

With these words the architect rose and went to the looking-glass. He stood there for a few moments viewing his features that were still contorted; obedient to the hand of the master, they laid themselves soon in the neat order which so well becomes an inferior, when he is to enjoy the privilege of high, patronising society.

Seiler dressed himself also now with that care which he always bestowed upon his exterior, though he seemed not to lay the least value upon it; and as he gave, with brush in hand, to his curly hair the finishing touch, an expression hovered round his lips, which also the most unskilled judge of human nature would have taken for a sign of great self-satisfaction. He then pushed aside the window curtains, and looked over to the opposite wing; but he saw nothing at the window but the green blinds, which were tightly closed.

"She is already in the parlour," thought the architect, and took his hat and went down.

When he entered the parlour, it was already lighted in the usual manner; three candles burned in the chandelier, and two on the table before the sofa, on which sat the countess and the baroness. On a cushion between them lay the favorite lap-dog, who received alternately the caresses of both ladies. Opposite to the pug dog, who was half asleep, at the other side of the table, with her back to the door, sat Thelma stringing beads, which Albano, standing by her side, took with his long fingers from a small box, and put on the table.

The old count, as he was always so called, though he was yet of middle age, and looked with his forty-nine years almost as young as Albano with his twenty-four—the old count was walking up and down the room with a long pipe, with a meerschaum bowl to it, in his hand, pointing out to old Borgstedt—who stood with his back towards the stove—in which direction the new road was to be laid out, so as to follow the border of the piece of land that did not belong to him.

The company having already welcomed Seiler, came, at his entrance, into no great commotion. Thelma, however, to whom her mother whispered: "The architect, my child!" rose and courtseyed politely, yet without being able to look at him. The thought that Albano was watching her embarrassed her still more, and hence it was, that her answers upon Seiler's polite inquiries after her health, and his congratulations on her betrothal, were very much confused. She was thankful when she could resume her seat, yet this she did in such haste, that the wide sleeves of her dress passed over the table, and brushed down all the beads which Albano had arranged in rows.

"But, dear Thelma, pray do look out!" exclaimed the baroness with an angry look.

"Oh, pardon me, good Albano!" said the confused girl, and bent down to pick them up. Albano was silent; some convulsive twitchings of his lips indicated, however, the violent excitement of his mind, which perhaps hindered him from assuring his love, that it was a matter of too little consequence to need an excuse.

Seiler and Albano were kneeling on the floor to gather up the beads. The latter observed how the architect every time he deposited his share into the box which Thelma held, cast upon her supplicating, speaking looks, which his betrothed, without looking up, seemed to answer by a light movement of the eye-lids.

At length the pearl-fishing was ended; and all sat again stiff and immoveable on the ottoman. Tea was now served, and Thelma found time to recover herself.

"Are you acquainted with this vice, Mr. Seiler?" asked the count, pointing at the same time to the gaming-table, which the servants were just putting in order. "It is our usual evening entertainment to make each other *bête*, and if you feel disposed, we will play a game."

The architect answered, with a polite bow, "that he had but little skill in playing at cards, but that he would take pains by attention to supply what he wanted in practice."

The old ladies began to seat themselves around the table on which the cards and masks lay waiting. The golden snuff-box of the baroness, and the crystal phial with eye-water for the countess, together with her cambric handkerchief, were put on the table—the spectacles were wiped, and the folds of the silk dresses arranged, and then a seat was given to the pug-dog on a cushion chair.

When the ladies were ready, the count and Seiler took their seats, they cut for partners, and the architect had the great fortune to become the partner of the countess.

"We never come out of the old order, sister," said the count, while he was shuffling the cards. The baroness nodded smilingly, and was so condescending as to offer a pinch of snuff to Mr. Seiler.

While the monotonous speeches of "Boston!—six trick!—I passé!—Misère," &c., were heard at the gaming table, a whisper might be heard from the sofa, which, heard at a distance, might have indicated the greatest familiarity, but which close by, proved to be an intentional belabouring on the part of Albano.

"Ah, sweet Thelma!" said he, "how industrious your fingers are. You work, indeed, with the speed of a machine. But your eyes will suffer from the exertion. Do let me see them—you do not turn your eyes from the flower there for a single moment."

"My eyes?—those you have seen often enough, Albano; they have nothing new in them for you."

Thelma worked even more busily; being a little vexed at Albano's suggestion, the reason of which she looked through, and he blushed slightly.

"Though there be nothing new in them for me, I would take delight in the sight of their beauty. You are more sparing with them to-day than usual; what is the reason?"

It was now utterly impossible for poor Thelma to look up. She began, for embarrassment, to count the stitches on the pattern "... One! two! three! four!" Her hand and needle trembled much.

"One, two, three, four! You seem not to mind a few stitches more or less, or you would not skip so many," said Albano, in a tone which he meant to be jesting, but which was sharp like a two-edged sword.

"But, Albano, you censure me!"

Thelma took away her pattern, and, with a displeased motion of her head, put it on the other side.

"I believe I am not so fortunate," answered he, ironically, and offered to hold the pattern for her.

"Ah, how warm it is here!" remarked Thelma, observing, with anxiety, the dark clouds that were gathering on the brow of her betrothed.

"You have been working at the eagle for a very long time," said Albano, after a pause, with calm composure, "and you have not even begun yet the swan. The pattern does not seem to please you at all."

"Though it does not please me, Albano, yet I work it because it pleases you. I prefer working at the other part which resembles so much the environs of the grotto."

"Do you also love the grotto, Thelma, and listen from there to the waves beating against the rocks? That is handsome in you, and I am glad that our tastes agree in this. We will often in the autumn visit it together, for it has the greatest charm just at that season."

Albano's eyes had a singular sparkle in them when he directed them upon Thelma to observe her closely; she, however, rose to get something, and when she returned, Albano troubled her no more. Sunk into a sullen brooding, he sat silent in the sofa-corner for the rest of the evening.

CHAPTER X.

MARIA TO BLOOM.

"Fredsburg, April 30, 17—
"MY NOBLE AND GOOD FRIEND,—Three months have not yet passed—
and three months are but a trifle compared to three years. But what
is it that I long for, and that is concealed behind the veil of these three
years? What else but the irrevocable decision of my fate? I do not long
for the judgment being pronounced which stamps the seal of lasting
pain upon my poor joyless life—no! that is not possible; this would be
an unnatural wish from which my feeble heart is recoiling. And yet I
count the slow hours of the day, the days of the week, and the weeks
of the month, and look up to God with gratitude at each evening sun
that sets behind the barren cliffs. Good Bloom, how is it possible that
a being without hope and without a future, like myself, can yet long
for any thing? I do not see it. It seems to me that all must be indifferent to me, and this is in fact the case; yet I am more impatient than
ever, and wish that I could give speed to the course of time. Were
I but able to comprehend my striving,—my longing! It is certainly
not aimed at liberty, for the bird whose wing is broken no longer
soars high—and I am, indeed, contented where I am, and must be so,
for I myself insisted upon leaving my quiet, neat household, Seiler's
home, and upon seeking another among strangers. Oh! and what
should I do in a place where every object that meets my eye, or that
my hand touches, speaks of him for whose faintest smile, for whose
slightest loving look, I would day and night lie at his feet like a faithful
dog, and serve him like the lowest of slaves?—But, Bloom, I was not
granted to win that heart which beat against mine with sincerity but
once, in the moment of separation, when I returned to him his vow.
Oh, it is hard to live, but also hard to die! I am yet so young, and time
passes so slowly; would I were old!—that it is, perhaps, Bloom, which
I wish for. I have certainly wept enough, suffered enough, to thank
God when I shall see, one day, the sun set for the last time.

"You will not recognise me, Bloom. You are not accustomed to
find me weak, and hear me complain hopelessly, nor do I this always.
But when I am alone with my God, and you, Bloom, the friend whom

I esteem above all other men, then I will not pass for better and stronger than I actually am. I will return your confidence and let you look into the most secret recesses of my soul.

"I am perfectly satisfied with all that surrounds me; it is quite suited to my state of mind. Believe not that I spend all day in sighing and dreaming, and that I have entirely lost the courage and power to bear my sufferings. No, Bloom, I still seek to apply my time in the most useful manner possible for me, and the good Eliza assists me faithfully. She is so simple, so pious, so true, and without possessing education so called, has so correct and sound a judgment, that I speak to her with pleasure on those things which can support the courage of those bent low. I take part in Eliza's domestic duties. I have taken her youngest child under my care, which is as old as my departed angel. He sleeps with me, and it is my pleasure and delight to behold the feeling of satisfaction in the little one, and to let his little plump hands toss about in my dishevelled hair. Almost every day I pay a visit to one of the fishermen's huts; and it is really soul-elevating to see how its inmates, now that the sun has thawed the ice, are preparing for new activity. The men put in order their boats and nets for fishing—the women help them in it as well as they can, and the outer walls gradually begin again to be covered with fishes of all kinds. All is activity and joy, thrift and contentment. I often feel almost envious when I see these housewives, accompanied by their joyous children, go down in the evening to the strand to receive their husbands who beckon to them at a distance, and point to their rich booty in the boats.

"When domestic troubles cloud over the heavens of life of these beings, they are borne by them with patience, for they know nothing of divorce; they feel, perhaps, less correctly; but they feel happier than we do. They demand of life no more than it must grant them. Are they not to be envied?

"On Sundays we go to the chapel. Althen, my honest host, is no orator; but he is a powerful interpreter of the word of God, and his audience understand him, for he knows them. There is the greatest harmony between the shepherd and his flock.

"One aim, for which I long, approaches nearer every day. I mean midsummer-day, a festival which we celebrate so beautifully in our old, dear Norway. They celebrate it here, also, but not in the same way. However, it can be indifferent to me. There are no flowers growing in my sandy desert. The roses in my heart are faded and scattered, withered like the fishes on our huts. I have, however, yet one joy, which is the thought of your visit here. I must be so candid as to tell you, that I miss you more than words can tell, and that I regret having chosen my residence at so great a distance from you. However, I have once chosen it and it cannot now be altered.

"Have you received any news from Seiler? You may communicate it to me without hesitation. Do not fear that you will give me any pain by a candid answer: this would be idle fear. A wound that has not yet healed cannot be opened anew. Oh, Bloom! you are a happy man not to know what it is to love, to love for ever—and without hope. The fate of the galley-slave chained all his life, is not more cruel than the certainty for a warm heart to be bound with invisible fetters to a cold one. It is hardly possible; and this union calls to my mind the horrible picture of a punishment in use with the ancient Egyptians, which always made a great impression on my mind;—this was that a living man was doomed, for certain crimes, to hold for three days a corpse in his arms. If we now substitute for three days a whole life, then this forced connection of one living with one dead, gives no improper emblem of the union of a warm heart with a heart that is cold and torpid.

"Perhaps this is a feeling and thought too fanciful to find grace before your calm and clear understanding. Pardon me, then, and remember that a woman is no man. She seeks a friend on whom she can lean all her life. Her heart will seize upon a cloud when reality flies; for alone—alone—she cannot be; she may be alone, indeed, with her pains, but not with her heart; some one must live there who fills it. And when the fair feelings have faded in it, then she seeks a substitute in recollection; if this no longer suffices, the thoughts stray even farther into the dark region of tradition. Do not blame the women for it, ye strong men who want nothing more than yourselves and the power within you, to drive away grief, or to silence it.

"Farewell, good, dear friend! The beams of the moon will shine upon the solitary Fredsberg only twice more before the festival of midsummer-day will come, and with it a joyous day for me; that of Bloom's arrival! I shall faithfully watch for you. Summer has also this advantage, that one needs but half so much time as in winter to make the way from you to me.

"Farewell! You will be welcome to

"Yours truly,

"MARIA."

Bloom had just returned home from one of his wanderings through his fields and meadows, when the mail-carrier from town delivered to him, besides various other letters, also the foregoing one from Maria. The noble Bloom was, just now, more than usually excited; his way had led him past Seiler's house, and he had not been able to resist the temptation to enter it. The restlessness which troubled his sick heart had increased only still more. Since his return from Fredsberg, he had received from Maria but a very short letter, and this soon after his arrival home. She had, however, promised more minute accounts, and with the fulfilment of this promise in his hand, he now entered his study, and locked the door after him.

The burning pain which breathed in every line of Maria's letter, found a response in Bloom's true heart. He suffered unutterably, nay, perhaps, more than she herself, as he saw that the gnawing tooth of grief was destroying the most beautiful of hearts with which he was acquainted; a heart whose most secret wishes it was happiness for him to fulfil. There was, however, also, a certain fortitude in this feeble being; this gave him joy. "But three years," thought he, "three years and more she cannot possibly stay in this solitude. I must see how I can bring her nearer; perhaps another abode can be found for her. She will become, in this solitude, a melancholy fanciful dreamer. Above all things I must go and see her." So thought Bloom. He had thoughts only for her, and not for himself.

A few days after he wrote an answer. It had cost him trouble and struggle to express in his letter all the truth and warmth which deep friendship can utter, without betraying, at the same time, the feelings which glowed in his heart. These remained always in the background, tearing the honest Bloom, who did not perceive that they, like the invisible fairies, hovered on his fingers and his pen, and dictated to him, and helped him in writing. The earnest Bloom had no suspicion of this jest. "It is nothing but friendship," said he, calmly, as he sealed the letter. It read as follows:

"Maria—(Let us state, in parentheses, that Bloom had puzzled himself very much how to address her—and this is, indeed, a very delicate matter, if one does not wish to say either too much or too little. Several letter sheets, with the trivial words—'Best'—'Good'— 'Dear,' &c., had been laid aside, because all these words did not sound to him so well as the one which he did not dare to write down. At last he had satisfied himself with the one stated, and he continued):

"The unlimited confidence with which you honoured me in...."

(At the word 'honoured,' Bloom sat a long time with pen behind the ear, staring at the ceiling of his room: 'honoured sounds so stiff;' but 'delighted' could not be used, since what was confided to him was not of a nature to give delight; he, therefore, retained 'honoured.')

"—with which you honoured me, has given me a few hours of the purest happiness, however sad it was in itself, since it came from you."

(How these words came to be on the paper so fast, Bloom did not know himself; his invisible assistants were guiding his hand.)

"O, Maria."

('O,' is an exclamation which all men make use of, and this, too, under all circumstances, in prose and poetry, in speaking and writing, in love and in friendship. It has been now adapted so generally, and has attained to just respect, that no one dares to attack it, wherever it may occur. It was, therefore, no question but Bloom, likewise, might use it.)

"O, Maria, what I have suffered the last three months from the thoughts of your solitary life, which I heartily repent having prepared for you, I cannot express by words. You will hardly believe this, since you think me so very cold. No, Maria, I am not cold—much rather— too warm; but in my serious manner, which is peculiar to me, there is that composure which you believe cannot be interrupted by storms. But you are mistaken; and you, above all others, should know, that a calm exterior is not always the sign of a calm, cold heart."

(Bloom now read over what he had written. It is good, thought he; a friend, a true brotherly friend, may have the right to speak of his heart. So far, nothing had been said in the letter that could offend, or from which the most sagacious understanding of a woman could have inferred that she was loved. No, not by any means! All was well considered, and suited to the relation between them.)

"But, Maria, let me now speak of you. I fear the solitude in which you live at present affects your body and mind injuriously. Though you

have not delighted me with any account of your state of health, yet
I fear that you have suffered from the manner of life which you now
lead, and that besides the grief which now overclouds the heaven of
your life, you have also bodily sufferings which affect your spirits, and
produce the sad tone which prevails in your letter. Maria, allow me,
your best friend, who neither will nor can flatter you, to tell you, that
a woman like you, a woman with that great power which I esteem
far more than the proud strength of man, should find in this power
a protection against the weakness peculiar to your sex, of indulging
in thoughts, and creating them, which nourish grief. I do not mean
to say, by any means, that you have lost this power, that you entirely
give way to your fancy, and give yourself up to gloomy ideas. Far
from it. But as I see you on the point of falling from the height of self-
control and fortitude, on which I saw you standing before, encircled
by a halo, I hasten to warn you, and beseech you to have regard to
your peace, your future, your noble and beautiful heart, and not to
sacrifice all this to an immoderate grief, which might, at last, destroy
your health, and bend your spirit, which has, heretofore, borne all
sufferings with so much fortitude."

(Bloom again ran over the thoughts he had committed to paper,
and was most particularly satisfied with this part of the letter, which,
with the exception of a few warm expressions, might pass for the advice of a Mentor. But he now approached a subject which was more
difficult to treat on. Maria desired information regarding Seiler. Every
mention of his friend, formerly so dearly loved by him, caused him an
uncomfortable feeling, and particularly when it was made by Maria.
However, this point had to be treated on; and, after he had tried the
pen several times, and mended it, and had rubbed his forehead almost
sore, he continued as follows):

"*One* thing in your letter I would call a weakness, Maria, if, in the
same moment that I feel tempted to condemn you, I was not forced
to own that your desire is natural and pardonable; I mean your in-
quiry about Seiler.

"I have received from him two letters; the first was written on his
journey through Denmark, the second from his present place of residence in Sweden. His mind was calm, it seems to me, so long as he
was wandering through Iceland and Fuhnen; yet this, I suspect, has
changed since his arrival at Hammarby; at present his state of mind is

a riddle to me, which cannot and will not be solved. However, what I may, in my opinion, safely assume is, that certain things, unknown to us, which for years have occupied his thoughts without coming to maturity, have now approached a crisis. I know not why, but I suspect that Seiler is playing in Sweden some hazardous game, which might easily give a blow to his future fame and fortune. I hope his honour may not suffer by it. Yet natures like his cannot calculate how far to go. In regard to the progress of the divorce, he expresses only in general, a great predilection for the Swedish laws, which settle such matters in shorter time."

(Here Bloom could not help but stop. He was by no means satisfied with what he had written, partly because he had come to speak on a subject on which he had often reflected himself—and partly because he found his words very cold, though they bore the stamp of truth on them. Yet he felt that the matter itself had something in it that admitted of no warmth of feeling, even if he wanted to try it. But it did not occur to Bloom, that this icy coldness was only to be found in his heart. He did not act, therefore, what he had written, and now passed over to the last point, which he began, almost without his own knowledge: 'Dearest Maria.')

"Dearest Maria, how kind you are, and how warmly I do thank you for the lines in which you tell me that you miss me, and long for the midsummer festival! God willing, I shall be with you on St. John's day, and I must not tell you how I long for this joy, and how I count every minute; for you would perhaps smile, and not believe that the calm Bloom knew what longing was. Yet you must believe it, knowing what a solitary life I lead here in Lindensberg, on my fields with my horses and hounds. It is true, I have formerly been just as solitary as now; but so long as Maria lived near me, I did not feel this solitude in such a degree, as now, that she is far from me, and no friendly voice gives me a welcome when I approach, from old custom, the white, small house, with green blinds. Though you intrusted to me the key to this sanctuary, yet I have not had courage to enter a single time into its solitary, grove-like recesses. What I should not at all be able to bear, would be the empty chair near the stove, on which you used to sit. Your image is connected in my mind too much with all the things and places of your house, to allow me to bear it without *you*.

"Excuse me, Maria, that I expatiate so much on what I miss. Man is always selfish, when his own dear self is the matter in question; and I would fain speak yet more on this subject, if I did not fear to incur your displeasure.

"I have a plan for the summer, which I will communicate to you when I shall have the pleasure to be with you. It concerns the change of your place of residence, at least for some time—for a journey to the baths or springs, or the like. You must leave these cold grey cliffs; your friend cannot allow that these should sway you entirely. The people around you deserve, no doubt, all respect, but their souls are all a little too narrow, they have not food enough for the mind. A noisy, changing life, I like as little as you do; but an almost cloister-like solitude, for a great length of time, is injurious, unless it is shared by another loving being. Last winter you needed the deepest quiet; but to stay for three years in the same place, where one is a stranger, would be a little too monotonous.

"God preserve you, Maria! For the happiness and peace of your future, you, yourself, can offer up no warmer prayers than are daily offered up with a faithful heart, by

"Your sincere friend,

"BLOOM."

CHAPTER XI.

THE EXPLANATION.

"UPON my honour," said the count, who, having returned from a journey, had just taken his seat at table; "I heard yesterday something very singular. Fill your glasses, children; I will first tell you my news, and we will then empty our glasses upon it."

They all looked very curious at the count, who continued with a significant smile:

"Yes, indeed, I, as every one, have my spies. A marriage, ladies and gentlemen! But the matter was kept so secret, as if the point was to get away the beloved of somebody else, rather than to keep what is already possessed. And whom do you think I speak of? Of nobody else but Mr. Seiler, who is married, though he lives here with us like a bachelor; and moreover, his wife is said to be a most charming wom-an. But, by my escutcheon of nobility! He blushes like a maiden. This is the handsomest sign of the love of a husband for his wife, which I ever met with."

"Is Mr. Seiler married?" asked the baroness and countess, as with one mouth. Albano opened his eyes wide with astonishment, and only Thelma looked with a pretty natural indifference upon the painting of her empty dessert-plate; but she thanked God in her heart for the talkativeness of her waiting-maid, without which she would not have been able to suppress evident marks of surprise.

The question, "Is Mr. Seiler married?" without being answered immediately, was followed by another.

"Why did you keep the matter so secret?"

With an unembarrassed look, a look that also in the worst case, knows nothing of confusion, the architect looked around and said, as indifferently as if the greatest trifle was spoken of:

"Yes, I have been married already four years; and the reasons why I did not speak of it are two of equal importance. The *first* is, that no asked me, and I could not, therefore, mention a circumstance which had so little claim to interest others; the second is, because I thought that delicacy of feeling would not allow a man, who is on the point of being divorced, to touch on a subject on which it must be equally unpleasant to speak himself, or hear others speak."

This declaration of the architect caused still greater surprise than the news of the count, with which the latter had intended to amuse himself and embarrass Seiler. He had heard nothing regarding the divorce; for otherwise his sense of propriety would have forbidden all allusions to this subject; he, therefore, said now in a tone half jesting, half asking pardon: "Then we cannot drink upon the marriage; I intended to congratulate you on the young wife; but as you intend to be separated from her, we had better let the matter rest, for such affairs do not bear the interference of third persons uncalled for, and I am sorry to have alluded to it."

The architect bowed in silence, after a few moments the count took the glass again, and said with that light ease which passes without difficulty, and from one to another:

"Let us not forget that we have to-day the first of May; we will drink to a good crop and harvest."

Every one passed the glass to his mouth with a certain embarrassment, for the tone had become more stiff and constrained than ever. They were, fortunately, already at the dessert. The countess ate as fast again as commonly, and the rest followed this example. As soon as the table was removed the architect went to his room.

"I made there a most horrid blunder," said the count, while he took a large pinch of snuff from the box, which the countess presented to him.

"Yes, indeed, but where did you get your news, my friend?" asked the countess.

"Yes, where? my dear brother," joined the baroness, who was highly envious.

"Where I got it? On the public road, I must say, as I rode yesterday to Babingsbro."

"But from whom?" asked the ladies, who demanded the most minute account.

"From whom?" repeated the count; "that is a different matter. I have already told you that it is a secret; and you must not think, my ladies, that I will betray a name when I promised to keep it secret. That is against the laws of honour, and I cannot consent to offend against them, though I should incur your displeasure."

The whole matter was simply thus: old Borgstedt had given a hint to the count on the real state of affairs, after he had received due information himself from his friend Captain Oernroos. Yet Borgstedt had not considered himself justified in touching upon these matters till he had observed, in his promenades by night in the court-yard, that the windows of the architect were kept open in the evening, too long for the cold month of April, which the kind old servant thought the more unhealthy, because the melting notes of a singing lady's voice from the east wing could be heard in this way distinctly in Seiler's room. On these promenades apprehensions arose in the mind of old Borgstedt. He believed that the architect could not be trusted, and the young lady must needs know of Seiler's marriage. The matter was, therefore, communicated to the count as a subject for joking, with which he might teaze the architect on account of his reverie. Old Borgstedt kept, however, to himself, that the latter had already cast his eye upon another one—nay, perhaps upon two. He exclaimed, however, the oftener when he was alone: "This architect is an abominable man! May God guard our young lady, the angel!"

The explanation which the count had given to the ladies did in no way satisfy them. They could not understand why so indifferent a matter, as whether the architect was married or not, should be a secret.

"He has himself given a very clear statement," answered the count.

"The architect is a man of tact; he would not be guilty of so great an offense against good breeding as to speak of his runaway wife."

"Yes, indeed, that is so; but you must grant, my dear brother, that the affair looks somewhat singular, at all events. I wonder whether the provost knows of it."

"No doubt he knows of it," answered the count, who did not suspect that he implicated himself by these four words, in a whole labyrinth of questions.

"Well, if he knows of it," answered the countess, in a tone which showed her wish to give the conversation a different turn, "why, then, has the provost kept the matter such a secret as if it were contraband? He generally likes to tell news whenever he can get any."

"No doubt he knew of the marriage," interrupted the baroness, who noticed what the countess aimed at; "no doubt he has known of it, since he made up his mind so suddenly to change the residence of the architect. And Alfhild's sickness, as well as Frenkman's embarrassment when he met the architect here last week, have likewise their reasons. The old Sebastian has, perhaps, played lottery, and come out with a blank."

"With a blank!" remarked the countess, in a very piquant tone; "I hope the provost and the girl will be on their guard."

"But, my dear brother, they know, no doubt, something certain about all these matters," continued the baroness.

The count stood as between two wells that have abundance of water. He would have liked best, if it had been proper, to have returned with both hands to his ears, as quick as possible to his own apartments. But he had too much gallantry for such an incivility; he, therefore, prepared himself to give as much as possible of the truth intrusted to him, and buy his liberty with it.

"Well, I will no longer make a secret of what I have heard," said the count, in a serious tone, "and this is, that the matter is just as you suppose; for the property of the provost, together with that of uncle Sebastian, and Alfhild's beauty, are sufficient to let one see into these matters. In fact, then, all explanations were superfluous, yet I will give them to satisfy you. People say that the architect paid last year a great deal of attention to his host's daughter, and even won, as people suppose, her affection; whether this happened with or without his endeavor, that is a matter on which neither I nor any body else can speak with certainty. In short, the provost heard accidentally that the architect was already married, and under these circumstances it was very natural for him not to let him reside in his house this year, and as well as for us to let him reside at the castle. One must always have a due regard for family secrets, and therefore, my opinion is, to keep perfect silence on this whole affair, with all its minor circumstances."

The countess and her sister were of entirely the same opinion, particularly since they now had all the information they wanted to see clearly. Their view was in regard to the architect, who was still in great favour with them, that he might very well marry the parson's daughter after his divorce was effected. Hereupon they agreed to act as if they had heard nothing of all these, and as if they had forgotten Seiler's domestic affairs long ago.

The baroness, the count and countess forgot them, indeed, yet the same week; for it was for them nothing but a little insignificant burglary affair, in which they might interest themselves for a few minutes, on account of its mysterious appearance; but no more.

Upon Albano and Thelma this news had an entirely different effect. To him all was like a dream, but like one from which one awakes with great surprise, without being able to recollect what one dreamed. The grotto, with all he had seen there, came before his mind. He tried to recollect the contents of the two mysterious letters. Some commission had been spoken of there, which was, no doubt, connected with Seiler's divorce; *this*, then, was meant by it, and the love, the storm in the architect's breast, which drove him to this step, was not caused by his love to Thelma, but by that to Alfhild. At least, according to all he had heard and seen, the one might be as much the case as the other. A ray of light fell into the night which generally prevailed in Albano's soul; he had in his breast a feeling of peace and reconciliation, which was rare for him.

"I did the man injustice," said Albano, half aloud to himself; "I did Thelma injustice; what I thought I saw was only a creation of my own mad fancy. Some future time, when I have entirely convinced myself of the fallacy of my apprehensions, I will make amends for it by a confidence which I hope will satisfy her."

This was the first time, for many years, that so peaceful, mild feelings, desired to be harboured by him, and found really a reception in the distrustful and dark heart of the sickly youth. He now imbibed this air of life in full draughts; his condition, perhaps, resembled that of a child which sees itself for once freed from its strict keeper, and now, in God's free nature, runs after a butterfly, in the full conviction of catching him.

But of what nature were the images that passed before Thelma's soul, and what thoughts kept the sway in her heart, after she had heard from Seiler's own lips the affirmation of his expected divorce?

On this point, one could not judge him like any common man; but even with the greatest indulgence towards him, one could not help but see something wrong and inexplicable in his conduct, which excited her indignation, though another stronger feeling hindered it from striking root in her heart.

What occupied her thoughts more than all the rest, was Seiler's relation to Alfhild, if there was, in fact, any relation between them. She had received so many silent proofs of affection from the architect, that she could not suppose that this was the case also with Alfhild.

But if this was so? Thelma was shocked at this double-dealing. She might, long ago, have obtained certainty on this, yet she did not dare, but avoided most carefully to mention Seiler's name in the presence of Alfhild.

A few days after these events, the architect one evening came home earlier than usual. As he entered the court-yard, he noticed Thelma and Albano sitting under one of the high linden trees. Seiler intended to continue, after a brief salutation, his way to the wing which he occupied; but the young count, with a complaisant politeness, called out:

"Will you not take a seat by us, Mr. Seiler? The evening is so beautiful, that my betrothed would like to spend it in the open air; and as I have to write a letter, I would request you to keep her company in the mean time."

Seiler bowed consentingly. Thelma looked with long and anxious glances after her betrothed, who walked up the staircase, and nodded to her once more, smiling, before he went out of sight.

This was the first time that Lady Ravenstein and the architect were left alone, without witnesses. They had never spoken together alone, and but very little in company. Thelma felt, therefore, in this remarkable moment, a restlessness which she strove in vain to conceal under the mask of forced indifference. She was now engaged. The serenades at the grotto, and the ardent looks which flashed from the eyes of the singer, ought no longer to be intended for her; and if anything gave her satisfaction, it was the circumstance that Seiler, whatever his feelings might be for her, had never expressed them in words, which would have certainly increased the embarrassment of the present moment.

"I would esteem myself happy," said the architect, as he took, in an easy manner, the seat near Thelma, which Albano had just left; "I would esteem myself happy, if I could make myself worthy of the confidence which the count was pleased to honor me with, by condescending to let me entertain his betrothed."

The words, "his betrothed," which Seiler much emphasised, sounded to Thelma, out of his mouth, particularly unpleasant. In a firm yet subdued voice, she therefore answered:

"Count Albano's betrothed has so few claims that they can be easily satisfied."

"If Lady Ravenstein would make but the least demand from her most obedient servant, he would esteem it the greatest fortune," replied the architect, with a bold finesse, using Thelma's words as a weapon against herself.

"I spoke only generally," said she, with a diminished gravity, but with deeply flushed cheeks.

"Is it possible that I have been so unfortunate as to offend you?" Seiler skilfully asked, in a different tone. "I should feel very unhappy to have been misunderstood; for can it be a crime to wish that you would make a demand, though ever so small, of a man who wishes nothing more fervently, than to give you some pleasure, though but for a few moments?"

It was Thelma's misfortune that she looked up just now, and saw the dangerous eyes with a supplicating expression, and at the same time with that of the greatest tenderness, resting upon her. In the insinuating tone of Seiler there was, moreover, a power over her soul from which she strove in vain to free herself. At this moment she could have wished that she could neither hear nor see; but she saw and heard against her will.

"You are no longer angry with me?" The architect bowed, at this question, so low that his locks almost touched the folds of her dress.

Thelma thought she should die. She recollected the evening when, sitting at Albano's bed, she felt herself suddenly clasped round by his arms, and she strove with all her might to free herself. It was now her soul which sought to unwind itself from a power which appeared to her almost like enchantment. She wished to rise and leave him, as her sensibility suffered by staying longer, and yet she felt herself held fast by invisible bonds.

She had never seen Seiler so closely. The wind was playing in the fine locks of his black hair; his forehead shone in the dark as white as marble; yet a singular cloud was resting on its arched brow; his eyes, as he turned them up to her, burned with a fire which she could not bear, and round his lips, that opened for a sigh, played a subtle pride, which was but ill-concealed under the mask of timid reverence.

The impressions she received now, were not of the same enchanting, lovely nature, as those at the grotto. There was always, and at present more than usually, an inexplicable charm for her in the manner of the architect; but as she now examined each of his features separately, they excited in her a fear for which she could not find the key; but, when looked upon together, they were irresistible for her.

No answer had as yet escaped her lips. She blushed at her silence, which was more speaking than words, yet she could not break it.

"You are not angry with me?" he repeated, and the respectful tone of his voice gave her courage to answer:

"No, not in the least," and thus put herself in a new and advantageous position towards her neighbour.

However, before another word could be exchanged, the old count entered the court-yard, and declared with a fatherly solicitude, that it was too cool for her to remain any longer out of doors.

Thelma quickly rose: she seemed to regard this interruption more with a feeling of satisfaction than regret, and hastened before them up the staircase, whilst Seiler, who had begun a conversation on the new out-building, slowly followed with the count.

CHAPTER XII.

ALFHILD VISITS SEILER.

"Come out of doors a little, my child, and see how finely your flower-bulbs are running up—you never had more beautiful flowers," said uncle Sebastian, as he entered, with hat and cane, Alfhild's room, to ask her to promenade with him through the garden.

The grief of the old man about his departed faithful quadruped, had subsided, and he now turned all his thoughts and care upon his only darling; "for," thought he, "I must take the child under my care, or she will die through all these troubles."

"It was only last evening that I was in the garden, dear uncle," answered Alfhild, and the tone of her voice showed distinctly that she wished to stay in her room.

"Last evening, my love? Do you call that having been in the garden? You turned round in the first path, saying that all was very beautiful, without looking round or being able to see, as it was dusky, and misty besides. No excuse, my child, you must see the flowers now. We have to-day weather which the very angels in heaven must be delighted with. The sun is not burning, but mild and refreshing."

Alfhild's bad cough, which even the warm air of June could not check, hindered her from answering. She put her head on her hand, and when she again looked up, her eyes were full of tears.

"The cursed cough will kill you yet," said uncle Sebastian, in a sad tone; he knew, however, very well, that it was not always the cough that filled the blue eyes of his darling with tears.

"Do you drink every evening your elder tea, with honey, my child?"

"Yes, every evening and morning," answered Alfhild, "but the cough will not yield."

"No, indeed—heaven knows. But you must not think, my child, that it will do any good, if you shut yourself up in this way; on the contrary, the best you can do is to be out of doors and breathe God's fresh air. Come, put on your bonnet, put your shawl on your arm, and follow me; for do not think that I will go without you."

Alfhild made no further objections, but yielded silently to the will of the old man, and they were, soon after, walking in the paths of the garden, which were neatly strewn with sand. Uncle Sebastian called Alfhild's attention to where some shrubbery was to be tied up, and some weeds had to be plucked out, and the like. She assisted him, and seemed to delight in the splendid colours of the flowers which fringed the footpaths—but—also in this delight there was a want of life and sympathy, which uncle Sebastian's most earnest efforts could not supply.

"Let us sit down a little while," said the old man, and he led her to the moss bank near the house, where she had sat last year, almost every evening, with Seiler.

Alfhild shuddered; she always avoided this place, and as uncle Sebastian drew her down against her will, she could not possibly conceal her emotion; she let her head sink down upon the shoulder of her faithful friend. The old man, as if suspecting what was passing in her mind, spread his kerchief over her face "that the flies might not trouble her," as he said, but in fact, in order not to see the outbreaks of grief which he could never look upon, without feeling himself a suspicious twitching in the eye-lids.

Thus they sat for a good while without speaking. The old man's heart grew softer; he ejaculated, however, at the same time one harsh soldier's expression after the other. "The rascal!"—this word was not a very refined one, but he had no other at hand—"to cause such a havoc in a heart which received him with so much confidence. Indeed, if I should get him for once in my clutches," muttered he; but immediately after he sighed deeper than ever, as he imagined himself a weak old man, opposite the powerful figure of him who was in his best years. This was an idle thought, and would have only exposed him to ridicule.

The provost had told Oernroos of his conversation with the architect, save only the points relating to the divorce, and his answer, that Seiler, after the legal affair had been settled, might ask once more for Alfhild's hand. Sebastian had approved of this; but when he considered that Alfhild's happiness was to depend, one day, upon a man of Seiler's character, then he shook his head doubtfully. He did not believe, however, that she would be able to bear this unnatural excitement for three or four years, and as often as he thought of it, and heard Alfhild cough, he wished the architect to the devil. At the same

time he was constantly thinking over how he might soothe the affliction of his darling, and at last he thought that another introduction
of Alfhild with Seiler was the most appropriate expedient for it. He
knew that Alfhild's grief had been increased by the conviction that
Seiler had left the parsonage in anger. She had told him—her uncle—
of their meeting, and of his cold departing look, which hovered continually about her. Seiler had not heard, it is true, her last word in the
matter, but perhaps he did not think this necessary, and thought all
settled; and she could not but believe that it was anger and not grief
with which he departed from her.

"Why, child," said uncle Sebastian, slowly, while he was taking
the kerchief from Alfhild's face; but suddenly, as if he had burnt his
fingers, he drew his hand back, and let the cloth lie, and was silent.
The old man held now in silence, the following conversation with his
two allies, weakness and reason.

"The cursed fellow! Upon my honour he is no better than a common scoundrel. I wish this had happened twenty years ago. Yes, by
heavens, I would have challenged him; for it would have been a trifle
for me, as it is now easy for him, to deceive poor Alfhild. Can then a
man choose no other sport, and especially one who has already his
position? But the girl here looked just now, when I raised the kerchief,
first crimson red, and then as pale as the lilies here in our garden.
This is, indeed, grief, and such an one as will consume her life. I wish
I but knew why he did not give her a friendly glance as he passed her
window. Women are now so fragile that they bend at once, like reeds,
when a wind blows on them. The provost, no doubt, provoked him;
but as he has given him permission to come again and ask for her
hand, I think it can do no harm—for the girl is, evidently, grieving
herself to death. Then, if I—indeed it can be no sin, especially as he
has given him this permission."

Uncle Sebastian's conscience seemed to be in conflict with his
desire to soothe Alfhild, and his sense of propriety which disapproved
of the step he was about to take. He could not, at the same time,
conceal from himself that he would not have thought of executing it
if the provost had been at home; but now—uncle Sebastian seemed
to have made up his mind. Things could not grow worse than they
were already, he thought, and taking the kerchief from her face, he
said,—

"Hear, my child; it occurs to me that we might take a walk to the building ground. We must see once more how far they have gone on with the new church; I have not been there for ever so long."

"To the new church, dear uncle! What are you thinking of?" Alfhild raised herself—a ray of joy flashed from her eyes; yet it soon disappeared again. She said with a sad smile: "That will not do;" and she relapsed into her former sadness.

"It will not do, that we see how our new church goes up? That will do very well. It is not at all certain that he is there—and if so, what then? You cannot avoid seeing him again somewhere; and your grief will be less if you know what made him so unfriendly at his parting. The man has a will of his own; but I know that a kind word from your lips will calm the storms in his breast."

"Yes, he often told me so himself, dear uncle—if I only knew that it was not wrong, and that I should not feel worse after it, then—And I should not be able to support another look like the one he gave me from here."

"No, certainly he will not do that. He was raging at that time, and you know men's eyes do not look love in such moments."

"That is true, uncle; but why has he not been since to see me?"

"Why has he not been to see you? How could he, since your father told him, he should not come and ask again till the divorce was effected? You must see that there is an end to his coming until then, as your father thought."

"Well, dear uncle, then it must be wrong for us to seek him at the building. God knows that I would give many weeks of my life for the happiness to refresh my heart once more by the sight of his endeared features; yet I will do nothing for which I shall afterwards have to reproach myself as being improper; nay, perhaps sinful."

"You draw on your fancy, my child; indeed you do. We will only walk about a little, enjoy the beautiful evening, take a view of the building, and speak a few words with the architect if we find him there. If that be improper or sinful, I do not know the meaning of either. Do, however, just as you feel disposed; I meant well towards you, and thought it would do your sick heart good."

"So it certainly would," answered Alfhild, with emotion; "and since you think, dear uncle, there is no harm in it, I am happy to go with you. I would like to comfort him a little, and be comforted my-self; then we both shall feel better."

They passed through the red painted lattice gate, and directed their way to the building ground.

The fresh glorious scenery before them had a soothing effect upon their minds. Alfhild had not seen it since June had clothed the fields and woods with its green velvet dress. She drank in full draughts the warm spring air which played in the foliage of the trees, and her locks. On the one side of the hill there lay the old grey church, and mirrored itself in the smooth surface of the calm lake, like an eagle whose wing is lamed by a shaft; on the other side rose the white walls of the new house of God, like a swan rising out of a lake from a bath, to lay himself on the moss of the green shore. In the back-ground appeared the large ruins of the old castle, and the new one shone in the rays of the evening sun. The whole was encircled by a frame of green hills, at the foot of which peaceful fields of corn and many coloured meadows wound themselves along. Nature seemed to hold a sabbath, so peaceful, quiet and beautiful was all around in her kingdom. But suddenly resounded from the building ground the confused noise of masons and workmen, who, after the vesper hour, continued their work with renewed vigour, and executed the orders of the architect, that were heard far and wide. He stood on the high-est scaffolding, with his back turned toward the approaching visitors. Alfhild's arm convulsively pressed that of her uncle.

"Do you see him?" she asked, almost breathless. "Is he not mag-nificent? Do you not find that as he is standing there aloft, waving his white handkerchief over his head, he looks like a..."

The maiden trembled at the bold flight of her imagination, and uncle Sebastian did not hear, for the present, to what she likened the architect. They drew nearer the scaffolding on which Seiler stood, in the most unrestrained position.

"For heaven's sake, look out!" the architect was heard to call out, just as a shower of gravel and sand was falling down. He was near losing his balance and falling down himself, when he discovered that it was Alfhild and her old friend who stood below. They had already stepped aside, and did not seem to be in any manner exposed to dan-ger. The architect saw that they would perhaps be reached by the falling stones. He called out, therefore, in a subdued voice, but in a cold and polite manner, while he took off his cap a little, and bent himself, as far as possible, over the scaffolding,—"The place there is unsafe; the lady and gentleman will please to go a little farther to the right." Hereupon he turned round, and continued to with the greatest calmness to give his orders, as if nothing had happened. Alfhild was scarcely able to hold herself upright; she trembled so much that uncle Sebastian's weak arm could no longer support her. They took, therefore, a seat upon one of the stone blocks that lay scattered about.

"Do not be grieved, my dove; I meant it well with you; but this man is a monster that would at last devour you if you should fall into his claws," said the old man, while he stroked the hand of his favourite which he held in his own.

Then they heard quick steps behind them, and the architect, red and heated, with his cap in the one, and his handkerchief in the other hand, stood by them.

"I beg your pardon a thousand times," said he. "I wished to be able to come down immediately, but my duty detained me yet for a few minutes; but now I am free, and it will give me much pleasure if you will allow me to accompany you a little on the beautiful way to the parsonage."

"Ah, you magician!" said uncle Sebastian, half aloud; yet he was glad of his coming; for did not the roses return on Alfhild's pale cheeks,—and did not a ray of sun flash through the mist which continually veiled her eyes? "Ah, what power has love!" murmured Sebastian, and pressed Alfhild's finger points in order to encourage her to speak. He himself had so great an aversion to Seiler, that he did not wish to engage in a conversation with him. But he might have pressed the fingers of the poor girl till blood had flowed without being able to open her lips, had not a particular circumstance come to her aid.

This circumstance was, that a workman came up to speak with uncle Sebastian, who was on all occasions consulted by all the parish.

"God bless your honour," said the workman, with a deep bow, while he busied his hands, for embarrassment, about the old fur cap; "could I speak a word with your honour?"

"O yes, why not, father *Anders?*" answered Sebastian in a friendly tone, and stepped aside with the man, who seeing the captain so very liberal with his time, improved the opportunity to unbosom himself, and in order not to be misunderstood, represented his affair from all sides.

When Seiler saw himself alone with the object of the warmest feelings of his heart, he felt himself entirely disarmed. Offended pride, distrust, petty revenge, all these low feelings were silent, and his spirit soared up free and spotless to the temple of sincere love.

"Oh, my Alfhild! my charming, pure angel," said he; "why have you been so long invisible for me? Why have you let me pine so long after a look from your eyes? They are the light of my life; I have been groping in the dark since I saw you."

"And yet, Seiler—how did you look at me when you left our house?" answered Alfhild, in a low voice, without looking up.

"Ah! do not mention that day. Your father, Alfhild,—Oh, he is an icy, cold man—had provoked me. He even intimated that your feelings towards me had grown cool from the time that you heard of the bond which will yet separate us for a certain time. In short, I knew how so skilfully to put all the feelings of my heart on the rack, that I left him provoked and more than cold; my pride then forbade me to come again."

"I supposed that my father was the cause; for you could not possibly be angry with me, Seiler."

"Be angry with you, my beloved? No, indeed, I never could be so. To be angry? No! But I could be wounded, deeply wounded and offended through your irresoluteness and your want of love; and I will not deny, that it was more this feeling than the conduct of the provost, which induced me to stay away so long. Consider yourself, Alfhild; you had sacredly promised to rely on my word. I deemed your love so strong that it might, like my own, bid defiance to every hindrance, not by strength and action, for these are demanded from man, but patience and confidence, which are the jewels in the crown of woman. I came to you with a heart full of love and tenderness—I expected to clasp in my arms,—my life and my world—and behold the viper of distrust had, during my absence, stolen into my paradise, poisoned all my flowers, and deposited her brood. Why love was no longer the only good of Alfhild; there was a word which she called alternately conscience and opinion of the world; this lay between us; this grew up to a wall, through which the warm language of my heart could no more penetrate to her heart. Alfhild, in that moment I experienced a pain, compared to which all that I had suffered heretofore, were but like the sting of a gnat. To be disappointed, and to see himself deceived in his hopes by that being for whom he had sacrificed all, a man cannot endure without losing the balance of his soul, and when the storms are once let loose, who can set them a limit where to stop?"

The architect was silent; his eyes with an indescribable expression sought those of Alfhild. And could she deny him a look? Seiler looked long and deep under the dark eye-lashes which veiled the sparkling stars of his life. Peace and conciliation, hope and trust, dwelt there.

"Alfhild!" the architect resumed at length in the gentlest tone. "You have come here, you have come here from your own impulse; tell me, are you come to make amends?"

"Ah Seiler!" she answered timidly, and fearful to rouse again the storm of passions which had scarcely subsided; "what can I answer? It was uncle Sebastian who persuaded me; I considered it wrong; but he knew what my poor heart needed, to be calmed and comforted."

"And what does it need, Alfhild?" asked Seiler with sparkling eyes.

"Certainty," answered she, "the certainty that Seiler does not think of me in anger."

"Nothing else?" exclaimed he, and a bright colour burned on his cheeks. "Needs Alfhild nothing more, to be calm, than to know that I am not *angry* with her? O maiden, maiden, does your look then deceive? Does not it speak another language from your lips? How can you thus sport with me?"

"Sport with you, Seiler! no, no—far from it."

Alfhild's tears fell hot upon the hand which clasped hers; yet they could not quiet the restlessness which began anew to stir in his breast.

"Is not this sporting with me in a double way?" asked Seiler in a bitter tone; "to show me these signs of a warm feeling, and yet to deny them with the lips?"

"I did not deny them, Seiler."

"Did you not? Well, God grant that my ear deceived me. But did you not say, that, persuaded by your uncle, you were come to inquire if I was angry with you?"

"Yes, Seiler, so I said; but this does not contradict what I answered just now, for one is not master of one's feelings. They come and lodge themselves firmly without asking permission; they are, therefore, not subject to any judgment. But they are subject to the opinion of our reason and conscience in their consequences and development. My feelings for you, Seiler, remain for ever the same; if I only know that you are not angry with me, I shall be composed, and wait patiently what the distant future may bring us."

A bitter smile trembled on Seiler's lips.

"You are satisfied, indeed, with very little," he answered, while he plucked with violence and tore the wild roses which stood at his feet; "yes, indeed, with very little, Alfhild. You will not know even whether I shall always love you and be faithful to you."

"No, Seiler; I do not wish to know *that*, nor have I a right to know it before—" she dropped her voice,—"what we feel in the depths of our heart, we must settle with God and ourselves; but we must not exchange these feelings between each other, and therefore, Seiler, let us part, it may be with pain, but not with bitterness. I am happy to have seen you; but do not destroy my happiness by giving yourself up again to the wild, gloomy outbreaks of passion, which I cannot understand, but from which I start trembling back. Promise me that you will apply your manly power and strength in a manner which is more consonant with what the milder feelings in our hearts command us."

Alfhild rose; she saw uncle Sebastian come back. The architect was silent; his eyes, however, expressed the bitter feeling, to see himself again disappointed in his hope. He knew now, it is true, that Alfhild would remain faithful to him; that she loved him beyond expression, and besides, he had the permission of the father, to ask once more for her hand; but, notwithstanding all this, his selfishness was wounded severely because Alfhild had *reason*, while he wanted her to have only *love*.

We will not be detained by reflections on the character of our young hero, neither in his favour or against him; but look into the heart of every man, and one will be convinced, that the pearls which are found there, consist but of a very dubious composition, notwithstanding all appearance of genuineness.

"Farewell Seiler!" Alfhild's hand pressed his. "Give me a friendly look at parting."

"Why, Alfhild, God bless you! I will do every thing not to leave your request unfulfilled." His voice trembled with emotion. "But recollect," added he, gently, "that I cannot always do as I will, since my good angel does not stand by my side, as formerly."

"But he hovers constantly around you," whispered she.—Long after the last beams of the sun had disappeared from the lake, the architect stood on the *same* spot, with his eyes fixed upon the bend in the road which had withdrawn Alfhild from his sight.

CHAPTER XIII.

BLOOM VISITS MARIA.

ON the peak of one of the barren rocks, on which the simple dwelling of the clergyman at Fredsberg lay, stood, on the morning of midsummer day, the graceful figure of a woman, motioning with a white veil, a welcome to a sloop, which came sweeping on with full sails. The nearer she came, the more distinctly could the waiting Maria distinguish all objects on it. The Norwegian red flag floated so friendly from the mast, and on a coil of rope, stood a man, with a spy-glass in his hand, with which he looked in all directions, till he had discovered the barren rock, on which Maria stood, waving her veil. Bloom let the spy-glass sink, quick as lightning, took off his hat, and answered with his handkerchief, the friendly salute. He had never before been so impatient, as he was during the short time which was required to make nearer the shore, drop the sails, and put out a boat. No sooner had this reached the landing, than Bloom sprang on shore, and was near kissing the Swedish soil, which now bore his adored friend. Following the direction of the veil, which now and then appeared between the dark cliffs, Bloom flew to the side from whence this friendly message had come to him; and though the climbing of steep and slippery rocks, was, to him, an unaccustomed labour, he soon approached his goal. Maria stood on a small projection, large enough to hold also Bloom. He leaped on it, seized Maria's hand, and pressed it, speechless, to his lips;—for who can have words in the first moment of meeting?

Maria, who cherished feelings only of gratitude and friendship, soon, however, recovered her speech.

"Good, kind Bloom, under how great an obligation am I to you, for the unwearied zeal with which you protect the poor woman, forsaken by all the world! My heart is so poor, that it has not even sufficient gratitude to be able to recompense you for your care of me...."

"Not gratitude enough?" interrupted Bloom, in so tender and trembling a voice, that Maria supposed he had grown unwell, "I wish no thanks for doing what—my duty as man—as friend demands of me." The last words were uttered rather brokenly and indistinctly. Bloom felt that it was not so easy to control feeling as he had before believed. They were not silent, though he enjoined silence on them; they secretly and openly rebelled against his commands. Bloom was dissatisfied with himself. Maria must be blind, thought he, if she does not now perceive what is going on in me. And was she, in fact, so blind, as not to suspect the storms of passion which raged in her presence? We do not venture to decide. It can be but a rare case for a young woman to be in a condition, to be obliged to be separated from a young man, whom she loves more than all on earth, and it might be rare that she should preserve her passion for such a man, yet after the separation.

"Well, I know full well," said Maria, with a friendly look upon Bloom, "that you men will never accept of our thanks. You, Bloom, at least do good for its own sake, and not for the feeble thanks from her whom you have taken under your protection. But now come, my best friend, let me give you another welcome in my little room there below. Our hostess, the good Eliza, has dinner ready, and I have no doubt you will relish it after your voyage."

Bloom nodded assent, and now skipped Maria on before him with skilled agility, whilst Bloom followed her with bold leaps. They had soon arrived on the small piece of ground before the house of the clergyman, which lay bright in the mid-day sun.

"Ah," said Maria, as she stopped to pluck a small moss flower, "it is sad, indeed, that no blade of grass grows here far and wide!"

"That is true," answered Bloom, "yet when nature substitutes in its place, I find also very interesting. Now, for instance, the waves of the sea lie quiet in the sun-light, playing with the coloured shells on the strand; to-morrow at this time they roll, perhaps, in the wildest storm, and cover the cliffs with white foam. And do you hear their syren-voices, which try with soft murmuring to allure us down into the deep.—That is magnificent!—To-day I admire the quiet music of the waves; to-morrow, however, when they swell with power and beat against my fragile vessel, I grow silent before them."

"You have grown poetical, Bloom," said Maria, smiling; "but what you say is true. I can judge of it best myself, since I have grown so familiar with this element, that it sometimes seems to me as if the spirit of my father is speaking to me from it—you know he was a bold sea-farer. But now turn your eye from the sea, and look how comfortable and neat these little huts are. All things in them are so white and scoured so clean that they might serve for a looking-glass."

"And see yonder a whole troop of those olive-coloured beings that look so much like the children of the hot zone," interrupted Bloom. "Only see how skilfully they climb about the huts to take off the dried fishes, and hang up fresh ones. Their dress, which consists only of a short frock, reminds one of our primitive parents in Paradise."

"Yes—but you must consider," answered Maria, "that this style of dress needs not to be envied. The children of our fishermen have only the advantage from it, that they can answer with the whole power of their lungs, 'here,' when they are called by their parents. But the clergyman is coming to meet us, and also Eliza already stands on the threshold."

They walked into the house; all was decked out in a festive manner; the floor was strewn with white sand, and fine sprouts of pine-tree, which had been brought here from a great distance, and the table was covered with simple but tasteful dishes, which the guest relished after his voyage.

When Bloom unpacked his trunk after dinner, he handed to his friendly hostess two bags with those blue grey children of the Orient, which seem to taste yet better when enjoyed in a cold land of rocks; nor did he fail to add the requisite sweets to them.

Radiant with joy, Eliza went with the coffee under the one arm, and two loaves of sugar under the other, into the little kitchen, where a bright fire soon blazed; nor did it last long before the pleasant, aromatic odour of the roasted coffee, which did not seem to be at all unpleasant to the inhabitants of Fredsberg, appeared through the whole house.

Bloom went in the mean time, after a short and friendly conversation with the clergyman, into Maria's room, and seated himself upon the sofa decked out with an ornamental cover, which had been the winter's work of Eliza, and the greatest ornament to be found in the whole house. The guest alone was allowed to take a seat on it, while the little child was not allowed even to touch it with a finger, and all the family considered it like something sacred.

"Is it not handsome, Cory," asked Maria, while she took Eliza's youngest child upon her lap, and covered its face with the ends of her shawl, and asked it to go to sleep.

"Wherever you are, there it is handsome, Maria; yet I do not think that it would be good for you to stay here longer. Pardon me, but I must be candid; your cheeks are pale, your hands have grown thin, and you are changed throughout."

"And this, you think, is caused by the sea-air and solitude of my residence? Ah, do you know the human heart no better? Though it be ever so strong, let but a worm creep in, he will gnaw at its root till he has destroyed it."

"No, Maria, he will not, unless he is left free to eat at pleasure, and to destroy. It is our duty, in my opinion, to preserve ourselves."

Maria shook her head. She had her own peculiar thoughts on this point; but since Bloom could not understand them, she was silent.

"Have you considered my proposition, Maria?" he asked, to give the conversation a decided turn.

"The proposition to go to some watering place?" answered Maria, dwelling on the words. "I have, in part, no disposition for such a journey."

"But, upon my honour, you require it—you must take care of your health," interrupted Bloom, with animation.

"Have I not opportunity here to take the best of sea baths?" objected Maria. "And if I required them really so much as you believe, why should I undertake a distant journey to obtain what I have here at hand? Indeed, I must confess, good Bloom, I do not like your proposal."

"Well, then, we will leave the baths out of the question. But then you must exchange your present place of residence with one in a near city, or on a larger estate. I have already regretted to have prepared this for you; it is too gloomy and solitary for your state of mind."

"At first, dear Bloom, I will frankly confess, it appeared to me like a dreary grave, but it does so no longer. It is uncertain if I should be happier and feel better on coming to a place where there is diversion, and things instantly change. It is ever dangerous to exchange what a man has, and he is contented with, for something he does not know."

Bloom appeared to be dissatisfied. "I am sorry—very sorry, indeed," said Bloom, "to have asked you in vain for what concerns your welfare. But you have to determine—I wish only to advise."

"Good, dear Bloom, my best friend, I did not mean to offend you. If you are of opinion that it would divert me, and be of advantage to me, then let us, now you are here with your sloop, sail for a few days to Stroemland or Uddevalla, and take Eliza and her child with us. I assure you, Bloom, a few days are more than sufficient; and, if the restlessness which I felt at first should come over me again, I promise you sacredly that I will inform you of it, and then we may think of another place of residence for the autumn. But having passed the winter here, I would like to spend the summer here likewise, which is by no means solitary and monotonous, as I see here from the rocks a number of vessels sail constantly by."

In the warmth of these assurances, and in fear of offending Bloom by a refusal, she had unconsciously put her hand into his, and he pressed it gently.

"Have my thanks," said he in a friendly tone, "that you think it worth while to console me for my little disappointment. All shall be arranged according to your wishes. We will make an excursion in the sloop, that you come for once from out of these rocks, which have begun to bewitch you."

Eliza with a face heated from the roasting of coffee, now announced that coffee was ready; and they went into the sitting-room where the fragrant beverage stood on a white cloth, encircled by the whole tea-set of the clergyman, consisting of four cups and three saucers of a yellow colour. Bloom and Maria looked at each other with a smile; Eliza appeared perfectly happy, and the good clergyman was occupied with preparing a pipe for his guest.

Toward evening they all went out to inspect the May-tree decked out with flowers, which was erected on the only level place in this region; and here was a merrier life than on many large estates where the lords give a feast to the peasants. The children, who were quite numerous, had joined hands, and were dancing round the tree; the young fisherwomen in their striped petticoats with white aprons, were dancing with the men in their blue jackets and trousers of seal cloth; a ragged musician called forth from the black strings of a violin the most ear-rending notes, which were taken for dance-music, and all were as much delighted by it, as if the numerous band of a regiment had played.

However, our readers, perhaps, do not take the least interest in these unimportant matters, though they bear the stamp of peculiarity; we will, therefore, drop them, and state that the excursions above mentioned were made, without Bloom observing, however, any favourable effect upon Maria's state of health or mind. The former was not so dangerous as Bloom had feared at first, and the latter could not be otherwise than it was. If she had not been possessed of so much strength of mind and resignation, he would have, no doubt, found her in an entirely different state. What tortures, however, Maria suffered in the solitary nights or in hours of day when she was alone, she kept to herself.

In the course of the summer Maria saw several times the well-known sloop with the red flag steer towards the cliffs of Fredsberg, and never without feeling a certain joy; Bloom, on his part, never landed on or departed from this coast without feeling distinctly, that he was labouring under a certain incurable disease, which increased with each new visit to his fair physician.

CHAPTER XIV.

THE DISCUSSION.

"I REALLY do not see why she should not ride if it gives her pleasure," said count Albano, one day, in the bitterest tone, when the countess found it advisable to remark that it was not proper for Thelma to ride on horseback, because the health of her bethrothed did not allow him to take part in this pleasure.

"How you do speak, good Albano," answered the countess, with all the regard in tone and look which she always observed when speaking to her son. "If a young girl was allowed all that pleases her and her whims suggest to her, this would hardly have a good end;—this is my opinion, at least...."

"Which I know how to estimate," interrupted Albano. "In the present case, however, I believe I must follow *my own*, and, therefore, Thelma shall have the permission to ride; and, if she wishes, four hours every day, for aught I care. As regards the *consequences* of the fulfilment of this, as well as many other of her innocent wishes, they will not, in my opinion, be so dangerous, if they should happen."

"As you think best," answered the countess; "but if she *shall* ride, she may do so in the park, and a servant may attend her."

"What!" Albano exclaimed with a sneering, cold laugh; "in the park! I hope she is not a mere bird that is permitted to flutter about in a cage. She shall ride where and whither she may please; and since no one but the architect, here, understands how to ride, I shall ask of him the favour to give her his company."

The countess grew pale. She appeared for a moment undetermined what to answer to dissuade Albano from this notion; but, knowing that the slightest contradiction had the opposite effect, she said in an indifferent tone: "Yes, that would not be bad, if the building gave him time for it. Your father feels great anxiety that he should always be on the spot to keep an eye on the workmen."

"Well, so far as that is concerned," replied Albano, "I can spur the people on as well as the architect, and I shall engage, therefore, to take his place at the building while he is riding with my betrothed, and takes *my place*; for he really appears well on horseback."

The countess began to perspire for fear. She by no means wanted sagacity, and she had observed, not only the ardent glances which Seiler cast upon her future daughter-in-law when he believed himself unobserved, but also the change of colour from red to white in Thelma's face, when in the evening at the hour of tea, the steps of the architect were heard in the entry. Her mother's heart expected nothing good from Albano's notion and his calm resolution, which was an extraordinary phenomenon in him. She felt a painful anxiety; to arrange these pleasure rides was challenging fate itself, which the countess always wished to avoid.

"Is there in my last proposal any thing that displeases my mother?" asked Albano, with a certain politeness.

"Well—and suppose I am displeased with something in it, dear Albano?" answered the countess.

"Then I will request you to tell me on what your displeasure is founded."

"But suppose I cannot do so—if it is a mere feeling which has neither form nor name, but is, nevertheless, strong enough to make me averse to your purpose—what do you say then?"

"Then I say with all due respect to yourself and your feelings, that such a phantom, without form or name, cannot influence the resolution I have formed. If you would allege facts, it would be different; but a mere feeling has no claim on my consideration."

The count bowed, and took his cap to go down into the court-yard. The architect generally came home about this time. The embarrassment of the countess rose with every minute; but to tell her son the reason of her displeasure would have been pouring oil on the fire. She was therefore silent, and repented having said any thing in this matter, and having made a vain attempt to bring him to a different resolution.

"Have you any thing else to say?" asked Albano.

"Not the least," answered the countess, with artificial composure.

Albano left the room.

"I will speak with my husband," said the countess when she was alone, and took her way, for the first time for a long while, to the apartments of the old count. She went through the ante-room, and knocked at the door of the cabinet.

"Walk in!" called out the count, but there was something declining in his tone. The countess, however opened the door, and the count was so much astonished at the unusual visit of his wife, that it hardly occurred to him to invite her to take a seat neat to him on the sofa. She seated herself, notwithstanding, and the count, who was not able to guess the cause of this *tête-à-tête* with his wife, only said: "Well, my dear friend—well, my good Henrietta, what is the matter?—what has happened?"

"Something very unpleasant indeed. I hope nobody can overhear or disturb us here."

The count got up and took the key out of the door; he looked at the same time as roguish as if a love affair had been in question.

"Well, Henrietta, come to the point; indeed, I do not understand it!"

"I believe that," remarked the countess, "you pay no attention to the trifles that go on around you; and they are, nevertheless, not without some importance."

"No flatteries, dear Henrietta. The time is past when, sitting here on the same place, you spoke to me in a very different way; and I recollect very well that when you reproached me, it was certainly not for my not having paid attention to what was going on around me. However, different times, different manners."

"There is now no time for jesting," answered the countess, vexed; "I have to communicate to you matters of importance, matters which require our serious deliberation. Albano has just told me of his intention to permit Thelma to gratify her singular fondness for riding on horseback."

"Well, my dear Henrietta, what is the harm in that?"

"Nothing farther than that he has selected Seiler as her riding-master and companion."

"Well, that is indeed more liberal in Albano than I should have ever expected of him. He begins really to leave off a good deal of his former foolishness, and I assure you that I desire nothing more."

"My dear husband, you are indeed struck with blindness; you have not the slightest conception of your rank and character, if you fancy that he could ever change. No, far from it: he only develops a new and more dangerous side of it; and thus by concealing his intentions, and nourishing, under the appearance of external calmness, a pride that will bring no good."

"Indeed I have not noticed this side of him," answered the count, and appeared to grow a little serious. "But I believe that what you tell me proves rather the opposite of your supposition. There is nothing secret in Albano's present way of conduct: on the contrary, I see only the most open confidence."

The countess shook her head with an expression of impatience.

"You ought to see, I should think, from what I have told you," she replied, in a manner somewhat piqued, "that I am persuaded that this proposal of his results by no means from confidence, but, on the contrary, from a secret distrust."

"Distrust of what?" asked the count, enraged.

"Of the real feelings of the architect towards Thelma, and of hers towards him."

"What are you talking there of feelings of Thelma and the architect? What nonsense! From what source should these come so suddenly?"

"From where improper feelings come," replied the countess, "I do not know; for, thank heaven, I never had any; but, indeed, I do not think that you are entirely inexperienced in this matter. However, the cause of them is of no consequence at present. But as regards your *other* remark, these feelings have come by no means so suddenly; they are already a year old."

"It is very extraordinary that I have not noticed the least of them," replied the count, pretending not to understand the bitterness of his wife. "The matter appears to me highly improbable. I thought the architect was reported to be in love with Alfhild. The fellow would be possessed if he could turn the heads of all women."

"I believe he is, in spite of his assumed and well-supported seriousness, a very frivolous person, who likes to pluck roses wherever they grow. And now you must see that these excursions on horseback are highly dangerous, and must be prevented."

"Yes, of course; I only do not know how. But are you certain that our little Thelma is disposed to flirtations?"

"Fie, how you speak, my dear! Who says that, or who should say so? Do you believe that a girl grown up under my eyes and those of my sister would be so frivolous a being? I had hoped, indeed, that you had more confidence in the sense of delicacy and judgment of your wife."

"But, I beg of you, what has your tender sense of delicacy, and your still more tender judgment to do with this? If you are so surely convinced that flirtation is entirely out of the question, what danger is there then? Let them ride together as much as they please."

"Indeed! and you think, then, that there is nothing else to fear? I tell you there is a kind of *Platonic* love, which is not mere jest; it is this I fear, and I wish to prevent its consequences so far as it is in my power."

"Bah! *Platonic* love! Nonsense, my dear friend; nothing else but nonsense, upon my honour. If there is nothing else, you may be unconcerned about the matter. It is always best upon such occasions to do as if one could neither hear nor see."

"As if I did not know that," answered the countess, vexed. "For this reason I have, for a whole year, neither heard, nor seen, nor spoken, even with my sister in regard to it. I know she would reproach the girl, and this is of no use. Thelma must remain in the illusion that no one thinks of the ridiculous idea that she, the betrothed of Count Albano, could blush and grow pale at the entrance of the architect."

"And have you really *noticed* that?" asked the count.

"Innumerable times," answered the countess. "I have noticed that on the evening of his arrival, she brushed, from sheer confusion, all the beads from the table which Albano had put there in order; I have noticed that the architect does not hesitate to look at her, as at one with whom one is in love; I have noticed that Albano grew pale, knitted his brow, and trembled with emotion, when he observed what he supposed he alone observed. But I need not recite what I have seen; suffice it that it is enough to fear the worst."

"Well, then, I say simply, that the architect cannot leave the building."

"I have already made this objection, but he replied that he would go himself and overlook the workmen. In short, my friend, it is a fixed idea which he has taken into his head, and to dissuade him from it requires both art and earnestness. I supposed you would know some expedient."

"Since you show so much confidence in my sagacity," replied the count, flattered, "I will prove to you that I deserve it in some measure. I will ride with her myself; then all harm is prevented."

"That would not be so bad; except this might cause him to suppose, which I fear he does already, that we suspect the danger. This would be very bad, and would increase his watchfulness, and seem to give more reason for it than there actually is."

"Now, may the deuce take me, if I do know any other advice. We will consider the matter till tomorrow."

"In the mean while they will ride out this evening, I really believe it is best for you to accompany her this time. You may, as if by accident, have your horse saddled about the same time. It is true you have, for several years, left off riding; but you have your own notions as well as other people."

During this conversation of the noble married pair, Albano walked up and down in the court-yard. The noon-bell rang, so that the architect must come home soon; but Albano almost died of impatience. For several months past he had, though with the greatest exertion, carried out the plan of concealing from his betrothed all struggles and gloomy outbreaks of jealousy, that he might the better be able to make his observations. The consequence of it was, that he knew no more now than at first; for the architect always entrenched himself behind an enormous wall of cold politeness, over which he ventured only now and then to cast some bold glances. As regarded Thelma, he perceived in her nothing else but what he had always noticed, namely, the anxiety with which she avoided being alone with Seiler. "I must have certainty; and may it cost what it will!" Albano had thus said to himself a thousand times. But as the opportunity to obtain it ever disappeared, he determined to lay his own hand on the wheel of fortune, and to bring it about. It occurred to him at last to use Thelma's innocent fondness for riding for a move, and with the thought he had also formed the resolution.

Having walked up and down in the court for a quarter of an hour, he heard the tramping of a horse's hoof, and a few seconds after the architect came flying along like an arrow upon a shining courser. Without noticing Albano, who stood in the shade of a linden-tree, he sent with his riding-whip a salute up to the east wing, as he left the saddle with an easy leap, and he sent then, after his salute, a polite bow and an ardent glance, whose rays fell directly into Albano's heart. He could not see whether she stood at the window; but he was sure that she had the dangerous enjoyment at this moment to observe his hated rival. He controlled his emotion with a strength which only the strong wish of examining the matter closer could give him; he therefore approached with a courteous bow, where Seiler was stroking the neck of his horse, and gave him to the groom that had come up in haste.

"You are a very skilful rider, Mr. Seiler," said the count; "it is a pleasure to see you on horseback."

"I have had some practice, and besides, I like to ride," answered the architect, thinking that only a common compliment was intended, which, however, struck him as something unusual from Albano's lips.

"In regard to your skill in riding, I have to request a little favour of you," continued Albano. "My betrothed takes particular delight in riding on horseback; but, as you can easily imagine, I am no proper attendant. The physician has, since my last sickness, forbidden me to ride at all; but as I do not wish to deprive her of this pleasure, I would request you to take a ride with her every day for an hour or two. You would very much oblige me by it, for I see that so skilful a rider as you are, might be of great advantage to her in this art."

"I feel very much flattered by your confidence, Sir Count," answered Seiler, without betraying by a single expression in his face, either joy or vexation, triumph or indifference; "and as regards my wish to justify your confidence, I hope I need not add, that my time and my little skill in riding are at your command."

"I thank you," replied the count. "I will inform my betrothed of it. If you have no objection, you may commence this very evening."

Seiler bowed in assent, and Albano went up to the parlour to await Thelma.

Evening came. The baroness who was always delighted to see her beautiful daughter on horseback, and had no objection to a thorough knowledge how to manage a fiery steed—particularly as this proposition came from the intended bridegroom himself—was exceedingly cheerful, and assisted her daughter in making her toilet. Thelma could not comprehend what had induced her lover to this singular notion; she did not dare, however, to oppose it, lest she might lead his distrust to the cause that could have induced her.

The horses stood saddled; Seiler was ready, and was walking up and down in the court, after he had examined the saddle and bridle on Thelma's horse. All was in order, only she herself was yet wanting. Now came Albano with his betrothed from the east wing of the castle. She wore a magnificent riding-dress, of dark-green velvet; on her head she had a small cap of the same material, which covered only half the locks that played round her neck. A black veil was fastened to it with a costly buckle, and flowed in ample folds from her shoulders. Count Albano examined with passionate looks his charming betrothed; and it was as if he flung her into the abyss on purpose and with fiendish pleasure. And he did all this, in order to obtain certainty on a matter which could only make him mad if he should find it as he supposed it to be. Moreover, who could ensure him the attainment of his purpose? He was not with them; they rode out alone and came back alone, without his being able to observe them secretly.

Albano's blood began to boil. He almost felt disposed to order the horses to be unsaddled; fear of making himself ridiculous overcame, however, every other consideration, and he handed Thelma to the horse.

"It would be remarkable," thought he, "if the architect could lift her into the saddle without my observing any thing."

Seiler stood aside. He seemed to expect that the count would perform this duty himself; but Albano stepped back, and said, with a disagreeable smile:—

"This honour belongs to the master."

Seiler now came up, and offered Thelma his hand with so easy and graceful a motion, that Albano's eyes sparkled with rage.

"Lean upon my arm, my lady," said Seiler, in a respectful tone. Albano went on the other side, that he might see this act the more closely. The architect appeared to great advantage. Thelma put the extreme points of her fingers on Seiler's arm and swung herself, light as a bird, into the saddle. Albano's breast became more and more compressed. The black veil had touched Seiler's face; and—was it imagination or truth?—it seemed to him that Seiler's lips had moved to kiss it.

"You must draw the foot a little back, my lady," said Seiler; "only the extremest point must touch the stirrup. Is it right so, or shall I shorten it? I believe the strap is too long."

"Yes, much too long," answered Thelma. "You will have the kindness to make it very much shorter."

Albano had now the highly disagreeable pleasure to see the architect take pains to put Thelma's foot in the proper position in the stirrup, at which he was not in too great a hurry. The earth began to burn under Albano's feet when he noticed that Seiler clasped Thelma's small foot with his hand, and turning it in all directions, while she blushed all over.

"Do I not now know enough?" asked Albano of himself, in wild self-defiance, when Seiler stepped back with a light bow, and received thanks from Thelma by a graceful motion of her head, which furnished a commentary to the secret thoughts of the tortured lover.

The architect now leaped into the saddle with great agility. Thelma's eyes followed his motions with visible delight. But when the dangerous ride was to begin, the groom brought a third horse out of the stable, and the old count appeared on the staircase.

"Will you take a ride also, father?" asked Albano, in a tone as if a load was removed from his heart.

"Yes,—I thought I must also wait, for once, upon my intended daughter-in-law, as cavalier," answered he, with a smile; and, after several attempts, he succeeded in getting into the saddle.

Seiler was too much accustomed to control himself, to betray even the slightest sign of disappointed hope in his features; he found, on the contrary, "the pleasure of the company of the count invaluable."

We do not know what Thelma thought; for though she said, "Ah, dear uncle, that is indeed very pleasant," yet she drew, at the same time, her veil so close over her face, that not a single feature could be distinguished.

The cavalcade now moved on; the countess, who had witnessed, behind the red silken window curtains, the whole scene, and Albano's emotions, breathed again freely, and thanked heaven that she had spoken to her husband; for if she was not entirely mistaken, her son was already entirely satisfied with the *first* lesson.

And so it was. Albano believed now that he knew all he wished to know, and spoke no more of riding out. He even answered several times very sharply, when the baroness afterwards began to speak of it. He now grew, with every day, even more gloomy and reserved; but did not attempt any longer either to bring about or to hinder Thelma's meeting with Seiler. His whole state of mind, all his expressions and thoughts, intimated a new stage of his unfortunate mental disease.

CHAPTER XV.

BANS PUBLISHED.

WEEKS passed by. The relations of persons and things, which grew intricate and entangled, at the castle of Hammarby, would not come to be unravelled, and the faint glimmer which the bright, warm summer days had spread on the horizon of the noble family vanished the nearer autumn approached. Seiler no longer enjoyed a gracious treatment as before; he had often to experience the taunts of high-born superciliousness, but he remained unchanged, always attentive and courteous in words and conduct. No one could make him definite reproaches; yet he was hated, particularly by the countess, nay, even feared, like a comet whose contact with any other heavenly body might fill all space with gloom and disorder.

Having such thoughts and notions, it is natural that she, with great impatience, looked forward to the season when the building of the church was to be suspended till the next spring, and then the countess was resolved Seiler should not put a foot in the castle, unless the young married couple were journeying. Albano's marriage with Thelma was to be celebrated in November. About this time Seiler was obliged to go on a journey, and the countess was resolved, though she could not tell her son so, not to hold the wedding before the departure of the hateful architect. But to the great surprise of all, days and weeks passed away without Count Albano's uttering a single word of wedding, bridal dress, or any other thing relative to his approaching marriage. He hardly spoke at all with Thelma any more, but, gloomy and reserved he walked in his spacious room up and down, casting now and then a glance in the large looking-glass, and smiling in derision at his figure and face, which grew every day paler, yellower, thinner, and more disagreeable. When he was in the parlour with the rest of the family, whole hours would sometimes pass without his doing anything but bite his nails, and looking from beneath his bushy red hair upon Thelma, with eyes that sparkled so fearfully that the breast of the poor betrothed grew ever more compressed—nay, she often felt as if she must suffocate for want of air. But the inexpressible tortures she suffered, so far from killing her, helped her, on the contrary, to live; man is not likely to die for grief. It is true Thelma lived, but she dragged on her existence like a tormented worm. And when her thoughts passed from the fearful intended bridegroom to the approaching wedding-day, then she seemed to herself like a bride of death, and shuddered for fear and horror. When Seiler came near her, to fill with a few drops of the dangerous poison from his lips the cup which she must empty, she felt, at the same time, a singular chill and heat thrill through all her limbs. The magic power which the architect exercised over her, appeared to her no longer the charming feeling of two consonant hearts that beat towards each other. No; far from it. She felt even a secret aversion toward the man who, united with another woman by the holy band of matrimony, nourished certainly a flame for a second, nay, perhaps for a third one. This appeared to her abominable, and yet she was enchanted by his voice, his look, and each of his motions. And with what delicacy and respect had he conducted himself of late! He showed his sympathy with her suffering in a thousand ways, observed only by her, and by no one else. The architect unfolded a satanic skill in the way and manner in which he treated her. She was to him like soft wax, that assumed different forms under his hand. He was able by a mere glance, a subtle smile, or a half-subdued tone of his voice, to raise her to the highest pinnacle of bliss; but when he flung her into the deepest abyss of misery by an icy coldness. When a painful grief was then painted in Thelma's features—when her eye then sought in vain for the cause of this sudden change, and Count Albano, from the sofa, would cast a fearful look upon the poor maiden, who was no longer able to control herself, then Seiler appeared the more satisfied; and the more violently Albano's torture was then expressed, and the more his lips quivered and his eyes sparkled with rage, the more subtle and fiendish was the smile of scorn which played round Seiler's mouth. He thought only on James Leganger's sufferings, and his better feelings grew more and more silent; with avidity he quaffed from the cup of vengeance.

"It is now time to think of having your bans published," said the old count, one day, as he was alone with his son, who sat, as usual, in the corner of the sofa, chewing on his nails. "It is high time, my dear Albano, if you intend to be married at the appointed time—namely, at the close of this month."

"There is no hurry for it," answered Albano, evasively; "my intended bride will not much long for it."

"That is a matter I do not know," replied the count; "but what I know," continued he, "is, that we should give the world an opportunity to laugh at our expense, if they saw or suspected that Count Albano, the heir to the castle of Hammarby, suffered himself to be supplanted with his beautiful betrothed out of fear of a rival, of a miserable architect."

"Out of fear?" exclaimed Albano, who felt himself wounded in the most sensitive spot. "The cunning, insolent adventurer does not frighten me in the least; and least of all in regard to my intended bride. How could my father come upon such a thought?"

"Your conduct, indeed, has given occasion to such suspicions; and if you will follow my advice, you will be published on next Sunday."

"That shall be done," answered Albano, with vehemence; "and since they think me so weak as to fear the architect, he himself shall be invited to the wedding."

"That would be entirely unnecessary in my opinion," answered the count.

"But as I am the bridegroom," Albano broke out with sickly impatience, "things must go according to *my* opinion. The architect may depart the day after the wedding, but he shall first see her as my wife."

The count did not wish to irritate the wild disposition of his son by contradiction to a violent outbreak, the consequences of which were always very dangerous. He was, therefore, silent, and on the following Sunday it was solemnly published in the church at Hammarby, that Count Albano, of H., intended to enter into holy wedlock with the high-born lady Thelma, of Ravenstein.

On this day there was, so to speak, an eclipse of sun and moon at the same time, at the castle. Count Albano stayed in his room with his doors locked, the architect likewise, and Thelma lay on the little sofa in her room almost without life, a marble-white victim of so many secret plans. The countess sat on the one side, the baroness, who could but with difficulty conceal her consternation, on the other; and it was as silent in the room as if the two ladies were watching by a corpse.

"How is your headach, my child?" asked the countess, whilst she held with motherly care, her smelling-bottle under her nose, and then poured a few drops into the hollow of her hand, to chafe with it the brow of the patient.

"My head is dizzy," answered Thelma, with a faint voice. "Will you be so kind, dear aunt, and have the light taken away, it blinds me."

"Your eyes are red and swollen with tears, my beloved child," said the countess, in a low voice. "Believe me, dear Thelma, they burn into my heart. My poor Albano has not the qualities that can win for him the heart of his young intended wife; but you will change him as much as his character permits by your gentle, good, and truly womanly manners. At least, I believe and hope it."

"Ah! dear aunt, I can neither believe nor hope it, I—good God, I myself need indulgence—I...."

She leaned her head upon the shoulder of the countess, her breast struggled for air, her heart longed for a being to whom she could unbosom herself. She suffered unspeakably, from the circumstance that she suffered *alone*, and in this condition she felt herself drawn more to the countess than to her own mother. It was an instinct-like feeling which told Thelma that it was motherly affection with the former, but selfishness with the latter, that decided her fate. Yet though the countess had a warm, feeling heart, she did not dare to go so far as to be the confidant of her future daughter-in-law in affairs of the heart, which would have been treachery to her own son, and she did not, therefore, encourage poor Thelma to confide to her her grief. This reservedness in a moment when a loving heart longed for a conversation on those things which were concealed from the countess by a thick veil was very fatal, and brought on consequences, of which the countess afterwards never ceased to accuse herself of having been the indirect cause. Having her thoughts bent only upon the present moment, she smoothed the locks of the young intended bride, and in friendly but wholly commonplace expressions, begged her to calm herself.

"You, good child," said she, "what could your innocent heart reproach you with? You are at present very much excited; but, believe me, that will gradually cease."

It did not cease, however. Thelma's anguish, her heart-rending torment increased with every moment that she approached the fatal day, and had an ever greater effect upon her state of mind. She was in an awful dream, which was soon to be reality. When her eyes fell upon Albano's form, that grew ever more dismal and gloomy, she shrunk back as from the sting of a viper; when she met the looks of the architect, now icy and then warm, her heart contracted convulsively. Had she been allowed but once to lay her head upon that dangerous being, whom she loved to idolatry—ah! had she been able but a single moment to experience the bliss, to press her half-broken heart to another which beat for her. But, no: solitary and forsaken, she was to pine and die. Even this very desire was a sin, which her own feeling condemned, and yet it was only human.

A number of dressmakers and mechanics were sent for from the neighbouring towns to prepare the necessary things, and arrange the rooms which the young couple were to occupy. The countess and baroness were constantly busily engaged; but their efforts to engage also Thelma in it were in vain. She would not employ herself in any thing, but stayed in her room with her door closed.

In this way the four weeks had passed of Thelma's noviciate for a more dreadful state than cloisterly seclusion.

It was now the evening before the wedding-day, the 15th of November, 1791, a day which is marked with indelible characters in the annals of the family of the count of H. The baroness had made the remark in the forenoon, that rain would have fallen on the bridal crown, if the marriage had been celebrated on this day; but now the heavens were entirely clouded over, and it was so dark that it seemed the sun would not rise at all on the wedding-day. A gale arose, and increased to such a degree, that it whistled and howled through the long corridors, and the lights had been blown out several times in the hands of the servants before they reached the room.

Thelma sat, with her hands in her lap, alone in the room; her eyes were directed upon the cloudy heavens, where not a single star would rise.

"Ah!" said she, half aloud, "all my hopes are vanished. I have now neither a hope nor a wish left; to-morrow is my day of burial; then my restless heart must be calm. Its account is closed, it begins to die already, for I no longer feel restlessness burn in my soul. I have no wish, not a single wish left,—I am very poor."

Some faint recollections now began to move in the back-ground of her heart, and the grotto came before her mind. Thelma had not visited it during the whole past year; but now—ah! she wished she might stand yet only a few minutes at the balustrade to listen once more to the well-known notes coming from the lake—though these were now out of the question, yet no one could object to her listening from thence to the howling of the storm.

"That would be beautiful—glorious!" said she. An irresistable desire awoke in her breast; she could not but visit the grotto once more. "I have then yet one wish—the last!" said she, and stepped to the window. "Huh! it is so dark without; but that is suited to my soul; there too it is dark. I shall go there—I must go. I will quickly fly on the familiar path through the park—the golden autumn leaves which cover it will give me light."

Thelma rang the bell, and her waiting-maid came in.

"Here, Anna!" said she with an agitated voice, "will you do me a great favour?"

"Ah, gracious lady! would that I am able to do it; I will do all that you desire."

"Well, then, I wish to go out for a little while, and take the key with me. If the countess or my mother should come, you must try to break them off in some way without betraying that I am not at home. You may say that I wish to be alone for a few hours. Will you do so, Anna? Can I depend upon you that you will not betray my absence; for it would only give them anxiety if they knew I had gone out in such weather."

"But, good heavens! what are you going to do out of doors? The wind blows so hard that you can hardly stand on your feet. Where do you want to go to, my lady?"

"I will only go down to my old favourite spot, the grotto. I have the greatest desire to see it once more before I.... in short, Anna, I *want* to go, and you will do what I asked of you out of love to me."

"Huh! to the dismal grotto at this time! I am afraid to go there in bright daylight; and I would not go there now if you would give me the castle of Hammarby."

"No wonder; you believe in ghosts; but I fear nothing, have nothing to fear; and, perhaps, I may feel better there. Give me the cloak and the black veil, and see whether there is any body in the court."

"Not a soul," said Anna, when she returned.

Thelma took the key to her door with her, and having been accompanied by Anna to the little garden door, she disappeared in the
darkness.

"May God protect her!" said Anna, who stopped a little while,
and saw the dark veil tossed to and fro by the wind, till she could no
more distinguish it.

Anna returned to her little chamber opposite Thelma's rooms,
where she continued to iron the lace collars and caps of her young
mistress. The restlessness she felt affected her so much that she
burned her fingers more than once, and spoiled a beautiful collar; a
mishap, which under different circumstances, would have caused her
tears, but her head being filled with superstitions of all sorts, she now
took it only for an evil omen which she could not prevent.

About half an hour had passed when Anna was most terribly
frightened by a knocking at her door.

"Who is there?" she asked, trembling for fear that it might be the
baroness, who wished to speak with Thelma; but the voice that answered, "It is I, open Anna!" caused her a still greater fright than the
presence of those ladies would have done.

It was Albano.

Anna tottered with difficulty to the door and drew back the bolt.
The little fire which glimmered on the hearth for the ironing threw a
faint light upon Albano's pale face. He appeared to be in a more excitable mood than commonly, and Anna perceived this at once from
the severe tone in which he asked: "Has the lady locked herself in, as
there is no key in the door?"

"Ah—she is not very well," stammered Anna in the greatest anguish; "she told me just now when I was with her, she wished to be
alone for a few hours."

"She is then now alone," answered Albano in a deep hollow voice;
"then I will speak with her. Go in and tell her that I ask for permission
to disturb her solitude for a few minutes."

"As your lordship commands," answered Anna, endeavouring to
collect her senses, and taking a candle she stepped out of her chamber; but the count, to her horror, remained standing on the threshold, and could not but observe, therefore, that she did not open the
door, which was impossible, since Thelma had taken the key with
her. Anna's embarrassment was great. She knocked—but as no an-

swer followed, she remarked, "that the gracious lady might have gone to sleep."

"She cannot sleep so fast that she did not hear your knocking; she is not asleep at all events!"

He himself now stepped to the door, and knocked three times, with his long hand, violently against it.

"Open, Thelma!" cried he, impatiently; "I want to speak to you on a matter which must be settled this day!"

All remained silent.

"Open—open!" cried he, with a wild voice: "you play with me in a double way. Open, I tell you, or I burst the door!"

As no answer came yet, Albano so violently pushed with his feet against the door that the lower part fell out, and he soon after stood in the middle of Thelma's dark room, with the light in his hand which he had snatched from Anna. He went to the bed, tore aside the curtains, and looked upon it—it was empty. He stood still for a moment, and gazed around him with looks in which was painted the surprise of a madman; but suddenly, as if the spirits of hell had inspired him, he uttered a fearful howl, while he seized Anna by the throat, and pressed her against the wall.

"Speak!" shrieked he, hoarsely; "where is the young lady? Bethink yourself—do not lie. Look me in the face; I throttle you if you do not tell me the truth!"

Half dead with fright, the unfortunate woman exclaimed: "For heaven's sake let me go—you shall know all!"

"Well."

He opened his long hand, and Anna then informed him that the lady had for a moment gone to the grotto,—but had forbidden her to tell of it, because her absence might cause anxiety.

"To the grotto! Ha! ha! ha!" laughed Albano, in the wildest tone. "I have once been there myself; this will be a beautiful scene. Well, I can speak to her there as well as here. But, that you may not betray your lady to any body else, you shall stay here till either I or she shall release you."

With these words he seized the trembling Anna, dragged her to Thelma's cabinet, pushed her into it, locked the door, and put the key in his pocket. Thereupon he stole across the court-yard to the west wing. All was dark there. Albano rubbed his hands, and seemed to feel a satanic joy. He now drew his cap over his ears, turned up his coat collar, and hastened, with winged steps, through the garden to the grotto.

CHAPTER XVI.

THE PARSONAGE.

THE architect had this afternoon, for the first time in the seven months which he had stayed at the castle, gone over to the parsonage to take leave of Alfhild before his departure. The building might have been proceeded with without hindrance from the weather; the count, however, was of opinion that, since the church could not be completed before the setting in of winter, the work might be discontinued for the present. Seiler knew full well the meaning of this, yet he was willing to leave a stage where he played a part which no longer agreed with his better self. Besides, he might presume that the evil seed he had sown would bring forth sufficient fruit. He wished not to see the effect of it, but to return to his native mountains, to seek there, peace; though as he justly feared it would flee him, perhaps, there also; for wherever he turned, his thoughts, past, present, and future, were enveloped in a dark veil; and he himself was like a riddle that moves about, inexplicable to himself and others.

The family at the parsonage were just sitting at coffee, when Stina rushed in, breathless, to announce that the architect was stopping at the gate, and asked for permission to pay his respects. Alfhild grew alternately red and pale; her trembling hand was near dropping the coffee-pot, if uncle Sebastian had not quickly taken hold of it, and put it in its place. The provost, who was of opinion that a visit of leave-taking could make neither him nor his family the subject of gossip, resolved to conduct himself like a man who knows politeness; and, as he did not wish to prevent either his daughter or Seiler from exchanging a few parting words, she was allowed to remain in the room and speak a few words with the guest.

Before a perfect equipoise at the coffee-table was restored, that is, while they were yet occupied with recovering a becoming composure, the architect came in, and saluted those present with a calm, grave bearing.

"Very glad to see you, Mr. Seiler," said the provost, and placed, himself, a chair near the table for the visitor. "Pour out a cup of coffee, Alfhild; it is, indeed, very cold to-day,—very rough. Winter is coming. Will you not take a pipe, Mr. Architect?"

Seiler declined, by a bow, as well the one as the other polite offer. He was so poor in words, that he was astonished at it himself; and his more than gloomy mind, which increased with every moment, seemed to have another cause than the bitter separation from Alfhild; but what it was he could not say himself. Whenever Thelma and her future came before his soul, he endeavoured to press these images in the back-ground. He had felt this pressure and anguish of soul ever since half-past six in the morning, when he was awaked by his watch, which lay on the table by the side of his bed, falling upon his forehead. This cold contact had struck him as very ominous, as it had awakened him from the most beautiful of dreams; and because this accident appeared to him very uncommon, he had let the watch repeat to learn the hour in which this wonderful sign was given him. He put the watch away, but was not able to drive away the thoughts which this occurrence had called up in him. He felt out of humour during the whole of the day; his bitter feeling was yet increased by the approaching separation from Alfhild, particularly as he saw her, in feeble health, approach a severe winter. All this taken together depressed his spirits; and, for the first time in his life, he was not able entirely to control himself, and as usual to command his countenance. Every one noticed that he suffered, and Alfhild was tormented by the bitterest feelings when she saw Seiler suffer, without being able to share his grief.

"Well, Mr. Architect, when shall we again have the pleasure of seeing you at Hammarby?" asked the provost.

"Next March," answered Seiler; "and if it be God's will, the church shall be finished in the course of next summer."

"That would be highly desirable," remarked the provost; "for I never step over the threshold of our old church, without imagining the possibility that it may fall in and bury us all. The vault has so many cracks, and the stones are so loose, that they appear only to hover in the air."

"Oh, there is no danger of that," observed Seiler. "The old walls will yet stand for half a century."

The conversation having gone on in this way for some time, Seiler began to move restless on his chair; he was about to go, but he was kept back by a natural feeling. He had not yet been able to speak a single word to Alfhild. The provost and uncle Sebastian, who noticed his wish, withdrew near the chimney. Seiler rose and went to the window where Alfhild sat in her usual place. She was busy with working at Thelma's bridal garters, which she wished to finish to-day.

Seiler admired the skilful texture of blue beads and silver threads.

"That is exceedingly beautiful," said he; yet his eyes no longer rested upon the work, but upon Alfhild's pale countenance.

"I believe myself that I have succeeded very well in this work," answered Alfhild, with a slight tremor in her voice. "I would be delighted if Thelma liked the garters."

"Alfhild will, no doubt, deliver them to her friend in person?" asked Seiler.

"Of course; though I have not been at the castle for a long time, I must go there now; for Thelma asked me, and the baroness honoured me with the commission, to be one of the bride's-maids."

"Alfhild will then come to the castle to-morrow?"

"Yes, and very early too. Old Borgstedt will come for me, just as in former times."

"Just as in former times, oh, Alfhild!"—Seiler's compressed breast gasped for breath. "We hope also for a *coming* time," whispered he, so low that she alone could only understand.... "Is it not so? Tell me that we may have in common at least the same hope."

Alfhild's look brightened by a clear ray which kindled also Seiler's eye, and was blended with his look; they seemed to wish never to separate, and their hearts interchanged new vows of fidelity in this happy minute.

"In February, my Alfhild, a year will have passed; and my heart can be sure of you, it has strength to overcome time. Only one anxiety will not leave me; your health, my beloved child, has suffered very much. I fear the evil will increase."

"I do not fear so, Seiler," answered Alfhild, consoling him. "I am recovering since we spoke together last summer, at the new church, and I have been so happy in the certainty that the dark spirits which you formerly complained of, have left you and given way to friendly, good spirits. Is it not so, good Seiler? No storms have raged in your breast since you promised me no more to give yourself up to their evil influences?"

"Ah, Alfhild, unfortunately it has been otherwise. I promised only to make the attempt, to control them; but I also said that I was not able to do so unless my good angel stood by my side. I have struggled; yet I have passed through many a bitter hour since the evening we spoke together."

Seiler spoke this in a tone of greatest pain; but what was done could not be undone; no complaining availed now. Nor was he such a man that he was dejected by a dissonance in his soul. Alfhild's eye searched in silence, in his; yet she did not dare to put a question.

"You angel," he again began, while his face and voice assumed the expression of what was at present passing within him. "You seek in me a response to the fundamental tone of your own being; this is not found in my soul at present, nor can it be found, for I am not pure and holy as you. But, my Alfhild, when the time comes that you always hover around me,—when your breath will drive away all dark images, and your lips kiss away the clouds from my brow; then I too shall be pious and worthy of you. Until then, my beloved, pray for me—I much need it."

Seiler felt himself almost overpowered by his emotion; he rose to take leave, while he whispered to Alfhild,—

"We shall meet to-morrow at the dismal wedding, and the day after to-morrow, when I set out, I shall pay you another visit;—may I?"

Alfhild lightly pressed his hand as answer, which he reached to her to bid farewell; and as Seiler stepped back to take leave of the provost, the latter invited him to stay for the evening. But he declined this, and after a visit of three quarters of an hour, Seiler galloped hastily from the parsonage to the castle, so that sparks flew to the right and left.

Having arrived in the court-yard he stopped his horse; it was half past six o'clock.

"What shall I do this evening?"

"I have no disposition to do any thing, nor have I rest," said he, while he walked a few times up and down the court, and gazed on the lighted windows in the main building. "Ha—I will take leave of the grotto. This weather and my state of mind are excellently suited to that gloomy place. There I will pass the evening and listen to the howling of the storm and the splashing of the waves. It is dark in the west wing; she is no doubt up there in the parlour, the poor victim— the bride of death—and the bridegroom lost in a fever of jealousy and mad love. Poor Albano! I believe James Leganger did not suffer more than you do."

The architect cast yet another glance up to the saloon where he supposed Thelma to be; he then opened the garden-door, and took the same way which she had taken a quarter of an hour before.

Seiler soon stood at the balustrade in front of the grotto. The fire which burned within his heart, seemed about to be quenched by the violent gusts of wind which raged around him. The waves of the lake do not go high even in a *storm*, but when they beat against the foot of the rock, and break at its projections, their noise sounds like the wailing of one about being drowned. It was this dismal, sin-gular tone, which the architect suddenly perceived. He looked over the balustrade to the foot of the steep rock, till he grew dizzy. This induced him to enter the grotto. He walked into it as far as he could, and seated himself upon the moss-bank. The sounds were now heard much fainter, yet they appeared to him like the cry for help of one in trouble. Full of thought, he put his hand on his brow, and was sitting there a few seconds in silence, when he perceived quite near him a half-suppressed sigh.

A shudder thrilled through all his limbs. He listened with checked breath—and heard a heavier sigh, yet still suppressed.

"Is any lady here?" asked he after a fearful pause, while he at the same time stretched out his hand as far as his arm could reach. He touched upon something soft, and immediately after these words came, in broken parts, from Thelma's lips: "It is I. For heaven's sake, Mr. Seiler, is it you? Leave me this moment!"

"Are you here, Lady Ravenstein—in this weather—at this hour? A foreboding tells me, that fate has not brought us here together without a particular purpose; and since such a moment might not be opened to us a second time, permit me to avail myself of it, to throw off a burden which weighs down my soul in the hour of de-parture, and to make a confession which must show you how little I deserved the favour with which you honoured me. I——O Thelma! I must say it! In this hour I am without a mask, without deceit. I have been more cruel towards you than an executioner. You have suffered with the patience of an angel; but I go away, loaded with the horrible feeling which but to-day has become wholly clear to me, to have destroyed your happiness for life. For, Thelma, know, in order to cool my revenge against your family, I deceived you; that by winning your heart I might lacerate that of your bethrothed. It was a fiendish plan; however, that you might despise me and quench the flame which I am not worthy of, I have condemned myself to the humiliating punishment to show myself to you without that false shining mask. Oh, if you knew what my pride suffers through this confession! But this remains buried in your heart and within these narrow walls. No human ear, except yours, has ever heard the language of repentance from my lips, and no eye, not even yours, has seen the blush of shame at myself, which is now burning on my cheeks. Oh, Thelma, Thelma! Speak you, speak to me but a single word. I have ill-treated you horribly—destroyed the peace of your soul. And yet, if you could understand to what a fantastic mind, like my own, can be brought when fate seems to conclude an alliance with its wild fancies...."

Thelma's lips quivered convulsively. She stood there annihilated. Of all the architect had said to her, she had comprehended only what was most terrible, that he had only carried on a fiendish play with her warm heart and her love. No one, except the mad Albano, had then loved her. She felt as if she herself was seized by madness.

"Thelma—Thelma!" continued Seiler. The tones of this dangerous voice never sounded softer and more soothing than in this moment; even now that she must hate him, he exercised a magic influence on her soul; but with all the strength she had left she pushed him back.

"Away!" was the only word she could utter with great exertion.

"Away, you say? No, Thelma! not now—not until you have collected yourself."

He would take her hand, but she tore it from his with her last remaining strength, left the grotto, and went to the balustrade, round which she clasped one arm to support herself, as she was near sinking down. Her breast heaved in violent emotion, it resembled the waves which broke at her feet; and as the moon now divided the clouds to look down upon the dark earth, she saw two marble, pale forms; one with loosened locks which floated in the storm, as if vieing with the veil which looked like a banner of death—the other with ice-cold drops of perspiration on his brow, bending, for the first time, his knee before a woman.

Thelma's arm clasped the railing even faster. She fixed her eyes upon him for a few seconds. Was it Seiler whom she now saw before her? The proud expression in his countenance, and the noble bearing of his body had disappeared—they lay in the dust, like himself; and yet his false love never spoke a more powerful language than his eyes did now, which sought to soften her heart, and entreated for a word of peace and conciliation.

She was carried away also this time by those eyes which had feigned love with the falseness of a serpent. Could she hate him? She fain would, but could not; for there is no hate in love, but only deep pain and infinite forgiveness.

"Have you in the same manner infatuated, derided, and deceived Alfhild?" asked Thelma, timidly.

"No, Thelma, I have not used these hateful weapons towards her; I love her with my whole soul. I saw Alfhild before I did you; she decided on my fate at once, in the first moment."

"But I was condemned to be a victim!"

These words she spoke so softly, that they hardly reached Seiler's ear; but yet he understood them, and saw the look which she cast from him upon the uproarious waves of the lake.

"In this hour," said he, with subdued but firm voice, "my future lies in your hand. Your forgiveness, Thelma, if it be at all possible, would resist, for ever, every feeling of revenge and bitterness which dwells in my breast. My heart would again be open to better feelings, which were heretofore excluded by stormy passions. Thelma, I am on a dangerous parting road; reach out your hand to me—and I am saved!"

Now her eye fell again on him. She was to influence his future by her forgiveness. What was to her the world and all compared with the blissful feeling of having been the saving angel of Seiler? Was not this sufficient to have lived for? Derided, deceived, with a breaking heart fastened to a chain which must oppress her life, she wanted certainty of having lived at least once, if she was not to despair, and believe her life was only a stray light, a thing without purpose and value. She trembled even more violently, her cheeks grew even paler, her locks, driven by the storm, flew more wildly about her brow!

"Seiler!" whispered she, while she bent down to the kneeling one, "my heart required the forgiveness of him who is to be my husband; it therefore feels the desire to forgive you. May also God forgive you! I will pray for you—here, and above, hereafter!"

"Angel, saint, whom my venomous breath dared to touch, but could not profane. Your spirit soars on high, free and pure; you cannot be unhappy; you are elevated from all pain; I can but adore you!"

The architect leaned his head on Thelma; she bent down to touch his brow; her loosened locks covered Seiler's face.

Now suddenly flashed two fiery balls near them, and a loud howl repeated Seiler's words: "I can but adore you!"—It was a fearful echo, which not even the loud storm could drown.

"Albano," sobbed Thelma, seized by convulsive contortions, and pressed her face on Seiler's shoulder. "He will…"

"He will avenge his honour, his spurned love, you faithless woman!" And with the swiftness of lightning the madman clasped his long bony arm round her body, and pressed so violently at the same time his nails into her side that she moaned for pain.

"Vengeance! Vengeance!" shrieked Albano, with fiendish laughter, and delighted a few seconds in her anguish; but then the architect seized him with a powerful hand, while he cried out to him:

"Let her go, madman! she is as innocent as God's angel. It was by accident that we met here, and—"

"And then you have worshipped her, wretch!—bent your knee before her!" howled Albano with increasing wildness. But suddenly a flash of light from hell seemed to shine on him: he grew quiet. His eye measured the athletic form of the architect: he must get rid of him.

"You are, then, innocent, Thelma?—Did you really come here only by accident?"

"By my eternal salvation, I did so!" stammered she. "But if you do not let me go, I shall die for fear."

"Nonsense! You said so also that evening when you sat by my bed. I will hear, without witnesses, from your lips, and on this spot where I have found you, what caused the scene before me. Have the kindness, Mr. Architect, to go before us to the castle; I shall follow with my betrothed."

"No, by heaven! I do not go from this spot," said Seiler, resolutely. "Do you think I would leave her alone with you? No, we go either all together or none."

"Thelma, will you deny this small request?"

Albano's teeth chattered; he bit in his lips that he might put this question with an appearance of composure.

She was silent.

"Thelma, bethink yourself!" continued Albano. "Shall the architect have the advantage, and your future husband stand here to be laughed at like the dupe in the play? Answer me. Grant my request, and I promise you never to mention to my parents what I have seen here."

This had effect upon Thelma; if any thing could be compared with the horrors of this fatal hour, it was the fear of the scenes that awaited her in the castle. In hope to escape these, she determined to remain alone with her excited betrothed for a few minutes, and she, therefore, asked Seiler to step into the grotto.

"Allow me to remain here," was all he answered; "you require my arm."

"No Seiler, I know him better," whispered Thelma, while Albano seemed to measure with his eyes the distance of the balustrade at the steep rock down to the water. "I know him; he will never forgive our refusing any longer to comply with his will. Go in,—I will try to speak to his heart."

The architect went with hesitating steps to the grotto; but Albano sprang forward like a tiger, seized the light Thelma, lifted her from the ground, and—threw her into the abyss where the agitated waves received his bride.

"Satan! you have drowned her."

These were the only words which Seiler uttered as he rushed forth from the grotto, pushed aside the mad Albano; and, without hesitation, sprang after the hapless maiden.

Albano climbed up the wide balustrade; there he stood and uttered a loud frantic laugh, which he intermitted now and then to listen to the deep beneath. A noise was heard below; it came nearer; finally the head of the architect seemed to emerge, and immediately after a long black veil was seen swimming behind a figure, whose form was, for the most part, covered by the architect; for he held her clasped round with one arm, while he strove with the other to work his way through the waves; but there was no landing-place on that side.

"Now adore her! now adore her!" Albano shouted with delight, and answered with a mocking laughter the cry of help which Seiler uttered now and then. He seemed now to sink, and then again to work himself out of the waves. Lights now appeared in the park; a confused cry of many voices mingled in the storm of the mocking laughter of Albano, who strove to drown all.

"They come! they come!—now they come all together!" shrieked the infuriated madman, and began to dance on the balustrade. His leaps grew wilder and more dangerous, and the voices grew louder in the park; Seiler's strength gave way, and ever smaller grew the black spot on the lake.

The castle clock now struck half-past seven—the cry for help ceased; and only Albano's laughter—the music by which he danced— resounded dismally from the grotto.

END OF THE SECOND PART.

PART III.

CHAPTER I.

ALBANO'S REVENGE.

On the evening of the sixteenth of November, there stood in the brightly lighted saloon of the castle at Hammarby, the Baroness Ravenstein, with her sister, at a table covered with gauze, laces, and brilliant silks, examining the bridal dress, which under the hands of the mantua-makers approached nearer and nearer its completion.

"These are excellent blondes. I had none like them on my wedding-dress," said the baroness, holding a garniture of them against the light. "Indeed they are superb,—almost as if woven of silver-air."

"And the garniture, I am rejoiced, has come out finely, though it was difficult to make it after the Paris journal of fashions," said one of the dress-makers, who wished to see her deserts placed in the proper light.

"Truly you have done that most admirably, Mademoiselle Péhl," observed the countess with a condescending smile, "and I am persuaded that my future daughter-in-law, the young countess, will never employ any other mantua-maker but you."

"At what time will the gown be so far completed that my daughter can try it on?" asked the baroness.

"Within half an hour, your ladyship. I have only to sew on the waist, and as the folds are already laid in, it will soon be done."

"We may then send to my daughter, and ask her whether she will try it on here, or whether she wishes to have the dress sent to her."

The baroness was just going to ring, when in the same moment Borgstedt entered with a face that looked as if he had just risen from the grave.

"Is the young lady here?" was the short, abrupt question he asked, while his eyes wandered about the room in anxious search.

"No, she is in her room," answered the baroness and the countess almost at the same time. "But what in the world is the matter, Borgstedt? You look, indeed, quite disturbed."

Borgstedt did not answer, but left the room, and ran as fast as his feet would permit along the corridor, and down the staircase. Having reached the court-yard, he ordered, with a trembling voice, two servants to light lanterns and follow him.

Borgstedt had shortly before seen a figure resembling Count Albano, take the path leading to the grotto. Urged by an inexplicably gloomy feeling, he had hastened to the east wing, and found both the rooms of the young lady and her chamber-maid dark and empty. The broken door of Thelma's sleeping-room left no doubt but force had been used; but how, and for what purpose, he had had no time to inquire. The old servant having satisfied himself that Thelma was not in her room, his apprehensions increased. Nor was the little Anna to be found, which was not to be wondered at, since she lay in a fainting fit in the small cabinet where Albano had locked her up.

"Make haste, children!" called out old Borgstedt, and hastened once more to the east wing to look into the sleeping chamber. It then seemed to him that he heard a voice in the closed cabinet. "Is any body here?" he asked, and knocked at the door.

"Oh, my God! it is I,—Anna, Mr. Steward. The ugly Count Albano has locked me in, and taken the key with him. I die with fear here in the darkness. For heaven's sake help me to get out!"

"Where is the young lady?" asked Borgstedt, in such a trembling voice, that Anna more guessed than understood what he said.

"Ah! good heavens!" complained the girl, "she wanted to go to the grotto this dark night, and then came the young Count Albano and wanted to come in, but the young lady had taken the key with her, and he frightened me so, that I shrieked till I fainted. Oh, good heavens! only help me to get out of this place."

But Borgstedt was occupied with different thoughts; he hastened off with the two grooms. "Has any one seen the architect come back from the parsonage?" asked he, casting a hasty glance up to the dark windows in Seiler's rooms.

"Yes," answered one of the grooms. "It is more than half an hour ago that I took his horse from him."

"Good God! There is no light in his room, and I did not see him with the ladies." It began to swim before Borgstedt's eyes, and a terri-

ble light dawned upon him, when, from the lake, the cry of help, mingled with Count Albano's laughter, resounded through the night.

"Make haste, my men; run as fast as you can. Some accident has
happened, some one's life is in danger; unfasten the boat, and go to
the grotto. Make as much haste as you can." The old servant of twenty years sank down at a tree, his strength forsook him and denied all
further service.

In the meantime alarm and commotion had also risen in the
castle. The count came down; they ran to Thelma's room, the sight
of which almost gave the frightened mother a fit of apoplexy. "My
Thelma! my Thelma! where are you? Answer me!" She ran about in
wild despair, and sought for the lost child in all corners.

"If you let me out I will tell all!" called out Anna, from her prison.

"Where is the key?" asked the count.

"Count Albano took it when he ran after the young lady to the
grotto."

"To the grotto?" A sad misgiving came over the trembling parents. The count rushed off, and the countess, with pale cheeks and
streaming hair, hastened after him. All the inmates of the castle followed them.

Only the countess sat, breathless, on the sofa, and pressed her
head against her violently beating heart. She recollected the day when
the bans were the first time published, and the hour when Thelma
wanted to open her heart to give herself comfort by communicating
her secret. The countess had held herself back, and avoided to speak
to her soothingly, and say to her a word of comfort. Left alone with
her grief, the unhappy bride had, perhaps, sought another bridal bed
than the one intended for her. Dark images floated before the excited
imagination of the countess. She trembled with cold in every limb;
but she had not strength enough to leave the room, whose broken
door testified to the dangerous madness that swayed over her son—a
madness from which the worst might be expected.

The park was now so light, from the many lanterns and torches,
one would have supposed, at a distance, that fire-works were going
off in its dark walls; but it was a fire-work of a very dismal kind; the
confused running about, and shrieking of many voices, gave it a wild,
fantastical appearance.

When the count had reached the lake, the two grooms who had unfastened the boat had just returned, and not with empty hands.

Seiler, holding in his arms the pale Thelma, sat at the stern, and gazed, with dark, piercing looks upon the people standing on the shore. He himself was a terrible sight. His countenance, at other times manly and fresh, was as white as the foam that floated around the boat; and his black, finely curled hair lay wet and matted on his cloudy brow.

When the boat touched the shore, all hands were stretched out to take the young lady; the baroness, however, thrust the people back, whom the count had ordered to take care of her, and pressed on toward the landing place. "Thelma! Thelma!" exclaimed she, with a heart-rending voice. "Answer me, my life, my light, my angel, answer your mother!" She wrang, in despair, the loosened braids of the long silken hair of her daughter, and pressed her fevered mouth, upon Thelma's ice-cold lips,—"Answer! answer! answer!"—And the echo alone gave back her wailing notes with terrible distinctness.

In vain writhed the proud baroness in the dust, at the feet of her daughter; no answer followed, and she had to be torn from her, that the ice-cold bride might be brought to the castle.

"In this general excitement, in this consternation, which makes my blood run cold," said the count to Seiler, "I can ask no calm question, nor expect a distinct answer. You have sacrificed yourself to save Thelma; but where is my son? Where is Albano,—do you know?"

"Ha! the raving villain is, no doubt, still standing on the wall before the grotto, laughing in scorn at his deed. It was he who sacrificed this charming being to his madness and jealousy,—he is her murderer!" answered the architect, convulsively, wringing his stiffened hands, while his teeth chattered, and he shook so violently with cold that one could hardly understand him.

"For heaven's sake, sir," whispered the count, while he eagerly seized his arm, "take care how you use expressions of this kind, I would advise you. We shall see how all has come about! Now follow the hapless train, whilst I see what has become of my son!"

The count, accompanied by a few servants, hastened to the grotto. When yet at a distance, he called out Albano's name, but no answer followed; and only the howling of the storm was heard. The nearer the count approached his goal, the more compressed his breast became, and the more difficult it became for him to breathe. With the wildest expression in his searching eyes, he looked in all directions, but he found nothing but the naked grey walls of the grotto. "Remain standing here," said he to the servants; "I will go in myself."

He crossed the threshold.—"Are you here, Albano, my son?" It was dark in the grotto; the count could distinguish nothing; and when all remained silent upon his repeated questions, he began to grope about with his hands; he found nothing but the cold, damp walls.

This was a bitter, dismal hour for the family of the count. The mighty, rich man stood, in the darkness of the night, upon the grotto, trembling with anguish, and bowed to the earth with grief. His son, the heir to his name, was gone. Perhaps he lay there in the watery abyss from which his bride had just been drawn forth.

The count seemed to suppose this; and, after a pause, he gave new orders accordingly; his people stirred anew; they ran more, many called out louder, in confused manner, than before; boats, oars, and poles, were put in motion, while the elements continued to rave, as if the last day of judgment was drawing near.

On the same table in the saloon, where the wedding-dress had just been shining, now lay the pale bride, on a bed of state. A great many people were around her, busied in rubbing and chafing her limbs. All attempts at resuscitation, however, remained without success,—no life returned to her broken heart,—no breath was perceived on the mirror that was held before her lips.

Thelma—the lovely revelation of an angel upon earth—had gone back to her home; whether she had breathed her last breath in the deeps of the lake, or on the man to whom she had devoted the rich love of her young heart, that only Seiler knew, and he buried it as a holy secret for ever in his breast. It may, however, be presumed, with probability, that she died in his arms, and on a place which she deemed heaven itself, though she could leave it but dying. Had she, at this moment, feelings and thoughts, they could have only been happy ones, for she believed she died with him.

But where can words be found of sufficient power to describe the state in which the baroness and countess found themselves—two mothers, in whose hearts despair was raging—the *one* convinced that the blow had struck—the other tortured by a fearful uncertainty, from which nothing could free her?

The grief of the countess was silent, immoveable, and almost as cold as the marble-pale Thelma, as she stood at the table and wiped her dripping hair. At times she passed the moist hand over her brow, and fixed a staring look upon the door; but the messengers who fled between the castle and the park appeared pale and like ghosts; fear, despair, and terror were painted on every face.

The grief of the baroness was more raving—it bordered on frenzy. With loud shrieks she plucked out her hair, and threw herself with convulsive motions upon the lifeless being whose young life she had constantly embittered by her pride and selfishness.

And what did the architect do?

Exhausted by the exertions of body and mind, he had sunk upon his bed; his limbs, but shortly before stiff and cold, now burned with a violent fever; his senses were confused, and the fire in his brain called forth the wildest phantasies. Now he would laugh loud, in imitation of Albano's voice, and then he listened and whispered, bending back his head and stopping his ears with both his hands.

"Hush—hush—hush!" said he then, softly, and began to work with his hands as if swimming.

"I see the boat—they push off—wait, wait!" Then he would spring up as if chased by evil demons, and exclaim: "Where—where?" Feeling round in the dark room, at last he struck his brow so violently against the stove, that he fell stunned to the floor. He passed his hand to the spot where he felt the pain, and it became wet with the warm, streaming blood. A momentary feeling of consciousness, an inexpressible fancy ensued. "Blood!" murmured he—"it is my blood—and yet it was not I who demanded this revenge; a higher will let the events come to pass, and give them free course—Ha! an awful event!"

He threw himself again upon the bed. The fever burned, and the blood was flowing from the wound unchecked; but these pains of the soul were drowned in a state of unconsciousness.

Some hours had passed in the most horrible suspense. The storm was still howling, mingling with the wild shrieks of grief of the baroness, in the dreary apartments of the castle of Hammarby. The countess stood motionless on the same spot, opposite the door; her strained look seemed to ask every one who entered for news regarding the life so dear to her mother's heart; but all lips remained closed.

Suddenly voices were heard in the court-yard; burning torches glimmered through the sight, but not a shout of joy was heard from the returning train.

"What is the gleam there in the court?" asked the countess, with vehemence, but in a hardly audible voice.

"Your ladyship, it is——," the dress-maker who had been spoken to, and was standing at the window, was not able to finish the sentence; it was only with some effort that she could suppress a shriek of horror at the sight that met her eyes.

"Are they coming back?" There was a heart-rending expression in the tone of the countess. The dignified, proud lady trembled like an aspen-leaf, yet no word of complaint passed her lips.

Miss Pehl answered nothing, except a long drawn out—"Ah, your ladyship!"

The countess put no more questions. She slowly left the saloon; like a shadow she walked through the long halls, and went down the lower entry. Here she met first her husband, who came toward her with a staring look, took her in his arms and turned her round. The countess, however, extricated herself from this well-intended restraint, and stepped to the train that followed the count. They were six servants of the house, who bore on their arms the last offspring of the noble family, the heir to the entailed estate, Count Albano, of H.

The countess only cast a glance upon the distorted features of the only being to whom she had given life. Without uttering a sound, she sank upon the cold stone floor. As the train passed by her, cold drops from Albano's red hair fell upon the face of the mother. The count and old Borgstedt lifted up the fainting lady and carried her away.

Days and weeks passed away before she awoke to a distinct consciousness of her dreary life.

CHAPTER II.

THE SERVANTS' HALL

On the left of the court-yard, at a short distance from the mansion, stood the house for the domestics, (a wooden building painted red,) whither we must for a moment, with their kind permission, conduct our readers.

It was about nine o'clock in the evening, a week after the events related in the preceding chapter. In a large gloomy room, with dark brown wooden walls, on which hung all the yellow leather breeches, the blue coats and hats of the servants, as well as here and there saws, axes, and other implements, in a motley mixture with the habiliments, there sat three figures at the chimney-fire, which was nearly burnt out, conversing together. They were the two grooms, who on that fatal evening had first unfastened the boat, and "Provost's Peter."

In the middle of the room stood an oak table—in one corner a planing bench, and near it an iron hook was fastened in the wall, holding a burning piece of pitch, which cast its red light upon a pendulum clock called a cuckoo—on another table near the window stood a wooden beer-can, surrounded by some dirty short pipes. The rest of the servants were sitting and lying on the benches, and in the beds, and listening attentively to the conversation of their more important colleagues, who held a sort of council near the chimney-fire.

"May the devil take me—if the affair should take a bad end. He never thought of that before, I warrant. He always was high in the instep, and proud as a prince," said Provost's Peter, while he thoughtfully burnished the brass chain to his watch.

"Noa—noa—he needn't be afraid," answered one of the grooms, who had taken the horse from the architect on the evening of his return from the parsonage. "Thank heaven, there is yet law and justice in the land though our lord is a count and Mr. Seiler only an architect. The architect is a whole man, I can tell you! He put many dollars in my hand, that I should keep his horse in good trim; and as true as my name is Boerse, they shan't get at him; for if they try it, I shall step up—I—and with my hand upon the bible I will swear, that it was the crazy young count who laughed so hard, though our gracious lord thinks it might have been somebody else."

"But if he was innocent, it would be rather venturesome to have arrested him," insinuated the Provost's Peter.

"Well—they can arrest him and hold him, God knows how long, if he is not able to prove his innocence as to the death of the crazy red-head. Besides, the count is on good terms with the judges; but to put his head before his feet they won't dare, if they don't get any witnesses who swear that the architect threw the young count into the water. And he didn't do that, I stake my head on it."

"But what business had he to be out there in the dark night? He looked as if he had some bad intentions when he rode from our house that evening. And he was as pale as death itself when he snatched the reins from my hand; and his eyes sparkled like a hawk's."

"Well, he was just so here," said Boerse; "but you told me, that all was now right and straight between him and Miss of the Provost, and that he was getting divorced from his wife on her account. Something, then, must have come across him that made his head so warm. The Frenkmans are just the fellows for that; they had rather say two words than one; and he may, perhaps, have told him that he loved his daughter too much to give her to a man who was divorced from his first wife."

"Ha, ha, that's it, no doubt! But look here, Boerse, how could the count arrest the architect, when he was sick?"

"Why, it is for that to be less wondered at. He thought the architect was, at all events, the cause of all the mishap, and he should never get out of prison except the day that he was led to the scaffold. And for that reason a watch was immediately put before the door, and the magistrate was sent for, who took down on paper all he was told. He, however, could not be examined, as he was too sick. He has not been off his bed yesterday and to-day, and to-morrow, at eight, the magistrate will come again and commence with his examination."

"But till then," said Sven, the other groom, (who had as yet been silent and absorbed in thought,) in a low voice, "till then, we must talk the matter over together, Boerse! For, look ye, if we keep our tongues I wouldn't give sixpence for his life; and I have no doubt that he would give us a good fee if we consented to state in court what we heard that evening."

"Hold your tongue and stop your cursed talk, or I'll make you do it," exclaimed the honest Boerse, in an angry tone. "You are a pretty fellow! You would, no doubt, have made better business than I, if the count had called you instead of me. I won't say exactly that he wanted to bribe and induce me to give false testimony—no indeed; but he took me aside and said: 'Hear, dear Boerse,' said he, 'is it not so,—you could not possibly hear the laughing at the great distance; you have, therefore, been mistaken at all events?' But then I said frankly,—'Your

Lordship,' said I, 'I'll stake my soul and salvation, that it was the young count in his own person who laughed and howled, and shouted there on the top of the rock, whilst the architect, together with the young lady, lay down below in the lake, and I and the steward and Sven, we all heard it,' said I.——'Ah, but Borgstedt is so old that his ears are not to be trusted any longer,' and then the count took out his purse is if it was accidentally—perhaps it was accidentally—and put it on the table. But I stuck to it: what I heard I have heard. Boerse will not keep his tongue if he can save a person by his testimony. And if you should take into your head to accept any money from the count, Sven, to testify against the architect, then we both, Peter and I, shall stand up against you, and tell in court what you have just now spoken."

"Don't you see, stupid fellow, that I only joked!" said Sven, angrily. "I think as much of my honour as you do of yours,—and you needn't at all come down upon me in that way." In his heart, however, Sven cursed his having been so foolish as to betray his plan by which he had, of course, cut off all possibility of executing it.

"The fox finds the grapes too sour, if he cannot reach them," remarked Boerse, and drew his coarse face into a sneering smile. "But, Peter, what did your people say when they heard of the story? I should not have wondered at all, if your Alfhild, who was already so weak that one might throw her down with the little finger, had died on the spot when she heard that her Seiler had been arrested, and that too for murder."

"And I can tell you, there was a great fuss at first. But the captain comforted her, and told her, heaven knows what! only so much I know, that our Miss was to come here to stay with the ladies at the castle, who don't know at present where their heads are. The provost would not allow it at first; but then she urged him with all her might; and then he called me and said,—'You must get the carriage ready directly; Miss wants to go to the castle.' I had the horses harnessed in no time—Miss came out well wrapped up, and got into the carriage, and then the captain wrapped a fur round her feet, and off we went. After we had gone on a little way, I said, as if talking to myself, 'I should be surprised if the architect, so handsome and fine a man, had really drowned the count and the young lady, as the people say.' 'No, Peter, you may depend upon it he is innocent,' said she then in so beautiful and dear a voice, that tears came into my eyes. My master would not let her come here, because he was afraid that she might have an interview with the architect."

"That is taken care of," said Boerse; "two men keep watch at the door by day and night, and besides, he'll soon be taken to gaol."

Here the conversation was interrupted by old Borgstedt, who came to tell the men that it was time to relieve the guard at the door of the architect.

Two of the servants who were lying on the beds, stretching themselves and yawning, got up, took a good pull from the beer can, and felt their pockets to see if they were provided with tobacco and matches.

"It will be pretty cold there at the architect's," said one of the servants;—"I hope Mr. Steward will be so good as let us have a bottle or two filled for us."

"I will try to grant your request, Lars, but make haste, children,— it wants but a few minutes to ten."

The men took large clubs with them, which served them instead of halberts, and went with Borgstedt to the west wing of the castle.

After the former guards were relieved, Borgstedt withdrew, soon returning, however, with a little basket which contained the evening meal for the prisoner.

"Look here, children, I have not forgotten you," said he, as he took from the basket a green bottle filled with the strong drink, which is not exclusively a cordial for the lower classes only. "Now drink courage for the night, for you will not be relieved before two o'clock."

The old man, hereupon, unlocked the door, and entered into Seiler's room.

The architect sat at a table covered with papers. One of his hands supported his head, while with the other he wrote some lines upon a piece of paper before him. A wax candle behind a green screen threw a pale, magic light upon his face, which, though wan, had resumed its bold expression of resoluteness.

"Good evening, Mr. Seiler," said the old Steward, as he put the basket upon another smaller table. "Will you do me the favour to eat a little?"

"I thank you, dear Borgstedt. In this cursed house I will eat nothing more but what is indispensably necessary for the support of life. The vilest prison-food will be to me a delicacy, compared with these poisonous dainties, which remind me of my poisoned life and the shameful violence which the count does to me. After the conversation we have had together, he is convinced as much as I am, that Albano, from mad jealousy, committed the murder of his bride, and he shall see in it the avenging hand of Providence. These papers, Borgstedt"—Seiler here snatched up a little packet containing Leganger's notes—"these papers give to him to-morrow, when I am gone; they will throw a light on things of which he has not the least suspicion now. But no more of this! Do you think that my wish will be granted, to be allowed to see once more the departed angel and Alfhild? With the latter I could speak in no other place with greater safety and less interruption than at night, and in the room where the corpses are lying."

"I have made all arrangements for it," answered Borgstedt, "Miss Alfhild had sufficient courage not to regard the place of interview, if she can only see you once more before…"

The old man hesitated to finish his sentence. The expression, of which he was going to make use of, seemed to him not sufficiently fine and chosen for the proud architect.

"Before my being carried to prison, where they will bring me like a common criminal," began Seiler, with cold scorn. "But this is not the first vulgar act which stains the escutcheon of the illustrious count's family. Or what do you think, Borgstedt, is not this a mere trifle compared to Leganger's history?"

An expression of perfect astonishment was painted on Borgstedt's old face, while he trembled in all his limbs. "Sir," asked he, pointing at the packet in Seiler's hands, "do these papers contain any thing concerning that history?"

"Every thing," answered Seiler. "And if the count finds any thing obscure in my conduct, his own conscience will give him light on it. The application will not be difficult after having read this."

"Have you ever once before had these about you, and forgotten them at some place?"

"Yes, one evening in the grotto; but those were the originals, from which this is only an extract."

"Father in heaven, thy ways are wonderful!" exclaimed old Borgstedt, passing his hand over his brow. "On the same evening that you forgot your pocket-book in the grotto, count Albano was there and had lighted a lamp. When I, late at night, sought and found him in the grotto, he was turning over the papers in the pocket-book which was lying before him on the table, and which he afterwards threw again upon the moss-bank. From his wild and distorted features, I perceived that he had read dangerous and forbidden things. It distracted his mind, for he was taken sick the very same night. Since that time he has never been quite right in his mind, and this has led, at last to the awful events which cost that angel and himself their lives."

The architect had risen from his seat. With his arms folded, his eyes flashing, and lips compressed; he placed himself before Borgstedt, who, with an expression of fear, was silent, and involuntarily drew back a step.

"You are right, old man—God's ways are wonderful! But another light dawns on me," said Seiler, slowly. "It was not these papers which he read—they were left untouched; this I recollect distinctly. But there were in this pocket-book letters which, without mentioning a name, spoke of my passion for an object which had awakened it. These letters were from one of my friends in Norway, and accidentally, of so mysterious a nature, that Albano, whose head was already full of thoughts of jealousy, saw in them a confirmation of his suspicion. Alfhild was the person in question, and he believed it was Thelma."

"But, Mr. Architect," interrupted Borgstedt, with a certain precaution, "I hope you will not deny, between you and me, that you were in love also with the young lady. I have often heard you sing at night before the grotto, on the lake, and seen the young lady steal regularly several times in the week to the grotto, to listen to your singing, which has caused her unhappiness, and at last her death. You will not, I hope, be offended at me for my saying so, for you know that if the young lady had not loved you so much, she would not have fallen into despair concerning her fate, to which she had reconciled herself before with submission. I mean to say that she would have stayed at home on that evening, and count Albano would not have fallen into that mad rage which deprived the young lady of her life, and has brought you into this situation, from which you will find it difficult to extricate yourself."

"You are not entirely wrong, Borgstedt. I shall never be able to clear myself from the reproach of having been the indirect cause of that awful catastrophe. But God knows that I have now given up all plans of revenge. That departed angel has already forgiven my guilt. A guilt for which I shall never forgive myself. We stood there reconciled, when Albano came, and, like a dark spirit, quenched the torch of peace. But—I will not recall those awful moments! I become almost frantic when I think of it.... Pardon me, dear Borgstedt—but I must request you to leave me alone. At what time will you come for me for the awful meeting?"

"About midnight I shall be here again."

Borgstedt, went out and locked the door, and Seiler walked with long steps to and fro in the room.

CHAPTER III.

THE CHAMBER OF DEATH.

At midnight, as the twelfth stroke of the clock of the castle died away, old Borgstedt, together with the architect, ascended one of the little stair-cases which led from the side wing into the lower storey of the main building. At the double door of a long hall, Borgstedt stopped and gave a gentle knock. Steps were heard, and a servant opened it soon after.

"Here, dear Bergman," said the old man, in a friendly tone, "you may go with your comrades and sleep a little for about an hour. The architect wishes to see the corpses, and I would not refuse his request. You may, therefore, rest for an hour; I shall come and wake you up."

The servant received, at the same time, an additional application in cash, which he quietly lodged in his pocket; he beckoned then to his comrades, and gave a free entrance to the visiters.

Their steps re-echoed in the empty hall, which was only lighted up by the faint light of a lamp. They stopped in the back-ground of the hall.

"It is a heart-rending sight; have you courage, Mr. Seiler?" asked Borgstedt, holding back the architect's hand, which he had just placed upon the door-latch.

"Courage?" exclaimed Seiler, with a sneering smile. "Let us go in!"

A moment after, they stood in a large vaulted hall, whose walls were covered with black cloth and rich silver fringes. On the floor were seen two elevations, likewise clothed in black, and on each of them stood a black coffin; upon both fell the faint glimmer of wax tapers, now burning low.

Seiler stopped at the smaller coffin. Borgstedt attentively observed his countenance, as he bent down to lay his head upon one of the silver plates. No visible emotion moved his body; but when he raised himself again, his face was as white as the bridal dress with which Thelma's corpse was adorned. Seiler stretched out his hand twice to lift the fine muslin veil which covered the features once so lovely; he manned himself at last and drew back the cloth. The angel of death had been forbearing in his work; yet he had put upon the sunken eye-lids a stamp sufficiently distinct to give to those who had known this charming being before, a feeling of deepest pain. Seiler's grief disdained words; he only motioned to Borgstedt to withdraw.

When the old man had closed the door behind him, the architect laid his face upon the small, cold hand, which, in its white glove, resembled a work of art in marble. The delicate fingers stamped fine icy spots upon his cheek, and on the point of each finger remained hanging a hot drop of perspiration. Seiler's feelings dissolved—here perhaps for the first time—into tears of repentance; they burned hot, but they were a relief to his soul, and he now looked more calmly upon the slumbering angel, in whose soft locks hung a myrtle wreath.

"*She is* happy"—thought he—"I know that she would rather have *died* near my heart than have *lived* near his."

Seiler rose. The thought of Albano filled his soul with wild emotions. He walked round the elevation and came to the other side, where he gazed with a menacing, challenging look upon the loathsome mass which formed the earthly remains of Count Albano.

"Even in death they united her with the being which caused her the greatest horror in life," he muttered, as he threw the white cloth again over the swollen face and red hair which, combed smooth and parted, lay on both sides of the brow.

Seiler walked, for a long time, buried in thought, between the two coffins. The wax candles shone ever fainter; a part of them had already burnt down, and mingled their smell with the stupefying odour of the inmates, when steps were heard in the adjoining room; yet Seiler was too much occupied with his own thoughts to notice them.

At last he felt a gentle touch, he turned round, stretching out his arm, and Alfhild lay on his breast.

All fear concerning his imprisonment, all considerations of propriety or impropriety, found in this moment, no room in Alfhild's soul.

As long as Seiler was free, esteemed, and beloved, she could willingly separate herself from him, but now that he was accused of murder, and in prison, where his honour was endangered to be stained by a shameful suspicion, and his pride must suffer under the treatment he received; now all doubts had disappeared, and she would not have shunned the greatest exertions to come to him, in order to comfort and assure him, by the soft grasp of her hand, and her love-laden look, that she believed him pure and free from every fault, though all the world should pronounce him guilty.

"My Alfhild, my adored angel!" exclaimed Seiler, clasping his arms ever faster round her slender waist, while she let her weary head sink upon his shoulders. "My Alfhild!" An expression of blessedness spread round Seiler's mouth, his cheeks coloured, and his eyes assumed a brighter lustre than they ever had before.

"Let us go into the hall—it is here so dismal," whispered Alfhild, and pressed closer to his beloved breast.

"Yes, let us go away from here; but first follow me to the coffin where Thelma slumbers, and promise me in her cold hand, that you will ever—"

"Seiler—no such vow," Alfhild interrupted; "why should we seal our love at a bier? And what need is there for a vow at all? You have, indeed, my whole heart, my soul, all my feelings and thoughts! I shall love you for us both—for us *both*, Seiler, for I have heard, what I did not know while she lived, that it was you that caused her the pain which struck her young heart still deeper than the awful connection with Albano; and therefore I believe it will give her joy to see that I have taken her love to you upon myself, and thus in me two beings love you."

The architect, open to any thing fanciful, seized upon this thought with eagerness. Such a feeling was suited to his thirsting heart. His heart beat on hers with strong throbs, and on his face was painted a proud satisfaction.

"I hope I need not assure you that I never sympathised with

Thelma's love?" asked Seiler, with a searching look; "and I hope you never believed so?"

"No; I never believed it, nor shall I ever believe it, though they here at the castle believe the contrary."

"Do you believe that Thelma, this noble being of fine feelings, could cling to a heart which never gave a response to her feelings?"

"Good God, Seiler, to what thoughts will you lead me? Have pity, and do not torment me with such suggestions! Thelma was good and pure as an angel—and that she loved you, she could not help."

"But I, Alfhild, am not pure and free! If I would deceive you in this hour, I were the most contemptible and abominable of men that the earth ever bore. Rather than leave you with the consciousness of having given you an erroneous impression, may the pain seize on your heart, even though it should die with bleeding. I feel now that your love to me is strong enough to bear the hardest trial. Know, then, my Alfhild, that I made her believe she was loved by me, not by words, but by subtle trickeries, which the spirits of hell insinuated to me; and after she had, without distrust, imbibed the poison, and this began to operate so that her betrothed perceived the destruction in her young heart, then I withdrew coldly, and increased or wounded his feeling for me alternately, as my fiendish humour impelled me. You shudder, Alfhild; you may, but you must love me notwithstanding, for I cannot live without your love, and could not do so from the first moment that I saw you, otherwise I should have deceived you too. But love surrounded you with a protecting armour. And my revenge would have spared also the angel of light who lies slumbering there, or would have, at least, brought her back from her error, if your father had not treated me in such a manner as called into life afresh all the dark thoughts of my soul. And you also, dear Alfhild, wounded my heart, when you refused me the vow of fidelity, and thought on right and wrong, whilst true and genuine love disregards all, and only follows its own promptings. Then a chill came over my heart, though a fire burned there which incessantly consumed its noblest feelings. I continued my old play, more from want of nobler employments than from vengeance.

"At last, however, the pangs of remorse came, when I was to separate from the innocent victim of my cruel revenge. On the evening when not even your eye, my dear Alfhild, could penetrate the dark clouds that enshrouded my whole being, after my return from the parsonage. I went to the grotto in order to take leave of a place from whence I had often lulled to repose her unsuspecting heart, by awakening happy dreams of hope. And here, Alfhild, in the deepest recess of the grotto I met her; I confessed to her my guilt. With her heart crushed she went out to the balustrade; I followed her, and your beloved, Alfhild, begged on his knees for forgiveness. Yet I shall never deem this a humiliation; no, I think of it with satisfaction, for—she forgave me—she felt that there was in love neither hate nor bitterness. But when the breath of peace now floated from her lips over my heart, the miserable, mad Albano appeared. She wished to remain alone with him to calm his wild spirit, that demanded from her this, as a condition of his silence, and yielding to her request I went into the grotto; but no sooner had I done so, than the awful sound of a body falling into the water, explained to me the revenge of the madman. In the depths of the lake, with the raging waves over me, I found the dear burden. Had a landing-place been near, and not rugged cliffs alone, I believe she might have been saved; but now——"

The architect was silent, and his eyes rested long on the white cloth which covered Thelma's face.

Alfhild had become, during the narration of her beloved, almost as pale and motionless as her friend upon the bier.

"Why—why?" These words came struggling over her lips, but she could not finish.

"Why I was such a fiend, you mean?" resumed the architect. "Alfhild, only the thirst for vengeance guided me. I had reasons to hate this race; but as it would be too long to explain them orally, I have written down these reasons, which will explain, though not justify, my conduct."

With these words, Seiler took from his pocket a large thick letter, and gave it to Alfhild. She concealed trembling, the mysterious papers which were to lift the unpenetrable veil that covered Seiler's conduct.

"And now let us leave this room," added Seiler. "My soul has opened itself to your love. However unworthy I may appear to you, do not reject my heart. Thelma has forgiven me. I told you that I loved only you; and has she not left to you her love as a dear legacy? Tell me, my beloved, will you also forgive? When all veils will be removed,—yet this will be done only there above, for who can already here below interpret the riddles of the human heart?—then, Alfhild, you will find that there was at least one firm, pure, imperishable feeling which animated my breast; a feeling which I never denied, nor ever shall deny; my love to you."

Alfhild had not strength to lend words to the violent sensations which stifled her. She only pressed Seiler's hand, and cast upon him a look that promised that his heart should not be disappointed; yet there lay in this look at the same time an expression of grief, which penetrated his inmost soul.

Seiler now conducted his beloved into the saloon, and took a seat by her side on a sofa, from where the door leading to the gloomy room of death could not be seen. She laid her head upon his heart, whose restless beating she alone understood how to assuage. The conviction, however, that he had acted towards Thelma as a man without principles—or with bad ones—left in her heart a great void behind, which nothing could fill up. But yet she was his. Through his misfortune, his crime, and punishment, she was bound to him threefold; and the great goal, which shone brightly behind the dark present, was for Alfhild's pious mind the hope of reconciling him to himself, and through her love and her unceasing efforts of banishing all thoughts which enslaved him in dark clouds.

Some minutes passed in significant silence, which was only now and then interrupted by sighs; and then they must separate.

"Have faith in me, and mistrust me not; you will hear from me, Seiler," said Alfhild sobbing on his breast.

"Thanks to you, my beloved! You will give rest to my weary heart, and this it needs sadly. Be not at the window, my Alfhild, to-morrow morning when they carry me, like a criminal, from a place whither my ill star led me. If the clattering of the vehicle should strike your ear, then remember that—as true as God may help me—I am innocent of the crime which they charge me with, to save the honour of the mad Albano. I would have sacrificed my own life to have saved that of Thelma; but he who murdered her is, no doubt already in hell, to receive the reward for his wicked deed. Well, do you hear, dear Alfhild? do not come to the window. Leave me time to become accustomed to my humiliation; for if I knew that you were observing me at that moment, I would——"

He did not finish; he had compassion on Alfhild's heart, that was already wounded too deeply.

The leave-taking was over. Alfhild was conducted to her room by Borgstedt, and Seiler walked the rest of the night up and down in his own. He was not able to close his eyes for a single minute; for the recollection of Thelma in her coffin, and the pressure of her cold fingers upon his cheek, as well as Alfhild's drooping form, and her panting look, which indicated a broken heart, and a speedy return to a better home, come constantly before his soul.

The thought of his being soon carried to prison had no share in his violent excitement; for on this point his manly fortitude was sufficient to console him in the wrong he suffered. He knew, besides, that he could not be found guilty; but in a threatening gloomy form came the thought before his soul, that he might not be able to prove his innocence, and clear his reputation of every suspicion.

The next morning, soon after eight, the low rumbling of a heavy waggon over the paved court-yard of the castle, and a small red-nosed man, in a blue frock coat with brass buttons, announced to the architect that it was time. The officer alighted, the waggon stopping at the west wing.

A wild smile played round the mouth of the architect. He trembled not with pain, but rage. The proud man was now compelled to bend to the iron necessity of fate. Every struggle was to no purpose. There was nothing left but to bear with fortitude what could not be altered.

When the officer, together with old Borgstedt, entered Seiler's room, all emotion was, therefore, suppressed, and his face did not betray the slightest excitement.

"Will the gentlemen please to be seated—I shall be ready in a moment," said the architect, in the indifferent tone of common politeness. Hereupon he examined his travelling baggage, and then took his cap without the slightest sign of emotion, pointed with a slight shudder to the door, and opened it.

The officer, who had not taken a seat, went out first. Seiler turned round once more on the threshold to shake Borgstedt's hand, and thank him for the sympathy he had shown to him, as a stranger, and whispered to him: "There in the drawer lies the packet. To-morrow when the bridal couple are buried, and with them the last hope of the noble family—to-morrow when the count awakes to a void, dreary life, then give him my compliments and this bundle." A bitter, almost malicious smile, curled round the lips of the architect. The honest old servant answered this request with a slight nod of his grey head.

In the next moment two vehicles rolled through the court-yard. In the best and most convenient one sat the officer alone; in the other the architect, and by his side was placed a man of dark appearance, whose dirty, coarse coat contrasted strangely with Seiler's fine, neat cloak, and whose disagreeable personal manners much annoyed him.

It was an attendant of the prison, who had been selected for Seiler's travelling companion.

No human being showed himself at the windows, and no one was in the court-yard; even the servants of the count had kept out of sight from a feeling of delicacy, in order not to offend by their presence the proud architect, who had always been liberal towards them.

Yet his departure was heard by many. But no one was affected so deeply by the rattling of the waggon as Alfhild. She lay in her room on her knees, and she pressed mechanically her hands to her ears, like a widow left behind in mortal agony, when the coffin of her husband is nailed fast, and with every stroke of the hammer, one fibre of her heart after the other is breaking.

On the same evening Provost Frenkman performed at the castle the church ceremony of burial. The funeral train was not long, but the number of spectators was so much the more numerous, when the large family tomb in the old church at Hammarby was opened to receive the heir to the estate, and his bride.

The following morning old Borgstedt entered the sleeping-room of the count. The faithful servant was moved in his deepest soul, when he saw the deep grief that spoke from every feature of his master, whose countenance was generally so friendly. Yet he had to fulfil his promise.

After Borgstedt had inquired after the health of the count, and the latter had answered, "Bad—it is over with me!" he delivered the bundle with the words, "From the architect, who sends his compliments."

The count looked at it with little attention, and then cut mechanically the thread, and examined the papers. On the top lay a paper with the words, "A greeting from the land of the dead."

"Leave me," said the count. "You may wait in the ante-room;— no one must disturb me."

That we may not retard the course of the story, we leave it to the fancy of the reader to paint to himself the astonishment and surprise of the count at the papers just handed to him.

EXTRACT

*From Jeames Leganger's Notes on a Journey through Sweden,
in the years 1741 and 1742.*

A LIGHT-HEARTED youth of three-and-twenty years, I wandered, with my knapsack on my back, and a few dollars—my whole property— in my pocket, out of the city-gate of Christina, taking the road to Goensberg, where my father, a skilful landscape-painter in his youth, had now, through poverty and weak eyes, descended to the humble, but reflection-stirring profession of a coffin-painter.

"Well, if a man has only his living, and this in an honest way," my mother used to say, "it is indifferent whether he paints canvass or wood."

My father and myself—as soon as I began to think and reflect— were of a different opinion on this point; as the old man was, at home, accustomed, in regard to my mother, to let "five" be even, he let also this assertion of his better-half pass unattacked.

On the long winter evenings, when I—then a mere boy—had to hold the light for him, while he painted the coffins, he told me of his beautiful former days, when he—a warm admirer of art—lived only for her alone, and he gave to his pictures such splendid colours as have never been seen in reality—the one richer and more beautiful than the other. I also received from him instruction in the art of handling the brush; but this was done in secret, for my mother thought that it only consumed time, which, when devoted to coffin-painting, was more profitable.

When my parents, however, perceived that my talents seemed to promise more and more every year, they resolved to send me to Christina to cultivate my abilities, which might, in time, bring in more than mere coffin-painting.

I was sixteen years old when I went to Christina. Through my industry I succeeded in making myself thought a pretty skilful artist, when I, in my twenty-third year, left the city to travel in foreign lands. This, however, could only be done on foot, for my small income only afforded me a sparing subsistence and an humble coat.

I had determined to visit Sweden first; afterwards to go through Denmark to Germany, and heaven knows where I, on the wings of my fancy, meant to travel; at least round half the world. Before I entered on this long pilgrimage, I wished to take leave of my native town, and my parents, to receive from them the only treasure they could give me—their blessing.

To see again the workshop where my father now, as formerly, sat among the dark coffins, with his grey locks playing round his furrowed brow, made a deep and never-to-be-forgotten impression upon me. Hearing my steps, he rose; and seeing his only beloved son approach, his still warm heart beat quicker than usual. We clasped each other in our arms.

"Come, now, let us go to your mother," said my father. "I will not have the joy alone. She has so many years shared my grief; she shall now share my joy."

It was a truly festive evening. The angels in heaven, no doubt, rejoiced in it.

The following morning my knapsack was unpacked, and all my sketches and pictures were examined. There were not many of them, for I had generally to sell them to procure my living before the colours were hardly dry. My father unrolled my things with the same delight that I had had at the sight of a sheet of pictures with stately lines of coloured horsemen with drawn swords. At the other end of the table on which the pictures were carefully laid, sat my mother, with spectacles on her nose, and her hands in her lap; only in this way she wished to enjoy the treasures which Jeames had brought for her. Their delight, however, was beyond bounds, when they came to an ivory tablet which bore the portrait of their son, who was now to go into the wide world. I found pleasure in portrait-painting, and I had, in leisure hours, painted this little picture, which I knew would be to my parents the dearest present I could give them before my departure.

I will no longer dwell upon the simple, but pleasant recollections of the years of my youth.

With the addition of three linen garments in my knapsack, and the blessing of my parents in my heart, I bade farewell to these never-to-be-forgotten beings, whose pure and deep love gave me my only comfort. When I thought of my gloomy fate, she gave me hope again, that on the firm bridge of faith I might, one day, soar up to Him from whom comes all good. But how many struggles are required to approach this bridge—how much skill to guide our little skiff of life, that it may not perish in the tumult of waves on the pathless ocean.

At that time, however, I did not think of those things. My spirit was light and elastic as my body; no grief or trouble affected me. Full of life and courage, I passed over the mountain ridge of the Fjellen, and I was well received wherever I came. The coin with which I paid for food and lodging, consisted in caricatures which I painted where I made a day of rest, and thus I passed through the world quite well. Only in cities I had to fall back upon my purse, which only contained two dollars. This wandering life was rich in changes and adventures; but my pleasure for it I lost in a time, which consuming the most vigorous days of my life, sucked with greedy tongue the blood from my heart, and left in its place poison, which burned and seared my nerves.

After having stayed for some time in Gothenburg, where my talent for portrait-painting procured me work and reputation, I again set out upon my wanderings, in spite of the urgings of my friends to remain in this place, yielding to my irresistible desire to travel. I now traversed Holland and Smoland, and was already, in my mind, with one foot in Schonen, when one evening, tired in body—(my mind was always bright)—I descried, to my delight, the spire of a church steeple, and a little further on, a large Gothic castle. At the sight of these alluring objects, I quickly retraced my steps from Schonen, and resolved to stay yet a little while in the province which had always shown itself so hospitable to me. I hastened my steps as much as possible, that I might not, at too late an hour, disturb my future hosts, and the sun had not yet entirely sunk as I sought, through kind and unkind words, to make a treaty of peace with the mastiff that watched the parsonage. This was, however, not easy; the dog barked terribly, and laid his fore-feet upon the fence, apparently determined to hold me by the skirts of my coat, in case I should endeavour to open the trellised gate. As my wardrobe allowed of no diminution, I had well to consider about what I should do. As I was deliberating, a young girl appeared at the open window; and, after her dark sparkling eyes had examined me for a few seconds, with a kind of roguish malicious joy, the window was suddenly closed, and the young maiden came out of the house.

"Hector—Hector! fie, for shame—into your house, back to your house, I tell you!" she called out to the dog, in a half-jesting, half-threatening tone. Hector crouched humbly at the feet of his mistress; the maiden opened the gate, and invited me to come in, a request for the repetition of which I did not give the least occasion.

As soon as I had crossed the threshold of the parsonage, I announced myself as a travelling artist, and requested hospitality for a few days.

The provost, a man somewhat advanced in years, in a very friendly manner granted my request, and also the beautiful Sigrid seemed to have no objection. In the course of our conversation at supper, the provost mentioned that the noble family at the castle had long wished to find a skilful painter, who would be willing to remain there for some time, partly to take the portraits of the present illustrious members of the family, partly to retouch the pictures in their picture-gallery, which, though very much neglected, still contained many valuable works, and particularly a numerous collection of ancestors and relations of the count's family.

I know not what gave me the wish of being engaged for this alluring work. Perhaps it was the hope to gain by it the means for a more comfortable continuation of my journey—perhaps also the pleasure I felt at the thought that I was going to live in that old Gothic castle, which appeared to me like a giant of the past, on the boundary between two epochs, motioning good bye to both. With great passion, I loved all remains of the past ages; and a Gothic, half decayed castle, could not but contain for me objects of the highest interest.

Whether beside all this—which for a burning fancy like mine was sufficient—there was still another secret attraction in my heart, I cannot say; for it would be ridiculous to maintain that I had, on the first evening been so caught in Sigrid's net, that I had not found myself able to extricate myself from it. This I should have no doubt been

able to do, if I had continued on my journey immediately on the following morning, and my head had not been filled so much with chivalric adventures, which, as I thought, were concealed in the castle,
and only waited for an opportunity to come to light.

The room which I was shown into, lay on the gable end of the
house. It was desolate, and contained nothing but a bedstead, and
some heavy chairs. Yet I liked it infinitely more now than at a later
time, when it was decked out for a bridal-chamber.

The following morning, when I entered the sitting-room, I found
Sigrid already waiting for me with the warm beer, which she handed
to me herself. Now the first opportunity I had had to look quietly
on her, and the impression she made on me, became lasting. Never,
not even in my fairest dreams, saw I such a picture. The fire of her
eyes burned my reason to ashes, and the smile of her mouth, now
as warm and lovely as the spring-sun, and then as cold as the eternal
snow on our Fjellen, now raised me up to heaven, and then brought
me back to earth again.

In the afternoon of the same day, the provost went with me to
the castle. Walking through its long, gloomy passages, it was as if I
was already living in the land of traditions; and I was wholly in it,
when two heavy folding-doors were opened, and we entered into a
large eight-cornered hall, whose gold-printed leather tapestry had
here and there got loose from the wall, and was now floating with the
whims of the whistling wind. The Gothic windows reached almost
to the vaulted ceiling. Our steps re-echoed on the polished floor. This
was unpleasant to me, for I had fancied that in this enchanted castle
one would hover like a spirit.

But my delight soon came to an end. My eyes had not devoured
one half of all the trophies, pictures, and curious things, when other
folding-doors were opened, and we stood in a room less spacious, in
the presence of the exalted occupant of this enormous ruin. On a
sofa covered with blue velvet, lay a tall, thin gentleman, examining
with a critical eye, the polished lock of a double-barrelled rifle, which
a young lad of about fifteen years had neatly cleansed and handed to
him.

"That is very well, Borgstedt! You may in time become overseer
over my armoury," said the count, without vouchsafing the deeply
bowing provost a look. "But now go, my boy," added he, "and tell the

sluggards, the boobies outside the door, they should look out that no one enter without being first announced. Ah! it is Provost Oernroos. Well, you are welcome! But what sheep have you caught there and brought with you? It is none of your flock, as I see——Was no one in the ante-room?"

"No, your excellency, no one by whom I might have sent in my name," answered the provost, bowing again most humbly. "I have been so bold to bring with me a young travelling artist from Norway, the landscape and portrait painter, Leganger. I thought your excellency might, perhaps, give him an opportunity to give a proof of his talents."

"Ah!—a landscape and portrait painter. I'm glad you remembered me, dear provost. My gallery, I have told you before, needs re-touching. The young man may make some trials, by which I may judge of his ability. My son will be here to-morrow,—he will tell Mr. Leganger what I want. At all events, the work may commence even to-morrow."

They now allowed me to follow my thoughts undisturbed. After the count had spoken a little while with the provost the audience was concluded, we returned to the parsonage, where, from this day, a new life began to bloom for me.

It would, perhaps, be too tedious to state minutely all the shades of my new condition. I resided at the castle, where I worked hard during the day, that I might in the evening give myself up without interruption to the pure enjoyment which my intercourse with the lovely Sigrid afforded me.

When I first came to Hammarby, the foliage had already assumed the tints of autumn. It was now spring. All nature was in bloom and splendour like my hopes. I did not believe that the gates of paradise could ever be closed to me.

Having finished my work at the castle, the provost invited me to pass some time, before my departure, at his house, and to continue the drawing lessons which I had begun to give to Sigrid and her younger brother, who had often carried the tender letters which passed between Sigrid and myself. I think it necessary here to state, that my fiery heart and lively fancy, had not rested till I had obtained the assurance that Sigrid returned my affection. Though our hopes, as may be supposed, were only built upon the future, yet we felt too happy during our present intercourse, to spoil our time by melancholy reflections. But it was not to remain so long.

I had pointed the portrait of my beloved, and placed it on the mantel-piece in my room. To this picture I could, when I did not enjoy the happiness of the presence of the original, speak in the most enthusiastic expressions of nature, which a young heart lends to its feelings, when it loves for the first time, and its passion finds an echo in another heart.

During one of these outbreaks of rapture, the provost happened one evening to enter my room. Surprised, he remained standing at the door, and gazed at me with a look which promised me no particularly delightful prospects for my wishes and the future.

"I have been blind, as I now see," said he, with an icy coldness; "but since the cataract is couched, I only wish to say that Mr. Leganger may pack his things up, and that the sooner the better; for no romance can be played in my house."

I felt my blood run seething through my veins, and every fibre in me quivered as I answered him: "I thought my feelings towards Sigrid had been long known to the provost, and, if I were to nourish no hope, had long expected a negative insinuation."

"By heaven, sir, you are impudent!" exclaimed the provost, in great anger. "Am I expected to go about in my own house like a spy, to ferret out things I never dreamed of? I could have sooner believed that... that... indeed, I know not what I could have thought of sooner than of the nonsense that you, an itinerant painter, could dare to think of becoming the son-in-law of the provost of Hammarby. Pack up your knapsack this moment, I tell you, or I shall send my men to help you."

Enraged to the utmost at the offensive treatment, and highly improper expressions of the provost, I was unable to utter a word; my conduct, however, showed clearly, that I was not inclined to lay his hospitality under contribution any longer. With vehemence I tore open the doors and drawers of the old oaken press, took out my things, and threw them in the middle of the room in a heap.

Being made contented by these preparations for leaving, he left my room and went down. No longer seeing the object of my just anger, I became more cool, and resolved before I packed, to get an interview with Sigrid.

It was just the time when the provost used to take a walk through the fields, which he never neglected. I flew down to the sitting-room, but was there surprised by a sight which had already affected me disagreeably—namely, by that of the young count from the castle, who was in an animated conversation with Sigrid, and at times gained a smile from her, which I thought belonged only to me. But Sigrid was of a lively temperament, and when her eye with the common expression of deep love fell on me, I reproached myself with the injustice I did her, by misrepresenting her conduct toward the young count, and trying to find in it a motive, which, as her caressing words afterwards convinced me, lay only in my jealous imagination. To meet the count just now was, however, more disagreeable to me than ever before, and this not only because he hindered me, for the moment, from speaking with Sigrid, but also because I thought I observed just today, distinct marks of coquetry in her whole conduct. As I entered I received a look which was as melting and charming as all those from which I had so often before imbibed poison. But as I turned aside to conceal as much as possible my excited feelings, I noticed in the looking-glass opposite me, that she gave the young count a look of a wholly different kind. It was an electric spark which kindled in his eyes the fire of passion, and in my heart the most vehement jealousy.

"Sigrid!" I exclaimed, not knowing what I was doing, "will you give me an interview for a few minutes? I depart this moment."

She turned pale—"You will leave?—and whither?" she stammered; and with an icy cold "excuse me, Count," which in some measure calmed my blood again, she went into a small side room, beckoning me to follow her.

"What has happened?—Is it again your freaks of jealousy that will disturb our happiness?" she whispered, taking my hands. "Can you believe that I take but the least interest in the count, although, on account of my father, and to entertain myself by his vanity, I sometimes cast a friendly look on him? How unjust you are to misjudge my love, and torment me with your imaginations! You have certainly no idea of setting off. No, that is not possible!"

"And yet it must be so, unless you can prevail upon your father to give his consent to our union. An outbreak of my feelings just now escaped me as I stood before your picture. Your father heard it as he unexpectedly entered my room. Explanations passed between us, and the end of it was, that he showed me the door in the most insulting manner."

Sigrid seemed to be in despair, yet she did not propose to attempt to pacify and persuade her father. When I asked if she had no courage to venture something for our love, she answered in a reproachful tone:

"Can you ask? Yes, I have courage; it is, however, not courage but madness to work against the stream in a moment when it threatens to sweep us off. Let us abide our time, my beloved. However hard it is for me, yet I must approve of your plan to set out. This yielding, I hope, will make a good impression on my father; and after his anger has subsided, and a calm succeeded the storm, I will try what my love and cunning can do to obtain our object."

"I must, then, depart and—separate myself from you! Oh, Sigrid, have you sufficiently considered what pain this will give us? Without you, my life is nothing; my strength will be broken, my feelings wither, and my energy to work dwindle by my fruitless broodings on our future."

"And will my lot be a better one?" answered she, lamenting. "No, Jeames, certainly not. You will travel, and the change of things around you will, by degrees, heal your sick mind; but I remain here in unchanging uniformity, and shall die with longing and sighing. You must write to me where you are; and if ever possible you will certainly hear from me."

Sigrid being so composed and strong, I blushed at my own weakness. With death in my heart, I embraced her for the last time. I do not know how I left the parsonage, nor how I found myself, a few weeks after, at Copenhagen.

Longer, however, the mind could not control the body. I sank into an idle, low brooding, which soon paralysed all my energy to work, and entirely disabled me to earn my livelihood. The only point round which all my thoughts was turning, was the hope for a letter from Sigrid. I had written to her several times without receiving an answer. At length a letter came, but it brought no consolation; she had not yet found a favourable opportunity to speak with her father. I was beside myself, for I feared, or rather saw distinctly, that she grew more and more cold towards me. The more fiercely burned the flame in my own breast. It threatened to destroy me, and what is still more, it made me an unnatural son. I wrote no more to my parents. Was I still the hopeful youth, full of life, who, with the blessing of his venerable parents wandered forth into the world to acquire honour and character? No, my passion had destroyed the good seed which had begun to come up. I had now neither strength nor will to raise myself again. Eight months had passed since my first arrival at Copenhagen. For the last quarter I had paid neither for my board nor lodging, and I sat within my four miserable walls where almost no ray of sun, and certainly no ray of life, did fall. My room was as dark as my soul. The only feeling which sometimes roused me from my stupefaction, was that of the total neglect of duty toward my parents; it only served to increase my torture.

I was sitting one forenoon on my miserable couch of straw, when the letter-carrier came in attended by my host. He had a letter for me; and as the seal bore the impression of a nobleman's crown, which gave my landlord some hope for the improvement of my sad circumstances, he had been so kind as to bring the carrier up to me. At my first glance at the seal, I recognised the coat of arms of the Count of H. and a letter from Hammarby, from whomsoever it might come, it affected me so much, that I felt as if a whole world of restless feelings rushed in my breast to burst it. I asked them, as a great favour, to leave me alone, and my host and the carrier went, after the former had promised to pay me another visit the next morning.

Now I could without witnesses open this mysterious remarkable letter, whose contents made my head dizzy and filled my heart with inexpressible joy. I thought I was dreaming; I feared that my excited fancy was only showing me deceitful images; I read the letter over and over again. It was reality—truth! I fell on my knees. The sudden transition from the torments of hell to the purest joy of heaven, again opened my heart to prayer, from which it had long been alienated. Here is the letter, word for word—it was from the hand of the old count:

"MY DEAR LEGANGER.—I have heard from my son that things at the parsonage are not in a desirable state, and that the fast waning health of the fair Sigrid threatens to give a severe blow to my honest Provost Oernroos. Being accustomed to look upon things in life more narrowly, it occurred to me that Sigrid's sickness might be connected with your departure, which must have been at all events brought about by some extraordinary circumstance, as it took place so suddenly that you did not find time to take your leave at the castle. Calling back to my mind your frequent walks to the parsonage, while you put in order my picture-gallery—(which, by the by, has gained you my confidence, and convinced me that some thing might be made of you)—I concluded that you might stand in some nearer relation with the beautiful Sigrid, and resolved, since this affair was on my territory, to take the provost into examination, to obtain some disclosure. He related to me the whole affair, and also specified to me the reason of his refusal, which, however, I found entirely unsatisfactory, as in my opinion, a skilful artist is a very proper match for a minister's daughter. It would lead me too far here to repeat what I said, to convince the provost of the absurdity of his determination to suffer his daughter to die with grief, and entirely to spoil the best years of life for a young man who was evidently destined to make a useful member of society. In short, he came back from his mistake. And as it is always a special pleasure to me to make happy those persons with whom I stand in friendly relations, or who know how, by a proper conduct, to gain my favour, I shall give to Sigrid, whose godfather I am, a little dower which will suffice for the beginning, to help you along. What I have once set my mind upon, I am accustomed to carry out as quickly as possible. Send me, therefore, by the returning mail, your papers, the certificate of baptism, and power of attorney for having the bans published, then will I expedite the matter, so that you can be married as soon as you arrive. I must not give Oernroos long time for deliberation; for however great my influence may be, still he is the father. Therefore be quick and brisk, my dear Leganger, hammer the iron whilst it is hot, and his paternal feelings are awake. Let me also know if you want money to come here. If this be the case, I shall send it as soon as I am in possession of your answer and papers. Do not fill your letter with idle expressions of gratitude. You are a good fellow, and such persons I assist whenever I can.

"WILLIAM J. H.

"Count of Gr. Hammarby."

"P. S. My son wished to be remembered to you.—He set out, a

few days ago, on a journey into foreign parts, which he had contem-
plated for some time.—Farewell!"

Only few men can ever have had as intense a joy, and such a feeling of unbounded bliss as I experienced when my senses could distinctly comprehend the heaven which was opening to me. I spent the
whole night in dreaming awake; if in depicting to myself my future
happiness, there was a light shadow, it was my surprise at Sigrid not
having also written. But perhaps she is so weak, thought I, that she
was not able to do it—as they have not yet disclosed to her our happiness.

At length morning came, and also my host, to whom I, in a few
words, communicated the sudden change of my circumstances in
consequence of my approaching marriage. He readily procured me
all that I desired, and after the lapse of half an hour, he carried my
grateful letter to the post himself. I had mentioned in it that my unhappy love had made me unfit for all work, and I had lost my custom
in consequence of it. I was, therefore, compelled to wait, though with
a burning impatience, for the supply of money so kindly offered me.

How I lived in an intoxication of happiness, which as little as my
previous grief, suffered me to come to reasonable thoughts. The answer arrived later than I had expected; but it contained, as set-off, a
news which almost made me crazy for joy. I had been already once
published, and to delight me with this intelligence, the count had let
some mails pass by.

As quickly as possible I arranged all my affairs at Copenhagen,
and also wrote during this time, a long letter to my parents, relating
the follies of the prodigal son, but at the same time, describing the
good fortune that awaited me. I put my wardrobe in order, took at
the first opportunity passage for Malmoe, and from thence travelled
by land to the place of my warmest wishes, the beloved Hammarby,
and hastened at last, with the lightest of hearts, through the alley
leading to the red gate of the parsonage. The coach came slowly after
me. I seemed to have wings, and the certainty not to find the young
count by my beloved, still increased my happiness.

Almost breathless, I reached the trellised gate. Hector was now
not so fierce as at my first arrival here; he recognised his old friend,
and barked for joy. But no Sigrid stood at the window, no light being

came hovering through the house-door to meet me and bid me welcome. Instead of this, my young friend, Sebastian, came springing, and warmly called out to me: "Papa will be here directly, but poor Sigrid is sick."

I was conscious of my growing pale; I was hardly able to approach the house where the provost was appearing on the threshold, and embraced me, saying—

"Times have altered, my dear Leganger. I could see the sufferings of my child at the loss of you no longer. And as the count, who wishes you well, likewise took interest in the matter, I have yielded, and now bid you welcome as my son-in-law."

"Oh, how kind you are, my father! I have no words to express my gratitude. Sigrid is sick—I hope not dangerously so. My heart is near dying in this frequent change of torture and happiness."

"Be calm, my son! When near you she will soon recover her bloom. In consideration of her present feeble condition, we could but by degrees acquaint her with the joy that is awaiting her; and notwithstanding our precaution, the joy has severely affected her. She is now sleeping. Within an hour I hope to be able to conduct you to her. Let us, therefore, in hope of a happy future, in the mean time drink to your happy arrival."

After a few hours of painful waiting, the provost, who had continually gone back and forth to Sigrid, informed me that she wished to see me. He led me to her room, and I shall never forget the impression made on me when the door opened which gave me entrance to the treasure so dear to me. My betrothed lay on the sofa, beautiful, but alas!—pale as a corpse. Grief had blasted the fresh roses on her cheeks and dimmed the lustre of her eyes. Dim and filled with tears, she cast them up to me, and instead of the delicate purple of happiness and joy, a deep blush covered her face. I went near her—I knelt down and took her hand pressing it to my burning lips, and to my faithful heart beating for anxiety. She looked at me, but her eye was without soul, and the smile which curled round her mouth, said nothing—at least, nothing that I was able to understand.

"My Sigrid, my dearest Sigrid, give me but a sign, a word that you feel at my presence, a share, however small, of the joy which I feel!"

"Happiness!"—exclaimed she, slowly; and again her brow and cheeks coloured deep red. "Are you happy, Jeames?"

"Can I be otherwise, since I can call you mine?—Does this question need an answer, my Sigrid? I am so happy that no one could compare his happiness to mine, if you were well, and could share it with me."

"I shall certainly do so," she answered, "after I am accustomed to the new change of my destiny. Have patience till then! My nerves are so feeble, so excitable, that I cannot bear the least excitement, the least emotion of mind. But it will grow better, Jeames. Believe that, and fear nothing; for your sorrow would still increase my bodily suffering."

"I will be strong, my beloved Sigrid, and God will grant my fervent prayers. You will soon bloom again the fresh rose that you were when I first saw you!"

"You find me then faded and sunken low?" she asked, in a hasty peevish tone.

"The white rose can be as beautiful as the red," answered I, affectionately; "but this one is the picture of health, and the other that of sickness."

She seemed to be satisfied. The provost now proposed to leave her, as she could not bear long continued conversation.

"Now come with me to see the newly-arranged bridal chamber," said my intended father-in-law, leading me to the room that I heretofore had occupied. Alas! there were none of the objects that had before been so dear to me, except the picture of Sigrid over the fireplace: indeed this was dearer to me than all the rest. In other respects all had changed. The dark wooden walls were covered with rich tapestry from the count's castle, and—(here follows in Leganger's notes, the description of all things which Seiler, on the morning of his arrival at the parsonage, yet found pretty well preserved.) And all these precious things, this finery, as the provost related with a father's pride, had been sent by the count from the castle, to show attention to the young future wife. For my own part I should have slept as well if I had found again the old oaken bedstead, and the heavy cushioned chairs; but in regard to Sigrid, it gave me pleasure. As soon as circumstances permitted, I hastened on the following day to the castle, to pay to my illustrious patron my most humble thanks.

During the whole of this day I did not see my Sigrid; but on the following Sunday, on which we were published for the second time, I was in the afternoon so fortunate as to spend a long time with her. She was by far more affectionate than the first time, and a natural colour on her cheeks proved that her health was improving. Later towards evening she rose several times, and walked, leaning on my arm, in the room up and down. With each succeeding day our hearts grew more intimate with each other, and Sigrid grew better. The only sign of sickliness, which would not leave her, was a continual chill; therefore her affectionate father advised her always to wrap herself carefully up in a shawl. This she did notwithstanding my suggestion that she might render herself too susceptible by it.

At length, a fortnight after my arrival, the wedding day came. I will not speak of my happiness; how deeply I felt it in my inmost soul, every one can imagine who has once loved himself. The marriage ceremony was to take place in the evening, and, according to Sigrid's and my own wishes, no other witnesses should be present, than the members of the family, a few neighbours, and the count, who made his appearance before the rest of the company. He brought with him two goblets of high value; they were intended for the bride and bride-groom,—in addition to the dower which the count had promised to my bride. Besides these mysterious tokens of favour, which I did not dream of when at my first visit at the castle, I saw the grave, haugh-tily-cold face of the count; he yet gave me the prospect of numerous orders through his influential recommendations to the first families, on account of which he advised, as soon as possible after my mar-riage, to take up my residence in one of the more important cities of the country.

In the course of conversation on these subjects, the momentous hour arrived. The few guests were assembled. The provost led his daughter into the room; the count took her by the hand, and after a lapse of half an hour, I found myself on the threshold of the wide opened gate of heaven. Immediately after the ceremony we sat down to a repast. As my poor Sigrid was so chilled that her white teeth be-gan to chatter, I wrapped closer round her shoulders the large costly shawl which the count had presented to her as a wedding gift. A ten-der, inexpressibly grateful look fell on me, for it fell from her tear-ful eyes. Why does she now weep? thought I. Perhaps it was only my imagination! But no—she actually did weep; for when the health of the bridal couple was drank, and we put to our lips those crystal cups, in which the red wine sparkled so beautifully, and I was about to touch glasses with my bride, two large clear tears fell into the goblet. This offended me, and I wished very much to be able right soon to speak with her alone.

The wedding feast seemed to me never to end. At length people began to move. The guests, with the exception of the count, soon took leave; and, after a ceremonious leave-taking from the count, and a paternal benediction from the provost, I led my young wife into the room on the gable side of the house. It was now *our* room,—ah, what worlds fancy can create!

My wife let herself be more carried than led to the sofa. Her tears now flowed unrestrainedly, and convulsive sobbing shook her whole frame.

"My Sigrid, my own beloved Sigrid," I asked, with warmth, "have confidence in your husband. What is it that torments you so much? Are you not happy? Am I nothing more to your heart, since you now, in the hour of union, after which we both formerly longed so fervently, suffer so much in body and mind? I conjure you, be sincere. I suffer the most fearful anxiety at your tears and pain, painted so distinctly in all your features."

She leaned her head upon my shoulder; her arms clasped me convulsively; but I did not understand a single word, though her pale lips moved as if speaking.

Thus an hour, most bitter to us both, passed away. "Jeames," said she, at last, in a low voice, "leave me alone for a moment. I shall be better able to collect myself when alone. Send our old servant up to me! Oh, if my mother was yet alive, I should not have become so unhappy!"

In her present excited state of mind, I did not dare to ask for a clearer explanation of her remarkable expressions, but went immediately to fulfil her wish.

While the old servant was up-stairs undressing Sigrid, I went into the ante-room. The servant had promised to call me when Sigrid had grown more calm. At my entrance, I was very much surprised to see the hat and cloak of the count lying there; he himself was not in the room. I was, however, not mistaken in hearing, soon after, his voice from the room of the provost.

Words came to my ear, which were almost unintelligible to me.

"Well, now I hope you are content, Oernroos?" asked the count, in a sneering tone, "The son-in-law is, indeed, a very handsome man, though no count. This time you fished in turbid water, and the cunning Sigrid likewise. How could you be so stupid as to think that my son, the heir of my name and property, would condescend so much as to marry a parson's daughter?"

"Still, however, he lowered himself so much as to reduce the innocent child, and make her unhappy now and in all eternity. For, do you believe that she entered, without burning pangs of conscience, upon your devilish plan, to deceive the fool who now represents her husband?"

Thus spoke the provost's voice, trembling from anger or grief; which of either was the case, I know not; for I was in a state of mind not to be described. I knew not whether it was a demoniac feverish dream that was raging in my brain, or demoniac reality. I drew nearer. With gigantic power I controlled my nerves, and pressed my hand so firmly on my betrayed heart that every fibre of it threatened to snap.

I was standing at the door. The words, the fiendish words, rushed in upon my soul, and burned themselves into it with ineffaceable, fiery letters. "What! ungrateful man?" resumed the count. "Is this the name my plan deserves, by which I have saved the honour of your house and daughter, at the sacrifice of my dignity and money? Is it my duty to meddle with the love affairs of my son, and to restore again to order what your carelessness brought into confusion? No, that belongs, by no means, to the duties of a father; and only to save you the shame that would fall upon you, if the matter should become known, out of regard for your clerical dignity, and the love which the girl formerly had for the painter, I devised this excellent plan, which has now completely succeeded. The poor devil who has nothing to think about but how to get on in the world, is not so very scrupulous about the matter. No doubt he would be surprised if he knew how the whole affair does stand; but then I shall yet give him a few dollars, and the whole affair is settled."

"Do you think so, gentlemen?" exclaimed I, with coldness and firmness in tone and manner, which I became possessed of the moment I burst open the door of the provost's room, and entered. "Do you think so?"

(Here, and in the succeeding pages, Leganger's own notes were almost illegible. Seiler, however, partly guided by the effaced writing, partly through information which he had collected in Norway, continued and finished the history of Leganger's fate, which he sent to the count through the old Borgstedt. This account of Seiler, with the exception of some attacks upon the count, we insert here.)

———

Leganger's wild rolling eyes darted flames of lightning upon both the associates in this satanic plot.

The provost lost all composure; but the count rose and asked, perfectly calm:

"Well, since you know the whole affair, Mr. Leganger, you may yourself fix upon a proper sum for indemnity; for you see that now all must remain as it is. It is best, therefore, you make as little noise about it as possible."

"You vulgar villains, who trample under foot every feeling, and disgrace the rights of man," thundered Leganger, in a terrible voice; "do you think that money can be here in question, when you have stolen the honour and good name of a man? And not only of his honour, but also robbed him of his peace of heart? But there lives an avenger above! You will surely not delight in the fruit which your villany will bear. There are yet law and justice in the land. You shall be sufficiently branded."

He rushed out of the room. He wished to see his wife once more, and bid her an awful farewell. As he passed through the sitting-room he noticed the two goblets on the table, which was not yet removed. "Ha! now I understand those false tears! My soul is burning, and my heart and lips are seared!"

He filled both goblets with wine, and quaffed one, and then the other, in hasty draughts. "Out of you I drank half an hour ago to the health of my bride and my own good fortune," exclaimed he, whilst he filled the goblets again. "The curse rested on you even then; for you were a gift from that wretch who deceived me beyond repair. I curse you now a second time! May you never bring good to him who shall put you to his lips, or shall but touch you!"

He emptied both goblets in haste, muttered a few unintelligible words, and hurried up-stairs, through the dark attic, to the bridal chamber.

The provost put his head carefully through the softly opened door of his room.

"He is gone, the madman!" whispered he to himself; "I hope he has not gone up-stairs to take revenge on the poor, unhappy victim! By heaven, your lordship," said he, turning to the count, "I say once more, this plan was fiendish—it could not but bring ruin to my family; and if he should carry out his threats, my grey head would hide itself for grief and shame from every honest man!"

"Bah, it has not yet come to this! After having slept on the matter he will change his thoughts. You may send me word to-morrow what end it has taken."

The count stepped into the sitting-room, put on his cloak, and got into his coach, that had stood in waiting for some time. He leaned back upon the cushions, ordered the coachman to drive on fast, and left the trembling provost in the solitary and gloomy marriage house.

In the mean time Leganger had entered the gable-room. Sigrid had exchanged the heavy, pompous bridal-dress for a white night-gown. She sat on a chair next the stove, and held her eyes, that were wet with weeping, covered with a handkerchief.

She heard her husband's hasty steps, but she had not the courage to look up to him. The violence, however, with which he closed the door, induced her so to do; and seized by a shudder, compared to which the coldness of death is warm, her staring looks remained fixed upon Leganger's wholly changed appearance. He stood close by her. An ashy paleness covered his face, which, but just before had been radiant with love for her. Dark blue veins appeared upon his brow and temples, and the eyes, before so beautiful and clear, shone like balls of fire from their sockets. His teeth chattered so vehemently, that in the fruitless endeavour to speak, he bit his lips, and one drop of blood after the other fell upon her white night-gown, where they shone blood-red, till her tears fell upon them, and quenched their deep glow.

"He knows all," thought Sigrid, and stretched her folded hands beseechingly toward him. "Pity—pity!" stammered she, with her pale lips. "Jeames, let me not die in this hour of anguish!"

"Outcast—you dare to beseech me!—one whom you deceived so shamefully! Is there no spark of shame left within you? has all womanly feeling vanished from your heart; is your recollection not strong enough to stifle every request for pity?"

Leganger's lips were distorted into an awful mocking laugh; pain and contempt struggled in his face.

Sigrid cast down her eyes. Dark powers contended with each other in her anguished heart.

"Jeames, they persuaded me to do it," she said in a low tone. "You saw my shame and anguish. Despise me—for I am the most miserable and contemptible creature under the sun; but yet I implore your pity—or I must perish in the storm that is raging here." She pressed her hand against her breast.

"You implore in vain! The rocks are not more insensible to your tears than my heart. Have you so acted that you can expect any thing else but harshness? Viper that I cherished in my bosom! The poison that you infused there, will burn in your own eyes. I go, never to return; but the law will separate us! And you, your seducer, your father, and the wretch who contrived this fiendish plan and executed it, you all shall be branded with disgrace which no time shall be able to efface!"

Leganger turned towards the door. He had loved the unhappy woman inexpressibly, and his heart had warmer wishes for her than he was able to utter; but his love, his honour, the peace of his whole life—all these dear treasures lay shattered at his feet. He remained unaltered, and revenge, only revenge—burned through his veins.

"Jeames, Jeames!" cried she, with a broken voice—"I will ask nothing for myself—I shall not long survive it; but for my poor father—oh, do not dishonour him!"

Her arms firmly clasped his feet. She uttered no word more, and her tears seemed dried up; but her dim, burning eyes, with an indescribable expression of grief, rested upon Leganger, whose just severity melted at the nameless pangs of the being once so warmly loved by him.

"Sigrid!" said he, and the tone of his voice called her back to consciousness: "Sigrid, I cannot remain here; but I will try to forgive. Not before you are again able to bear any emotion, shall this unnatural bond be severed. More I cannot do. Yet one more thing I can do—I will pray for you, unhappy woman!"

At these last words, he freed himself from her arms, that strove to hold him back with force, and, without looking behind him, he rushed into the dark, cold night.

Leganger knew not whither he was going. He roamed about in the fields, till in the darkness, he violently struck against a tree, and sank down powerless. A severe wound on his head bereft him of the little consciousness that had remained to him; and not till the following morning was he found in this sad condition by a peasant, who came to the wood for timber. The peasant brought the painter, whom he recognised as the son-in-law of the provost, to his own house, that lay near the parsonage. After he and his wife had endeavoured in vain to restore the sick man to consciousness, and to learn how the bridegroom had come into the woods, some one was sent to the parsonage to inform the provost of what had happened.

The greatest consternation reigned in the mean time in the parsonage. They had watched all night by the young woman, who had been found lying on the floor, in fearful convulsions, and who had now fallen into a state of stupefaction, which promised no good result.

The painter lay more than six weeks at the house of the farmer who had taken him home. The wildest feverish dreams raved uninterruptedly in his brain, and not a single bright moment let him feel his deplorable condition.

At length, however, his sickness must exhaust itself. It was one Sunday morning, that he looked round the room, for the first time, with recovered consciousness. Every object was strange to him, and only by degrees came the images of the past, one after the other, before his soul. Some appeared in a clearness only too awful, others were enveloped in an impenetrable veil of mist; the recollections which they called forth, threw him back almost into the same state from which he awoke. In what manner he had come to the place where he was at present, he could not explain to himself; his conjectures, however, came ever nearer the truth, as he recollected to have run, like a madman, from the convulsive embraces of his wife, into the woods. But how much time had passed since then? What had be-come of the unfortunate woman? He wanted certainty on this point. He motioned the only person that was in the room, an old woman, to come to him. She came near the bed.

"How long have I been here sick?" he asked.

"Well, God be praised, that you at last begin to speak," the old woman answered. "It is more than six weeks since, that my son brought you here, out of the woods."

"Who is your son? I should like to speak to him."

"Yes, you shall, when he comes back from church; but I suppose he will first go with his wife to a funeral."

"A funeral?" All the blood rushed to the sallow emaciated face of the painter. "Who is to be buried?"

"Bless me!—it was stupid in me to talk of it; but, good God, you must hear of it some time or other. It is your poor wife, who died a few days ago. She lived but a few moments after she had given birth to a little girl. But the child is weak and miserable, so that it will soon follow her to the grave. Yes, indeed—the folks at the parsonage talk about some curious things; but I suppose you know best how the matter stands!"

The old woman now was silent, for the sick man darted, at these last words, looks at her that made her blood run cold, and frightened her, as she was all alone with him. But he remained lying quiet; he had folded his hands, and his look turned upward, seemed to make peace with the departed one. From time to time, however, he put his hand upon his heart, where he seemed to feel a piercing pain. But what are the sufferings of the body compared to those of the soul? Leganger's deeply wounded feelings, sought after a place in his heart for the unhappy woman; but it was entirely filled up with the most direful tortures that can befall a man. The all-reconciling angel of death, however, spread his snowy wings over the storm of passions. Leganger prayed—he prayed for her who had gone to everlasting sleep, as he had promised.

Towards evening his young host returned, and Leganger received a letter, that had been waiting for him for a month. He had not suffi-cient strength to break it open, immediately. The following morning, when he was alone, he opened it, and read the following scarcely leg-ible lines, from Sigrid's hand:

"JEAMES!—Look not with anger and hate upon these words from the wretched and criminal Sigrid. You said you would pray for me, and since you promised me this, I know that your heart, which once beat for me full of love, will not, after I am gone, break its vow, as I did mine. Jeames, I pray to God for my poor soul! I have sinned much, and deeply, and great is my guilt against you. But I have done penance, through sufferings, which words cannot describe. It would be too bold in me to ask for your forgiveness; no, I cannot be so happy as to carry this with me to the grave. Yet, when I am gone, you must not banish all recollection of me, although my guilt is greater than you suspect. Now, that death already stands at my door, I will not deceive you. Know, then, that I received Count Hugo's attention before I knew you. But it was you who taught me to love. I loved you, I loved you unboundedly; yet selfishness destroyed the best and purest part of my feelings; and toward the end of the time that you stayed at Hammarby, I already was in a secret understanding with the count. My father and myself both believed that his passion would raise me to the high position to which I aspired. And in order to obtain our object, I gladly seized upon the discovery of the relation that existed between us, to remove you from Hammarby.—Oh, Jeames, I have nothing further to add!

"The punishment did not fail—my father raved—the young count set out on travels, and the old count contrived the plan, which I was so weak and wretched, from fear of shame, as to assist. But I am not able to express what I suffered from the day that we were first published, till the fatal night of our wedding. If it is possible to atone for a part of our guilt, by mental suffering here on earth, let me believe, Jeames, that I did it.

"*You will pray for me!* These words return continually to my memory; they are the only comfort which instils a drop of balm into my heart. But, my father, for him I feel great anxiety. He was in this affair, only an indulgent, yet blind father, who would sacrifice every thing to his own and his child's false pride. Let me yet add, that he was willing, several times, to disclose to you the whole affair; but the persuasive power of the count, and the fear of the shame that must fall on his whole family, held him back. You, Jeames, were sacrificed! But death reconciles many things; the tie will be severed. Be merciful towards the unhappy and suffering old man. The burden of his own conscience, which he has in future to bear, will be heavy enough. You will not wish to increase it, for you are too high-minded to take revenge.

"I wrote these lines on my knees—my last words are: Pity and forgiveness to the criminal, penitent, and dying

"SIGRID."

"Indeed death reconciles many things!" sighed the painter, and pressed, with deep emotion, the letter to his lips. "The love of God has mercy on every penitent soul; how could I then disappoint the confidence of the departed! The tie is severed, my heart has already pardoned her who was guided astray. I leave vengeance to the hand of the Lord."

And Leganger kept his word. As far as his strength permitted, he visited Sigrid's grave, where he renewed once more his vow. He then took leave of the provost, with a few lines, in which he told him that he should leave vengeance to Providence. Hereupon he wandered one evening, with his knapsack on his back, past the red-painted fence of the parsonage, where he stood eighteen months before, for the first time, and believed to behold in Sigrid an angel of heaven. He heaved a deep sigh. It was dark. He came to the church-yard. The wind sighed through the poplars, and they seemed, as it were, to beckon to him. He entered, took his last leave of Sigrid's grave, and then proceeded on his pilgrimage to his native land.

Not having retained a farthing of the blood-money which the count had given him, he was compelled to seek, as before, his support by painting. He found little work, and could not hope to arrive before autumn, unless he adopted other measures. He saw himself obliged to dispose of his watch and other trinkets. He was, nevertheless, constantly detained by sickness, and the leaves had already began to change, when he arrived, one evening quite late at his father's house.

A light was shining in the work-shop. Leganger softly opened the door, and behold!—his father was sitting among the dark coffins, just as at the time when he took leave of him, two years before.

"Good heavens," thought he, "how much altered does the son return who went into the world to gain glory and wealth!"—He was overpowered by his feelings. "Father, prepare for me a resting-place in one of your coffins," said he, all at once with a stifled voice, and sank down among the piled-up coffins, which came down with a great crash and noise.

Trembling, as if seized by the shudder of death, the old man looked round.—"Was not that Jeames?" said he, almost startled at his own words. "Jeames—my son! Is it you, or..." and the eyes of the sire fell with a searching expression upon the moved heaps of coffins.

It was a dismal meeting, and it lasted long before father and son were able to call words to their feelings.

"Oh God—my forebodings!" exclaimed old Leganger at last, and pressed Jeames's hands into his own. "They whispered to me that your letter, for which we waited nine months, promised nothing good notwithstanding the golden castles of air which you painted therein. I felt as if all was not right; and I see by your looks, my poor boy, that I was unfortunately not mistaken."

The kindness of his father, disappointed in all his hopes, moved Jeames deeply. For his own misfortune he had had no tears; but seeing the resigning sorrow of his father, all grew dark before his eyes, and two large, clear tears dropped upon the withered hands that were hardly any longer able to ply the brush, the old true friend that now for many years had provided his master a scanty livelihood.

"Oh, my father!" said the son, with his head bent down—"You were right! I have been dreadfully deceived. Sick, poor, bereft of my honour, my love, and my peace, I come back—and these are the treasures which I bring for you."

"But I hope you bring a pure conscience with you, Jeames?—Answer me candidly;—if you have sullied your hands with a crime, I will have nothing more to do with you." With a searching look, the father regarded the deeply-moved youth.

"No, my father—I intended to take revenge, but death spread his expiating hand between me and her who prepared for me all those withering pangs. I have forgiven her, and she besought me in favour of the others. My hand is disarmed, and I leave vengeance to the Lord."

"It is well, Jeames! I now bless you as I did when you left me. After you have grown more calm, you may tell me the circumstances. The Lord is powerful in the weak. You will surely rise once more."

Jeames dejectedly shook his head. "Let us go to my mother; but go you first, father; I fear to alarm her, for I am so altered..."

"Oh no—you will not alarm her," answered the old man with suppressed emotion. "She has already obtained what is yet wanting to us—rest."

"What, my father?"—Jeames grew still paler than before. The thought of his unnatural levity, of having given himself up, in Copenhagen, to his unhappy passion, in such a manner, that he forgot every duty in consequence of it, came before his soul, and made his grief still greater. Was it not his long silence that had dug the grave in which his mother now lay? He had thought himself so unhappy, that he believed nothing would increase his burden—and now he stood there, gasping for breath, to take the new load which his conscience added to the old.

"Jeames, my son—compose yourself! She had been sick long before. Let us not murmur. She sleeps—we wake; but the Lord looks upon our distress. Let us be comforted! The storm will be succeeded by a calm—though it be not till we slumber by her side."

In silence stood father and son—breast to breast. The cold dew on Leganger's brow moistened the grey locks of his father.

Now sounded from the next church-steeple the hour of midnight; soon after a loud, thundering report was heard—it was followed by the dismal ringing of the bell, and the cry of "Fire—fire!" ran through the streets.

The next moment after, father and son were blinded by a bright glare of light; the neighbouring house was on fire. Iron necessity tore them, who held each other locked in their arms, asunder—they were now called upon to save their house and their little goods.

In the morning they stood, without shelter, before the smoking heap of ruins into which their dwelling was turned. They had now nothing left; no house, no home, no bread—the one sought for comfort in the other's looks of despair.

"God be praised that your mother went before us!" said old Leganger. "Do you see, Jeames, it was only yesterday that your grief at it was beyond bounds; today you must acknowledge that what the Lord does is well done. Let us go to the church-yard to her grave— this is now our home."

They went there. Jeames knelt on the green mound. The grey

mist of the damp autumnal morning cooled his burning face, and the imperishable love of the departed brought peace into his troubled soul. His heart became filled with nameless forebodings, earth with her struggles and sorrows vanished, and his spirit soared in those regions above the stars, where the tears of remorse burn no more, and the light of reconciliation shines on him who returns.

A light sobbing, however, soon recalled him into the world of reality. He looked round; his father also had been disturbed by it in his silent devotion. Both now observed on a grave near to theirs, a little girl who, lying on her knees and weeping, scratched with her hands at the sod, as if she would take the slumberer beneath out of the earth, that he might rise and comfort her.

Jeames went to the child. "Poor child," said he gently, "whom will you awake?"

"My father—but he cannot wake up. And mamma is burnt up in her little room last night—and I am now all alone—entirely left."

She trembled with grief and cold; the loosened locks floated in wild disorder round her half-naked shoulders, and were caught by the rose-bush which she herself had lately planted on her father's grave.

"Poor child—have you no relations, no friends?"

"No, none—not a single one! My parents came from a land far, far from here—I do not know from where."

Jeames looked at his father. "We ourselves have no place where to lay our heads," said the latter; "yet as long as we are able to gain a piece of bread through the labour of our hands, she shall share it with us. She will have in us some protection, and we in her a being that we can love."

They took the child with them; and after having sold the little household goods of the painter, which they had saved, all three set out on a journey in the country, where they took up their abode for the winter in a small village. Old Leganger again painted coffins, and Jeames made little pictures, which Nikoline, their ward, carried about for sale. Thus they helped themselves till spring came—and then they wandered farther.

Many years passed away in this manner. At last the poor family of Goensberg owned once more a little dwelling far from their home, where peace and harmony reigned. Jeames and Nikoline now kept their house alone; the old father had continued with industry to paint coffins, and the last which he painted became his own. After Jeames and Nikoline, who had in the mean time reached her nineteenth year, had buried the old painter, they deeply felt that the best link in their life's chain was broken. They stood alone. In Jeames's breast the grief at his despised love, the mortification of the wildest feelings of his youth had never died. But time had blunted the sting of sorrow and revenge. He had succeeded in obtaining information from Hammarby.

The provost and the count had gone to give account of their deeds before the highest judgment-seat; and the young count, the wretched violater of his honour, revelled in all the enjoyments and pleasures which his riches could procure him. He was married, and had already a son and heir to his illustrious name. The illegitimate offspring, Sigrid's child, was brought up at the parsonage by its uncle, the Provost Oernroos, whose name it bore; for Jeames had threatened them with a degrading law-suit if they should dare to give the child the name of Leganger. The whole episode of Sigrid's horrible marriage had at length become an obscure tradition, which lost itself more and more, for both at the parsonage and the count's castle there were but few persons who were acquainted with the real state of the whole affair.

When Jeames now sat at the easel, and gave colour and life to the forms which he invented, his eye often rested with true delight upon Nikoline, who busily plied the spindle or the needle.

The flower of love was withered in his heart for ever—it had been destroyed to the very root; yet a quiet desire for domestic happiness developed itself in him. He had accustomed himself to the friendly care of the charming maiden; moreover, he had educated her himself, and knew that she was free from all guile, and loved him from her heart. "Many marriages are built on a foundation less firm," thought Jeames, and ventured the trial. Nikoline became a true sample of a housewife, and the little household thrived under her management.

The birth of a daughter soon crowned their domestic joys.

And Jeames could now, as husband and father, look back more calmly upon the past, the incidents of which he wrote down and made over, at the end of his life, in his testament, to his grandson, the son of his daughter—Rudolph Seiler.

Here end Leganger's notes. A continuation of the events up to Seiler's appearing in Hammarby, and the formation of his dark plans, with which the reader is already acquainted, is now required no farther. We shall therefore take up again the thread of our narrative, and request the reader to accompany us on a visit to the architect in his prison.

CHAPTER IV.

MARIA AND ALFHILD.

SOME months after the architect had been arrested had passed. His case had been examined in court several times; and though no sufficient proof against Seiler could be produced, and moreover, the testimony of Borgstedt, and of the two grooms, spoke in his favour, yet the suit threatened to be protracted.

On a cold afternoon in the month of February, the architect sat in his cell at the window, and busied himself with scratching letters on the frozen window panes, which admitted but little light into the narrow cell. His appearance was not much changed; he had only grown a little thinner; but the holding of his head, and the bold, animated look of his eyes, were yet the same; besides, the neatness and exactness of his dress proved that he had not yet sunk into that dull indifference into which many people are apt to fall when fortune turns her back on them.

After a short while, Seiler rose and began to pace his narrow room, yet more, as it seemed, to warm himself, than from any inward emotion, as the thermometer stood twenty degrees below zero, and the fire in the chimney was long ago burnt out.

When Seiler felt the beneficial effects of his exercise by the faster coursing of his blood, he sat down at a small table on which writing and drawing materials lay. He wanted to do something to kill time. Every stroke upon the paper, however, proved clearly that the hand which made it was too stiff to show its common skill. Vexed at it, he took up a little bell that stood upon the table, and rang it violently. Immediately after the gaoler appeared.

"You must make up a fire," said the architect; "it is colder here than in a dog-kennel."

"Fire?—You think that nothing else is required for it but to order it?" answered the gaoler, morosely. "It was only last evening that you had some wood."

"But I have given you money enough. I think I may expect, at least, a warm room for it."

"It is true you gave me money; but you demand too much for it to hold out long, and I have now neither wood nor money."

Seiler perceived that this was only said to extort some more money; without entering, therefore, into any further discussion, he threw a few dollars on the table, and fifteen minutes after a bright fire diffused a comfortable warmth through the room.

The architect seated himself in an old easy chair, covered with leather, and stretched, for some time, his feet towards the flames. He then folded his arms, and observed with a steadfast look, the strange figures which were formed in the sinking coals, till the magic illusion was covered with ashes.

"Thus fall at last to ashes, also, the hopes of men, their works, and the recollection of them," said Seiler, half aloud to himself. "What is this impulse to live—this striving for honour and glory—this labouring for joys of the heart, and the union with the being whom we exclusively love? Perhaps—instinct! No, that would be too beastly. A divine spark lies at the bottom of all impulses of the soul; but as the different feelings must be weighed against each other, and the impulses are so various, they get easily into conflict and confusion, which has a baneful effect upon the actions of men. The bond between spirit and body is so delicate, and yet so strong at the same time, that we try in vain to separate them. One half of our being belongs to earth, and it often draws the other half with it into the dust."

Sunk into these thoughts, which occupied him intensely, the architect did not notice that his gaoler, who had now grown very polite, repeated several times the words, "Mr. Seiler, here is somebody who wants to speak to you." As Seiler did not answer, the gaoler came up to him, and putting his hands upon Seiler's shoulders, he said, "somebody wishes to speak to you."

"I do not wish to speak to anybody," answered Seiler, in a refusing tone.

"As you please. I will tell her, then, that the gentleman does not wish to receive her."

"Her! Is it a lady?" The architect sprang up, and a deep colour suffused his cheeks. "Bring her in directly. For heaven's sake make haste!"

"As quick as I can."

The gaoler shut the door, and Seiler with strained eyes and violently beating heart, stretched out his arms to receive the dear object of all his feelings—the being for whose presence he had longed for months.

"Oh, come—come—do not delay," said he, full of emotion; and at the thought of her, the otherwise proud man forgot all other things around him. He saw no longer the dusk of his prison, for bright sunshine smiled within him. The close walls of his prison no longer oppressed him, for there was for him neither time nor space at this moment.

In this suspense a few minutes passed slowly away; then he heard in the passage elastic soft steps, and behind them the heavy tread of the gaoler.

"Here, Miss," said the latter, turning the key in Seiler's door. The architect stood there in breathless expectation. "My—my...." He hastened toward the door, but he suddenly dropped his arms and started back pale as death, when not Alfhild but Maria, his wife, stood before him.

Maria saw that the disappointed hope threw a chill over Seiler's countenance, which just now had been full of animation. He did not bid her welcome even here.

"Rudolph," said she in a low voice, "I thought you stood in need of me. I hoped, that here, in a foreign land, forsaken and without friends, you would not despise her whom no circumstances can hold back from you."

"Best—dearest Maria, your kindness—your self-denial——indeed, I cannot express my gratitude; but you see me in a condition in which...." He was silent; his pride awoke, as the beaming star of love went down. The prison grew again gloomy, the cell close, so close that he was hardly able to breathe in it. Sensitive to the highest degree, he suffered in this present position by contact with any stranger. What torments, then, must not he suffer now, when he was wounded by a thousand thrusts, by the little demoniac powers whose names are remorse, bitterness, and displeasure.

"Ah, Rudolph! do not look on me so dark." Maria seized his hand and pressed it gently. "I come here not with the claims of your wife to share your prison; no—no one shall know that I am or was your wife. But I conjure you, do not refuse my care. It would be my greatest happiness if you would allow me to attend you, and keep you company in so far as your state of mind will bear it."

"By no means, dear Maria. Do you not know I am accused of murder; that I am charged with having killed two persons, and that I am not able to prove my innocence. It may be that my blood will stain the hospitable Swedish soil, and my name will be branded...."

"Stop!" asked Maria, in a reproachful tone. "You know, Rudolph, that it cannot come to this. It is, indeed, awful enough as things stand now. But just on this account you want a person to be with you, though not all the time. And, believe me, we may perhaps understand each other better now that we need no longer consider each other as husband or wife, than when a forced bond tied us together."

"Ah! Maria, thou high-minded, resigning woman! The man for whom you have already done so much, and wish to do still more, is not worthy that you should waste the rich feelings of your heart upon him. But believe me, your conduct touches deeply his heart and conscience, and this the more, as he is not in a condition to recompense you for it."

"To recompense!" exclaimed Maria, and a brighter red suffused her cheeks than the severe cold had produced on it. "Rudolph, I have told you already, that we do speak of recompensing. I will take a small room in the city, and only by degrees accustom you to my presence."

"No, Maria, you will never prevail on me to give my consent to it. Do you believe, that in the present condition of my misfortune and humiliation, I am able to receive favours from her whom I rejected, perhaps from cold selfishness, in the days of freedom and fortune—do you believe that her noble sentiments and self-denial could soothe my present sufferings? No; by the Almighty God, this might only increase the burden which I have at present to bear. Forgive me for this view, Maria. I respect, honour, and esteem your noble mind not less on that account. But in this narrow room there can exist beside myself but one being, whose presence will not offend me; for it is only by her whom man loves most on earth, and hardly by her, he can bear to be seen in a condition like my own at present."

What Maria felt at this cruel declaration she alone, with her uncommon power of self-control, was able to conceal. With a gentleness, void of all bitterness, she said:

"Pardon, Rudolph, that I obtained information of your condition, and believed you would not reject my wish to share it with you. But since you have done so, I will torment you no longer. Only allow me one question: has she been to see you?"

"No. As I hear, she has been sick—very sick. Perhaps she is so still; besides, she depends upon a father, who goes strictly by the dictates of the world. He will not allow her to meet a man whose condition is, at least, very doubtful. But, dear Maria, seat yourself on the only chair which I have to offer you. I am exceedingly sorry that I must wound your sense of delicacy so deeply. Yet it is my firm conviction that one must act candidly in so rare a case as the present; for the least dissimulation here would be a greater sin than the speaking of truth, though it should wound ever so deeply."

Maria did not answer; it was, however, evident that she was induced to take the offered seat, more through her failing strength of body and soul, than from free choice. Seiler seated himself upon the bed, and as he looked upon the high-minded woman, whom he wished to have never known, a fire glowed in his eyes, which, when it was observed by Maria, softened the hard words which he had just spoken to her.

"From whom did you hear of the sad misfortune that has befallen me?" asked Seiler, after a long pause. "I hope you did not travel alone? Did not Bloom accompany you?"

"Nobody accompanied me," answered Maria. "My host had, on a journey through Uddevalla, read of your arrest in a newspaper; and if a severe indisposition had not prevented me, I should have been here long before now. I did not wish to inform Bloom of my resolution; for I could infer from his great caution of not having informed me of this subject, that he would have taken pains to dissuade me from it."

"Great God! you are, then, entirely alone in a foreign land, to visit a husband who destroyed your happiness of life, and is now himself so miserable that he can offer you neither protection nor shelter.

Oh, Father in heaven! there are trials which it requires more than human power to bear!"

Seiler's deeply wrinkled brow, and the swollen veins on it, proved distinctly what he suffered, when he thought of her who, without protection and assistance, had sought her way to him, and who now, crushed and rejected, must return to her solitary abode, whither his cruelty drove her.

"Have no anxiety about me," said Maria, consolingly. "I know the way, and am not without means. Also for you, Rudolph, if you need assistance, and will not indignantly refuse it...."

"For heaven's sake, no farther, dear Maria!" Seiler made a violent motion with his hand, and turned away his face which glowed with the deepest blush of shame. To take pecuniary assistance from her whose slightest feeling he could not recompense—a thousand times rather starve! So the architect thought, and therefore he suffered at Maria's offer as violent pains as if he were on a rack. Seiler had never had any emotions that could be compared to those of the present moment. He would rather have lain fifty fathoms deep in the earth, to be spared the humiliation of seeing Maria, and being seen by her, and this in a state in which all his strength and manly firmness were not able to save him from the feeling of his own abasement.

Before the fearful storm within him had been allayed, the gaoler again opened the door with the words: "Here is yet some other person who wishes to see Mr. Architect!"

Seiler slowly raised his eyes, and it appeared to him now, perhaps for the first time in his life, that he lost his composure, which never forsook him even under the most extraordinary circumstances. All began to swim before his eyes—the damp, cold stones burned under his feet like glowing coals, and piercing pains shot through his heart, when he suddenly saw himself in the presence of his wife and his beloved.

It was Alfhild, or rather Alfhild's shadow, that appeared in the door-way, and fixed a staring look upon Maria's lofty and expressive figure.

What Maria felt and suffered, no one saw. She rose with an astonishing strength and calmness, and with a light bow, and a trembling "farewell," she strode through the door in which Alfhild was yet standing. A few moments after the ringing of the bells of a sleigh announced Maria's departure.

Seiler's hand, with which he had during the whole of this time rubbed his eyes, now sank down, and a deep sigh struggled forth from his breast. His eyes sought those of his beloved. Alfhild was quite near him; she was kneeling before the chair on which Maria had sat, leaning her forehead against it.

"Alfhild, my life!" he said slowly. "Can you look at me? It was Maria; my former wife. She wished to visit me from kindness; but I bear no generosity unless I can expect it from returned love. Only from you, from my Alfhild, I bear that sympathy and care which she wanted to bestow on me. Then we do not *bear*, that is not the right word—we *feel* only then, that all around us is pleasant and peaceful—that our being is doubled—that we are not alone."

Alfhild was not able to raise her eyes. The blow she had suffered had been too hard for her strength. She had only tears—but neither reproach nor comfort—not a single word for her beloved.

Seiler lifted her up, and took her in his arms. "Are you afraid of me, dearest? Are you afraid of the darkness of this prison? Do you dare no longer to lay your brow on my breast? Oh, then, my Alfhild, all that I have suffered in these three months is nothing compared with the tortures of this hour! I have firmly relied on your love, when the storms without threatened to break my inner strength; and if I no longer possess this love, or if it is mingled with a feeling of contempt on account of my present wretchedness, then—if the best and noblest feelings of a woman can waver and perish in a trial—then I have lived enough—then I need not wait for my condemnation or acquittal."

Alfhild sank on the bosom of her beloved. The storm in her breast gradually abated, and passed over into a quiet but deadly pain, when Seiler beheld the destruction which the last three months had made on Alfhild's cheeks, where already the roses had faded.

"You ought not to have given me this happiness, beloved Alfhild," said he, tenderly. "I shall now suffer tenfold, when I think on how much strength this journey will cost you."

"No, Seiler, I do not believe it will injure me; but to see you here, to see...." She trembled like a frightened dove.

Alfhild possessed not Maria's heroic strength and firmness. She was a delicate being that required support, and she was perhaps loved so much by Seiler on this very account, who could never bear the thought that the object of his affection could equal him in any thing but in love. His character and nature could not bear to see any body's power dare to compete with his; for, according to his view, this detracted from his sole sway.

"It is my usual fate that brought Maria here today," said he, in a caressing tone. "She will never come again; her pride forbids her to repeat these noble, but rejected offers; and her appearance and strength on this occasion proves that she has a soul that is sufficient for itself. But do not weep so, my Alfhild. Each tear that falls from your eye upon my breast, burns there a spot like those...." Seiler did not express his thoughts; he thought, however, on the fine icy spots which Thelma's cold hand had pressed upon his cheek.

"Uncle Sebastian, who is waiting below, will think, no doubt, that I stay too long," whispered Alfhild, whilst she cast upon her beloved an inquiring look. She feared to offend him, and provoke his restless disposition.

"Are you already tired of the short meeting, my Alfhild?" said he gently, and without reproach.

"No, far from it, Seiler; but I am so excited, and my blood rushes so violently through my heart, that I feel as if it would break out in flames; and if I could die so with my head upon your shoulder I should be happy; for you see that we can no more hope for any true happiness here on earth. I feel that Thelma's shade, and Maria's lofty form, will never leave me, and besides, we are now enveloped in darkness, out of which I see no opening."

"Not here, in this country; but when you are well again, my Alfhild, and have the courage to follow me into a new home, then we have no reason to distrust the future."

"I shall not want the courage to follow you when you are free from all bonds, if my strength will only not fail. I have promised you to love you in life and death, and I will keep this promise. Death alone can build up a bar between us."

"Which I will break down," Seiler interrupted, with an enthusiasm into which excitable men will sometimes fall. "I will seek you in the kingdom of the dead, if I do not find you in that of the living."

Alfhild's hand pressed his. Somebody knocked at the door.

"Uncle Sebastian grows impatient; he fears I may take cold in the evening air. I must...."

"Yes my Alfhild, you must go; but you are mine in life and death."

"In life and death, Seiler!"

She tottered out of the cell;—the architect sank with his face upon the hard pillow of his miserable couch.

"I have destroyed also her life!" sighed he. "I shall perhaps see her for whom I sacrificed every thing fall into the dust like a withered flower. Is there then in my breath a destroying power? I shudder at myself; for I cannot hold the being for whom my love wished to make a heaven upon earth. And if she too does vanish—if there be in the whole wide world not a single tone that finds response to my own heart, then—then....

"But no, I despise to die like a coward! It is easy to throw off the burden of life if one is too tired of it; it is much more difficult to bear the burden if death be a benefit."

CHAPTER V.

UNCLE SEBASTIAN.

"WELL, my dove—you have now had your will; but I do not believe that you feel better after the excursion," said uncle Sebastian, as he and his darling got into their sleigh again, which flew swift as an arrow along the road to Great Hammarby.

"Ah, dear uncle, but I have seen him!"

"He deserves indeed that you see him. All the gaol will speak of it, that the daughter of the provost has been there to comfort the imprisoned architect, and that uncle Sebastian, the old fool, accompanied her."

"Heaven grant that people do not speak of me *worse things*," sighed Alfhild. "He receives visits from all sides, for it is known he is innocent. But did you see the stranger lady, dear uncle, who just left him when I came?"

"Certainly I did see her, and had my own thoughts about it. Do you know who she was?"

"His wife," whispered Alfhild, casting down her eyes to escape the searching gaze of the old man.

"Well, that was a fine meeting!" murmured Captain Oernroos. "May the plague come upon me, if I would, for all the treasures of this world be in the place of this man! But I must say that you are not so weak as I believed you to be, if after such a meeting you could come down the stairs unsupported. But now I make a vow, and shall keep it, that I will say 'no,' if you expect of me another such a folly as to-day's visit: indeed, and if you should beg for it on your knees. I will rather see you stiff and white as the fresh fallen snow there, than expose you once more to such excitement."

"Dear uncle, if you love me at all, then do not grumble any more. Believe me, I suffer enough without this."

"There you are right, indeed, child; and taking it all together, you could not help that an unlucky fate should bring his wife in your way. But it is highly unpleasant, after all, that you should meet her with him. However, it has been, and is still my opinion, that this whole unfortunate affair with this confounded architect is nothing but a punishment from God for the treachery which was practised in our family upon his grandfather. And from the moment the architect entered the parsonage things were not as they should be. On this account it must happen that you broke the goblet on the day when the place for the new church was selected—on this account the bishop must propose just the Norwegian adventurer for the architect of the church. Indeed—our misery began from that moment, and heaven knows when it will end."

Alfhild's lips quivered much.—"I now recollect also," said she, after a brief silence, "what I read in the papers which Seiler gave me the night we met at the coffin of Thelma for the last time. Leganger cursed the goblets, and drank out of them a toast of vengeance. Ha, uncle Sebastian! I begin to fear and tremble when I think of it, and I never put a foot into the gable room, since I learned what had taken place in it. Indeed you may believe me, I have scarcely courage to look up to the gable; for my imagination constantly brings before my mind the white form of Sigrid, beckoning me to make good by Seiler the wrong she had done to his grandfather. But, uncle Sebastian, do not reproach me any more for my love to him. Do not tell me that it is sinful, for surely God demands a sacrifice for the wrong of my grandmother. I am the sacrifice. My love does not prosper, for it sprung up under gloomy auspices, and has been nourished under like dark circumstances."

"Nonsense, child! Our Lord does not demand from us, miserable creatures, such sacrifices; it is easy for him to exercise his vengeance in some other way. But guilt is guilt, and it is to be fully paid for now, it seems, at least on the part of the count's family; but also *our* old remaining debts, it seems, are now to be collected. You, child, our only pride, our only hope, you dwindle away as if you lived in a grave—almost as in former times a nun who was immured alive on account of some great crime."

Alfhild answered only by a deep sigh; uncle Sebastian's comparison made a deep impression on her.

When the travellers reached the parsonage, they were received by the provost, who friendly stepped to the sleigh, and assisted his daughter in alighting.

"God be with you, my child!" said he, with great earnestness, after Alfhild had kissed his hand. "How did the journey agree with you? May uncle Sebastian not repeat that, persuaded by you, he used the same means, to entice likewise from me, consent to a journey which I could grant only from fear that your condition might grow worse."

Alfhild pressed her lips upon her father's hand with heartfelt gratitude. She was not able to utter words, for her father's gentle treatment moved her so much, that she could answer only by an expression of her feeling.

She had made an agreement with uncle Sebastian not to mention her meeting with Seiler's wife.

"Well, how does the prisoner fare?" asked the provost. "Does he hope that the disgraceful examination will soon be at an end?"

Alfhild now recollected with anxiety that she had not spoken with Seiler a single word on this subject. They exchanged only the feelings of their hearts, but had not thought of the examination. She therefore answered, somewhat embarrassed: "Seiler appeared to be in good spirits. His looks and his unshaken firmness, showed that he thinks his delivery from the unmerited imprisonment is near at hand."

"Well, but he can wait yet some time for this," observed the provost, "however eloquently he may plead his own case, and in spite of

the incontrovertible facts which speak in his favour. Suits of this kind
are always very ticklish, and, in my opinion, he can never come out
of it entirely exculpated, though the count is at present less urgent in
the matter than might have been expected from his first zeal."

"And do you know what is the cause of the present dejection in
the count's life and conduct?" asked uncle Sebastian, as he threw himself into the sofa-corner, lighted his pipe, and seized his beer-glass.

"Not exactly; but I can think that Seiler, after having finished his
part at the castle, perhaps disclosed to the count the old connection
in which his family and ours stand with that of the architect. And
it is very natural that this should affect the count, who now sees in
the awful death of his children a dispensation of Providence, if not a
sentence of punishment."

"So it is," said Sebastian. "After the count had read the papers
which the architect had entrusted to old Borgstedt, the grief at his
double loss has been increased by a consuming pain that is gnawing
at his heart. It is true the count had heard some whisperings about
these old stories; but it is of course an entirely different thing whether
they are looked upon from the point of view in which Seiler represents them, or from that of the love-chronicle of the noble family.
From Seiler's point of view, illusion is easily distinguished from truth,
and one can perceive from his representation, that all misdeeds are
avenged, though it be not in the life-time of the offender. According
to what Borgstedt tells me, the count would like, if possible, to take
back the complaint against the architect; but the matter has gone too
far now and must be carried on to final judgment."

"Indeed, the count's family presents a mournful aspect," the
provost interrupted. "The count has withered, and resembles more
a shadow than a man, when he is creeping through the rooms to
the picture-gallery, where he now passes most of his time. The eyes
of the countess, that were not well before, are almost extinct from
uninterrupted weeping. She sits in her cabinet hung with green taf-
feta, dumb, like a mummy. The baroness, this proud and supercilious
woman, has grown mad, at least her wits have suffered so much, that
she will never recover the complete use of them. She runs all day
about in her rooms, and seeks her daughter in every corner, who, she
maintains, has hidden herself. But when any body enters, she springs
up and flies into the furthest chamber, where she throws herself into

a chair, and covers herself with the black veil which Thelma wore when she was taken out of the water."

"The hand of the Lord is heavy upon them," remarked uncle Sebastian, in an unusually mild and conciliating tone. "God grant them peace. But I see Alfhild has gone away; she did not wish to listen to our conversation. Yes, indeed—her burden is heavy enough—heavier than the young shoulders are able to bear."

On the same evening that Alfhild, almost lulled to sleep by uncle Sebastian's voice, lent scarcely half an ear to his stories by her bedside,—on the same evening that Seiler, sleepless, tossed himself on his couch,—Maria travelled alone with the coachman, through the wild, desolate fields of snow, on which the road could scarcely be discovered.

"Is it yet far to the next stage?" asked she with difficulty. The sharp cold and the whirling snowflakes almost took away her speech; the limbs of her delicate body grew stiff—she was hardly able to hold her cloak closed with her hands.

"You ask if it is yet far?" answered the coachman. "Yes, upon my soul, that it is. You ought not to have set out, for this is no weather for ladies."

"But the last inn was so uncleanly; and it did not snow when we left."

"*Uncleanly*, you say? You will see something different in the next inn, if we can reach it at all."

"Is it still worse than the other?" Poor Maria's teeth chattered, and she was not able to move her feet, which had no other protection from the cold than some hay.

"I warrant you it is!" answered the coachman. "But you should move your feet, or they will be frostbitten."

Maria suffered in body and soul, but her courage had not left her. She did not repent that she had undertaken the journey, however badly she had been repaid for her kindness.

They reached at last a small grey house, with one of those wide, low doors, which are commonly found in this region. It looked very smoky, and the interior of the house entirely corresponded with its exterior. The coachman lifted poor Maria out of the sleigh, and opened the door. In a dark, low room, sat eight or ten coarse, suspicious looking men, smoking their pipes, while they had frequent recourse to the brandy glasses which almost stuck to the table, which was drenched with this liquor. The whole room was filled with dense clouds of smoke, which darkened the light from the two thin tallow candles, which, in the absence of candlesticks, were stuck into two beer-bottles.

"Here is a lady that wants a night's lodging!" cried out Maria's coachman, whilst, in a crouching position, he struck, repeatedly, his arms round his body, to warm his hands.

"A night's lodging!" shrieked a piercing voice, which came from a corner near the chimney-fire, and Maria, who, almost suffocated by the smoke, had stopped at the door, saw a tall, dirty female form come up to her, and announce herself as the hostess.

"Can I have a warm room?" asked Maria.

"Oh, yes, if it is here warm enough for you, I will make you a straw bed in yonder corner. Besides this room there is but one other partition in the whole house; but it is there as cold as out of doors, for the corpse of my mother-in-law has lain there on the straw till this evening."

"But I suppose it can be warmed?" remarked Maria, who would rather try it in this partition, than stay longer in the smoky room.

"Oh, yes; if you are willing to stop there, we can make up a fire. All shall be in order directly."

With these words the hostess took a long piece of pine-wood, kindled it, and led Maria into the partition, from which a horrible smell of death came towards her. The white walls were covered with all kinds of signs, names, and figures.

"No, no! it is impossible to stay here!" exclaimed Maria, holding her handkerchief to her mouth, while she stepped back horrified.

"Then, if it is impossible to stop anywhere, you do best to travel on," said the hostess, sensitively.

"I am not in a condition to do that; I will sit down by the fire for a few hours."

"As you please."

They went back to the sitting-room; the hostess stirred up the fire, and gave her guest a chair, and Maria was obliged to take a seat in the clouds of tobacco-smoke and fumes of brandy. The loud conversation of the men, the bad smell and the heat, soon gave her a violent headach.

A sigh came struggling over her lips. But as forsaken by all the world, and with the most bitter feelings in her heart, she seated herself by the fire, she heard a strong manly voice call out the word "Horses!" so loud, that it re-echoed in the room.

"He seems to be in a hurry," remarked the hostess, and prepared to go out.

Maria also had got up. The voice seemed to her familiar. She rushed out of the room, and sank with a cry of joy into the arms of Bloom.

"Good God, Maria, must I find you in such a hovel!" He pressed the forsaken woman, who had in the whole world no one else but him, to his heart. It beat with noble, proud satisfaction that he was indispensable for her, at least in this moment.

"Oh, Bloom! heaven has not forsaken me, since he sent you to me. Without informing you I had taken a resolution for the execution of which I have been severely punished. Forgive me, and I give you a sacred promise, never again to undertake any thing without your advice."

"Here cannot be the question of forgiving, dear Maria; but you have given me unspeakable anxiety. Apprehending that certain rumours might come so far as your distant Fredsberg, I hastened there to prepare you for them; but you were gone, and already two days; having travelled, however, by day and night, I am so fortunate as to overtake you."

"No, Bloom," said Maria, with a sad but calm expression, "you have not overtaken me, for I am already on my return home."

"What!" A ray of joy which Maria, however, could not see in the darkness, flashed from his eyes.

"It is so, Bloom; and now, I beseech you with all my heart, bring me back to my solitary abode. I shall not freeze in your warm and comfortable sleigh. But let us depart immediately; for I long to be out of this horrible house, in which I should have hardly lived to see the morning if you had not come to take me away."

"And do you wish to go back, Maria?—Will you not repent of it when we are on the way?—Have you considered all well?"

"Every thing, Bloom!" she put her mouth towards his ear: "I have seen Seiler for the last time. I do not wish to see him again!" The last she pronounced with a decision which suppressed all fear in Bloom's mind.

He was, however, not selfish enough to forget his former friend in his present happiness. Having brought Maria into the neat, small town, and taken for her a warm convenient room, he persuaded her to stay twenty-four hours to recover, as he had to settle some urgent business in this part of the country.

Maria understood her friend, and promised to wait for him here. Bloom then went to see Seiler, and their hearts soon became again reconciled. The architect knew how to value the noble efforts of his friend, who did not make use of a single offensive word in developing his point of view from which Seiler should start in his defence; and Bloom respected the fortitude and manly courage with which Seiler bore his burden, and the intense warmth which yet burned in each of his words when he spoke of his plans for the future, in a fresh active life. According to what he said to Bloom, he intended to settle in Denmark, where he, during his last visit, had found a place which particularly attracted him. There he intended to live with his Alfhild, and enjoy domestic happiness, for which he had fought so many battles.

The few hours, which Bloom could devote to him, passed quickly by, and after a brotherly embrace, they parted in the hope of meeting each other again in better circumstances.

When Bloom had left, the fire in Seiler's eyes died, and the fanciful images which his fancy had conjured up in the moment of the joy of meeting, began gradually to fade, and sank at last into a grey sea of mist. Only one form remained behind clear and bright; it was Alfhild's image—the only star which shone in the dark night, in the heart of the prisoner.

CHAPTER VI.

THE MAJOR.

ON a rainy, autumnal evening, in the year 1794, a female figure, who, so far as one could see by the faint light, was something between "lady"

and "madame,"[1] stepped along on the driest stones in the neighbourhood of the red sluice at Stockholm. She carried in one hand a set
of dishes, of which, however, only one-half was filled; and with the
other she lifted up the poor fur-lined cloak, to guard it against all
improper communication with water or dirt. Our new acquaintance
came out of Soedermalm's cellar, took her way across the sluice, and
stopped at a book-store to buy, in passing, a copy of the Stockholm
Mail Gazette, which she folded up carefully, and put it away—and
hereupon she continued her way; passed by the treasurer's office towards the Oesterlong-street, where she entered, at last, an old-fashioned, smoky house, and climbed up five flights of stairs to an attic
chamber. Here she appeared to be at home, if we may judge so from
the bold knocking at one of the doors.

"Is it you, Madame Lisa?" asked a voice which seemed to have
been harsh by nature, but had grown milder.

"To be sure, it is I; I think Sir Major might hear that by the knocking," answered Lisa, while she entered the room through the hastily
opened door.

It was a small square apartment, of about eight feet by eight. The
furniture consisted of a field-bed, with a silken cover that had once
been blue,—an easy-chair, two cushioned chairs, a coarse table, and
a press. In the middle of this poor parlour stood a man of about fifty,
leaning upon his crutch-cane. His figure, of middle height, showed
that there was yet power and strength in his muscles; but one of his
legs being shortened by some inches, had brought him on the list of
invalids, and forced upon him a crutch-cane, as a constant companion.

"Welcome Lisa! you stayed away very long it seems to me, or
time has passed much slower than usual during your absence," remarked the major, and gave a friendly nod to his companion through
joy and sorrow. "I fear you have been in Soedermalm's cellar."

"And if it were so?" asked Lisa, smiling.

"Why you had done so against my will. You know, Madame Lisa,
that though I find, as ever, the cooking best in Soedermalm's cellar,
we have not at present means enough to follow our taste, and...."

---

[1] The women of the higher and middle classes are addressed, in Sweden, by
"lady," those of the lowest, by "madame." [Translator's note.]

The major saw a light cloud on Lisa's brow, which induced him to drop the subject.

Madame Lisa, or Madame Lindborn, as she was called, if the major spoke to her as servant, had, as the story went, been very near the heart of the major twenty-five years ago. What truth there was in the rumour, of course cannot be accurately ascertained. It is only certain that young Lisa married and became soon a widow, when she became the leader, as housekeeper, of the bachelor's hall of the major, and there ruled uncontrolled so long as the major had any thing left. Madame Lisa had followed her master into the Fianic war, had cooked and washed for him, and faithfully kept by his sick bed, when he returned shot and maimed, and shifted along on a small pension as well as he could. Afterwards the condition of the major had grown worse and worse; one piece of furniture after another had to be sold, that Lisa might procure some conveniences for the money, to which he was accustomed; and from year to year he moved, when he changed his dwelling, ever higher up, till he found himself, at last, six flights of stairs high, in an attic chamber.

One must not think, however, that the major, if he wished, could not have had things a little more convenient; for he had rich and high relations who would not have refused him assistance. But they did not seek the major, and the major was too proud to seek them. He would rather eat half a plate of beef with gravy—the other half was for Lisa—from his own means, than a whole plate of roast, with sauce, through the gifts of others; and, however much he liked a glass of wine, he took rather a glass of water from Lisa's hand, than a glass of wine (which he could not pay for) from that of another.

Madame Lisa put off her cloak, and put the dishes upon the stove; she then went into the adjoining partition, which served at the same time for her kitchen, pantry, and sleeping chamber. From this holy of holies she brought a napkin, knife and fork, and put then the dishes and a warm plate on it.

"You have got your feet wet, Madame Lisa," observed the major, full of anxiety. "I am in no hurry; you may first change your clothes."

"Oh, no; I am not wet. You must eat, now that it is warm. Here are sour peas and boiled ham; that is a glorious feast. Our dinner was not very good to-day."

"I thank you, Lisa; you excellent soul! If I had not you, or if you should die, it would not last long with me, either. Well, since you do not wish me to wait, give me your plate; we will share this fine dish."

"No, no; that cannot be done on any account!" exclaimed Lisa, in a very decided tone. "I have yet some of the gruel which I cooked for us last evening. I do not take a single bit; that is certain."

"Well, then, you may take the whole of it away, and I go to bed without supper; for see, Madame Lisa, I do not relish a mouthful if you do not take your share."

"Well, then, I must do as Sir Major wants me to," said Lisa, smiling, and looked so kind and friendly, that the Major repeatedly nodded to her. She took a small piece of ham, and a few tea-spoons full of peas. "Well, now I have my share," said she then, and seated herself with it on a cushioned chair between the table and press.

After the scanty supper was eaten, and Lisa had regaled the Major with a glass of beer, the latter seated himself in the large easy chair which Lisa put near the table, and began to draw with a piece of chalk, the plan of the battle of Perkumaski, in which he had been. And he now explained to his housekeeper, at least for the fiftieth time, all the positions and movements of both armies, and held at the same time, as usual, a great eulogy on the brave Stedingk. To please the Major, Lisa listened attentively, yet did not omit to ply her knitting-needles busily in the woollen stocking, that she might not lose this time entirely.

"Will Sir Major not smoke his evening pipe?" asked Lisa, and made a movement to go for it.

"Keep your seat," answered the Major, "I will save it to-night."

"Why that," asked Lisa. "There is yet tobacco."

"I know it, Lisa; but see, I have so much accustomed myself to read the newspaper with my pipe, that since the time we are no longer able to keep it, I relish no more the evening pipe."

"Why—only try!"

Lisa got up, filled the old pipe with the meerschaum bowl, which had faithfully accompanied the Major through all stages of fate.

He could not refuse his Lisa any thing. He therefore took his pipe; yet a light sigh, which he tried in vain to suppress, escaped him, as he took up again the piece of chalk to continue the explanation of the battle, in want of better pastime.

But now Lisa stepped with a cheerful triumphant air behind his chair, held the newspaper high over his head, and let it drop upon the table, as if it came floating down from the clouds.

"Lisa!" exclaimed the Major, and looked with a joyous grateful look in her face. "I cannot comprehend how you manage my small pension, always to have something left to give me some unhoped-for joy. I can never save anything for you," added he, dejectedly.

"Why, how you talk. Did I not get on my birthday, a new snuff-box, and on my name's day, two pounds of coffee? I hope I shall not hear this again. Read quietly your paper; I have, in the mean time, something to do in my chamber."

When the Major had the lighted pipe in his mouth, and the newspaper in his hand, Madame Lisa could be certain of not being disturbed for the first hour. This time, however, she had no sooner closed the door behind her, than the Major suddenly called out with a loud voice, and half out of breath: "Madame Lisa—come here—come here!—A wonder—God's dispensation,—a *great* news!" And as Lisa entered, the Major stood in the middle of the room, with face all red, and holding the newspaper high in the air.

"What is the matter? What in the Lord's name has happened?" asked Lisa, and dropping the duster, which she had just handled.

"Listen, Lisa," said the Major, and read in a solemn voice.

" 'Deaths. The Chamberlain and Knight of the Northstar order, Count William Hugo of H., died at castle Hammarby, the 30th of October, aged 40 years and 7 months.' "

"What do you say to that, Lisa?"—The Major dropped the paper, sent a look to heaven, in which shone a tear, and folded his hands with an expression of silent devotion.

"Oh, heaven! what shall I think of that," exclaimed Lisa, with glistening eyes. "The deceased count was, indeed, a cousin of Sir Major, but I do not know whether the lieutenant, who had not visited us for a year past, is not nearer related to the late count."

"No, Lisa, that he is not. The stupid fellow hardly bows to me when he meets me in the street. He has grown four inches taller since the news of the death of young count Albano. See, Lisa, then all shops and purses opened for him, 'Take, take,' people said; 'when you are the occupant of Great Hammarby, you can pay.' No one thought of the poor, dismissed Major, in the attic chamber, who is nearer to the deceased than the brother's son; but I suppose no one thought that the count would die in his best years. They believed the old invalid would go before him; and then, to be sure, the lieutenant would have been the next of kin. But God willed it otherwise; and now, Lisa, we can move to-morrow into better quarters. I shall not be in want of credit till I take possession of the inheritance of Hammarby; but God forbid that I enter the castle, so long as the widowed countess and her sister, the baroness of Ravenstein, wish to occupy it."

Lisa floated on rosy clouds. In her mind she saw herself already as the mistress of a great, splendid castle. Her will was law,—her nod was command for a countless train of servants. All honoured Madame Lisa; she ruled within and without the castle as far as the territory of Hammarby extended.

Indeed, that would be another way of managing, than in the small miserable kitchen. Madame Lisa was an excellent woman, but she too had her share of vanity, for which nobody could blame her, for she was a woman.

During the night there was not much sleeping in either of the attic chambers. Lisa had scarcely got up on the following morning, and put on her best cap and dress,—she had scarcely put the Major, who wanted to go into the city, into his uniform-coat, when three knocks at the door announced a visit.

"You will see, Lisa," said the Major with a satirical smile, "that is the lieutenant."

"Shall I not say that your honour has gone out?" asked Lisa in a tone which betrayed her wish to turn him off.

"No, that you shall not do," said the Major, good-naturedly. "He is, upon my soul, punished enough, that the majorat slips through his fingers for this time at least."

"Well, as Sir Major wishes."

Lisa opened the door, and immediately after a young military officer entered the chamber.

"What joy, my dearest uncle, to find you at home. I come to bring you news, which, though it crosses my own hopes, yet causes me the greatest joy, since you without doubt, deserve such a fortune more than I. And I have been running about in the city for a whole day to find out your lodging."

"This last circumstance proves, my dear Linus," replied the Major seriously, "that I have but now become your 'dearest uncle;' otherwise you might now and then have sacrificed a few hours, which you devoted to pleasure, to entertain the old invalid. I know the news already which you mean to bring me. And though it may change materially my outward circumstances, yet it cannot exercise the least influence upon my life in general. I am now accustomed to solitude, and I have no intention to give up my old habits."

"Can I assist my uncle, perhaps, in the settling of business?" asked the undaunted lieutenant, without allowing himself to be at all disturbed by the grave utterance of the Major.

"No, I thank you, I shall go to a lawyer for business of this kind; to the rest I attend best myself. I am yet so fleet on my feet, that I hope to look, God willing, on this world yet twenty and some years to come."

"May my uncle live yet thirty years," answered the lieutenant, with a generosity of despair. "And if you look on only ten years more, I hope to get board and lodging at some other castle than great Hammarby."

"I think also of being married," continued the Major. "It will give me particular pleasure to see a little heir of the Majorat play with my crutch-cane."

"You said just before that you wished to adhere to your old habits, dear uncle," remarked the lieutenant, while he strove to hide his vexation under a forced smile.

"No rule without an exception," answered the Major, calmly. "And one can live with a young, handsome wife, as retired as an old bachelor."

"Certainly—certainly! Retirement would then be even a *necessity*," observed the lieutenant, ironically; "for if old gentlemen want to keep their young wives to themselves, nothing else is left for them."

"Right, right!" laughed the Major. "But I am just on tip-toe; you will excuse me."

"Pray do not let me detain you; I only come to give you my congratulation."

The lieutenant bowed and withdrew, and soon disappeared on the dark staircase.

"Upon my soul!—I have comforted him," exclaimed, triumphantly. "But he deserved a punishment for his overbearing manner with which he treated me heretofore."

"That was right," said Lisa. "And as regards the marriage—"

"That was only a jest—you may imagine. In the fifty-seventh year, and being invalid besides, one does not think of it."

"All true; but the matter about an heir to the majorat of your own remains to be considered. Hammarby would then remain in the family; and the lieutenant who had not so much politeness as to say, 'good morning, Madame Lindborn,' would have to wipe his mouth with the large silk handkerchiefs which he has borrowed at Bildberg's. But he will yet see, that—"

"You grow warm, Madame Lisa," interrupted the Major. "We eat beefsteak for dinner, and drink a bottle of Madeira to it."

CHAPTER VII.

THE NEW LORD.

SHORTLY after Christmas the new lord of the Majorat made his entrance into the castle of Hammarby. Borgstedt, who had grown much older, but was still active, stood with head uncovered at the great staircase, to receive the Major. "Put your hat on!" were his first words, and then followed a representation of Madame Lindborn: "My housekeeper—my right hand," he said, among other things.

Madame Lindborn, in a stately cloak and new plush bonnet, nodded friendly to the old steward. Her eyes appeared to express distinct assurances of her favour.

The Major being tired, he allowed "his right hand" to walk alone through the innumerable rooms of the castle; and, after dinner, he seated himself in the small parlour well known to us, and put his head in the same sofa corner which formerly Albano used to occupy.

"Take a seat by my side, dear Borgstedt," said the Major inviting him friendly. "I have had so little intercourse with my relations, that I do not know scarcely any thing in regard to their circumstances. Tell me something of them—it will entertain me. For instance, where have the two ladies taken up their abode?"

"They have moved to Engelbro, an estate which his lordship, the late count, had bought as her widow-estate, in case he should die before the countess. It is a very fine manor, and lies about nine leagues from hence."

"How is the health of the two ladies? I have heard that they are not very well since the great calamity."

"Yes, indeed, Sir Major, it is bad enough with them. The countess is mourning so deeply, that she has entirely withdrawn from the world. And the baroness, who had for some time lost her reason, has given herself up to religious fanaticism. They, two noble ladies, weep together, and their feeble health does not allow them to receive company."

The major sighed with sympathy. "They have not had much pleasure from their large property," murmured he. "But do tell me, dear Borgstedt, how is it now with the law-suit? The count had the architect arrested, I remember, and if I mistake not, they meant even to put his life in danger."

"Oh, no; he is still alive as ever," remarked Borgstedt. "He was confined in gaol for more than a year; but they could prove nothing against him; on the contrary, it was shown, and proved as certain, that Count Albano himself had thrown the young lady over the balustrade, in a state of frenzy, and had then either jumped after her, to assist the architect in rescuing his bride, or had stumbled while he was dancing on the wall in the dark. It was not easy to settle this matter; but since the count did not wish to have the examination continued, and the judge found no sufficient reason to find the architect guilty, he was acquitted. Proud as he had come, he left the land. The count sent him a well-filled purse, with travelling money; but he rejected it with disdain. He sent word back, 'no gold could remunerate him for the fourteen months imprisonment, which he had suffered innocently.'"

"Well, I am not surprised at that. He did right, upon my soul! No man in the world can make the architect restitution for what he suffered in his honour. It was wrong of the count, from the beginning, to have the examination commenced."

"Yes, it was rash in the count, and he afterwards often repented his hastiness; but the commencement was made, and he could do nothing more than declare himself willing to drop the suit, since no proof could be brought up against the architect."

"It is very handsome in you, Borgstedt, that you defend your deceased lord; however, before a man attacks another man's honour, he must take it into full and mature deliberation. Was the count sick long?"

"Yes, pretty long—in fact, he has constantly been sickly, ever since the fatal evening, the 16th of November. It was, however, a fit of apoplexy that gave him the last blow, and put an end to his life, which—as far as I know—gave him not much pleasure at last."

"I mean to take a view, some day, of the fatal grotto. The provost is said to be a very nice man?"

"Oh, yes—a very fine, respectable, and trustworthy man. Provost Frenkman was always much liked in the count's family."

"I suppose he has a family?"

"Only one daughter; but there lives besides, at his house, a relation, an old Captain Oernroos."

The Major put yet a great many questions, all of which old Borgstedt answered with the greatest accuracy. The old servant went to rest this evening with a lighter heart than he had done for a long time. He had to-day saluted the fourth possessor of Great Hammarby; and as he compared, in his mind, the cunning Count William, the proud, frivolous Count Hugo, and the Count William Hugo, who only strove for outward appearance, with the kind Major, he felt more comfortable than ever. Though he deeply sighed at the recollection of the tragic event which caused the extinction of the count's family, yet he gave himself joyfully up to the hope of a freer and pleasanter life. The manner of the Major had a friendly condescension; one felt in his company, that one man stood opposite another.

On the following forenoon, Provost Frenkman paid his respects at the castle.

In the small parlour, where the provost—who, in parentheses, had remained just the same, and had only grown a little fleshier—was wont to salute politely the countess and baroness, there on the same carpet, before the divan, on which the delicate feet of the ladies had rested, now stood the large, black cushions, which constituted the lower part of Madame Lindhorn's body. Lisa, who had nothing more

urgent to do, than to make herself acquainted with her domestic duties, was just engaged in examining one of the beautiful sofa-cush-
ions, in which the moths had taken delight. "Fie, a shame," exclaimed
she, "not to look better after these fine things."

Here she was interrupted in her soliloquy by the provost, who
said to her in a polite tone: "Your most obedient servant. Am I so
fortunate as to have the honour to see Lady Lindborn?"

The provost who was courteous from custom, and besides had
acquainted himself with the widely extended sphere of Madame
Lindborn, found it advisable to address her in this manner, which
must convince her of the respect which the provost entertained for
his new patroness.

Madame Lindborn found the tone of voice of the provost very
agreeable, and the choice of his words highly pleasing.

"Lady Lindborn—hem—why not? This gives the people, if possible, still more respect, and is more suitable to the new position, than
the former Madame."

"Yes, my name is Lindborn," answered Lisa, with a friendly dignity. "Our provost, I believe?"

Let no one blame the good Lisa for the *our.* She was so much
accustomed to speak in the plural, that another number did not at all
occur to her.

At the same moment the Major came in, and all seemed to wish
to be on a friendly footing with the provost. The unfinished church,
of course, formed the first topic of their conversation.

"To-morrow I shall come to the parsonage, and then I shall take
a view of the building," said the Major. "Pity, that we cannot retain
the same architect; I take great interest in the man. Is it not possible
to make him consent to complete the work he began?"

The provost shrugged his shoulders. "He is not likely to do it,"
he then answered. "He has been involved here in Sweden in some
very unpleasant circumstances, as you, Sir Major, no doubt are aware
of, which must naturally make, for a man with his pride, his stay in
this country very unpleasant. I am convinced he would refuse the
offer; and besides, he is at present very advantageously employed in
Copenhagen."

"You correspond then with him, Mr. Provost?" asked the Major.

"Not exactly that; some business which we had to regulate together, required the interchange of some letters, and his last informs me, that he was then in full employment."

"We must then look round for another architect," remarked the Major, and with this the whole matter was settled.

While the gentlemen at the castle speak politics, and relish the dinner prepared by Madame Lisa, we will pay a visit at the parsonage.

Alfhild, who we saw the last time, pale, sick, suffering, and almost in the arms of death, had recovered her strength and the rosy colour of health on her cheeks. This life which awoke again the very moment that it seemed to die for ever, and in general the whole reformation of her person, had its cause in Seiler's acquittal. The day on which Seiler's fate, through his acquittal, had taken this favourable turn, had also brought about the total change of Alfhild. From this moment ceased the consuming heat in her breast, the sharp stitches no longer troubled her, the snow colour on her cheeks gave way to the hue of health, and around her lips, which almost for two years had opened to no smile, a slight sign of cheerfulness again showed itself; they were the passing sunbeams of a young spring-day.

"God's wonder!" often exclaimed uncle Sebastian, with folded hands, when Alfhild now again sometimes plucked, jestingly, at his beard, or looked into his eyes with animated glance.

"You are right, dear uncle; God's wonders are great!" answered she, as on the afternoon that the provost paid his respects at the castle they sat cozily together, and conversed with each other. "The kind Father there above has given me new life, a new soul, and I believe even a new body; but I am now also convinced that Seiler will become a calm, rational, and true man. You cannot imagine what excellent qualities he possesses; what pure and warm feelings he cherishes in his heart, if one is only able to subdue the impetuosity and fire of his temperament, and the restlessness of his soul. But that shall be my care. I will immediately study his character till I know it thoroughly, and you will see—or at least you will hear it said—that your Alfhild is an excellent housewife."

"Child, child—you will then venture the bold game, you will go with this bold adventurer from your father, your home, and your uncle, into a foreign land where you will have no one to understand you?"

"Where no one understands me, you say, dear uncle? Do you believe that Seiler, who so fervently loves me, could ever cease to understand me? No, never. I feel it as certain in my soul, that in order to become one of the best of men, he only wants a being who loves him with her whole heart, and that is capable of returning his affection as warmly as he demands and deserves. No one can understand him as I do, and on this account he will not be able to do without me."

"But we, your father and myself, do you think, child, that we can do without you?" said uncle Sebastian, in a reproachful tone.

"Must not the wife follow her husband?" whispered Alfhild, intercedingly, while she hid her face on her uncle's breast.

"To be forsaken by him afterwards," objected the old man, in a sharper tone than he was wont to use generally towards Alfhild.

"That you do not believe, uncle Sebastian," answered Alfhild, with a certain feeling of self-respect. "I am convinced you do not believe that.—Do not judge of Seiler too harshly. He has failed, and failed much; but his temperament, and the most unfortunate circumstances in the world, had conspired against his better feeling, and you know, indeed," she added, with a bashful countenance and soft voice—"he never loved Maria."

"I perceive that his eloquent tongue has gained power over you. You spoke very differently when you at first heard of his being married."

Alfhild blushed. "Dear uncle," said she, in a hardly audible voice; "do not think, that my feelings on this point are not less bitter now; but I did not know then that he was on the eve of being separated from her, still less, that his fidelity could bear such a trial as he has gone through; nor had I read the ominous story, which has bound me to him as by a spell. But this enchantment lies, I suppose, only in love. I do love him—I will share with him joy and sorrow—I will die with him!"

Old Sebastian shook his head. Such ideas, though they are natural enough to a young mind, which lies open to all impressions;— such ideas uncle Sebastian could not comprehend. "Alfhild, child!" said he, with an almost trembling voice—"the evening when Seiler came here to take leave of you, has entirely changed you. It is true, you always had a feeling heart and warm sensibility; but I have never heard you speak in this manner. You have trusted to the words of your old friend, and never quarrelled with him, as if he did not wish for you the best."

Alfhild clasped her arms round the neck of the old man. "Pardon me, uncle, if I defended him with too much warmth," she entreated, warmly. "And if you will not say any more that he will forsake me, I will patiently listen to all the rest. But it pierces my heart, uncle Sebastian, if you think ill of him I love."

"Well—well, my dove; if he is better than his *actions*, I have certainly no objection to make; but see, my child, it is these by which I have judged men all my life, and they are in general the best standard which can be applied to the character of a man."

"That is true; but, dear uncle Sebastian, there are also circumstances—*you* know that best since you have lived in the world so long—which look gloomier than they are; and if we could look into the inner soul of man and discover all the causes, which lay at the bottom of their actions, we would judge of them less severely."

Uncle Sebastian smiled. "You have learned to plead well, my dove; still I will not say that you are entirely in the wrong. There can exist such circumstances, though he whose actions appear ambiguous, is generally held by public opinion to be a man of ambiguous character."

Alfhild sighed, and a few tears which the grief forced from her, because she was not able to convince uncle Sebastian, fell upon his hand. "You are very harsh towards me," said she, in a reproachful tone; "you will never allow me to be in the right."

"God grant that you are right, child. You can wish it not more so than I do," replied Oernroos, whilst he friendly wiped the tears of his darling. "But you must also understand that your old friend has a feeling of bitterness, perhaps of *envy*, when he sees how joyfully and willingly you give up the old, dear bonds, to enter into new ones, whose strength, at least, you cannot have tried as much as the former."

"Oh, indeed, you are right; it is heart-rending!" exclaimed Alfhild, before whose soul suddenly came all the pains and struggles which the future must bring her, compared to her present calm condition. "But my given promise! Ah, dear uncle, I must follow him though my heart and yours should bleed to death through it. But it is yet some time till then; who knows what God may let come to pass before I put on the bridal wreath?"

"Very true, my child! But we will not embitter the present by thoughts on the future. When you are married, Uncle Sebastian, perhaps, sleeps already under the turf."

"Or, perhaps...." Alfhild was here interrupted by the so called "new Holsteiner," who came running into the court. A few moments after Provost Frenkman alighted, and came into the parlour, friendly nodding to Alfhild and Sebastian.

"Well, what do you think of the lord of the castle?" asked Oernroos, as he judged from Frenkman's contented looks that all was well.

"He seems to me to be a gentleman in the fullest meaning of the word, though he has not a spark of the deceased count's refinement in manners and appearance," answered the provost.

"Did you speak about the church?" asked the captain, who took great interest in its being completed.

"Yes, certainly we did. The Major sends for a new architect with the next mail; and we can hope, with God's help, to consecrate our new church next autumn."

CHAPTER VIII.

THE CONSULTATION.

"Here, Lisa," said the Major one day to the confidential mistress of his house—"I do not know how it is, but time hangs often heavier on me in this large empty castle, than formerly in my small attic chamber. And yet I read here my newspapers, drink my bottle of good wine, converse with the provost, and drive daily in my commodious carriage to the building-place, to delight myself with seeing the progress of the church—and yet the day often appears to me longer than in former times, when I, instead of all this, marked with a piece of chalk the plan of the battle, on the table, and explained it to you. And you, Madame Lisa, have now less time to listen to me than formerly. You are too much overladen with business to have a quiet moment."

"Oh—one cannot say that," answered Lisa. "But I will explain to Sir Major how that happens. When we lived five flights of stairs high in the attic, our chamber was so small that two men were sufficient to fill it, and feel comfortable in it. But it is something entirely different, Sir Major, when one is the lord of a large castle, and has a count-less number of empty rooms. To feel comfortable in them requires people. When I am absent, Sir Major sits alone, or has, at most, old Borgstedt, and now and then the provost to converse with; but this is not sufficient. It would be by far better—"

"What would be better, Lisa?"

"It would be better if—Sir Major would get married. What are fifty years? Why, good heavens! a man is then in the prime of his years. And if we had a young wife in the house, we should have here an entirely different life!"

"Perhaps only too much, Madame Lisa. You and myself, you would see, were then nothing but ciphers in the house. God preserve us from such folly. A man in the prime of his years, you say? A fine man—with a lame leg—who walks with a crutch-cane. Indeed these are things that can charm a young woman. No, Madame Lisa; this time your kindness has made you lose sight of prudence."

"I did not say that she should be a young chicken; we always call a wife that is just married, a young wife, though she is no longer young in years," said Lisa, somewhat vexed at the Major's contradicting her. "In short, Sir Major would, if married, have by far more joy of life and his riches."

"But you, Lisa, would *you* also have more joy, if you came under the commands of a wife, whom you had to obey?"

"O yes, if she made Sir Major happy, I should become used to it," answered Lisa, in a tone of submission, which indicated that it would be a sacrifice at all events.

"But I would not be able to bear that my wife should command you. No, Lisa, your proposition is not good at all, and must be wholly rejected."

Lisa appeared to be somewhat offended—"I had already made a plan how to arrange the choice," observed she, half loud.

"Well, and how then, Lisa? You can tell me that at all events—though it be only in jest."

"Well, I thought of this plan. Sir Major has made his visits in the neighbourhood, and has been invited by all the world, without having yet reciprocated the favours. It is now our turn. We give a dinner to all our neighbours, and according to the information I have obtained, there is among them a host of elderly and young unmarried ladies.

When they are all seated at the table, we hold a review, and select the one that pleases us best. The rest would come in time of itself."

"As regards the dinner, Madame Lisa, I see no objection. I have never given a large dinner; but I believe it must be entertaining enough, though I always dislike long dinners at other people's. And as regards the ladies, we may, at all events, look at them—that will do no harm."

Lisa's eyes sparkled. Her soul was too noble, even to think with envy of her who might, perhaps, pay her with ingratitude for her warm efforts for the happiness of the Major. Lisa always put her own *self* in the back-ground; and as the happiness of the Major was in question, she gave no hearing to her self-interest which whispered to her, that her authority could only suffer through the marriage of the Major.

The great dinner was appointed for the 17th of May, and a week before, cards of invitation flew in all quarters and directions of the neighbourhood. The object of this great feast was to remain a secret. Madame Lisa had, however, communicated it, under the seal of secrecy, to Borgstedt, who found the affair so peculiar, that he told it, the very same evening, to his friend Oernroos, who, according to his old custom, informed Alfhild of it. (The matter would not have gone round farther, if accident had not willed that the little Anna was in the adjoining room while it was told, and heard it likewise. She had been dismissed from the service at the count's after the great catastrophe, and found a new place at the parsonage.) She could not possibly keep such a secret, which Captain Oernroos had given a comical air by his way of relating it. When she went to church on the Sunday following, she told her news to three or four servant-girls, and the rumour ran like a wild-fire, from place to place, that the old Major would hold, on the 17th of May, a great bridal review, in consequence of which, the unmarried lady who would find favour in the eyes of the Major, was to be the mother of a new race of lords of the Majorat at Great Hammarby.

What talking and whispering, what stir and motion, in all places where one of those interesting invitation cards was sent! All the young ladies over twenty-five years of age read from the card, instead of the simple invitation to dinner, the by far pleasanter invitation to exchange their present title for the by far more interesting one of "gracious lady;" and all mothers whose daughters were no older than sixteen, seventeen, or eighteen, an age in which the advantages of such an election-day are generally not sufficiently appreciated, spared no pains to make to them the meaning of it clear and evident. It was already known that Madame Lisa was a highly important person, and that her voice in this matter would, perhaps, be of greater weight than even that of the major, and therefore all the young ladies received, both before and during the visit, particular instructions how to behave toward Madame Lindborn.

On the morning of the fatal day, while Lisa was most busily engaged in the kitchen, and the servants were occupied spreading the table in the large dining hall—while Borgstedt superintended with a skilful eye the arranging of the wine bottles, and the Major lay, with all composure, in the window smoking his pipe, a carriage drove into the court-yard, and stopped at the castle door, from which a young military officer sprang.

"Ah, my soul!" said the Major, with a good-natured smile—"was not that Linus, my nephew? Well—he will make a long face when he hears what is going on here."

Soon after steps were heard in the entry, and Lieutenant H. stood, with a somewhat doubtful face and bearing, before the master of the house.

"Pardon, dear uncle, that I came to visit you here for some time; and I will confess at once, that my visit here will not be short. The matter is this: after the rumour of the impending marriage of my uncle was spread through the whole city, my *bears* have been attacked by a cruel, rapacious desire, and as one must never neglect any duties due to one's self, I have taken, in order not to be devoured, a long furlough, which I mean to spend, with permission of my uncle, at Castle Hammarby, where there will be no want of room for the nephew of the Lord of the *Majorat*."

In the tone of the lieutenant there lay a mixture of bitter defiance, and a kind of despairing impudence, at which the Major was too good-natured to be vexed. He said, in a friendly tone: "You are welcome, Linus; but first put yourself on a better footing with Madame Lisa—Lady Lindborn as she is called here at the castle—than you have done heretofore, or your stay here might be very unpleasant, and last a shorter time than it seems to be your intention."

"Ah, dearest uncle," exclaimed the frivolous lieutenant, who felt himself transferred from hell into heaven, while he powerfully shook the hand of the Major; "your kindness is equal only to the greatness of my gratitude, and since you are so kind yourself, to give me a hint in regard to the right way, I will prove that I am the most docile young man that ever appeared as a hopeless pretender to a beautiful Majorat. Where, dear uncle, do you order me to establish myself?"

"Establish yourself wherever you please, except in my room and in the dining-hall, where they are just busy with spreading the table. I give to-day a dinner to my neighbours."

"That is only what I know already," answered the lieutenant, with a peculiar smile. "The whole country speaks of your bridal re-view, and, in fact, I drove day and night only to be present at such an extraordinary affair."

"What bridal review are you talking of, Linus?" The Major was si-lent with astonishment when the light flashed upon him. The deepest secret which had been spoken of between him and Lisa, only with-in the secret walls of his chamber, was betrayed—nay, had perhaps formed the universal subject of ridicule in the correspondence of his neighbours with the capital. The Major blushed, and stroked his mustache, as if he wanted to pluck it out, and the more he thought on the ridiculousness of the whole undertaking the more vexed he grew, since he must believe himself to be at present exposed to the mockery and laughter of his acquaintances.

Linus observed with the greatest triumph what was going on in his uncle's mind and determined boldly to turn the circumstances to his advantage.

"My dear uncle," said he, with a slight shrug of his shoulders, "we will not speak any more of the matter; for, upon my honour, you would certainly, and though you were personified patience, get angry at the barefacedness of people. They cannot stop at all their tongues in regard to the ridiculous manner in which you seek a wife. But you ought to have kept the matter more secret. However, excuse me, dear uncle. I am as hungry as a wolf; I will pay my respects to Lady Lindborn."

The Major remained standing at the window, and rubbed his forehead, without being able to comprehend how the matter could have got abroad, and particularly who could have given it this ridiculous air. He was then thought an old fool, who had not the courage to take a single step without first consulting his housekeeper.—"Stupid, cursed stupid, was the whole business!" thought the Major; "but I will spoil them the pleasure in the election day; they will then deem the matter a mere rumour, and gradually forget it."

While the Major made these reflections, Linus hastened to that part of the castle where kitchen and store-room were. He opened with bold hand the door leading to Lisa's empire, and saw her, with her back turned towards the door, and her cap on one ear, being very busy keeping, with all her might and main, the long stick of the churnel in motion.

"Your most obedient servant, my good Lady Lindborn. Excuse the boldness with which I come into your kitchen, entirely unexpected; but, as I have to ask your pardon for my neglect at our last meeting, when vexed through many annoying things, I did not know where my head was. I did not wish to defer it till dinner, but flew, after I had saluted my uncle with a few words, to the hostess of the house, to entreat her most friendly, to show me a room in my new home."

"What—new home? Was there ever heard any thing like it!" Lisa's eyes sparkled like the fire on the hearth. "The Sir Lieutenant, indeed, comes, as he says himself, *quite unexpected*. You cannot possibly have so bad a memory as not to recollect that?"

"Best Lady Lindborn," said Linus, interrupting her, "you can, indeed, be convinced that I should never have taken this liberty if my uncle had not told me, just now, 'You are welcome, Linus, and may stay at Hammarby as long as you please; that is, if the hostess, my faithful Lady Lindborn, is well disposed towards you.' We will see, said I, whether as regards the forgetting of all petty anger, she does not resemble her illustrious predecessors at castle Hammarby. I run down immediately to try it.—And now I stand here, humility itself, and ask for a word, for a slight sign of the old sins being forgiven."

"And do you think I have nothing more to do today?" answered Lisa, evidently softened, as well by the submissiveness of the lieutenant, as by the handsome conduct of the Major, which Linus knew how to put in the best light. "But so much is certain," added she, with a mixture of pretension and pride; "I have lived long enough in the world to have learned that servants must not oppose the will of their master. And if the Major has bid you welcome, then—I have no objection."

"After so much generosity on the part of Lady Lindborn," replied Linus, "I venture to hope that the complete contract of peace will be signed and sealed with a small breakfast."

"If Sir Lieutenant will go into the small parlour, I will presently send him something."

"No, by no means, my best Lady Lindborn. I am too much convinced that you have too much to do on a day like this, to have any thing to do with so insignificant a person as myself. Allow me that I cut off some bread myself; for I cannot allow you to take the least pains about me."

The Lieutenant now rose ten per cent. in Madame Lisa's favour; she, therefore, put some plates upon a waiter, and went herself into the store-room, to get the best delicacies. When she came back into the kitchen, Linus, who had put on a white apron, stood at the churnel, and churned with all his might and main.

"But, good heavens, Sir Lieutenant, what are you doing there?" cried Lisa, laughing. "That is, indeed, pretty work for an officer! Here, take your breakfast, and eat it where you can find room."

"Ah! Lady Lindborn, we shall become friends," cried Linus, in a prophetic tone, and disappeared with the result of his first trial.

CHAPTER IX.

THE DISAPPOINTMENT.

THE guests were assembled and seated at the richly laden and beautifully ornamented table. Silk dresses rustled, flowers, pearls and feathers decked the hair of the ladies, each after her age and taste, and all were strutting with jewels and heavy goods. But at the one side of the table sat a young maiden in a simple white dress, who wore in her locks nothing but a natural lily. The proud, rose-decked young noble ladies, regarded her with envy, for the Lieutenant v. H., most assuredly the handsomest young man of the company, and the most attentive vice-host, had his eyes continually fixed upon her. As she drew her small rose-coloured lace-shawl closer round her on account of the draught of air, he even sprang up and took, without mistaking, her warm shawl, and handed it to her with a polite bow.

"He certainly does not know who she is," whispered a young lady to another.

And so it was. Lieutenant Linus did not learn who this charming girl was, till a lady near him nodded to the object of his attention, with the words,—"How is your health now, my dear Miss Frenkman? A rose in your hair would have become you better than a lily."

Alfhild blushed. But without waiting for her answer, the lady turned to one of her neighbours to discuss with her the head-dress of a young lady sitting opposite to her.

"The daughter of the provost? An excellent pastime during my stay in the country," thought Linus, and directed his attentions to the beautiful girl to the great chagrin of the rest of the ladies.

The mothers, however, had their eyes constantly fixed upon the Major, who, seated between a lady-general, round as a ball, and a dressed-up baron's widow, sighed under the heavy load of fulfilling his duties as host in the best possible manner. His two fair neighbours laid constant claim upon his attention, insomuch that with his best will he was not able to see any other of the young ladies but those pointed out to him by the stout lady-general and the lean baron's widow, and what they showed to him had so little attraction, that he thanked heaven when the table was removed.

The rest of the day went off rather tedious and heavy; all attempts of the mothers to draw the Major into a conversation with their daughters, failed completely. The Major smoked his pipe in company with the gentlemen, and left to his nephew to represent him with the ladies. The lieutenant, a selfish soul, however, did only what pleased him; he had eyes only for Alfhild. All the other ladies, without exception, appeared to him either too old or too ugly, or too uninteresting, to fascinate a young gentleman from the capital.

Also, the last attempt failed. In a room adjoining the dining-hall, stood Madame Lisa, and served coffee. One lady after the other repaired to this room, and all could not admire enough the good coffee and the excellent arrangement of the dinner. They patted Madame Lisa's shoulders in the most condescending manner; but Lisa having received, before the arrival of the guests, a hint from the Major that their plan was betrayed, she too was out of humour, and saw in the polite attentions nothing but what they actually were, endeavours to gain her favour. But they did not succeed. Madame Lisa had never in her life been in so bad a humour as to-day, and no one could boast of a friendly word, except Alfhild, who assisted her in pouring out coffee, as she alone could not fill the cups as fast as the guests emptied them.

With a feeling of discomfort and dissatisfaction, in consequence of the disappointed expectation, the elegant ladies put themselves again in their coaches, and the Major's dry, "I thank you," upon their sugar-sweet invitations, was so repulsive, that it was the general belief the story about the election-day had only been a joke which some malicious wag had set on foot. This circumstance easily explains that every family who had been present at the dinner, took particular pains to suppress these rumours, and there was, before long, no affair which one had so much to avoid speaking about as the so-called election-day.

He who gained most from the unhappy result of the brides-show was the lieutenant. "My best uncle," he began, the following morning at breakfast, "do tell me, above all things, which of the ladies with whom I had yesterday the fortune of becoming acquainted, will be my new aunt? Lady T——is very handsome, and has also a good figure, but she squints dreadfully, and her sister, the widow in mourning, looked so languishing, that I myself was near pining away whenever I came near the magic circle controlled by her charms. And Lady B——, and Lady O——, and Lady R——, and so on, one and all."

"For heaven's sake be still! You'll burst my ears with your nonsensical talk!" said the Major, in a tone unusually severe and forbidding. "Whoever wishes to stay in this house, must not mention a syllable of the foolish affair which one could read in the faces of all mothers who had a daughter to marry."

The lieutenant felt satisfied. He carved with much agility the wing of a turkey. "Allow me, dear uncle, that I help you. Upon my honour!—does it not taste better so than if here...."

"You rogue," said the Major, and again looked as friendly and good-natured as ever, when nothing annoyed him.

Not a word passed between Madame Lisa and the Major, on the failed speculation, and a trifle of ill-humour prevailed between them for several days after. During this time the lieutenant knew how to make himself indispensable to both—with the Major, by exaggerated praises which he bestowed upon Lisa's excellent qualities, and her perfect disinterestedness regarding the marriage project—and with her, by speaking of the great confidence and friendship the Major entertained for her, of which—as he maintained—each of his actions gave a distinct proof. Things stood, ere long, again as they had been, nay, ever better; for Linus brought life into the castle, which had been wanting heretofore. He was much in the fields to assist old Borgstedt, and to show at the same time to his uncle, that he understood something of agriculture, and loved it too. Besides, he played in the evening at drafts with the Major, and listened with the greatest attention and patience to the reports on those battles in which his uncle had been, and at the same time did not neglect showing to Madame Lisa those little attentions which never fail of their good effect. If his uncle missed his snuff-box, Linus immediately sprang to fetch it; if some household schedule was to be made out, it was Linus who took pen in hand and wrote what Madame Lisa dictated; and in all things that were undertaken at the castle; he was an indispensable person, insomuch that he soon raised himself to a favourite from having been a common, hardly welcome guest. From the time that Linus felt himself safe in Lisa's favour, he feared no longer a new aunt at the castle. He was firmly convinced that she had for ever given up the idea of the Major's marrying again.

But the activity which the lieutenant displayed at the castle did not by far consume all his time, nor was he in any way satisfied with it. No, indeed; he wished also to become the favourite, and was daily at the parsonage, whither the beautiful Alfhild drew him with irresistible power. As the Major also liked the provost and his family, he often accompanied the lieutenant at his visits, and while the provost, old Oernroos, and the Major, were absorbed in talking politics, the heir to the Majorat, as he was now every where called, sat by Alfhild at the same window, where the architect in former times had so often whispered to her the tenderest words of love.

Lieutenant v. H. had not the regularity of features of the architect, and still less his beautiful figure and his manly imposing manner; but as to pliability and boldness, he would compete with him throughout. Besides, Linus was a very pleasant and handsome man, and accustomed to meet with success with ladies. Under these circumstances, he must feel particularly vexed to see that his attentions were wholly lost upon Alfhild. Whatever he spoke to her, nothing would make an impression upon her. In former times, a man with his light and cheerful temperament might have captivated her mind; but now Alfhild's feelings were devoted so exclusively to him whom she had loved and could love alone, that every attempt to win from her a look, or the faintest smile, must fail.

Resistance has always been an incentive, even for such butterfly natures as Linus, and he began at last to believe seriously, that he actually loved Alfhild.

"I cannot conceive," said the Major one day on their way home, "why you always plague the poor girl with your flatteries and empty compliments. An honest girl of the country does not care about such nonsense, and you might see that yourself, my dear Linus, if you would open your eyes but a little."

"Upon my honour, there is not one girl in a hundred but is pleased with flatteries," remarked Linus; and he added with a certain self-complacency:—"How many of these country samples of virtue would, in your opinion, be able, my dear uncle, to resist me if I took serious pains about them?"

"How many?" replied the Major. "That is more than I can say. I now speak only of what I know, and this is: that your pains to please Alfhild Frenkman, have no more effect than if you threw water on a goose!"

"You mean to say, then, dear uncle, you think that she is a goose?"

"Far from it. She is a girl uncommonly well educated for her station; and neither I nor any body else will deny that she is handsome, pleasant, and amiable. For me she has still another most particular value, that of domestic industry; and of the heartfelt, childlike love with which she treats old Oernroos and his weaknesses. In short, I never found any woman, excepting my old Lisa, who could be compared less to a goose, than the daughter of the provost."

"Well, my dear uncle, if she is a refined, amiable, and intelligent girl, she must also have a little taste; and to show it, she has here the best opportunity."

"I think she does so," replied the Major, with a somewhat dry smile. "I should think it proves understanding, if a young girl knows how to distinguish the jests of a frivolous cavalry officer from the sincere attentions of an earnest man. Alfhild has intelligence enough to do this. It gives me, indeed, great joy to observe the fine manner in which she knows how to check the lieutenant; upon my soul, she understands it better than many ladies of *ton*, who have been educated after the rules of art."

"But, my dear uncle, from what reason can it give you pleasure to see me treated so? I cannot comprehend, besides, what possible interest you can take in this relation."

"See, Linus, it has given me pleasure all my life long, to observe how young conceited gentlemen burn their fingers when they approach the fire too near. You play so often and meanly with young hearts, that the whole sex is under obligation to her, who, like Alfhild, knows how to maintain and defend her dignity and rights."

"But, dear uncle, what then, if it were no mere play—I only suppose the case—if it were earnest, what would you say then? I know that certain prejudices, and more particularly those relating to the difference of ranks, cannot be found in a man like my uncle."

"Nonsense!" exclaimed the Major, while he drily laughed and looked in another direction.

"That was a very undecided answer," remarked the lieutenant, somewhat offended.

"Ha!" said the Major, and looked very serious.

"You have suddenly grown quite taciturn, my dear uncle. The provost is said to have quite a large fortune, and old Oernroos, likewise, is a man of no small means."

"Certainly not without means," interrupted the major—"he is a man of the genuine make. It is really a pleasure to hear him speak of the campaigns which he passed through before my time."

"That is, no doubt, very interesting; but I found our former subject of by far more solid interest. Would you not, dear uncle...."

They now met one of the farmers belonging to the manor, to whom the Major had something to say, and before the lieutenant could resume the thread of his former conversation, the carriage stopped at the staircase of the castle, where Madame Lisa stood and gave a welcome to the gentlemen.

On the same evening there was a long consultation held in the room of the Major between him and Lisa. We do not know what was the subject of the deliberation; however, when it was finished, and Lisa had left the room, the Major said these words to her: "I depend entirely upon your shrewdness, Lisa. You must feel their pulse, but carefully. I have still fresh on my mind the election day with all its fooleries."

"And I, likewise," answered Lisa. "But we will do it this time more shrewdly."

Madame Lisa walked in her room up and down. She looked as if she would alternately weep or laugh; she was evidently much occupied with her thoughts, and resolved a number of things, which she in her wisdom would, however, yet sleep upon.

CHAPTER X.

AN INTERVIEW.

SUMMER was now in the full bloom of its beauty, and had reached the point from where it must, according to the eternal laws of nature, slope gradually downward.

In the grand, but wild country, near the castle of Hammarby, lay the great ruins of the gigantic Gothic building which stood here in former times, and looked far upon the lake. When the new castle was built, a large quantity of building materials had been taken from the old mansion, and what remained formed, on this account, only a dilapidated ruin, a mere shadow of what the building had once been.

On a quiet, beautiful summer morning, when the ringing of bells from two distant church steeples re-echoed in the old walls, the form of a man was seen walking slowly in the ruins. He would now ascend, with precaution, a piece of wall jutting forth, in order to send a look to the country around, and then again he disappeared in the dark shadow of the grey masses of stone.

In a few moments the rattling of a coach was heard, and soon after the yellow painted chaise of the provost was seen stopping near the ruins.

"Why am I to stop here?" asked Peter, who had been ordered to drive Alfhild, the daughter of his master, to the neighbouring church.

"It is so long since I visited the ruins," answered Alfhild, "that

I wish to look at them once more. You may drive on to the church; the weather is so beautiful that I prefer going the rest of the way on foot."

"Why, dear me, miss! what brings that into your head?"

"I feel now to-day disposed to walk, dear Peter; drive on unconcerned; I shall follow you unharmed."

Peter shook his head; but Alfhild spoke in a tone so decided, that he was forced to obey, and he was, therefore, soon with horse and chaise out of sight.

When the cloud of dust raised by the vehicle had settled, Alfhild took the way to the ruins. The form inside the old stone heaps began to move, and hastened to meet Alfhild, and when she entered the ruins, she was clasped round by two arms, and in the same moment she lay on Seiler's breast.

A few minutes, in which Seiler and Alfhild forgot earth and its cares, flew away on invisible wings.

The two lovers then seated themselves on a stone covered with moss, and after their eyes had satisfied themselves by a mutual gazing upon each other, their feelings found words.

"You see, so your father wrote," said Seiler, "and, therefore, I shall not put a foot over the threshold of the parsonage till I have the decree of divorce in my pocket."

With these words Seiler unfolded a letter, and read the following passage to Alfhild.

"Mr. Seiler will, no doubt, see himself, that under present circumstances, a father may entertain doubts which are in conflict with his former promises. The exceedingly unpleasant affairs in which you have been involved, will always be of incalculable consequence, notwithstanding the examination has resulted in your acquittal. For this reason I hope to receive back, from your well-known sense of honour, what my own sense of honour forbids me to demand distinctly—namely, my promise given to you, &c."

Seiler folded again the letter with a contemptuous smile, and without uttering a word, put it back where he had taken it from.

"Did my father write this? He has not told me a word of his resolution. He well knew it would have been my death."

"But this cannot be done on any account," said Seiler, in a fearfully decisive tone. "He has once permitted me to come again when

I should have the decree of divorce; and I will come—rest assured of that, my Alfhild—yet before autumn will have scattered from the trees the last yellow leaves. I shall then demand the fulfilment of his promise, which he, at the time, confirmed with his word of honour. I hope to God he will not refuse it. But if he should do so, depend upon it, I will not have struggled four long years for a happiness, to see it suddenly consumed in smoke and flame by any wilful caprice."

"But what will you do, Seiler?" asked Alfhild, and her voice trembled with fear.

"What will I do?" The eyebrows of the architect contracted. A dark cloud shaded his forehead. "Let us not speak of it now," answered he. "Your father will not dare to break his word,—he will not dare to provoke me."

"Certainly he will not wish to destroy my happiness and my life," whispered Alfhild, and placed her hand, calmly, upon the heart of her beloved.

"Perhaps that, neither," said Seiler, while he touched the caressing hands with his lips.

"But are you certain," began again Alfhild, after a short pause, "that your affair will be finished so soon? May I hope that you will return in autumn?"

"You may rely on it, my beloved. No further hinderance stands now in the way of dissolving a band which Maria is now as willing as myself to break. The three years required by the Norwegian law, will expire in February next, and then the suit will proceed without delay. The forms alone are yet to be complied with, and they will be done with, in the slow course of law, in a few months."

"Oh, Seiler, God grant it! How grateful and happy shall I be, when all the darkness, which now surrounds us, shall have vanished,—when I can openly call myself before God and the world, your betrothed. You cannot think how painful it is to me to be obliged to envelope us in this obscurity which I hate,—and how bitter it is to me, in spite of the bliss of our meeting, to meet you here in the ruins, and far from my relations. I wonder whether uncle Sebastian has not suspected something, when I so obstinately insisted upon attending service in the neighbouring church, instead of dining with my father at the castle, where we were all invited to-day."

"If you have no courage to encounter for my sake, a few little inconveniences, how will it be, when I shall carry you away from all those to whom your heart is now allied?"

Alfhild felt, with a bitter pang, the sadness of what Seiler remarked. She thought of the words of her uncle, and her eyes were filled with tears.

"Was I harsh towards you, my beloved? Excuse my violence and my self-love, which can never be satisfied with a divided heart. Oh, Alfhild! If you could feel all the struggles I passed through, on your account—if you knew of what I am still capable, in order to reach the goal after which I am striving,—then you could understand how much I may ask of you and your fortitude, but still more of your love."

"And, for the sake of love, I am willing to suffer all," replied she, and looked cheerfully into his eyes.

"Suffer, Alfhild? How did you come to use that word? Do we suffer, when we sacrifice ourselves for the being that we love more than our lives? I do not think so. This suffering, as you call it, is happiness for me."

"I can be happy, and yet suffer," said Alfhild, compromising. "I am, indeed, happy and glad, to follow you to the distant home, which your love prepares for me in a foreign land; but, notwithstanding, I suffer at the thought of being separated from my father, my beloved native home, and, perhaps, most from uncle Sebastian. Ah, Seiler, if you knew how the noble old man has cared for me from my childhood, if you had seen how often he has sat at my sick-bed, sacrificing his own rest, and told me his history,—how friendly and kindly his eyes looked at me, when I awoke, and how many little troubles he helped me to escape, when he could, or has shared with me, if he could not avert them;—and if you knew how his heart has grown entwined with mine, and that I am his only joy here on earth, and constitute so entirely a part of his happiness of life: then, Seiler, you would, certainly, not be angry that I suffer at the thought of being obliged to leave all that is holy and dear to me. It grieves me, particularly to let the old friend die alone, without that the familiar voice shall read to him the last prayer, or wipe the sweat of anguish from his brow."

"I am not angry, beloved Alfhild," said Seiler, soothed by the gentle tone that spoke to his feelings, and the mild clear words that penetrated to his heart. "No, not anger, my dearest, only an unbounded envy of all, to whom you are attached in love, comes over me against my will. It is true, I shall soon bring you into a foreign land, and among strangers, where you love no one except myself, where I constitute your life, your world, your heaven, and your all. But a gloomy, fearful thought rises in my soul, a thought that has never occurred to me before. Though you may have strength of body and soul, to bear the separation from those whom you love so fervently,—will this struggle not deprive you of the last remnant of your weakened strength? Shall I, perhaps, carry away in my arms only the dying victim, only the angel who is near returning to its heavenly home?"

"Oh, no, Seiler, do not believe so. The separation will give me pain, but you will have indulgence with my first pain. On your breast I shall soon recover,—and I shall receive new strength of life, through your love and tender care. Have I not once before hovered on the brink of the grave, and have I not been called back into life through love? God is merciful and kind towards us weak, and whatever he does is well done."

"Is that also well done, if he takes you from me,—if he turns to dust the hopes which I have carefully cherished," asked Seiler, and looked with a painful expression, in her beautiful, tear-laden eyes.

Alfhild was silent. A powerful, holy feeling moved in her soul, and it seemed to her as if secret voices whispered to her, "yes!" Her lips, however, refused to pronounce this singular message before her beloved. With a sigh, without uttering, however, a syllable, she leaned on Seiler's shoulder.

Then the architect felt a convulsive quiver run through his body. His cheeks grew pale, paler than those of Alfhild; single drops of perspiration broke out and covered his brow. He raised Alfhild's head with his hand, and put his lips on hers; and having convinced himself, as it were, that there was still warmth in them, he whispered in a melancholy tone: "Do you prefer the cold bridal bed under the turf, to the place on my warm bosom?"

Alfhild was violently moved by Seiler's serious question. In this moment it was love to him, and this alone, which gained power over her. She clasped firmly her arms round his neck; it was so warm on his heart,—it was heaven for her.—"Do not torture me so unspeakably," begged she, with fervour. "I will live and die on the place where I am now."

A smile of happiest satisfaction hovered round Seiler's lips. Vernal images from the dream-world of the future passed through his breast, and a quiet, holy happiness was felt by both, undisturbed. But the moment of most intimate and closest union was immediately succeeded by that of separation. The time had long passed, that Alfhild must go away.

"In a few months we shall meet again," said the architect, comforting, as he accompanied Alfhild to the entrance of the ruins—"but before we part, pray tell me what you think of the new inmates of the castle?" Seiler could not, at these words, suppress a sigh, as the family came to his mind, which had lately perished.

"Oh—I like them very well.—The Major is an honourable gentleman, and Madame Lisa, his housekeeper and right-hand, is a woman of the kind that is found but seldom in these days. But the lieutenant".... Alfhild drew the words a little. She knew nothing to say against him; Linus did not please her, however, because he busied himself, next to his own person—most with hers.

"Well, the lieutenant—how is it with him? According to what I have heard, he cannot be compared with Albano; or he would have no great success with the ladies; but he is said to be a real heart-breaker. Has he already turned his attention to any charming object in the neighbourhood?"

"I believe not," said Alfhild; but feeling she had said an untruth, her cheeks coloured crimson. Lieutenant Linus evidently distinguished her over all other young ladies in the neighbourhood. She could not help observing it very well; but she did not like to tell Seiler of it.

"Is it then any white lily which has supplanted in his eyes the rose?" asked Seiler, without the least sign of excitement. "The colour on your cheeks lets me suppose so, my beloved."

"Well—yes; it almost appears so; I only feared you would——"

"I should be jealous?" interrupted the architect, with a subtle smile. "However natural it may seem to you, that a man of my violent temper be subject to it, it is not the case with me. My pride, or if you please, my self-love, prevents me from believing that a woman that gives me her love could sigh for any other man. No, dear Alfhild—on this point you may be perfectly calm. The butterfly Linus may flutter round my white rose as much and as close as he pleases, he will not be able to tear a single leaf from the charming flower. And besides, all dark spirits have withdrawn from my breast. In it dwell only my beloved and her knights,—*love* and *confidence.*"

A livelier and brighter fire shone in Alfhild's eyes, than Seiler had ever seen; the burden she had felt weighing upon her breast, disappeared through the words of her beloved, as if by magic. So happy as in this moment, she had never felt before.

They now stood on the parting road. They looked on each other in silence, to impress deeply upon their memories the beloved features.

"I know not," said Seiler, "what restless feeling now comes over me. Just now I was perfectly quiet—and a few months soon pass away, when the goal of happiness is so near."

"Ah, yes—it is but a short time, compared with the long years during which we struggled, suffered, and waited," answered Alfhild; but she, too, was seized with a singular anxiety. And as they embraced each other to bid farewell, the two beating hearts pressed each other with a kind of fear.

Now the bells of the neighbouring church resounded, and the ringing struck upon the ears of the two listeners with remarkable distinctness.

"Ah," sighed Alfhild, "thus they also rang on the evening that you came to Hammarby for the first time. It was a wonderful foreboding, together with the rattling of the coach. Do you recollect? I still hear distinctly how it mingled with the chiming of the bells."

"O be quiet—be quiet; do not speak of it. There is nothing so wonderful as our love, that has passed through so many trials," whispered Seiler, and pressed a long kiss upon her lips, that of parting—of separation.

Alfhild stepped over the threshold of the ruins, and was separated from Seiler; yet she turned round once more, and stretched her hands out after him. The full light of the sun fell upon her pale tear-covered cheeks; the architect thought to see before him a transfiguration of the earthly into the heavenly.

Their hands united once more for a hearty grasp.

But when Alfhild had gone, and Seiler had returned into the dark walks of the ruins, a light whirlwind rose, and effaced the foot-prints in the sand where the two lovers had stood.

CHAPTER XI.

LADY LINDBORN.

Lieutenant Linus v. H——. To His friend in Stockholm.

I WISH, my dear Azel, you were here, that you might admire my diplomatic skill. By my honour, and all things holiest I wot of, by the Majorat of Hammarby, I must admire myself, and am firmly convinced that I was mistaken when I adopted the military career. It is as clear as the sun I should have made the best diplomatist that ever received a mission to a foreign court. "Well!" you exclaim—"wheel about, it is not too late yet." But, my friend, it *is* too late. I hope, if God willing, very soon, as a powerful magnet, to let my voice sound forth at the hall of knighthood, and at the interval to rule here at the castle, as a king does his submissive vassals. And how have I acquired these glorious prospects of these beautiful dreams which will soon become the most enchanting reality? What do you think, my friend? By nothing but my unheard of diplomatic finesse, with which I understand to insinuate myself with the present queen of my future kingdom—with Madame Lisa. She certainly is no Madame Maintenon, but she unquestionably exercises as great an influence over my uncle, the major, as the French lady did over Louis XIV. And you will grant, that all means are good which lead to our ends.

Having by some sarcastic sallies at the ridiculous election-day, on which my good uncle intended to select his better half, totally banished out of his and Madame Lisa's mind all thoughts of marriage, which he never harboured in real earnest, I began my operations.

It was very difficult to tear up the deeply-rooted prejudices of the old man, which he had conceived of me, as being a frivolous, incapable, and supercilious sprig, which he thought me to be. At length, however, I succeeded in convincing him that a new spirit had taken possession of my body. And the good gentleman observed with attention and delight, the development of my good qualities, which, you well know, are acquired very naturally, when one sees all day only good examples, and not as in Stockholm, also bad ones now and then, which, by the by, I do not mean for a hit at you.

But now, listen, Azel. If you were not as great a fool as I have ever been, and if I were not a little ashamed of unfolding the truth before your profane eyes, I would tell you in confidence, that in fact this example, with the beautiful prospects of independence, has had a wonderful influence on—you may laugh if you choose—my better feelings. The deuce may know what is the real condition of the human heart; but I believe it is not quite so bad as we take pains to make it. I, for my part, must confess that the country air, the intercourse with my good-hearted uncle, and with Madame Lisa, an excellent woman, and with the old steward, Borgstedt, as well as the daily interesting sight of the beautiful castle of Hammarby, have produced an effect upon me which I can only call beneficial—and it extends over my whole character. But, Azel, you must come yourself, and have an ocular proof of all this; you must be persuaded by yourself, that in such company, a man as light-minded even as myself, might become very rational, that is, if the old evil spirit does not maintain his sway.

However, enough of this. I will turn over to another chapter, and cautiously show you a new page of my present life; a page which I believe will not look very badly in the future, if all that is now anticipation should be realized.

I will not consume time by telling you of the influencings of angels upon the fibres of our hearts. Angels are a kind of beings with which, you know, I have had very little to do heretofore; but when they sometimes revealed themselves in the form of a delicate woman, on whose lips they put their sweetest smile, and in whose eyes a poor sinner could read something of the mysteries of heaven, then I have drawn near, to adore; yet beyond adoration my wishes have never heretofore strayed. Often I have bowed down only at a distance before these angelic beings, who seemed to me too holy to excite a livelier interest. But as I said before, the country air in which Amoo's attendant spirits have a freer scope for their activity, must have succeeded in opening in me certain pores which were heretofore closed up in the bad city air. In short, I believe firmly and devoutly, that I am in love, and this really and entirely; for feelings such as I cherish now, were as yet entirely unknown to me. But unfortunately, the angel is not one of the merciful kind. She lets me sigh, pine, nay, die, if I should choose to do so, and only smiles and looks in the almanacks whether the days really pass by. The poor child, her eyes have not yet been operated upon; it is a pity that the beautiful eyes have the cataract. But, upon my honour, I will become her oculist, and have already made a good beginning—only listen.

After my roundabout ways and attempts to win the heart of my uncle, for my plans had worked on his stubbornness, doing just as if he did not understand me, my good spirit suggested to me the plan of applying to an authority, whose opinion, if it should turn out in my favour, would build the road to my fortune, or at least must smooth it. You, no doubt, guess, I mean Madame Lisa, our amiable and respected lady.

A few days ago when, under the pretence of drinking some raspberry juice, I had followed her into the pantry, the following conversation was held between us:

To begin the conversation, I ejaculated a long-drawn "Ha—hoh!" and then said:

"Oh, my chest! I shall yet die for want of air."

"God forbid!" exclaimed Lisa. "You, indeed, moan, lieutenant, as if you were in a consumption. You must not drink such heating things. The beer, of which you daily drink a couple of flasks, is much too strong to pour it down like water."

"Ah, dearest Lady Lindborn, but it does my poor breast so much good. Believe me, I am much worse than I show it; for it is not becoming in a man to wail and complain like a sickly girl. But here it is so charmingly real—here the air is so pure! I cannot conceive how it is possible to keep a pantry in such order; so much is certain, that I feel better here than in the most beautiful state room; and if my dear Lady Lindborn permits, I will seat myself upon the chest. To be candid, I have long wished to speak a few words in private with the person in whom I have the greatest confidence. You are of such delicate sensibility, my dear Lady Lindborn—you have so much experience of the world and knowledge of men, that it would be a real comfort to me to be allowed to lay for once before you some of my troubles."

"Well, well—if that can give you relief, my dear lieutenant, then speak by all means," answered the excellent Lisa, while she seated herself upon a bag of peas, standing opposite me. "I have long noticed that all is not right with you, and perhaps I do know already where the shoe pinches; but it is not my disposition to meddle with other people's affairs without being called on to do so."

Lisa gave a significant nod, and as she at the same time gave herself up to the enjoyment of a pinch of snuff, some phrases harmoniously escaped her lips, of which I understood only the word "parsonage." Enchanted that our thoughts met, I exclaimed: "Yes, indeed—nothing escapes your sharp eye. We understand each other I see clearly; let me then speak with you without further ceremony, and with all frankness. What else can I expect for my love in my present condition, but a life without comfort and joy? Just like my uncle, the nobleman, I shall pass the best years of my youth, forsaken and destitute, on the thorny road of want, and be yet more unhappy than he, for God in his mercy has given me no Lisa, whose fortitude might give me courage when the strength of my soul fails me. But I am candid enough to own that I do not deserve such a blessing."

Lisa, who felt herself touched on her most sensitive point, dried her tears with the corner of her apron, and said in a pious tone, "May God preserve you from so dark and bitter a life as that which the major was compelled to lead in his youth and as a man. It is true, praise and thanks to heaven, that I made many hours easier for him, but still it has been miserable enough notwithstanding, and we will hope, with God's help, that, lieutenant, after having become a rational and proper man, you will fare better in the world."

"Ah, dearest Lady Lindborn, how could I hope for that without being infatuated by my imagination,—a poor devil like me, over ears in debt, and without any prospects but a free lodging in the debtors' gaol? Oh, my situation is desperate, and I almost despair entirely!"

"Oh, heaven forbid, lieutenant; you must not look upon the matter in so dark a light. Time brings its own help, says the proverb. We will see what can be done. At all events, the debtors' gaol shall be out of the question, so long as Lisa has yet to say a word here in this house. And, as regards the other matter, if it really is your earnest and determined wish to marry the girl, and live here as a quiet and orderly man, till the Major shall—which may God prevent—one day bid a farewell to earthly things, I think that, with a little sagacity, all can be managed as you may wish."

"Good, best Lady Lindborn!" I moved my chair much closer to the bag of peas, which gave me an opportunity of taking the hand of the old lady, and shaking it heartily. "My best Lady Lindborn, your words are a soothing balm to my troubled heart!"

Lisa smiled complacently, and I now saw that my affairs stood on a firm ground; however, to be on the safe side, I said, with the greatest earnestness, and with humblest expression: "May heaven grant, my good Lady Lindborn, that I do not misunderstand you. Did you not mean to say that, out of Christian charity, you would take my part in this delicate affair?"

"Since you give me your confidence, I will do whatever is in my power. But we must break off now; the Major might wait for me." Hereupon Madame Lisa rose,—the time for coffee had arrived, and I went away light of heart, for I could now consider my game as won.

And, Azel, I was not mistaken.

The Major and Lisa held long sessions; this I perceived every time I came into the room unexpectedly; and I learned the result of it yesterday after supper, when my uncle called me into his chamber, and stated to me, without any preamble, as follows:

"Lisa thinks herself convinced that you have become a better man; and that, moreover, years and a domestic life might have a beneficial effect upon you. I know not if she is right;—the result of such a trial seems to me, at least, very doubtful. However, I have confidence in Lisa's judgment, and if she did not misunderstand you, you may rely upon my not opposing your wishes in regard to Miss Frenkman."

A shining sea of hopes lay at these words, open before my sight. As soon as I had his permission to marry, it followed, as a matter of course, that I was to live at the castle, and might consider myself as heir to the majorat, and need fear no other election day.

"My dearest uncle...." But enough of this. I was tenderly moved, Azel, and, therefore, will not repeat what I said; for know, I have yet some sensibility, and if all goes well, I will henceforth be what is called a rational man. I, therefore, intend to visit Stockholm only on the days of diet, to gratify my long-cherished wish, to make a speech in the house of lords as a member of government, and then to take a walk with my beautiful wife on the Norrbro, that people may admire and envy me. But I had almost forgotten—it will be yet some days before the Major drives over to the parsonage to ask from her father, Alfhild's hand, and I will not transport myself on the wings of my flighty imagination, into the future and reality, before I have the consent of father and bride.

I have no other news to tell you except that our new church will be consecrated a fortnight from next Sunday. If God willing, the bishop, who is coming here, will publish us, the future patrons of the new church, on that occasion for the first time.

But this is, indeed, a letter far too long. After I am married, I will be less talkative. I shall then have enough to do with giving to my pale and silent wife a little more animation and *tournure*; at all events, she shall then not read in the almanack. Heaven knows what pleasure she finds in turning over the leaves of the cursed book, even when I am sitting opposite her.

Farewell, Azel.

In conclusion, I will tell you yet news, which will put quicksilver into the paws of my *bears*. It is as certain as Amen in church, that the Major will pay all my debts before I kneel with my bride upon the fair cushions, which were made for the intended wedding in the former family, and still found at Hammarby. You no doubt recollect the terrible history of Count Albano and the beautiful lady Ravenstein. I begin to feel curiously whenever I think of it, and I never stand before the grotto and look down the abyss, without imagining I hear the cry of woe from below. You shall hear the old steward tell about these things.

Come here, Azel—come and hear yourself the wonderful stories connected with castle Hammarby, and I will also relate to you a number of things about the main actor in that awful event, the well-known architect, Seiler. His part is now finished; he has never shown any thing of himself in this country since he was acquitted.

Once more farewell, and remember

Your friend

Linus v. H.

CHAPTER XII.

UNEXPECTED PROPOSITION.

Alfhild sat in her chamber window working, in secret, at a scarf for Seiler. This was her dearest employment during her leisure hours, in which, with longing in her heart, and newly awakened pain in her breast, she looked forward to the time when the autumn winds would shake the leaves of the trees, which already began to change colour.

This time was now come, and while Alfhild busily plied her needle in the meshes, she looked now and then out upon the red-pointed trellis gate. A sudden confusion of mind broke in upon her musings, to which she gave herself up. She thought to see Leganger as he entered the first time the trellis gate. The dog-kennel, and the mastiff who was just barking on account of the approach of a beggar, tended to complete the deception. Also Sigrid's form appeared at the window, and Alfhild trembled at these ghastly recollections. The window at which she now sat was the same; this little chamber having always been occupied by the daughters of the parsonage.

"No, I am not able to look at the trellis, however much I wish," said she half aloud, and turned her back towards it.

"How can you, in this position, have light at your work, my dove?" asked, in the same moment, uncle Sebastian, who had just entered, and took a seat by his darling.

"Oh, I can do it, dear uncle, whether it be day or night."

"I have no doubt of it—if it be for *him*; you then can force every thing by your feelings," remarked old Oernroos smiling, and pinching her cheek in jest.

Alfhild, however, did not smile, but sighed, while she seized the hand of the old man and pressed it to her burning lips.

"What is the matter with you, my child? Are you not well?" asked uncle Sebastian, afflicted. "Your lips burn, indeed, like fire, and your eyes have a feverish lustre. What is the cause of it? Did you not confide to me yourself, that you expect him every day? What then are you grieved at?"

"Because I do not know whether father will keep his promise; and, if he does keep it, because I must then part from him, from my home—from you, my best and dearest uncle." She threw her arms round the neck of the tried friend, and wept as bitterly, as if the hour of separation had already struck.

"Do not move me, girl!" said the old man, in a tone which proved sufficiently that this warning came too late. "The day of separation has not yet come; let us save our strength until it has come. And as regards the circumstance of your father breaking his word, be not concerned about that. If the architect does not give him back his promise of his own free will, he is too honest a man to refuse the fulfilment of obligations he has made."

"But you know, dear uncle, papa has of late uttered very strange and ominous things. He has, when we were alone, alluded to the duty of a father of not exposing his child to dangers which can be avoided; and there was something determinate and threatening in his allusions which frightened me, and caused me to fear that they were nothing but messengers of a serious declaration in the alluded manner."

"You must not be frightened by mere appearances, my dove," interrupted uncle Sebastian. "Believe me there is time enough to be grieved and sick when there is another cause for it, than mere fear of evil. And I tell you now in earnest, if you love me, then do not always sit alone and give yourself up to your sad thoughts, for you will soon fall back into the miserable condition in which you were a few years ago."

"I will try to banish the grief from my mind," replied Alfhild, "but whether I shall succeed is a different question; for you know, uncle, I am rather peculiar. Though I had not the slightest reason to be sad, yet a consuming restlessness and secret pang befalls me as soon as the pains in my chest return, and they have been more fierce for the last week than ever, though I could walk about. But what noise is this? A coach!" She sprang up, and the blood rushed to her face, when she heard the gate open. But it was not the light vehicle of the architect, but the heavy coach of the Major, which came rattling into the court.

"It is the Major," said Alfhild, dejectedly. "Ah! I believe...." she did not say what she believed; uncle Sebastian, however, knew what she had believed and hoped, for she trembled in every limb as she leaned against his shoulder.

Oernroos did not leave his darling; the provost, however, ran quickly out of the house, and gave welcome to his worthy guest.

When the gentlemen had entered the sitting-room and taken a seat, the Major said significantly: "I come to-day on business."

Provost Frenkman's face assumed, at this remark, so beaming an expression, that it reminded one of the full moon. "On business?" remarked he, smiling. "Your honour has only to command."

"No, indeed, I shall not do that. We both may bespeak the matter, but must remain neutral, since the determination does not depend upon us, but upon a third person. In short—I have always been an enemy to circumlocution—and I, therefore, ask without farther ceremony, whether you think that your daughter is somewhat favourably disposed toward my nephew, who loves her, and asks through me for her hand."

Provost Frenkman was, in spite of his gown, more a man of the world than a clergyman. The prospect of seeing Alfhild one day as the mistress of the castle, a hope which he had secretly cherished for several months, was too alluring—nay, irresistable for him, not to overlook, for its sake, many things which might otherwise have given occasion to objections. It was, however, not so easy under the present circumstances, to find an answer to this straightforward proposition, because he would not, for any thing in the world, give a dubious one.

The provost therefore, answered, well considered: "Your honour has in a very extraordinary manner, surprised me by the entirely unexpected proposition, which reflects great honour upon my daughter; and my joy, my gratitude, is greater than I am able to express."

The Major moved impatiently to and fro in the sofa-corner; the stilted phrases of the provost appeared to him like empty foam; he, therefore, broke in upon him without further ceremony: "the question is not honour and joy, but about the acceptance or refusal of my offer. Do you believe, Mr. Provost, that Alfhild will accept Linus? As regards myself, I think it very doubtful; you, Mr. Provost, must, however, know better the inclination of your daughter; and I, therefore, desire an open and frank answer. If she does not want to—well then, I come away with a bag, for she shall not be forced."

This determined manner drove the provost into straits. "Scenes" he hated once and for ever, and in case he should inform Alfhild without preparation, of his intention to recall the word he had given to the architect, a scene of a truly tragic nature would be the consequence of it; he knew this as well as that twice two were four. And if the Major should witness this scene, it was as certain that he would return home and throw up the matter. He had to prevent this. He asked, therefore, with the greatest calmness, "whether his honour wished to have an answer this very day?"

"Why, certainly, Mr. Provost. Yes or no is easily said. The only question is, whether she loves him. No affection is the birth of a moment; if persons have had so many opportunities of seeing each other, as Alfhild and Linus, this point has long been settled. If there should be no love now, it is not to be expected that there ever will be; and it is my opinion, therefore, that you ask your daughter simply for this, and no more. I shall stay here below, in the mean time, and smoke my pipe."

The provost rose and made a deep, polite bow. A satisfied, pleasant smile hovered on his lips; but in his breast dwelt a feeling of dejected anxiety, wholly unknown to him before, while he strode through the small room which separated Alfhild's chamber from the parlour.

"Great God," said Alfhild, when she heard the well-known steps of her father, "what is the meaning of this, uncle Sebastian? The Major is here—papa—my breast—ah! what is moving here so violently?" With an expression of deepest pain, she put the hand of the old man upon her breast—"Do you feel how my heart is beating? Ah—ah—it is as if something was breaking under your hand. But what does papa want? He delays—now he is at the door?—God, you will see——"

Alfhild had no words left. With a convulsive motion she clung closer to uncle Sebastian, who, infected by her anguish, and frightened by her feverish state, trembled likewise with fear. Oernroos, however, tried to control himself, and said in as firm a tone as it was possible for him:

"What is the matter with you, my dove? I have never seen you so. I suppose there is nothing else the matter than that papa wishes to entertain the Major well in some manner, and wants your assistance."

"In that case he would not delay entering so long; but now—now!"

"What is the matter?" asked the provost, who now entered, and looked with a dissatisfied countenance at Alfhild, who leant on uncle Sebastian's shoulder, and stood there motionless. "What is the matter?" he asked once more, as no answer followed.

"I should think you could see that *yourself,*" answered the captain briefly. "The girl is sick; that has been evident for several days, but this afternoon she is in a very bad state."

"Ah—I hear nothing else now-a-days but whining and lamentation of not being well," exclaimed the provost with a dark look. "I suppose it is not so bad that you may hear what I have to say to you." He approached her, put his hand under her chin, and raised her head, while he said in a much milder tone; "How is it with you, my child?"

"I am not well, dear father. I feel I am really sick; but I cannot say what is the matter with me, in fact."

"Ah, nonsense! You were perfectly well a few hours ago. Be reasonable, and do not simper; I have to speak with you on a very important matter. But I believe it is better I speak with the girl alone."

The provost cast a significant look upon Oernroos; but as Alfhild's arms clasped him still faster, and she whispered with quivering lips: "For God's sake do not leave me. I die for anguish if you go, dearest uncle!"

Oernroos said in a determined and firm tone: "If you have any thing to say, do so; I am no stranger, and shall stay where I am."

"But you spoil Alfhild, and make her think she is sick, when she is as well as a fish in the water. There is no use in it. You have always found a pleasure in destroying what I sow, and for this reason there is at once a howling and lamenting when I say a word."

"Ah, dear father,"—Alfhild seized with deep emotion the hand of her father and kissed it,—"do not be harsh towards uncle Sebastian!" she entreated fervently. "He cannot help my being sick, and so weak and fragile a creature."

"But you were not so formerly. It is the unfortunate affair with the architect that has turned your head, and made yourself and your heart sick. But, Alfhild, my child, I often told you that this match would be your ruin. Seiler's violent temper, and his ambiguity of character and conduct, are little safeguards for a woman that will intrust him her whole future. Women are near-sighted, and for this reason, because they have more feeling than understanding, which, to be sure, you cannot help, since the Lord ordained it so. But see, my child, when he did so, he put you under the guidance of fathers and men. He charged them to watch over the weaker sex. I, therefore, follow God's commands, as well as my own conviction, when I hinder you from falling into the deep abyss, which you cannot see in your blindness."

Alfhild did not utter a word of contradiction. She pressed even closer to uncle Sebastian's breast, and her hands burned so much, that Oernroos, who felt them clasped round his neck, thought them glowing coals lying there.

Provost Frenkman, who was prepared for tears and entreaties, and had hardened himself against them, began to take courage in proceeding with his proposition.

With greater assurance, and far less heartiness in tone than at first, he continued:

"Since we have settled this matter for ever, in which you have behaved with a judgment that does honour both to your understanding and the careful education you have received, I will inform you that an extraordinary honour and great fortune has lighted on our family. The Major...." Here the provost made a pause, for Alfhild suddenly started up with a violent motion; and, as the father saw the cheeks of his child pale as death, and her eyes shine with a feverish fire, he gasped for breath, and added, in a half-loud, deep voice: "My child, the Major asks for your hand for his nephew, the bright, amiable, and joyous lieutenant, the heir to Great Hammarby." A deep, heart-rending sigh escaped Alfhild's lips; anguish of death was painted upon the look she fixed upon her father.

"The misery was not yet great enough," murmured Captain Oernroos; "they now wish to take also her life. But then," he added, in a loud, reproachful voice: "How can you break your word entirely, arbitrarily, and because the spirit of haughtiness comes over you? Remember that speculations of this kind have failed in this family once before. And I consider it most just and best, that marriages are made by affection, without any calculation of worldly pride and interest."

"I knew very well," interrupted the provost, with great bitterness of feeling, "that you would give me good advice, and encourage the girl in disobedience. Answer, my child! I hope you will not put your father in the embarrassing situation to be obliged to refuse the honourable proposition of the Major, and to have no other reason for declining it, than your disobedience to my open and distinctly pronounced will."

"Oh, my father!" said Alfhild, with the greatest exertion. "You have given no promise to the Major, but Seiler has your word. And I—great God!—at least do not desire that I should break mine! That I cannot do. My father, have pity on my suffering, on my poor heart, which, otherwise, will break with grief! Say that you will not sacrifice your child—be kind to him I love. Should Seiler have struggled and laboured, for four long years, to be deceived in the end?"

She looked up to her father with eyes in which was painted all the fires and pangs of love, while she stretched her hands in supplication towards him. But at this moment the provost was a hard man. His heart was shut against the grief of his child; for his fancy showed to him, in ever livelier colours, the great fortune that would visit his house, if he could one day, with a satisfied father's pride, salute his daughter as the future lady of the castle, where he had often stood with wounded feelings, in the humble position of an inferior. What a triumph over the nobility in the vicinity!

"What are you talking of *sacrificing?*" exclaimed he, harshly. "It would be more becoming in you to speak of *obeying.* But the moments are counted—the hour is decisive; the Major is waiting for an answer, and it can be only one."

"Well, then, let it be a *negative* one!" replied Alfhild, in a remarkably firm tone. "You will not listen to the entreaties of your daughter, my father; she must, therefore, appear disobedient. If I cannot become the wife of Seiler, I will, at least, never belong to anybody else."

"You will not?" asked the provost, whose blood became excited. "You break, then, the fourth commandment, without consideration, and openly? But take care, girl; you might miscalculate if you rely on my indulgence. Weakness is no love to children; and if God willing, you shall be published with the lieutenant a week from next Sunday, when the bishop is here to consecrate the new church."

"Published?—No, father, that I do not believe. I feel something here," said Alfhild, with a faint dying voice, "which gives me the assurance this will not be done." She sank down and clasped her father's feet. "Be kind, father—be indulgent to your child. Do not think of the lieutenant. Use no force—I—I—" She grew pale, and her head sank faint upon her breast.

"I use only *reason*, and with this you may live and prosper." The provost would free himself, but Alfhild's hands did not give way.

"My father—my father," moaned she, "bethink you what your child is now suffering. Give no promise—you will—not be able—to keep it!"

"I shall *give* and *keep* it!" exclaimed the provost, determinedly, while he tore himself with vehemence away from his daughter.

Alfhild fell to the floor. When the provost closed the door upon her, he heard a hollow tone in the room of his daughter; but it was not her voice, but that of uncle Sebastian.

Frenkman stepped into the parlour. His brow was again smoothed down, and his mouth was smiling; yet the words came out rather disjointedly, as he said:

"My daughter—the surprise caused her one of those nervous fits to which she is liable—and unfortunately prevents her to-day from expressing her gratitude in person. I hope, however, that she will, to-morrow, be so far restored as to be able to pay a visit at the castle."

"Well, does she accept him?" asked the Major, who found the answer a little obscure.

"Of course, your honour! That was hardly to be questioned; that is a matter of course."

"Hem! I do not see that exactly. But I suppose she will not be offended, if I go to see her for a moment." And before the provost was able to stammer forth that his daughter could not possibly receive the Major, he had already left the parlour and opened Alfhild's room, with the words: "Almighty God, Mr. Provost, where have you your senses?" he pushed the perplexed father into the chamber, closed the door, and returned to the parlour, where he walked up and down by his cane, in the greatest excitement.

But in Alfhild's chamber, all remained quiet till late at night. The provost forgot his guest—forgot all; and those that listened at the door, heard the deep sighs which struggled forth from his breast.

The physician for whom the Major had sent, had been there and had left—the Major likewise. At the parsonage all seemed to lie under the hand of death; no sound, no whisper was heard; Stina sometimes crept on her toes to Alfhild's door, and put her ear to listen.

When day began to dawn, and the clouds of mist gave way before the rising sun, a low noise was heard, and uncle Sebastian came into the parlour.

"How does she do?" asked Anna softly.

The old man answered not a word; but two large tears ran down his furrowed cheeks. He did not wipe them off—his strength was gone; and like a shade he disappeared on the dark staircase which led to his room.

Anna looked through the half-opened door into Alfhild's chamber. She saw nothing but the provost's black gown that seemed to be spread over Alfhild's bed, and a black arm which lay close to her pale face.

"Oh God!" said Anna, with subdued voice, and pressed Stina's arm. "God be merciful to us!"

CHAPTER XIII.

THE CONSECRATION.

ON Sunday, the 27th of October, 1795, a light travelling coach was seen rolling along the road to Great Hammarby. In it was a man of tall powerful stature, with animated looks, and a healthy, sun-burnt countenance. It was the architect, who, with the decree of divorce in his pocket, and pride and joy in his heart, came to demand of Provost Frenkman the fulfilment of his promise, and—the hand of his daughter. "Drive on, my friend—drive as fast as you can," he cried out to the postillion; "I will give you an extra fee far beyond your expectation. The church yonder is being consecrated to-day, and I should like to be present!" and on they went like the wind; stones and earth flew to the right and left up to the travellers; but Seiler did not think of throwing his cloak round him; his thoughts were with her whom he was to see again shortly. He wished to surprise her with his presence in the new church, partly built by him.

"Shall I turn in to the parsonage?" asked the postillion.

"No,—drive right on to the new church." The architect took the reins into his own hand with impatience. When they came nearer, he rose, and viewed with pride and satisfaction the beautiful house of God, with its lofty steeple, built in the noblest style.

"This is a glorious sight!" exclaimed he aloud; but immediately after he murmured something about "the roof projecting too much" which had been added by the *new* architect.

The coach stopped. "All the world is in the church," said Seiler to himself, as he alighted and walked with hasty steps to the new church, which lay close to the old one in brotherly harmony.

The new house of God was entirely filled with people; and the architect, succeeded only by means of his powerful elbows, to make his way to the main aisles. The holy ceremony of church consecration itself was already over; however, the sonorous voice of the bishop was still heard.

It grew dim before Seiler's eyes. A cold night breeze stole over his heart; he pressed forward ever more eagerly, till he stood at last pretty near the altar.

Being a head taller than the persons around him, he saw a coffin, before which the bishop stood. The golden cross shone on his breast, and in his right hand he was holding a black iron spade. Pronouncing the significant words of the bible, which express the affinity of our body to dust, he threw earth upon the coffin.

When it rolled down on both sides with a hollow sound, Seiler, in unspeakable anguish, directed his eyes upon the bright brass mark on it; but he stood too far off to be able to distinguish the letters on the plate and read the name. Not a syllable passed over his quivering lips; but with a giant's strength he pressed down those standing before him. He now saw a myrtle wreath upon the coffin, and read the inscription on the plate. It bore—*the name of his bride.*

The mourners, who were gathered round the coffin, as well as the bishop, looked up, and a shudder seized them when they beheld a head with pale cheeks, dark lips, with eyes glowing ghastly in their sockets, and with an expression of wild, annihilating anguish, peering over the rest.

He saw, however, this ghost-like countenance, for a moment; it seemed suddenly to disappear. And when the architect turned round to leave the church, the congregation gave way as if touched by an invisible power, to the pale form, which went right towards the door and stepped out.

The deep emotion of the provost, which the sight of the architect had caused him, was clearly visible in his features, distorted by grief. His eyes sought, with humble resignation, the old, tried friend, who had faithfully shared with him joy and sorrow. But uncle Sebastian's deeply-bowed head, proved that he had but one only feeling left— that of yearning to be re-united with his darling.

The funeral train passed from the house of God to the church-yard, and stopped at a newly-made grave. But when they were about to sink the coffin in it, the grave-digger suddenly stopped, with trembling arms: the place designed for Alfhild was already occupied.

A living mass was moaning in the grave. It was the architect. Blood streamed over his pale face, and coloured his dark locks; yet no instrument or weapon was seen with which he could have destroyed himself. When they lifted him up, however, they noticed that a pointed piece of iron, which stuck in the ground, had inflicted a deep wound in his head. It was supposed that the architect had fallen backwards into the grave, and wounded his head dangerously.

"God's wonder!" said Captain Oernroos, with trembling lips, "it is a piece of iron from Sigrid's coffin."

The by-standers looked awe-struck into the grave.

Seiler yet breathed. With the strength peculiar to him, which did not leave him even in death, he made signs to be carried into the church.

He was put upon the black pall which had but just before borne Alfhild's coffin. The hue of death sank on his face, yet no pain, no struggle, was painted there.

The bishop bent over him, and now Seiler's lips began to move.

"God's judgment!" he whispered. "Punishment of self-vengeance—yet the punishment was merciful. Since she has departed, I had no other wish but to follow her."

An expression of peace and faith transfigured his countenance; all storms were silent. He folded the blood-stained hands upon his rattling breast.

The bishop gave a sigh, and the holy mysteries, in which man thinks the heavenly united with the earthly, were brought. A deep stillness, unbroken by any sound, reigned in the church. Seiler's features spoke the greatest gratitude, when the bishop, after a short prayer, reached to him the cup.

After he had touched it with his lips, and his head sank back again, a ray of purest blessedness seemed to shine forth from the breathing eyes of the architect.

"The organ!" he whispered, almost unintelligibly.

When the mysterious tones re-echoed in the high vault which he himself had erected, he lifted himself up once more, yet sank back again immediately, and with the conclusion of the grave choral melody his heart had ceased beating.

———

Five years after this event, a gentleman with a lady on his arm, were seen one evening walking about the grave-yard, and reading carefully the inscriptions on the stones. The lady was of uncommon beauty, and led a boy, about three years old, by the hand, who often freed himself to tumble about to his satisfaction.

"What name stands there?" asked the lofty lady, looking at her companion.

He read:

"Sebastian Oernroos, the 1st December, 1795."

"Praise and thanks to God—he did not mourn long!" whispered she.

They now stood on the grave, on account of which they had come here.

Both knelt down in the small path between Seiler's and Alfhild's graves.

"Do not weep so much, my beloved," said the gentleman, and he laid his arm gently round the slender figure. "Both could not have become so happy here below as they are now."

"So I also think," answered she, with a mild, confident voice. "But the evening is damp; we must go; and the child might take cold."

"Oh, there is no danger for him. But allow me to put the shawl round you, dear Maria!"

APPENDIX: Review of *The Magic Goblet, or The Consecration of the Church of Hammarby* (the U.S. version of the English translation) from *North American Review* 60:2 (1845), pp. 492-493.

The Magic Goblet, or the Consecration of the Church of Hammarby. By Mrs. Emilie Carlen. Translated from the original Swedish. New York. 1845.

WE have shared in the pleasure so generally diffused in this country by the writings of Frederika Bremer; but if her stories have opened the door for an inundation of such novels as this, we could earnestly wish that her name had never reached our shores. Mrs. Carlen is not destitute of invention. She has made machinery enough, but has forgotten to supply a sufficient motive power. We have followed the development of the narrative with constantly increasing dislike; it is all a wild phantasmagoria of unmixed and unaccountable evil. The good spirit which, in some shape, everywhere prevails in the productions of Miss Bremer, and in whose protection for our favorites we have learned to confide, is, in Mrs. Carlen's wisdom, left out of the account. Evil predominates, and admiring virtue bows before it. Among other scenes described are some love passages with a married man who makes no concealment of his guilt, which are an outrage on all womanly delicacy; and an accidental meeting between the noble and deserted "wife and the beloved," the heroine, who has watched and waited for her ruin, and who has come to receive vows of eternal fidelity from the husband of another woman. There is a murder, too; and this same husband, the prime cause of all the wrong, is blessed in the conviction, that a beautiful girl, another victim, is at least happy in the "consciousness of dying in his arms." This hero may well put to shame the worst of Bulwer's highwaymen; and it may be doubted if the vilest of his works has brought to our unguarded homes a more dangerous lesson than that which is taught through the whole book of this Swedish authoress.

The Magic Ring

Baron de la Motte Fouqué

Edited by Amy H. Sturgis

It is the twelfth century, the era of Richard the Lion-heart and the Third Crusade. Along the Danube, the tranquil world shared by the young squire Otto and his cousin Bertha is changed forever when they witness a knightly contest for possession of a magic ring. Soon both are drawn into a quest that transforms them and endangers all they love. The resulting adventures lead each to different paths of enchantment and peril, from the mysteries of Moorish Spain to the birthplace of Norse mythology. While navigating an ever-changing sea of allies and foes, both natural and magical, the two seek love, honor, survival, and a ring that possesses more power than either can possibly understand.

A seamless blend of medieval quest, epic fantasy, and Gothic nightmare, *The Magic Ring* draws on an impressive host of inspirations, such as Germanic folk tales and Icelandic sagas, Arthurian romance and Gothic horror. This novel has earned its place as a text of considerable historical significance, and yet it continues to offer an exhilarating reading experience for the modern audience.

This edition includes the complete original text of the first English version of *The Magic Ring*, the 1825 translation by Robert Pearse Gillies, as well as a scholarly introduction, a glossary of literary influences and references, and the complete text of Fouqué's 1820 short story "The Field of Terror," also translated by Gillies.

ISBN 0-9777841-2-6, 388 pages, trade paperback, $18.95

For more information on this and other titles, visit valancourtbooks.com

9 780979 233296